The Rise of the City

NEW HORIZONS IN REGIONAL SCIENCE

Series Editor: Philip McCann, *University of Groningen Endowed Chair of Economic Geography, Faculty of Spatial Sciences, University of Groningen, the Netherlands*

Regional science analyses important issues surrounding the growth and development of urban and regional systems and is emerging as a major social science discipline. This series provides an invaluable forum for the publication of high quality scholarly work on urban and regional studies, industrial location economics, transport systems, economic geography and networks.

New Horizons in Regional Science aims to publish the best work by economists, geographers, urban and regional planners and other researchers from throughout the world. It is intended to serve a wide readership including academics, students and policymakers.

Titles in the series include:

Creative Knowledge Cities
Myths, Visions and Realities
Edited by Marina van Geenhuizen and Peter Nijkamp

Societies in Motion
Innovation, Migration and Regional Transformation
Edited by Amnon Frenkel, Peter Nijkamp and Philip McCann

Innovation, Global Change and Territorial Resilience
Edited by Philip Cooke, Mario Davide Parrilli and José Luis Curbelo

The Regional Economics of Knowledge and Talent
Local Advantage in a Global Context
Edited by Charlie Karlsson, Börje Johansson and Roger R. Stough

Entrepreneurship, Social Capital and Governance
Directions for the Sustainable Development and Competitiveness of Regions
Edited by Charlie Karlsson, Börje Johansson and Roger R. Stough

The Geography of the Internet
Cities, Regions and Internet Infrastructure in Europe
Emmanouil Tranos

Social Capital and Rural Development in the Knowledge Society
Edited by Hans Westlund and Kiyoshi Kobayashi

Regional Competitiveness and Smart Specialization in Europe
Place-based Development in International Economic Networks
Mark Thissen, Frank van Oort, Dario Diodato and Arjan Ruijs

Agglomeration, Clusters and Entrepreneurship
Studies in Regional Economic Development
Edited by Charlie Karlsson, Börje Johansson and Roger R. Stough

Regional Development and Proximity Relations
Edited by André Torre and Frédéric Wallet

Knowledge, Innovation and Space
Edited by Charlie Karlsson, Börje Johansson, Kiyoshi Kobayashi and Roger R. Stough

The Regional and Urban Policy of the European Union
Cohesion, Results-Orientation and Smart Specialisation
Philip McCann

Innovation and Entrepreneurship in the Global Economy
Knowledge, Technology and Internationalization
Edited by Charlie Karlsson, Urban Gråsjö and Sofia Wixe

The Rise of the City
Spatial Dynamics in the Urban Century
Edited by Karima Kourtit, Peter Nijkamp and Roger R. Stough

The Rise of the City

Spatial Dynamics in the Urban Century

Edited by

Karima Kourtit

Department of Urban Planning and Environment, School of Architecture and Built Environment, KTH Royal Institute of Technology, Sweden and Adam Mickiewicz University, Poznań, Poland

Peter Nijkamp

Professor of Regional, Urban and Environmental Economics, VU University Amsterdam, the Netherlands and Adam Mickiewicz University, Poznań, Poland

Roger R. Stough

School of Policy, Government, and International Affairs, George Mason University, USA

NEW HORIZONS IN REGIONAL SCIENCE

EE Edward Elgar PUBLISHING

Cheltenham, UK • Northampton, MA, USA

Published by
Edward Elgar Publishing Limited
The Lypiatts
15 Lansdown Road
Cheltenham
Glos GL50 2JA
UK

Edward Elgar Publishing, Inc.
William Pratt House
9 Dewey Court
Northampton
Massachusetts 01060
USA

A catalogue record for this book
is available from the British Library

Library of Congress Control Number: 2015935893

This book is available electronically in the **Elgar**online
Economics subject collection
DOI 10.4337/9781783475360

MIX
Paper from responsible sources
FSC® C013056
FSC www.fsc.org

ISBN 978 1 78347 535 3 (cased)
ISBN 978 1 78347 536 0 (eBook)

Typeset by Servis Filmsetting Ltd, Stockport, Cheshire
Printed and bound in Great Britain by T.J. International Ltd, Padstow

Contents

PART 3 URBAN SYSTEMS, INFRASTRUCTURE AND SUSTAINABLE DEVELOPMENT

Contributors

Åke E. Andersson, Jönköping International Business School, Sweden
Ake.Andersson@jibs.hj.se

David Emanuel Andersson, International Business School Suzhou, Xi'an Jiaotong-Liverpool University, China
David.Andersson@nottingham.edu.cn

Marlon G. Boarnet, Sol Price School of Public Policy, University of Southern California, USA
boarnet@usc.edu

Ana Maria Bonomi Barufi, Department of Economics, University of São Paulo, Brazil and Department of Spatial Economics, VU University Amsterdam, the Netherlands
ana.barufi@gmail.com

Stephan Brunow, Institute for Employment Research (IAB) and Otto-Friedrich University Bamberg, Germany
stephan.brunow@iab.de

Roberto Camagni, Department of Architecture, Built Environment and Construction Engineering, Politecnico di Milano, Italy
roberto.camagni@polimi.it

Roberta Capello, Department of Architecture, Built Environment and Construction Engineering, Politecnico di Milano, Italy
roberta.capello@polimi.it

Andrea Caragliu, Department of Architecture, Built Environment and Construction Engineering, Politecnico di Milano, Italy
andrea.caragliu@polimi.it

Zhenhua Chen, Sol Price School of Public Policy, University of Southern California, USA
zhenhuac@usc.edu

Zara Daghbashyan, Department of Industrial Economics and Management, KTH Royal Institute of Technology, Sweden
zara.daghbashyan@indek.kth.se

Chiara F. Del Bo, Department of Economics, Management and Quantitative Methods, Università degli Studi di Milano, Italy
chiara.delbo@unimi.it

Richard K. Green, Sol Price School of Public Policy, University of Southern California, USA
richarkg@usc.edu

Eduardo A. Haddad, Department of Economics, University of São Paulo, Brazil and NEREUS – The University of São Paulo Regional and Urban Economics Lab, Brazil
ehaddad@usp.br

Björn Hårsman, Department of Industrial Economics and Management, KTH Royal Institute of Technology, Sweden
bjorn.harsman@indek.kth.se

Kingsley E. Haynes, School of Public Policy, George Mason University, USA
khaynes@gmu.edu

Noriko Ishikawa, Faculty of Economics, Konan University, Japan
ishikawa@center.konan-u.ac.jp

Karima Kourtit, KTH Royal Institute of Technology, Stockholm and Adam Mickiewicz University, Poznań, Poland
k.kourtit@vu.nl / k_kourtit@hotmail.com

Johan P. Larsson, Jönköping International Business School, Sweden
johan.p.larsson@jibs.hj.se

Miruna Mazurencu Marinescu, Department of Statistics and Econometrics, Academy of Economic Studies Bucharest, Bucharest University of Economic Studies, Romania
miruna.mazurencu@ase.ro

Valentina Miersch, Institute for Employment Research (IAB) of the Federal Employment Agency, Germany
valentina_87@gmx.net

Peter Nijkamp, Faculty of Economics and Business Administration, Department of Spatial Economics, VU University Amsterdam, the Netherlands and Adam Mickiewicz University, Poznań, Poland
p.nijkamp@vu.nl

Amy Rader Olsson, Division of Urban and Regional Studies, KTH Royal Institute of Technology, Sweden
amy.olsson@abe.kth.se

Roger R. Stough, School of Policy, Government, and International Affairs, George Mason University, USA
rstough@gmu.edu

Marina van Geenhuizen, Faculty of Technology, Policy and Management, TU Delft, the Netherlands
m.s.vangeenhuizen@tudelft.nl

Renato S. Vieira, Department of Agricultural and Consumer Economics, University of Illinois at Urbana-Champaign, USA
schwmbc2@illinois.edu

Yuyuan Wen, School of Economics, Renmin University of China, China
wenyuyuan@ruc.edu.cn

Hans Westlund, Division of Urban and Regional Studies, KTH Royal Institute of Technology, Sweden and Jönköping International Business School, Sweden
hans.westlund@abe.kth.se

Qing Ye, Faculty of Technology, Policy and Management, TU Delft, the Netherlands and China Europe International Business School (CEIBS) Shanghai, China
yeqi519@gmail.com

Introduction

Karima Kourtit, Peter Nijkamp and Roger R. Stough

> We come from different nations, from different cultural backgrounds. Our politics differ, our professions are various. But we believe that the problem of human settlements is a general and fundamental problem in our new dynamic world and that it must be viewed and studied in such a way that it will, in common with all great scientific disciplines, transcend our local differences. We agree that the practical implementations of policy – in such vital fields as land use, the location of investment or the planning of cities over time – will be determined by domestic politics and needs, and as citizens we pledge ourselves to attempt to bring these issues into the active political dialogue of our local societies. But we are not divided in what we wish most strongly to affirm – that we are citizens of a worldwide city, threatened by its own torrential expansion and that at this level our concern and commitment is for man himself.

This statement on urban dynamics was formulated half a century ago at the Delos Symposium (Doxiadis 1963, pp. 22–23) in Greece. This symposium found its origin in the intellectual views and organizational capacities of the great Greek urbanist Doxiadis, the founding father of the Ekistics association. The results and recommendations of the Delos Symposium can be found in the Newsletter published by Doxiadis Associates, Athens, 1963.

The surprising feature of reading at present the Delos Declaration (Doxiadis1963) is that over the past 50 years the concern about the future of human settlements has not declined; on the contrary, it has become even more manifest. The message of the Delos Symposium was that cities are bound to adapt themselves to the dynamics of modern times, as otherwise the city being the cradle of civilization and progress would turn into a source of socio-economic and ecological catastrophe. Today, the emerging megacities, especially in the developing world, tend to become high-risk agglomerations for millions of citizens, as a result of environmental decay, social stress, ecological damage, or natural disasters. The dramatically needed change towards survival, called for by Doxiadis and his supporters, has, however, not materialized.

Admittedly, urban agglomerations show – in addition to shadowy sides – also many sunny sides. Agglomeration advantages are in many cases abundantly present and are a driving force for structurally continuing urbanization processes and ongoing increases in urbanization rates (see Kourtit 2014a,b). One might argue that a modern city may find itself as an epicenter of antagonistic forces with many diverse and sometimes contrasting movements which are difficult to control.

The concern about urban dynamics and its urgently needed strategic policy on urban agglomerations has prompted a new interest in future research challenges in the urban domain. In a "Scoping Report on Research Priorities" by the UK Economic and Social Research Council (ESRC) (2014), various thematic research priorities were formulated. The following three themes were identified as key areas for social science research in this field, viz.:

- Social innovation and digital technology.
- Environment, resilience and urban vulnerability.
- Urban economics.

In addition, two cross-cutting themes were proposed, viz:

- Inequalities, diversities and difference.
- Politics, contestation and governance.

In a study of the Commission of the European Communities (CEC) on *Cities of Tomorrow* (2011), various pathways for innovative and challenging research endeavors on cities were identified, in particular:

- The balance between competitiveness in the global economy and the need for sustainable local economies.
- The creation of a resilient and inclusive economy.
- The potential of socio-economic, cultural, generational and ethnic diversity.
- Combating spatial exclusion and energy poverty with better housing.
- Design of a holistic approach to green and healthy cities.
- Recognition of the importance of thriving and dynamic small and medium-sized cities.
- Design of attractive open public spaces to promote sustainable, inclusive and healthy mobility.

Finally, in a study by Bouton et al. on "How to Make a City Great" (2013), various challenging messages – with far-reaching research implications – were formulated, from the perspective of the achievement of smart urban growth. Four routes were proposed:

- Adapt a strategic approach (in particular, identification of competitive clusters, investments to support growth, think client service).
- Plan for change (e.g., make planning an inclusive process, keep urban plans flexible).
- Integrate environmental thinking (in particular, plan and build green infrastructure, safeguard resources).
- Insist on opportunity for all (e.g., connect the city outskirts, promote social integration, build affordable housing).

Clearly, the research agenda on the future and strategic challenges emerging in our "urban century" is vast. But from reading various research policy documents and many social science research contributions on the architecture and working mechanisms of the "new urban world" (Kourtit 2014a,b), it becomes clear that the city is a source of great inspiration for advanced and policy-relevant research on urban affairs, in both the developed world and in emerging economies.

The present volume on *The Rise of the City: Spatial Dynamics in the Urban Century* aims to offer a systematic collection of original and advanced contributions to enable a better understanding of urban dynamics in an open space-economy. These contributions cover various geographical areas in our world and serve to highlight the use of new methodological tools so as to enhance our insights into the complex constellation of the "urban century."

This volume is divided into three parts. These building blocks of this book center on the following main themes:

- Part 1: Urban creativity and growth.
  This part highlights the role of creativity and knowledge in relation to spatial clustering in agglomerations and the dynamics of urban areas (including smart cities).

- Part 2: Cities, innovation and productivity.
  In this part of the book the competitive performance of cities is examined, in relation to entrepreneurship and innovation of firms in the context of favorable seedbed conditions.

- Part 3: Urban systems, infrastructure and sustainable development.
  This section addresses the long-range external conditions of successful cities, such as accessibility, transportation investments, quality of life (health) and energy savings initiatives.

We now briefly summarize the individual contributions in each of the parts 1–3 of the volume. Part 1, on urban creativity and growth, commences with a study by Åke Andersson, David Emanuel Andersson, Björn Hårsman and Zara Daghbashyan on complexity, creativity and urban cluster formation. Industrial investments in research and new product development have been the key factors behind economic growth in recent decades. They have also been the most important causes of the changing comparative advantages of regions and countries. This chapter aims to generate theoretical insights into the mechanisms behind the spatial clustering of research-dependent production and the impact of the increasing complexity of products and production technologies. The authors claim that increases in product complexity in information and communications technology (ICT), biomedicine and other high-tech industries necessitate closer co-operation with basic science and interdisciplinary research in universities. At the same time, statistics on the allocation of research and development (R&D) investments between industry and universities show that in most countries the share going to university-based research is quite low. This is especially marked in the cases of South Korea and Japan. The Andersson et al. study offers three key policy conclusions. First, governments should increase their funding of scientific research, which would provide a stronger knowledge infrastructure in support of industrial R&D investments. Second, increasing scientific complexity implies a need for more support of projects with scientific *diversity*. Such projects will tend to have leadership that can integrate different disciplinary perspectives. Third, from a European perspective, there is a particular need for greatly expanded increases in science and R&D investments in many countries in southern and eastern Europe. Otherwise there is a real possibility that scientifically peripheral regions will lag even further behind northwestern Europe in the future than they do at present.

Next, Ana Barufi and Karima Kourtit present an overview of concepts and theories on agglomeration advantages of cities and metropolitan areas, in relation to Smart City concepts. The authors argue that agglomeration advantages are a key force in shaping cities and metropolitan areas. Next to system-wide benefits of such urban externalities generating intra-urban and extra-urban advantages, such agglomeration forces have also had a thorough impact on the local labor and housing markets, in terms of wage formation, spatial disparity and quality of life. The United Nations (UN) objective of making urban areas inclusive, resilient, safe and sustainable calls for effective initiatives. A contemporaneous response to this global challenge is given by the "Smart Cities" movement, which aims to turn urban agglomerations into knowledge-based, innovative, environmental and equitable concentrations of human and business activity. Based on the notion of urban system capital, this chapter critically reviews and synthesizes the current literature in this field.

The concept of Smart Cities also plays a key role in the subsequent contribution by Andrea Caragliu and Chiara Del Bo. They start from recent EU policies, prompted by the European Commission, which revolve around the word "smart" and are aimed at stimulating the best from each region and city. At the urban level, several policy initiatives are focused on the concept of Smart City, which initially developed around the relevance of ICT infrastructure as a means of connecting cities and, thus, empowering their growth capabilities. More recently, the "smart" label has also been applied to regional policies. "Smart Specialization Strategies" were originally conceived in terms of industrial specialization and are a currently a highly debated topic in regional science, both in terms of steering policy making and eliciting academic studies. Despite the popularity of these concepts in the policy domain, only a few attempts have been made to properly ground the concept of "Smart Specialization Strategy" in a comprehensive theoretical framework, and none has been made to explain the difference between the concepts of a Smart City and a Smart Specialization Strategy. This chapter attempts to fill this gap by framing both concepts in a single fused framework. A previous definition of Smart City is the basis for the construction of an urban indicator of smartness, while a new empirical methodology to identify Smart Specialization Strategies among regions is proposed. By combining the two levels of analysis, empirical results suggest that EU regions appear to be on a Smart Specialization path and that Smart Cities are more likely to emerge in regions where Smart Specialization is taking place ((semi-) mature stage) or being implemented (introduction stage).

The final study in Part 1 is contributed by Roberto Camagni, Roberta Capello and Andrea Caragliu. The main hypothesis investigated in this chapter concerns the fact that decreasing returns related to urban size can affect not only large but also small cities; for the latter, decreasing returns are occurring at smaller-sized cities. The existence of one single optimal city size for all cities is questioned: as empirical analysis shows, agglomeration diseconomies can take place in small cities as well as in large cities. In addition, in each city agglomeration diseconomies can be turned into agglomeration economies by reorganizing urban activities towards higher value-added functions and networking with other cities as suggested by urban economic theory. These propositions are empirically tested on a sample of 136 European small and large cities, showing similar patterns of structural dynamics. These patterns, however, show specific properties for each urban class.

Part 2, on cities, innovation and productivity, starts with a multi-level modeling experiment on metropolitan performance analysis carried out by Karima Kourtit, Miruna Mazurencu and Peter Nijkamp. This study examines the relative competitive performance of a set of metropolitan areas in our world by means of multi-actor explanatory models. These models are a specific class of a much broader technique known as multi-level modeling. In this study, extensive databases on 35 world cities are derived from the Global Power City Index (GPCI) database created by the Institute of Urban Research of the Japanese Mori Memorial Foundation. These data served as input for comparative models addressing the multi-annual performance growth of these areas. A fixed effects modeling approach is then used to identify and assess the determinants of urban performance from the perspective of different classes of stakeholders. An empirical application using R software is carried out. The study highlights the importance of different stakeholders in assessing the performance of metropolitan areas.

In the next chapter in this part of the book, written by Amy Rader Olsson, Hans Westlund and Johan Larsson, the issue of entrepreneurial governance for local growth is assessed. Taking as their starting point the general literature on entrepreneurship and the growing body of literature on entrepreneurship among public sector actors and institutions, the authors offer a conceptualization of entrepreneurship and metrics that can capture municipal propensity to launch local development initiatives. Results of an initial survey of Swedish municipalities indicate that there may be important differences in the way larger and smaller communities of various types introduce new initiatives and leverage local resources. They conclude that not only do local governments contribute to the creation of communities that support entrepreneurial firms, but also act in entrepreneurial ways. In particular, they create new institutions as a response to the risk and uncertainty associated with new development ventures and due to local resource constraints.

Next, Marina van Geenhuizen and Qing Ye analyze the role of cities as seedbeds of innovation. They argue that in transitions towards higher sustainability in our society, the quality of space (place) has rarely received attention or has received no attention at all. Rather, the focus has been on the national innovation system, thereby overlooking local/regional specificities that enhance or block developments towards higher sustainability. This chapter deals with a specific category of young, high-technology firms involved in responsible (sustainable) innovation, namely, spin-offs from universities, and it explores whether the city is a locational attracter for these firms and whether the networking by these firms makes a difference to their growth and potential contribution to higher levels of sustainability. The authors' work starts with a conceptual reflection on responsible innovation and what the role of cities as seedbeds could be according to various spatial-theoretical perspectives. Then the chapter proceeds with an exploratory analysis of growth among university spin-off firms active in responsible innovation in two contrasting cities, a core metropolitan location and a peripheral city in Europe. Regression modeling and retrospective descriptive analysis of six case studies are used. The study concludes with a discussion of the implications and research needs and a more comprehensive measurement of responsible innovation.

The final chapter in Part 2 is written by Stephan Brunow and Valentina Nafts. Their study starts with the observation that innovation is a key driver of technological progress and growth in a knowledge-based economy. There are various motives for individual firms to innovate: improving quality, introducing new products and adopting new technologies. Much empirical work using binary logit or probit models has been conducted to identify variables that affect the likelihood of being active in one of these fields. Firms, however, can perform innovation activities in one or more of these areas or in none of them. The question then is what variables are associated with innovative processes in these areas? This is answered by constructing a measure that counts the number of actually performed innovation types. The measure of active research fields serves as a proxy for the establishment of specific innovative capacity. For this purpose the authors employ plant-level survey data and combine it with administrative data from Germany's social security system. An ordered logit model is estimated using a variety of characteristics which describe the workforce diversity and other establishment-related variables, the regional, intra-industrial environment of establishment's location, as well as industry and region fixed effects. The empirical evidence from this study suggests that workforce diversity is relevant for innovative processes. The location itself does not lead to higher propensities to innovate; however, being located in an intra-industrial cluster provides a positive spillover effect, highlighting the importance of regional innovation systems.

The third and last part of this volume, Part 3, addresses issues of urban systems, infrastructure and sustainable development in relation to urban dynamics. The first chapter in this part, contributed by Zhenhua Chen and Kingsley Haynes, explores the public surface transportation investment impact on economic output, using a Granger approach. The chapter investigates causal linkages between surface transportation infrastructure and economic performance in the northeast corridor in the United States. To improve the validity of estimation, financial data for highways, public rail and transit are measured in real monetary value. The panel Granger causality test shows that the endogeneity between surface transportation input and the regional economic output does not exist with statistical significance in this analysis. Surface transportation infrastructure is found to "Granger cause" the change of employment and personal income per capita whereas the reverse effects are not found.

In a subsequent study, Renato Vieira and Eduardo Haddad present an accessibility index for the Metropolitan Region of São Paulo. The objective of this chapter is to elaborate on an index for measuring accessibility to jobs. The index follows a gravity-based formulation, weighting the opportunities according to the impedance to achieve them. The authors define "opportunities" as the number of jobs in each zone, and "impedance" as an inverse exponential function of travel time between each pair of zones. Two indices were calculated, one for trips by private vehicles and a second one for public transportation. The study concludes that: (a) accessibility is usually higher for zones nearer to the city center; (b) the spatial distribution of accessibility is different between the two modes concerned, because accessibility by public transportation is strongly related to the subway and railway network; (c) there is a significant spatial correlation between income and accessibility.

Urban systems may also exert differential effects on human health. In a chapter on urbanization and quality of life, Noriko Ishikawa, Karima Kourtit and Peter Nijkamp offer an overview of health effects on urban and rural residential patterns. It is well known that there exist considerable inequities in health within and between countries. A number of studies have shown that health outcomes are affected not only by individual socio-economic status, but also by the physical environment, and socio-economic and political circumstances. Most of the effects on health outcomes of socio-economic circumstances, commonly referred to as contextual factors determined by spatial and environmental characteristics of the area itself, seem to be intuitively plausible, except for the effect of urbanization. This chapter offers an inventory of many studies that have addressed the relationship between urban conditions and human health, to examine why the estimated effects of urbanization vary among countries and studies. The finding is that it is difficult to draw accurate conclusions as to whether contextual factors might precisely and steadily affect health outcomes, mainly due to a variety of health outcomes and a lack of appropriate criteria classifying the arena into urban and rural areas. The authors also argue that area-based differences are masked when using the urban–rural dichotomy because of the existence of intra-regional heterogeneities. Therefore, it may be important to find a more accurate classification scheme or a proper analytical method that minimizes the heterogeneity within regions rather than evaluating the usefulness of dichotomous and continuum classifications. The authors argue that health studies should reveal which and to what extent regional components affect health outcomes. Consequently one should decompose regional characteristics into relevant components in order to identify more precisely which components have a critical influence on health outcomes. Finally, the authors propose six critical contextual factors which may affect health outcomes in relation to urbanization.

Cities are also large energy consumers. In his chapter Yuyuan Wen offers an interesting dynamic analysis of energy rebound effects in the megacities of Beijing and Shanghai. This chapter, employing both nested CES and Cobb-Douglas production functions, estimates the energy rebound effects for Beijing and Shanghai in the period 1990–2011, as well as for the country as a whole. The findings are as follows: (a) short-term rebound effects in both Beijing and Shanghai are higher than in the country as a whole. Their values are under 100 percent and experience only a small increase between 1990 and 2011, which indicates, at least theoretically in the short term, that improvement in energy efficiency can reduce total energy consumption; (b) long-term rebound effects in Beijing, Shanghai and the country as a whole predominantly show a decreasing trend between 1990 and 2011, which suggests that China's energy saving policy has yielded positive results since the mid-1990s. However, how to overcome energy "backfire effects" in the long-term rebound effects is a difficult issue for the megacities and the country as a whole to address in the future; (c) due to the rebound effects, technology progress, economic structure adjustment and institutional transformation should be taken into consideration when developing an energy-saving policy.

The final contribution in this volume is produced by Marlon Boarnet and Richard Green. They raise the question of how cities should manage economic development in the future. They argue that economic development policy and real estate development are closely linked, often conflated, and exist in a politicized environment where the need to "do something" too often trumps insight from theory. The authors suggest that the economic rationale for public sector efforts to promote economic activity can and should be based on theories of market failures. They further note that government regulation of the land market can either help or hinder economic development efforts. In turn they propose real estate regulatory principles that are consistent with effective economic development policies. These insights from theory are combined with summaries of experiences from four U.S. cities – Austin, New York, San Diego and Washington, D.C. – to develop policy recommendations for economic and real estate development.

After this panoramic overview of the rise of cities, their underlying mechanisms and the possible effects on the urbanized space-economy, the question emerges: which lessons and trends have been uncovered.

The opening chapter by Andersson, Andersson, Hårsman and Daghbashyan argues that industrial investments and new product development have been key factors behind economic growth in recent decades.

This is an important observation and implies that economic growth in cities has come primarily from R&D investments, that is, research and technology development. This is one of the basic ways that economic growth occurs; the others are through physical resource extraction and education. Resource extraction plays a minor role in general urban economic growth today. Education that produces improved human capital has long been a source of economic development in modern times and also has likely contributed to urban economic growth, but this driver of growth has been evolving for a long time; at least since the rise of industrialization. What is new is that recent urban economic growth appears to have come primarily from the development and adoption of new technology that has been concentrated in urban places. But why has this occurred and will it continue?

Sifting the substance of the contributions of this book and recognizing both the stated and hidden assumptions upon which its contributions rest one concludes that the recent evolution and adoption of ICT combined with telecommunication developments are the primary drivers of the continuing growth of cities (urban places). These developments have resulted not only in the creation of huge new amounts of information and knowledge but, perhaps even more important, the reality that this corpus of knowledge can be accessed more broadly and deeply than at any time in history. This fact has had profound impacts on nearly all processes in urban (as well as rural) existence. Consequently, most processes that undergird sustained societies have become more open than in the past. Thus we see openness, broadening participation and increasing transparency occurring in such urban and social maintenance processes as governance, big project/infrastructure finance, management, planning, transportation, government service provision, education as well as in R&D. While such processes have historically been more closed, they are becoming increasingly more open and this openness is occurring most in urban places. So why is this so?

Thomas Friedman (2005) recently wrote a book in which he argued that the "world is flat." His argument is that the merging of ICT and telecommunications technology evens the knowledge playing field so that all places (all people) have similar access to information and knowledge. Yet, if that is the case, then why are cities and urban places growing? It is because in most cases not all locations have the same ability to convert that knowledge into new economic growth. The counterargument to Friedman's influential book put forth by Richard Florida (2005) and others is that "the world is spiky" and continues to become more agglomerated in the knowledge age. Urban places are expanding and evolving because proximity of people, knowhow and resources remains an important factor in economic growth even in the knowledge age. As people congregate in urban places, demand for products not only grows in quantity but it also diversifies and together these factors create increased demand for a broader array of goods and services. This creates a fertile bed for innovation and entrepreneurship and the development of new goods and services. As this demand is met, new jobs are created which in turn attracts more people to fill those jobs. Further, proximity is important for the innovation process. Proximity makes it easier to recognize the new and diverse opportunities because there are always fine grained local factors (e.g., tacit knowledge) that are required as inputs for the successful innovation and entrepreneurship that create the new goods/services. These factors have a higher probability of being known and used in urban places because of the proximity of people and knowledge. In short, a self-reinforcing or positive feedback system arises in urban environments that attracts people, creates new demands and responses to meet those demands, which in turn produces new jobs and which in turn creates new and diverse job opportunities, and thus more people are attracted to fill the jobs and growth occurs. This line of reasoning is that offered by the new economic geography and new international trade theory (Krugman 1991).

In the knowledge age the growth of cities begins, for the most part, where cities are already located and where proximal advantages already exist, and consequently this is where the forces of the knowledge age are themselves amplified and focused. The result is growth due to increased knowledge fueled by continuing advances in ICT and telecommunications technology. Because of the concentration of new opportunities in cities and their potential for exploitation it is not surprising that scholars and observers note that creative people are increasingly attracted to cities or as Florida (2005) observes – "Spiky Places." What is important not only about the overall continuing growth of cities and their attraction for entrepreneurs, innovators, inventors and creative people is that the positive reinforcing and positive feedback nature of cities in the knowledge age is likely to continue for some time. This growth and the forces producing it are driving increasing openness in the processes that serve to govern, manage and undergird the urban reality. This evolving openness and how to use and manage it is a huge dynamic that underlies "cities in transition." The contributions of this book all in one way or another are important because they provide a window into the adjustments that are, or are not, taking place in urban and city spheres.

REFERENCES

Bouton, S., Cis, D., Mendonca, L., Pohl, H., Remes, J., Ritchie, H. and Woetzel, J. (2013) How to Make a City Great, McKinsey & Company, http://www.mckinsey.com/~/media/McKinsey/dotcom/client_service/Infrastructure/PDFs/How_to_make_a_city_great_v2.ashx.

Commission of the European Communities (CEC) (2011) *Cities of Tomorrow: Challenges, Visions, Ways Forward*, Commission of the European Communities, Brussels, http://ec.europa.eu/regional_policy/sources/docgener/studies/pdf/citiesoftomorrow/citiesoftomorrow_final.pdf.

Doxiadis, C. (1963) *Newsletter on the Delos Symposium*, Doxiadis Associates, Athens.

Florida, R. (2005) The World in Numbers – The World is Spiky: How Globalization has Changed the Economic Playing Field, but hasn't Leveled it, *Atlantic Monthly*, October 2005, 47–51.

Friedman, R. (2005) *The World is Flat: A Brief History of the 21st Century*, Farrar, Straus & Girous, New York.

Kourtit, K. (2014a) *Competitiveness in Urban Systems: Studies on the "Urban Century"*, VU University, Amsterdam.

Kourtit, K. (2014b) *The "New Urban World": Economic-Geographical Studies on the Performance of Urban Systems*, Adam Mickiewicz University, Poznań, Poland.

Krugman, P. (1991) Increasing Returns and Economic Geography, *Journal of Political Economy*, 99(3), 483–499.

UK Economic and Social Research Council (ESRC) (2014) Urban Transformations Scoping Report on Research Priorities, http://www.esrc.ac.uk/_images/Urban-Transformations-scoping-report_tcm8-30925.pdf.

PART 1

Urban creativity and growth

1. Complexity, scientific creativity and clustering

Åke E. Andersson, David Emanuel Andersson, Björn Hårsman and Zara Daghbashyan

INTRODUCTION

By the late 1960s, economists and policymakers realized that manufacturing employment was stagnating in many of the most developed countries. In a pioneering study of the American economy, Fritz Machlup (1980) concludes that what he calls the "knowledge industry" already accounted for close to 30 percent of America's gross domestic product (GDP) in the 1970s. Using a definition of knowledge-producing occupations that included both occupations assumed to produce new knowledge and those involved in transferring knowledge and information, Machlup also showed that this group of occupations had grown faster than other groups for several decades. Åke Andersson (1985) provides a broad historical overview of creativity, infrastructural change and economic growth, suggesting that an assessment of the relative knowledge orientation of an economy should exclude occupations that focus on information transmission. Andersson's definition of "knowledge-handling occupations" is thus a subset of Machlup's knowledge-producing occupations, and mainly consists of workers in education, research and the arts. Andersson and Persson (1993) show that the number of workers in this occupational category is growing faster than other categories in Sweden and other advanced economies.

In a more detailed study of different industries, Christer Anderstig and Björn Hårsman (1986) show that the percentage of "knowledge-handlers" is increasing in manufacturing as well as in services; they further show that this expansion is fastest in large metropolitan areas. Edward Glaeser and David Mare (2001) and Richard Florida (2002) elaborate upon these early findings in an American context, with the conclusion that U.S. metropolitan areas increasingly depend on highly educated workers or a new "creative class."

In the 1970s and 1980s, producers in the electronic, pharmaceutical, optical and transport industries were becoming increasingly aware of the need for research and development (R&D) in order to secure dynamic comparative advantages in their location and trading decisions. Public policy, however, lagged behind. It was only later that actors in the public sector realized that there was a need for a corresponding shift in their education and science policies. The European Institute of Innovation and Technology, EIT, a body of the European Union, can be looked upon as a political manifestation of a perceived need for increased collaboration between universities and industry to enhance the competitiveness of Europe. Through long-term and large-scale investments in "knowledge and innovation communities," EIT aims at fostering the innovation capacity of Europe. The communities or so-called "KICs" are run and co-funded by university and industry stakeholders, integrating higher education, research and business. By way of example, the EIT ICT Labs include universities in Berlin, Eindhoven, Helsinki, Paris, Stockholm and Trento and firms such as Ericsson, Siemens, Philips and Nokia. The budget for the EIT ICT Labs amounts to about €70 million per year. Figure 1.1 is an attempt to visualize the relationships among the different aspects of knowledge, research and production (Andersson and Beckmann, 2009).

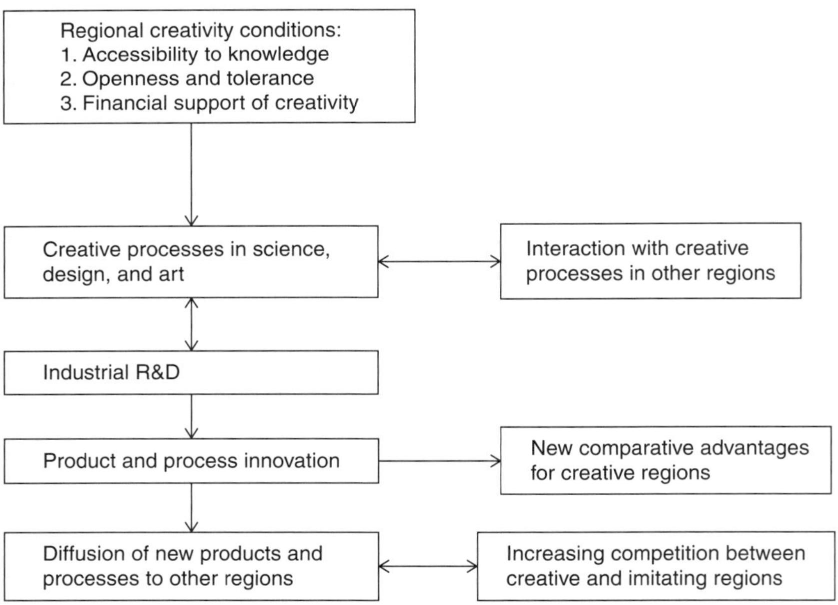

Figure 1.1 Creativity, research and new comparative advantages

Creativity in research is nowadays a precondition for industrial R&D, in contrast to the situation in earlier stages of development. In early industrial society, there were clear "stages of innovative production" whereby the lone inventor (often with some short engineering education) provided the industrial entrepreneur with the key input for a successful innovation. Science was for the most part external to this production process. Even today the managers of some high-technology firms have tried to cut off the links to science by planning the whole process from scientific inputs to innovative outputs. It is likely that such strategies misallocate knowledge resources. The increasing complexity of products and production systems necessitates a stronger interaction between the creativity of basic science and the technological R&D of firms.

Our contention is that scientific creativity is becoming increasingly important for industrial research and innovation. This will not only affect the location of industries and their knowledge capital. It will also change the location of scientists. A study by Hans Lööf and Pardis Navabi (2013) quantifies the benefits of knowledge-intensive locations. They analyse 10,000 Swedish export firms over a twelve-year period in order to estimate the relationship between productivity and innovations. Their conclusion is that both persistent and non-persistent innovators benefit from a knowledge-intensive local environment of universities and other scientific research institutions. Additionally, this type of external knowledge influences the productivity growth of those firms that are classified as persistent innovators.

FROM SCIENTIFIC CREATIVITY TO INDUSTRIAL R&D

Fundamental creativity in the sciences is shaping the future comparative advantages of industry. The intermediate factor is industrial R&D, with product and process innovations as direct outputs. Still, scientific research accounts for only a modest part of overall spending, even in those economies that are most "science-intensive." Spending on industrial R&D—which tends to be more incremental and short-sighted than scientific research—is more than five times greater than spending on scientific research in the Organisation for Economic Co-operation and Development (OECD) countries (see Table 1.1).

As Table 1.1 shows, the public sector—which is the main source of research funding in the higher education sector—attaches less importance to basic research than the private sector attaches to applied industrial research (or, in some cases, than the public sector attaches to applied military research). There are at least two reasons for this.

Table 1.1 Research and development spending in the OECD countries, 2008–2011

Country	Overall R&D (percent of GDP)	Scientific research (percent of GDP)
Sweden	3.43	.90
Denmark	3.06	.90
Finland	3.89	.79
Netherlands	1.83	.75
Switzerland	2.97	.72
Austria	2.71	.72
Canada	1.80	.69
Iceland	2.64	.66
Estonia	1.62	.62
Portugal	1.59	.59
Norway	1.69	.55
Australia	2.18	.54
Germany	2.79	.51
Ireland	1.79	.51
France	2.12	.48
United Kingdom	1.70	.48
Belgium	1.97	.46
Japan	3.33	.45
OECD	2.17	.44
New Zealand	1.30	.43
South Korea	3.58	.40
United States	2.28	.39
Spain	1.34	.39
Turkey	.84	.39
Italy	1.25	.36
Greece	.60	.30
Slovenia	1.85	.29
Czech Republic	1.56	.28
Poland	.74	.27
Luxembourg	1.56	.19
Slovakia	.62	.17
Hungary	.23	.16
Chile	.39	.16
Mexico	.37	.10

Source: OECD (2012).

First, scientific research tends to adopt a much longer time perspective than industrial R&D. There is consequently greater uncertainty of success in the sense of Ramsey (1927, pp. 153–170; see also Sahlin, 1990, pp. 88–94). Second, science focuses less on financial or private returns and this characteristic induces an evaluation problem among policymakers. Third, scientific returns are in general public in their effects, as a consequence of scientists' preference for open-access dissemination of their results.

Politicians and bureaucrats often assume that heavily marketed "national innovation policies" are best at promoting future comparative advantages. The implication is that they tend to support industrial R&D rather than scientific research, in spite of the (potentially) much greater and more widespread social returns that scientific creativity brings about.

William Baumol (2004) suggests that policymakers should distinguish between inventors' inventions, entrepreneurial innovations and firms' R&D-based inventions and innovations. Though corporations may employ large numbers of scientists and operate research centres in different countries, independent inventors and firm-external entrepreneurs provide disproportionate numbers of radical—as opposed to incremental—innovations. Baumol (ibid., p. 8) writes that

> the R&D divisions of the large firm tend primarily to require personnel who have undergone training for mastery of extant information and analytic methods, while the work of the independent entrepreneur and inventor may prove to be more effectively facilitated by avoidance of that sort of preparation to the extent that it impedes imagination and originality.

A counter-argument to Baumol's hypothesis is that increasing complexity may lead to the demise of the classical independent inventor, working alone in some minimally equipped laboratory. As Rogers Hollingsworth (2007) points out, the increasing complexity of fields such as biomedicine means that large and multidisciplinary science teams are becoming increasingly important for basic scientific research, which is the domain that has always been responsible for the most revolutionary creative breakthroughs.

Economies and their research organizations are becoming increasingly complex. We therefore need an understanding of what the increasing complexity of products and processes imply for the organization of economic life. There are numerous proposed definitions of complexity. Most of these are somewhat intuitive. Ray Solomonoff (1964), Andrey Kolmogorov (1965) and Gregory Chaitin (1966) provide a mathematical and precise definition of complexity. They claim that complexity is measurable and defined as the minimal length of a program or algorithm that yields an exact solution to a pre-formulated problem. This can be clarified with a few simple examples. An illustrative problem is to find the shortest way of generating a given sequence of numbers.

Example 1: 1010101010. . .
Example 2: 0020003000040000050000006. . .
Example 3: 121543699821345798709812699943 33.

It is easy to identify formulae or algorithms that are shorter than the series of Examples 1 and 2 and that yield the same unique number series. Both of these formulae of minimal length are short and thus of low complexity. In contrast, no formula shorter than the series itself can identify Example 3, which is a random series of numbers. Example 3 is thus more complex than Examples 1 or 2. Example 2 is, however, more complex than Example 1.

It is possible to generalize the complexity of mathematical expressions and computer algorithms to phenomena such as blueprints and production process instructions (Casti and DePauli, 2000; Solomonoff, 1964). Standard goods must follow strict and stepwise (i.e. algorithmic) rules of composition. A simple example is a baker's recipe. For example, the recipe for a standard American brownie is less complex than the recipe for the *Sachertorte* of the Hotel Sacher in Vienna (we believe rather than know this, since this particular *Sachertorte* recipe is a trade secret). But despite the clarity of this example, it also alludes to numerous limitations of the computational complexity measure.

The first limitation arises from the difference between numbers in an algorithm and ingredients in a cake. Cake ingredients have much greater *scope* than numbers; they are heterogeneous rather than uniform in having an open-ended set of underlying attributes.

A second limitation is that cakes, unlike numbers, are sensitive to the skills of the individual using the recipe. A recipe-using individual is not as homogeneous as an algorithm-using computer. A skilful worker can adjust the recipe if the delivery of an ingredient is delayed or if an ingredient is of superior or inferior quality (in one or more of its intrinsic attributes). The structure of inputs in the production process is thus a function of algorithmic complexity, c_A.

Baumol (2004, p. 8) captures the skill change that accompanies changes in algorithmic complexity when he writes that

> incremental improvement of complex products may require mastery of far more demanding technical information and techniques than was needed for the original ideas that resulted in the invention of those products. The technology needed to improve the design of a Boeing-777 passenger airplane is obviously enormously more complex than that underlying the Wright brothers' first vehicle.

The *cost* of production will thus depend on (at least) three factors: the complexity of the recipe (composition or design); the quality attributes of the ingredients (land and physical capital); and the skills of the worker (labour or human capital).

Besides the complexity of production there is also the complexity of consumption. These two types of economic complexity do not coincide. More complex production often causes *less* complex consumption. One example is computer-assisted automatic transmission systems in cars. The production complexity is substantial, but the user derives utility from this *high* production complexity to the extent that s/he values *low* consumption complexity, c_{IJ}. This implies that revenues as well as costs depend on both production *and* consumption complexity.

We can assume that consumption complexity is a function of production complexity, as specified above. This means that we can now formulate a profit function, Y, for a given good as follows:

$$Y = R(\mathbf{q}, c_U(c_A, \mathbf{v})) - C(\mathbf{q}, \mathbf{v}, c_A); \tag{1.1}$$

where

$\mathbf{v}$ = a vector of ordinary inputs (dependent on the prevailing complexity levels);

$\mathbf{q}$ = vector of scales of production of the given set of products.

In the short term, we treat the complexities of the products as given by earlier investments in new knowledge. In the long term, algorithmic complexity, input structure and skills can all change as a result of creativity in science and in applied research. Such changes are possible only on much slower timescales than the typical timescale of ordinary business decisions, which in this case includes R&D-induced incremental improvements.

The accumulation of scientific knowledge thus occurs through a slow and creative process that changes the algorithmic complexity of a given good:

$$\begin{aligned} \Delta C/\Delta\tau &= F(C, S_r) \\ \Delta c_A/\Delta\tau &= G(c_A, C); \end{aligned} \tag{1.2}$$

where

C = scientific creative capital;

S_r = funds allocated to scientific research;

τ = a basic long time period.

We assume the functions to be concave with respect to C, S_r and c_A, ranging from R^+ to R^+. In addition, τ = kt, where k is a constant transforming ordinary time (say years) into the much longer time periods that new scientific breakthroughs usually need in order to mature and gain acceptance in the community of scientists. By adiabatic approximation $(G, F) \approx 0$, implying that firms will treat the current stock of established scientific knowledge as a fixed constraint on their opportunity set. We may therefore treat the algorithmic complexity of a specific long time period as the knowledge infrastructure. Firms treat this infrastructure as a stable basic input into the much more rapid industrially applied and incremental research processes that transform scientific results into product and process innovations.

CREATIVITY AND COMPLEXITY

There are numerous contemporary examples of how the creativity of scientists, designers and engineers has increased product complexity and necessarily *preceded* industrial innovations. The most important example is the information and communications technology (ICT) industry. One should keep in mind that recent rapid increases in the product complexity of computers and ICT systems would not have been possible without the scientific creativity of Alan Turing and John von Neumann in the 1930s and 1940s.

The transport equipment industry is another example of this process of increasing interdependency between science and industrial technology. A modern airplane is more energy-efficient and easier to fly than vintage airplanes from the 1920s. But it was only through a massive and protracted accumulation of science-based novel electronic and hydro-mechanical components that this combination of high production and low consumption complexity was made possible. It is also noteworthy that workers in contemporary airplane manufacturing plants have more advanced technical skills than their counterparts in the 1920s.

The trend towards increasing levels of complexity, which is now evident in most industries, eventually caused a restructuring of both scientific and industrial research. It also gave rise to the spread of higher education and the current popularity of national and regional innovation policies.

Although the Second World War accelerated the integration of scientific creativity and product development in the military, a more wide-ranging civilian integration only began in the 1970s. Two industries were then at the forefront, integrating science, industrial research and technological innovation.

The computer industry is one of these industries. It emerged from the rather simple office equipment industry. The British mathematician Alan Turing supplied the key scientific input. Turing had been analysing the mathematical properties of digital mathematics in a simple but very general algorithm, which was later to be known as Universal Turing Machines. Basing their work on Turing's theorems, two Princeton mathematicians, John von Neumann and Herman Goldstine, provided the original inventive input in the 1950s: the first prototype of the programmable computer. It was only later—and sometimes with great resistance—that industry became engaged in the development of programmable computers.

The increase in the product complexity of computers since the 1950s has been staggering. Algorithmic complexity has been increasing at an unrivalled pace from the 1950s onward. It was not only Turing, Neumann and Goldstine who made the resulting "information revolution" possible. Their scientific predecessors also contributed to the necessary conditions of this particular scientific breakthrough. Examples include Sir Isaac Newton (the Newton–Raphson technique for solving non-linear equations), George Dantzig (the simplex method for solving linear programming problems) and other algorithmically oriented mathematicians.

Information technology is but one example of this type of process that connects scientific breakthroughs with increasingly complex products. A non-exhaustive catalogue of creative activities in sciences which have caused increasing downstream product complexity would include aerospace engineering, architecture, astrophysics, biochemistry, chaos theory, meteorology, electrical engineering, financial engineering, geophysics, integer optimization, molecular biology, pattern recognition, physics, robotics, systems engineering and transport engineering.

The algorithmic complexity of computer programs has relied on the increasing hardware capacity of computers as well as on the need for decreasing consumption complexity. The user-friendly laptop computer is one outcome of this parallel development. Perhaps the most important aspect of the dynamics of hardware complexity is ever-increasing storage capacity. IBM introduced the 350 Disk File in 1956. This hard drive had a total capacity of only five million characters. In 2011 Hitachi introduced the first four-terabyte hard drive, and in 2012 Victorinox began selling one-terabyte USB flash drives (one terabyte or TB corresponds to one trillion bytes or eight trillion single characters of computer text).

Greater speed has accompanied greater storage capacity. A research team at the University of California, San Diego has for example developed a "phase-change memory solid state storage device," which is thousands of times faster than the fastest conventional hard drives. Another team at Johns Hopkins University has discovered some previously unknown properties of a common memory material (GST), paving the way for the development of novel memory drives that store and retrieve data more quickly, as well as being more durable. These examples illustrate how scientific breakthroughs cause new inventions, and how subsequent product innovations depend on interactions between parallel increases in algorithmic complexity, (physical) input complexity and skill complexity.

Another example of an industry which had an early start in the integration of scientific and industrial creativity is the pharmaceutical industry. Decision-makers in that industry early on identified and acted on the need for an integration of medical, chemical and biological science with firms' research and innovation strategies. Yet another example is the medical equipment industry, whose constituent firms have developed elaborate strategies for using relevant results from physics, computer science and cognitive science.

This raises the question of what type of organization is best able to cultivate the scientific breakthroughs that firms subsequently use in their product development efforts. Hollingsworth (2007) addresses this question by connecting scientific complexity to the frequency of creative breakthroughs and the internal organization of universities, research institutes and laboratories. His focus is on biomedical science, which is unusually concerned with understanding and predicting highly complex systems. Hollingsworth (ibid., p. 129) notes that "high cognitive complexity is the capacity to observe and understand in novel ways the relationships among complex phenomena, the capacity to see relationships among disparate fields of knowledge. And it is that capacity which greatly increases the potential for making a major discovery."

Hollingsworth's empirical analysis distinguishes between two different types of laboratories (A and B). He starts by asking (ibid., p. 131) the following question: "What were the characteristics of the culture and the structure of the laboratory where the [breakthrough] research occurred?" The initial finding was that most labs never made any major discoveries, including illustrious ones such as the Royal Society or the National Academy of Sciences. Meanwhile, there was a small subset that did in fact produce revolutionary scientific results. Hollingsworth labels the creative type of lab "Type A," while he calls the relatively uncreative lab "Type B." As it turns out, labs which produced creative breakthroughs had similar Type A organizational attributes, although most Type A labs were unsuccessful. More significantly, *none* of the conventionally structured Type B labs ever produced a truly revolutionary biomedical finding. Table 1.2 illustrates the organizational attributes of Type A and Type B labs.

Hollingsworth's results are striking. He writes (ibid., p. 132) that "almost all of the 291 discoveries in our project were made in Type A laboratories . . . Type B laboratories are at the opposite end of the continuum on virtually all the lab characteristics. Significantly, none of the 291 discoveries in our research occurred in Type B labs." Hollingsworth's

Table 1.2 Organizational attributes of Type A and Type B laboratories

Attribute	Type A lab	Type B lab
Cognitive	High scientific diversity	Low or moderate scientific diversity
Social	High and diversified network connectivity	High network connectivity within a single discipline
Material	Access to funding for high-risk research	Limited funding for high-risk research
Personality of the lab leader	High cognitive complexity; high confidence; high motivation	Low cognitive complexity; risk-averse
Leadership	Excellent grasp of how different fields may be integrated	Not concerned with integrating distinct scientific disciplines

Source: Hollingsworth (2007, 2009).

findings imply that one may doubt the wisdom of the current tendency towards increased specialization in the sciences, which has been the normal outcome of the interplay of relevant forces such as monopolistic competition among scientists, the funding policies of science foundations and universities' hiring strategies.

On the basis of these results, we conclude that the development of science towards increasingly complex theories, models and products causes a need for more complex cognitive capacity among individual creative scientists as well as within laboratories and other research organizations at the micro level. Moreover, the increase in expected (but uncertain) individual creativity that accompanies good access to new and diversified knowledge (cf. Andersson, 1985; Florida, 2002; Hollingsworth, 2007; Simonton, 2011) provides strong arguments for locating such micro research organizations in large, open and diverse cities.

THE GLOBAL AND REGIONAL DISTRIBUTION OF CREATIVE SCIENTIFIC CAPACITY

The most systematic studies of the global distribution of scientific creative capacity are all based on Thomson Reuter's Science Citation Index, which records publishing and citations in peer-reviewed scientific journals.

Table 1.3 Science output in Europe's 25 leading regions, 2008–2010

Rank	Labour market area	Country	SCI publications
1	London	United Kingdom	96,856
2	Paris	France	77,007
3	Randstad (Amsterdam–Rotterdam–Utrecht)	Netherlands	65,527
4	Moskva (Moscow)	Russia	45,857
5	Madrid	Spain	41,926
6	Berlin	Germany	41,923
7	Øresund (København–Malmö–Lund)	Denmark–Sweden	38,970
8	Milano (Milan)	Italy	37,917
9	Roma (Rome)	Italy	37,681
10	Barcelona	Spain	36,657
11	Stockholm–Uppsala	Sweden	35,257
12	München (Munich)	Germany	32,132
13	Oxford–Reading	United Kingdom	30,374
14	Manchester–Liverpool	United Kingdom	30,144
15	Dortmund–Düsseldorf–Köln	Germany	29,351
16	Edinburgh–Glasgow	United Kingdom	29,151
17	Cambridge	United Kingdom	26,927
18	Frankfurt	Germany	26,221
19	Genève–Lausanne	Switzerland	25,996
20	Zürich	Switzerland	25,720
21	Wien (Vienna)	Austria	24,084
22	Mannheim–Heidelberg	Germany	23,324
23	Sheffield–Leeds	United Kingdom	22,306
24	Basel–Mulhouse–Freiburg	Switzerland–France–Germany	22,295
25	Bruxelles–Antwerpen (Brussels–Antwerp)	Belgium	21,957

Source: Thomson-Reuters (2012).

Admittedly, only a very low percentage of published papers are truly creative. Although the world's highest ranked universities according to popular league tables are mostly located in a few American and British regions, the density of research output in some of the smaller European countries such as Denmark, Sweden and Switzerland is quite remarkable. But even in Europe, the distribution of research output is heavily concentrated in large metropolitan areas and a handful of college towns. Table 1.3 gives the total number of publications registered in the Science Citation Index (SCI) from 2008 to 2010 in European urban regions. The regions are delimited according to the spatial extent of a time distance of forty-five minutes from the regional centre by the fastest transport mode.

Historical data (Matthiessen et al., 2011) show that there is considerable stability in the geographic distribution of European science production, with centres of gravity—both in terms of mass and network connectivity—in the three leading nodes of London, Paris and Amsterdam (Randstad).

Denmark and Sweden spent the most money on scientific research relative to GDP, while Switzerland (ahead of Denmark and Sweden) produced the most SCI papers relative to population between 2008 and 2010 (Andersson and Andersson, 2013). As Table 1.3 shows, the Øresund region (which includes Copenhagen in Denmark as well as Malmö and Lund in Sweden) is Europe's seventh largest agglomeration of science production, while Stockholm–Uppsala is in eleventh place. More detailed national statistics show that Sweden's science output is disproportionately located in Stockholm (narrowly defined) and in the two university towns of Lund and Uppsala (Matthiessen et al., 2011). There is also an over-representation of scientists in other Swedish regions with research universities, for example in Göteborg (Gothenburg), Umeå and Luleå. But what *mechanisms* cause scientists to locate in one rather than another region?

ACCESSIBILITY AND CLUSTERING OF SCIENTISTS—A THEORETICAL APPROACH

Assume space to be subdivided into N regions. The scientist must select one location from these N regions. One location preference argument is thus the accessibility to other scientists from a region i to all N areas. Scientists can be expected to prefer other scientists to have proximate rather than distant locations. Similarly, scientists are expected to aim for the greatest possible number of other scientists at a given distance.

The definition of accessibility to scientists from area i is

$$a_i^x = \sum_{j=1}^{N} f(d_{ij}) x_j \tag{1.3}$$

where
a_i^x = accessibility to scientists, x, from area i;
$f(d_{ij})$ = a strictly decreasing function of the distance between two areas i and j;
x_j = the number of scientists in area j.

The positive convex distance function $f(d_{ij})$ implies that the accessibility to a given number of scientists decreases with increases in the distance between regions i and j.

A reasonable and commonly used measure of $f(d_{ij})$ is

$$e^{-\beta dij} \text{ with } \beta \geq 0 \text{ and } d \geq 0. \quad (1.4)$$

Here d is defined as the time distance by the transport mode that scientists normally use. This functional form implies that accessibility is a spatial analogue to the discounted total value of revenues in capital theory. An advantage of this functional form is the property that $e^{-\beta d}$ has the limits 1 if $d \rightarrow 0$ and 0 if $d \rightarrow \infty$.

The second important factor in scientists' location choices is the scientific infrastructure in terms of labs, libraries, supercomputers and other large-scale science machinery in universities and R&D-intensive firms. Examples of large-scale infrastructures in science include CERN in Geneva, the new ESS unit in the Øresund region and the IBM research facility in Connecticut.

Scientific infrastructural accessibility can be denoted as $a_i^s = \sum_j^N e^{-cdij} S_j$, where S_j = scientific infrastructure in region j. The valuation of accessibility to such infrastructure would of course decline with increases in the number of users, as a reflection of bottlenecks and other congestion phenomena.

A third key factor in the choice of location is the relative level of science subsidies in region i, W_i. We may further assume that the level of algorithmic complexity, c_A, is fixed in the short run and acts as a vector of level parameters in the **Q**-mapping.

It has been shown that a non-linear Eigenvalue equation determining the endogenous clustering has an equilibrium solution with a positive equalized rate of return ρ on the associated positive human capital vector **x** in:

$$\rho \mathbf{x} = \mathbf{Q}(\mathbf{x}, a^s, \mathbf{W}, c_A); \quad (1.5)$$

where $\mathbf{Q}(\mathbf{x})$ is a continuous, quasi-concave mapping from R^+ to R^+ (Nikaido, 1968). For such a system, we can use one of Nikaido's (1968) theorems as follows.

Assumptions:

a. $\mathbf{Q}(x) = (Q_i(x))$ is defined for all $x \geq 0$.
b. $\mathbf{Q}(x)$ is continuous as a mapping $\mathbf{Q}$: $R_+^n \rightarrow R_+^n$ except possibly at $x = 0$.
c. $\mathbf{Q}(x)$ is positively homogenous of order m, $0 \leq m \leq 1$ in the sense that $\mathbf{Q}(x) \geq 0$ and $x \geq 0$.

Theorem:

$$\text{Let } \Lambda = \{\boldsymbol{Q}(x) = \rho x\} \text{ for } x \in p_n \tag{1.6}$$

where

$$p_n = \left\{ x | x \geq 0, \sum_{i=1}^{n} x_i = 1 \right\} \tag{1.7}$$

is the standard simplex. Then $\mathbf{Q}(x)$ contains a maximum characteristic value which is denoted $\rho(\mathbf{Q})$. Furthermore, if $\mathbf{Q}(x)$ is homogenous of degree 1, that is if $m = 1$ as a special case of assumption (c), then $\rho(\mathbf{Q})$ is the largest of all the Eigenvalues of $\mathbf{Q}(x)$.

Proof: Nikaido (1968).

In the vicinity of an equilibrium, $\rho(\mathbf{Q})$ can be locally linearized as $\mathbf{Q}(x) = \mathbf{Q}(x^*)$, where x^* is x in equilibrium. We then have the Eigen-equation

$$\rho \mathbf{z} = \mathbf{Q}(x^*)\mathbf{z} \tag{1.8}$$

with the equilibrium growth rate $\rho(\boldsymbol{Q}(x^*))$. Applying the Frobenius–Perron theorem we can conclude that the rate of return to scientific capital, ρ, will increase with

a. an increase in the scientific infrastructure in any region,
b. a decrease in any distance, d_{ij},
c. a decrease in the general distance friction, β,
d. an increase in the rate of subsidies to scientific research in any region.

Changes of types a–d, as specified above, influence the rate of return to science capital in all nodes to the same extent—but only in the long run after attaining general equilibrium.

CONCLUSIONS

Inventions and other forms of creativity depend on external support in the form of funding. In recent decades this has become a policy priority in government and industry, reflecting a search for dynamic comparative advantages. Nevertheless, the relative share of R&D expenditures allocated to basic scientific research in universities is between 10 and 30 percent in most countries. This share is especially low in East Asian countries such as China, Japan and Korea. One possible cause of the low share allocated to the scientific infrastructure is the myopic nature of political decisions as compared with the necessary foresight of more than a decade in high-tech industries focusing on increasingly complex products and production systems.

In this chapter we propose a new approach to modelling the complexity of products. The approach uses definitions that were originally proposed in another context by Chaitin, Kolmogorov and Solomonoff. The basic idea is that the slow and steady accumulation of scientific research generates increasingly complex theories. Such theories and models are potentially useful for the more rapid industrial R&D of products and production systems. In our model, the decision-makers that shape firms' R&D strategies treat established scientific theories as a fixed knowledge infrastructure.

Hollingsworth has shown empirically that the organization of complex scientific research projects that aim at scientific breakthroughs has to be carried out by teams that are much more interdisciplinary and open-minded than is normal in firms' R&D efforts.

We conclude that the development of science toward increasingly complex theories, models and products causes a need for more complex cognitive capacity among individual scientists as well as within laboratories and other research organizations at the micro level. Moreover, the increase in expected (but uncertain) individual creativity that accompanies good access to new and diversified knowledge provides strong arguments for locating such micro-level research organizations in large, open and diverse city regions.

Hence we expect science to be clustered in space. In line with this expectation we formulate a spatial general equilibrium model of science clusters. This model is a non-linear Eigen-equation, in which scientific collaboration gains, R&D support systems and the level of complexity of products and production systems act as joint determinants of scientists' clustering patterns.

Statistics on the scientific output of European city regions show that the distribution is clustered in a limited number of regions. Twenty of the twenty-five leading regions are located in the north-western quadrant of Europe, alluding to a future super-region of comparative advantages in the production of science and complex products that encompasses leading city regions in Benelux, Britain, northern France, western Germany, Scandinavia and Switzerland. There are few regional analogies in the south or east, and none at all in the south-east.

Some policy conclusions can be formulated. The first and most obvious conclusion is related to national knowledge policy. Scientific research has in contemporary times provided the knowledge infrastructure of industrial R&D investments. The importance of this infrastructure for the productivity of R&D in the industries is growing with the growth of complexity of products and production systems. However, most of the OECD countries spend a very small part of total R&D investments on scientific research. An increase is urgently needed in most countries and especially in Japan and the Asian tiger economies.

A second policy conclusion is related to the growing contradiction between scientific specialization to gain comparative advantages and the need for diversified science laboratories and institutes to handle the increasing complexity, as shown by Hollingsworth. The current focus on publication quantities and citation frequencies by university and research-funding administrations in their selection of scientists to be supported tends to favour scientific specialists, with detrimental consequences for creativity in complex research fields. Much more of the science resources should be allocated to projects that have secured scientific diversity. Such projects usually have leaders with a demonstrated capacity to handle cognitive complexity by integrating different disciplines and fields.

Finally, it seems especially important from a regional development perspective that most areas outside north-western Europe increase their spending on basic science and applied research.

REFERENCES

Andersson, Å.E. (1985). *Kreativitet – Storstadens framtid*. Stockholm: Prisma.

Andersson, Å.E., Beckmann, M.J. (2009). *Economics of Knowledge. Theory, Models and Measurements*. Cheltenham, UK and Northampton, MA, USA: Edward Elgar Publishing.

Andersson, Å.E., Persson, O. (1993). Networking scientists. *Annals of Regional Science*, 27(1): 11–21.

Andersson, D.E., Andersson, Å.E. (2013). The economic value of experience goods. In: Sundbo, J., Sørensen, F. (eds.), *Handbook on the Experience Economy*. Cheltenham, UK and Northampton, MA, USA: Edward Elgar Publishing.

Anderstig, C., Hårsman, B. (1986). On occupation structure and location pattern in the Stockholm region. *Regional Science and Urban Economics*, 16: 97–122.

Baumol, W.J. (2004). Education for innovation: entrepreneurial breakthroughs vs. corporate incremental improvements. *National Bureau of Economic Research* WP No.10578.

Casti, J.L., DePauli, W. (2000). *Gödel*. Cambridge, MA: Perseus.

Chaitin, G.J. (1966). On the length of programs for computing finite binary sequences. *Journal of the ACM*, 13(4): 547–569.

Florida, R. (2002). *The Rise of the Creative Class*. New York, NY: Basic Books.

Glaeser, E., Mare, D. (2001). Cities and skills. *Journal of Labor Economics*, 19: 316–342.

Hollingsworth, R. (2007). High cognitive complexity and the making of major scientific discoveries. In: Sales, A., Fournier, M. (eds.), *Knowledge, Communication,*

and Creativity. London, UK and Thousand Oaks, CA: Sage Publications, pp. 129–155.
Hollingsworth, R. (2009). The role of institutions and organizations in shaping radical scientific innovations. In: Magnusson, L., Ottosson, J. (eds.), *The Evolution of Path Dependence*. Cheltenham, UK and Northampton, MA, USA: Edward Elgar Publishing, pp. 139–165.
Kolmogorov, A.N. (1965). Three approaches to the quantitative definition of information. *Problems of Information Transmission*, 1(1): 1–7.
Lööf, H., Navabi, P. (2013). Increasing returns to smart cities. *Regional Science Policy & Practice*, 5(2): 255–262.
Machlup, F. (1980). *Knowledge: Its Creation, Distribution, and Economic Significance* (Vol. 1). Princeton, NJ: Princeton University Press.
Matthiessen, C.W., Schwarz, A.W., Find, S. (2011). Research nodes and networks. In: Andersson, D.E., Andersson, Å.E., Mellander, C. (eds.), *Handbook of Creative Cities*. Cheltenham, UK and Northampton, MA: Edward Elgar Publishing, pp. 211–228.
Nikaido, H. (1968). *Convex Structures and Economic Theory*. New York, NY: Academic Press.
OECD (2012). *Science and Technology Indicators*. Paris: OECD.
Ramsey, F.P. (1927). Facts and propositions. *Aristotelian Society*, Supplementary Volume 7.
Sahlin, N.-E. (1990). *The Philosophy of F.P. Ramsey*. Cambridge, UK: Cambridge University Press.
Simonton, D.K. (2011). Big-C creativity in the big city. In: Andersson, D.E., Andersson, Å.E., Mellander, C. (eds.), *Handbook of Creative Cities*. Cheltenham, UK and Northampton, MA: Edward Elgar Publishing, pp. 72–84.
Solomonoff, R. (1964). A formal theory of inductive inference, part II. *Information and Control*, 7(2): 224–254.

2. Agglomeration economies and smart cities

Ana Maria Bonomi Barufi and Karima Kourtit

1. URBAN AREAS IN ECONOMIC THEORY

Cities all over the world are in a state of flux and tend to exhibit in most cases a steadily growing pattern. Apart from a few exceptions ('shrinking cities', 'cities in decline'), the global map shows an increasing urbanization. Clearly, cities may turn into diffuse urban agglomerations (including suburban urban areas, poly-nuclear satellites), but the trend is undeniably towards a rise in urbanized settlement patterns. This trend is caused by the fact that urban areas may be characterized as powerhouses with unprecedented agglomeration benefits of all kind (see e.g. Combes et al., 2012). Of course, there are also negative agglomeration advantages (see e.g. Fragkias et al., 2013), but as long as the positive advantages supersede the negative ones, the urbanization trend will continue (see Kourtit, 2014a,b,c; Kourtit and Nijkamp, 2015; Van Geenhuizen and Nijkamp, 2012; Nijkamp, 2008).

The conceptualization and measurement of agglomeration (dis)advantages has prompted a wealth of urban-economic research (see e.g. Duranton and Puga, 2014; Glaeser, 1998; Henderson, 2010). In addition to standard economic agglomeration indices, alternative, mainly non-economic, indicators have been developed, such as the Human Development Index (HDI) and the Happy Planet Index (HPI). These indicators are rather informative, but deserve to receive a more specific urban focus. It is evident that the spatial influx of people and activities into urban agglomerations presupposes high agglomeration benefits, while such benefits prompt in turn new waves of people and economic activity into urban areas.

In fact, urbanization is a structural process in motion all over the world, especially in developing countries (Glaeser, 2011; Kourtit and Nijkamp, 2013a; Nijkamp and Kourtit, 2012). This movement towards cities happens in spite of the rising costs of large urban areas, related to land use, housing, transportation and labour force (van Oort and Lambooy, 2014). It is noticeable that there is not only a trend towards mega-cities, but there are also many movements directed to smaller agglomerations (with less than 500,000 inhabitants), which may also act as relevant drivers of urban growth (UNFPA, 2007).

The industrial composition of these urban areas may vary, with small and medium-sized cities possibly achieving a status of specialized centres, in contrast to more diversified and larger ones (Henderson, 2010). In such conditions, it is important to understand not only why there are cities and how economic agents benefit from them, but also how the modern city can reinvent itself to become more sustainable and to better accommodate the needs of a modern society.

The question regarding the existence of cities and the consequent trade flows between them has been largely debated in the literature on urban and regional economics. However, this has not been the case for studies based on the competitive paradigm of neoclassical economic theory (exemplified by Arrow and Debreu, 1954), as they could not properly include space and increasing returns as additional dimensions of economic modelling (Fujita and Thisse, 2012).

In more detail, even if spatial interdependences are considered in the neoclassical model as additional characteristics of the choice of place to work and consume, space is still taken as homogeneous (it does not affect the utility of consumers and the production set of firms, and consumers do not have any a priori preference for a specific location). As shown by Starrett (1978), under a homogeneous space with a finite number of locations, transportation frictions and locally non-satiated preferences, there is no competitive equilibrium with goods transported between locations (the 'Spatial Impossibility Theorem'). In these models, trade is substituted for the mobility of production factors and all the local consumption is satisfied by local production.

Relaxing the assumptions of the neoclassical model, one of the possibilities to understand cities and their trade flows is to allow for spatial heterogeneity. Nevertheless, this factor has less variation within countries, making it more appropriate for modern urban economic theory to consider increasing returns to scale as an explanation for the existence of cities (Brakman et al., 2009). Such agglomeration forces are generated by non-market interactions between economic agents. Another possibility is that under imperfect competition, firms are price-makers (by product differentiation or oligopolistic strategies), meaning that their spatial distribution along with consumers will determine regional prices and may generate agglomerations (Combes et al., 2008). This last approach is more related to economic geography and spatial competition models.

The focus here will be on the second modelling strategy discussed above (based on urban-economic theories), as our interest lies in the urban level of analysis. In this context, agglomeration economies are defined as external economies of scale generated by the spatial concentration of economic agents. Therefore, individuals and firms may benefit from being concentrated in cities by obtaining higher wages and higher productivity levels, respectively.

The next section will discuss how agglomeration economies are generated, along with their measurement. The third section explores the concept of knowledge externalities and how new technologies can change their formation. The concept of smart cities and how they can deal with the problems posed by large urban areas while fostering the generation and exchange of knowledge is discussed in Section 4. Next, Section 5 will highlight the rich potential of digital technology, while the final section presents the main conclusions and final remarks.

2. MICRO-FOUNDATIONS AND THE SCOPE OF ANALYSIS OF AGGLOMERATION ECONOMIES

The concept of agglomeration economies is strongly tied to the idea of proximity, as they result from the 'interaction (often involuntary) among economic agents made possible by the lesser amount of spatial friction that occurs in concentrated locations' (Capello, 2014, p. 163). They are of particular interest due to their positive effect on the productivity of firms and the utility of individuals. Among other advantages, they present a hedge against uncertainty in the economic relations (Gordon and McCann, 2000). Models of economic growth have been focusing mostly on the gains generated by knowledge externalities and innovations, which are classified as dynamic externalities, as they increase the innovative capacity of firms and aim to explain not only how cities form, but also why they grow (Glaeser et al., 1992; Pessoa, 2014).

It is noteworthy that static externalities are associated with an increase in the efficiency of technologies that are already in use, explaining the existing distribution of economic activity, productivity and amenities, but not their growth. Among these, there are urbanization and localization externalities, which refer to the co-localization with firms from many sectors or from firms of the same sector, respectively. In the case of urbanization economies, an increase in urban scale or population density may allow firms to increase their production without improving productivity or efficiency (de Groot et al., 2009).

Therefore, spatial equilibrium models applied to an urban context are usually concerned with how dynamic externalities can affect the distribution of economic activity and the interactions between economic agents. Glaeser and Gottlieb (2009) develop a basic model to understand the effects of agglomerations on productivity and income, which should encompass the production side, individual utilities and the housing market (inspired in the Rosen-Roback tradition). Departing from a basic production function with an explicit term related to the productivity level, the labour demand function derived from the optimization process of the firm will present a positive relationship between wages and productivity. In a dynamic setting, the model includes urban changes and an adjustment of the local economy caused by migration and changes in the housing market. Agglomeration economies are multipliers of the exogenous factors that affect productivity, population, wages and prices, amplifying the relationship between amenities, housing supply and the economic agents.

The measurement of agglomeration economies requires a better understanding of the mechanisms that generate them. In this context, there has been a large discussion in the literature on the micro-foundations of agglomeration externalities. Marshall (1890) identifies three main channels through which proximity can lead to extraordinary gains: it makes possible the exchange of information and knowledge; there are potential benefits from labour market pooling; and firms may share inputs, specialized or not. These interactions are stronger between firms belonging to the same sector and they happen outside the traditional market mechanisms, without prices.

With a slightly different and broader perspective, Glaeser and Gottlieb (2009) argue that such externalities can be associated with the reduction of transportation costs of goods (greater proximity between intermediate goods supply and demand), people (labour markets are more efficient in urban areas and service providers have greater access to their clients), and ideas (stronger knowledge exchange between people and firms).

Duranton and Puga (2004) and Puga (2010) present some more specific concepts that are focused on the mechanisms driving the theory: (i) sharing (facilities, gains from individual specialization and variety, and risk – labour pool); (ii) matching (higher matching quality and quantity among workers and firms); and (iii) learning (knowledge generation, diffusion and accumulation). Finally, Rosenthal and Strange (2004) consider additional elements that generate agglomeration economies, such as local natural advantages, home market effects, consumption externalities and rent seeking.

It is worth mentioning that there may be agglomeration diseconomies in bigger cities associated with pollution, congestion and higher costs (of land, labour force and transportation), which can lead to negative externalities for firms and individuals (Glaeser and Maré, 2001). Moreover, the cost–benefit functions faced by different groups of economic actors in large urban areas are expected to present a certain degree of heterogeneity, determining distinct locational choices (Fujita and Thisse, 2012).

The exchange of knowledge and ideas is a common element of the different mechanisms underlying agglomeration externalities, being related to the productivity shifts discussed above through the creation and adoption of new products and processes. This concept is central to studies investigating the industrial scope of agglomeration economies (Rosenthal and Strange, 2004), especially for the comparison between specialized, diversified and competitive urban structures. In this context, the MAR model[1] advocates that industrial specialization fosters the generation of knowledge spillovers, as the similarities between firms facilitate their interactions through the circulation of workers, imitation and business relations (Glaeser et al., 1992). Furthermore, a certain monopolistic power can be more suitable for innovation, as it increases the capacity of firms to internalize knowledge externalities (Capello, 2014).

Alternatively, according to Jacobs (1969), the source of knowledge externalities is external to the industry, being related to industrial diversity. A higher variety of industries can generate more opportunities to create, share and combine ideas and practices, as well as to exchange skills. In this case, competition is viewed as an incentive for firms to innovate and to adopt new ideas, and usually industries that share a common science base can profit further from a diverse environment.

The third main theoretical perspective concerning the generation of knowledge externalities is based on Porter (1990). In his view, a competitive environment fosters economic growth, as it gives incentives for firms to innovate and to promote technical progress. This process is stronger in a specialized economy, as knowledge spillovers occur mainly within vertically integrated industries.

These different perspectives can be harmonized by considering that the maturity and the technological content of a certain industry can affect the way it benefits from the different types of agglomeration economies. Standardized manufacturing with well-established firms may derive higher benefits from the agglomeration of their own industry (specialization), while innovative and high-technology industries will tend to locate in larger and more diverse urban areas (Beaudry and Schiffauerova, 2009; Henderson, 2010).

This discussion shows that it is important to understand not only how productivity is affected by city size, but also to what extent the sectoral composition of an urban area may be more or less beneficial to

[1] Marshall-Arrow-Romer, referring to the Marshallian externalities discussed above, combined with more recent advances in economic growth theory.

firms in specific industries. In this sense, agglomeration economies can be studied simultaneously by their direct effect over productivity and by their industrial scope. Nonetheless, the current empirical literature is still facing difficulties in finding consistent results, requiring a careful re-evaluation of concepts and methodologies (van Oort and Lambooy, 2014). One of these new concepts refers to 'smart cities' and will be discussed in Section 4.

An additional aspect to be mentioned is that the present section has been mainly discussing agglomeration economies generated by geographical proximity (Capello, 2014). However, there are different dimensions through which individuals and firms can interact, especially in relation to dynamic externalities and knowledge exchange. Section 3 will present a contribution to this issue and how new technologies can change the role of space for the generation of these externalities.

3. KNOWLEDGE EXTERNALITIES, PROXIMITY AND NEW TECHNOLOGIES

The previous section has discussed dynamic externalities and their relationship with knowledge creation and exchange. In spite of the clear importance that these elements have for the local competitive advantage (Beaudry and Schiffauerova, 2009), there are many aspects of knowledge externalities which are still unclear in the framework of the theoretical and empirical literature. Among them, there are the reach of spatial spillovers (Krugman, 2009) and the relative importance of different types of proximity (Boschma, 2005).

There is a first distinction to be made between different types of knowledge, namely the distinction between tacit and codified knowledge. While the former refers to a person-specific knowledge, requiring direct contact between individuals to be transmitted, the latter can be transacted in markets and easily transferred among individuals (van Oort and Lambooy, 2014). Furthermore, tacit knowledge is acquired through learning-by-doing or learning-by-using, and its transmission requires proximity in different dimensions, such as spatial, cultural and social (Boschma, 2005).

In this context, face-to-face (F2F) contact is usually associated with the transmission of tacit knowledge and is related to the different mechanisms of generation of knowledge externalities. The main advantages associated with F2F involve allowing the communication between different agents even with non-codifiable information, reducing the problems with incentives and lack of trust, the evaluation of potential partners and socialization, and improving performance by giving incentives for greater effort and motivating the individuals (Storper and Venables, 2004). Therefore, the spatial dimension has a crucial role in the exchange of knowledge, especially in its tacit version. The exchange of codified knowledge may also require spatial proximity, because the interpretation and assimilation of this kind of information can depend on tacit knowledge (Howells, 2002).

The literature on spatial spillovers and agglomeration economies has focused significantly on space as the main source of interaction between firms and agents. In recent years, however, there has been a shift in the perception of the types of proximity which are essential to the promotion of knowledge spillovers and innovation. For instance, the endogenous growth literature highlights that innovations are determined by increasing returns, which are associated with spatial, relational and institutional proximity (Capello and Nijkamp, 2009). In this sense, there are different factors in motion to promote innovation, with proximity being considered a transitional concept between socio-economic and spatial interactions (Stimson, 2014).

Therefore, proximity is not exclusively a geographical concept anymore, being accompanied by other relevant dimensions (cognitive, organizational, social and institutional). In this sense, there is a high degree of complementarity between the different relevant dimensions, but even if geographical proximity can be substituted by a combination of other types of proximity in the learning process (Boschma, 2005; Torre and Rallet, 2005) there is still a great deal of knowledge exchange associated to space (Camagni and Capello, 2009). Combining the different perspectives seems to be the most interesting way to proceed in order to model and estimate innovation and knowledge generation (Capello, 2014).

Another relevant discussion in this subject relates to the role of geography in innovation systems under the rise of information and communication technologies (ICTs) that have emerged in the past few decades, accompanied by an increase in the globalization of economic activity (e.g. Cairncross, 2001). These transformations are said to be changing the requirement of proximity in space by altering the way knowledge and information are produced and exchanged, based on the concepts of tradability and codification. The codification of information and meanings allows the transformation of complex and unfamiliar coordination tasks into routine activities, which can be placed in cheaper and remote locations. This reinforces the tendency of de-agglomeration of activities with codified knowledge.

On the other hand, new activities are created through innovation, and usually the tasks related to them are complex and unfamiliar, requiring F2F contact and geographical proximity in general terms. Tacit knowledge will permeate these new activities, meaning that the knowledge required to conduct them is usually embodied in high-skilled workers (Storper and

Venables, 2004). Moreover, the quality of F2F interaction is higher than the electronic one, and they intersect in a complementary manner to lead to knowledge and information creation and diffusion. In this sense, digital technologies are usually able to maintain but not to create communities, while information may be easily diffused, but not necessarily understood (Morgan, 2004). Recently, highly detailed data on digital interactions between individuals started becoming available for an empirical evaluation of the relevance of space under the new technological paradigms. The first results show that spatial and organizational proximities are still relevant to determine the strength of digital networks (see e.g. Tranos and Nijkamp, 2013a).

In summary, urban areas still constitute an essential ingredient for the generation of productivity gains associated with the production and exchange of knowledge, even with the reduction of the cost of long-distance contacts caused by recent technological advances. Moreover, other types of proximity are also relevant in this context and should be controlled for in an evaluation of the role played by space in economic interactions.

The recent technological development enabled the creation of more efficient and sustainable urban centres, which are being studied within the concept of smart cities. Among their main characteristics, there is the strengthening of interactions between economic agents, especially those involving knowledge transmission, reinforcing the formation of agglomeration economies. The next sections will explore this concept and how digital technologies can provide tools for analysing smart cities.

4. SMART CITIES

The 'urban century' has led to an increasing research and policy interest in urban agglomerations as fireplaces of economic wealth and growth (see also Drobniak and Brandenburg, 2012). The strategic position of these areas has prompted the popularity of a new concept, namely, the 'smart city' (see e.g. Hollands, 2008). In the meantime, a great variety of definitions of a smart city has emerged. Ingredients of a smart city are inter alia: advanced telecommunication, knowledge intensity, sophisticated environmental management, high efficiency or productivity, cohesive social capital, a high quality of human health. An example of an often quoted definition can be found in Caragliu et al. (2011): a city is smart if 'investments in human and social capital and traditional (transport) and modern (ICT) communication infrastructure fuel sustainable economic growth and a high quality of life, with a wise management of natural resources, through participatory governance'.

According to Nam and Pardo (2011), a smart city is an organic entity, characterized by three fundamental factors: technology (e.g. digital networks), institutions (e.g. regulations) and human factors (e.g. suprastructure). The authors also refer to related concepts, in particular: digital city, intelligent city, ubiquitous city, wired city, hybrid city and information city (see also Roche, 2014). It goes without saying that a smart city derives its welfare-enhancing and innovative potential from information technology, including e-services and digital communication services (see e.g. Akman et al., 2005; Batty et al., 2012; Nixon and Koutrakou, 2007; Schaffers et al., 2011). It is thus clear that smart cities and urban ICT use are two parallel phenomena.

According to Paskaleva (2013) the characteristics of a smart city can be categorized as follows:

- exploitation of networked infrastructures to improve efficiency and to enable the social, environmental and cultural attributes of urban development;
- a vision and strategy for creating a competitive city, with the smart city taking the opportunities ICTs offer to increase local prosperity and competitiveness;
- an approach to sustainable and inclusive cities, placing the main weight on the social capital of urban development.

A more comprehensive overview of concepts and policies of smart cities can be found in Deakin (2014). The latter study contains a wealth of reflections and case studies on smart city initiatives. Smart cities are not evolving in a wonderland of no political dimensions, but are shaped through dedicated policies. The challenges faced by smart cities are in particular:

- a strong knowledge orientation based on creative classes and innovative minds;
- a dynamic perspective on new opportunities based on a learning policy mode;
- a strong sense of entrepreneurship based on competitive business strategies in open urban systems;
- a strong focus in the public sector on ICT and digital technology based on e-management of the urban area;
- a rigorous choice for quality of life and sustainable development of cities based on e-awareness;
- a sophisticated use of digital data based on a geo-science orientation using the city as an advanced digital data machine (the city as a 'big data' producer).

Smart cities are places which through the application of ICT and knowledge-based activities are more efficient, more sustainable and safer. In such places the economies of density, proximity, accessibility and connectivity are of crucial importance for urban vitality and creativity. Clearly, the modern digital technology allows also for external connectivity, so that smart cities are not islands of isolation, but hubs in a global open network of cities. The various dimensions can be summarized in Figure 2.1.

Smart cities are based on smart infrastructure and supra-structure connecting the physical and the virtual world. In this context, Tranos and Nijkamp (2013b, p. 5) argued: 'The physical world of urban (infra)structure and transport, and the virtual world of urban communications and interactions, are often regarded as two disjointed domains.' Structuralist explanations for the spatial constellations of cities – such as Von Thünen's concentric model or Burgess' ecological layout of cities – did not take into account the close interwovenness between the real and the cognitive dimensions of city life. In the past years, the emergence of ICTs has prompted an overwhelming interest in the cyber-constituents of modern cities (see e.g. Cohen et al., 2002; Cohen-Blankshtain and Nijkamp, 2004; Cohen-Blankshtain et al., 2004; Graham and Marvin, 1996; Melody, 1996). It turns out that ICTs do not only generate benefits of all kinds for the urban economy, but also act as a driver that shapes novel urban structures and influences its metabolism.

It is evident that ICT plays a critical role in the functioning and governance of smart cities. Concepts like e-democracy, e-learning or e-care would not have emerged without the presence of modern technology. The use of digital tools for smart city studies and governance will be discussed in the next section.

5. DIGITAL TOOLS FOR SMART CITY ANALYSIS[2]

5.1 The Digital Urban World

In recent years, the popular concept of smart cities has often been linked to advanced ICT use in cities, with the aim to enhance efficiency (e.g. competitiveness) and sustainability (e.g. energy saving). Smart cities arise because of intelligent use of digital information, for instance in domains

[2] This section was inspired by several studies that have been produced in the context of the Joint Programming Initiative 'Urban Europe' (see in particular Nijkamp and Kourtit, 2011, 2012, 2013; Kourtit and Nijkamp, 2013a,b,c,d, 2015a,b; Kourtit et al., 2013a,b, 2015a,b) and other related documents produced in this context by the author (see in particular Caragliu et al., 2012; Kourtit, 2014a,b,c; Kourtit et al., 2014; Kourtit and Nijkamp, 2015).

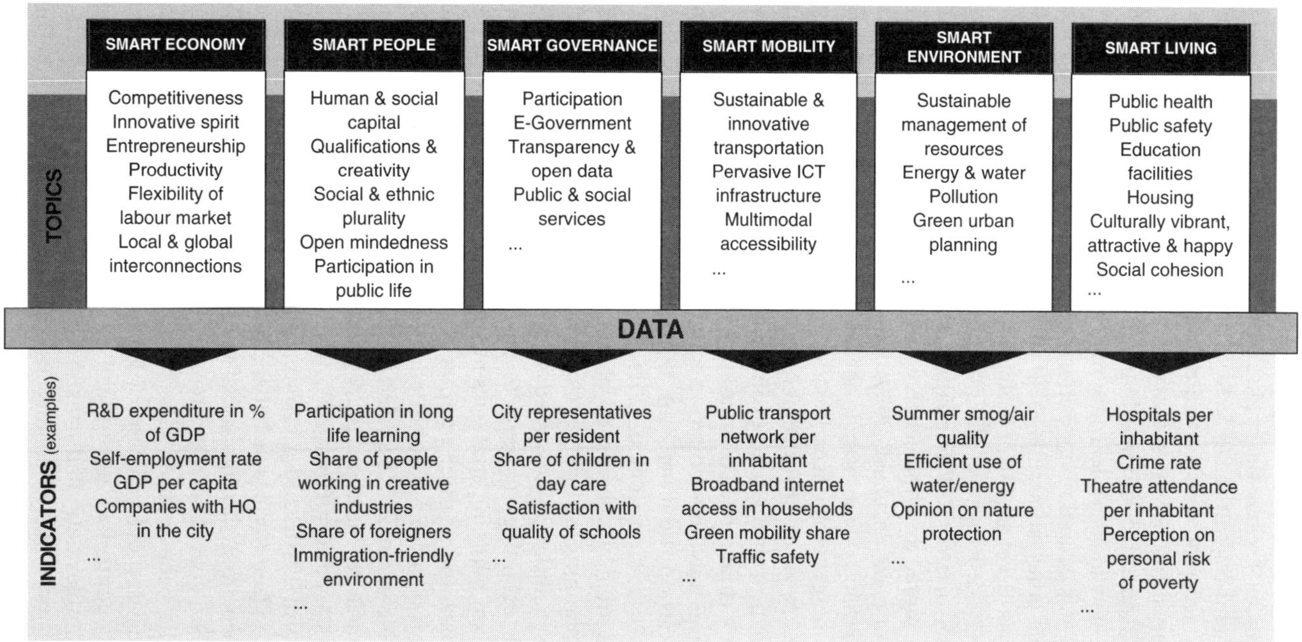

Source: Giffinger et al. (2007).

Figure 2.1 The 'smart city' constituency

like human health, mobility, energy use, education, knowledge transfer and urban governance (Arribas-Bel et al., 2015; Caragliu et al., 2014; Castells, 1998; Kourtit and Nijkamp, 2015; Kourtit et al., 2015a). ICT has turned into a rapidly accepted and systemic innovation that has penetrated all domains of public and private activity in urban agglomerations. It has also become an indispensable tool in urban and regional planning, especially in the context of new ideas on learning regions and smart cities. Clearly, the advent of ICT has caused many opportunities to design and realize smart and sustainable cities, sometimes also called digital cities or cyber-places (see also Arribas-Bel et al., 2015; Hollands, 2008; Komninos, 2006; Kourtit and Nijkamp, 2015; Kourtit et al., 2015a,c).

The increased use of ICT in shaping the modern and complex urban system has prompted an unprecedented volume of digital data (sometimes called 'big data'; see Barabasi, 2009; Kourtit et al., 2015b,c). Such data may pertain to many phenomena in the city, such as use of public facilities, traffic flows, emergency services, weather conditions, entertainment events, mobile phone usage or crowd emergence, often in a real-time context. Digital information through accessible wireless communication networks may become a virtual replica of human space–time behavioural patterns in urban areas, and may hence offer an important source of real-time information on 'cities on the move' (see also Arribas-Bel et al., 2015; Kourtit and Nijkamp 2015; Kourtit et al., 2015c).

Digital data are nowadays essential and provide a new tool for efficient and effective planning of urban space, inter alia in the field of transportation, public facilities or advanced services to citizens (see also Roche, 2014). Digital technology appears to create novel pathways for contemporaneous urban planning strategies in smart cities. The use of ICT reinforces the impact and position of smart cities, not only from an efficiency perspective, but also from a social cohesion perspective (cf. Lewis, 2008; Ratcliffe and Newman, 2011; Sadler, 2005; Westlund, 2015). Social media is one of the most recent and rapidly growing phenomena (Facebook was launched in 2004, Panoramio in 2005, Twitter in 2006, FourSquare in 2009 and Instagram in 2010), and is essential for the generation of bottom-up real information (see Arribas-Bel et al., 2015, p. 2).

Virtual information through social media is likely to change the functioning of urban spaces, as a permanent flow of interactive information will change the behaviour of citizens, firms and visitors into dynamic urban consumerism and behaviour (Pentland, 2009). Smart cities tend to be increasingly controlled and influenced by – top-down and bottom-up organized – complex data platforms. Access to and smart use of such data platforms will most likely become critical success factors for the urban future of our planet (see Arribas-Bel et al., 2015; Kourtit et al., 2015c).

Although a rising share of the world population is moving to urban areas – which may likely become socio-economic and political powerhouses in a globally connected planet – it is noteworthy that spatial concentration and connectivity do not only manifest themselves physically: virtual flows of information in and between cities are becoming more important than traditional material appearances or modalities. And such virtual flows are less visible: cities tend to become cyber-places. The analysis and management of such complex data systems call for new data techniques (e.g. data mining, agent-based modelling) based on virtual data (Global Positioning System (GPS), Global System for Mobile (GSM) communications, observatories, among others). Geo-science – in particular, geodesign and geo-imaging – may then provide new urban management tools, in which various stakeholders are involved, often in interactive environments and dialogues. Examples can be found in recent 'urban facebooks' and 'urban dashboards'. This development will cause a revolution in the management of complex urban systems and prompt the emergence of 'smart or intelligent cities' (Kourtit and Nijkamp, 2015, p. 3). Essentially, a smart city emerges when urban intelligence is added to information. This information is created by sensors of several forms and stored in 'electronic warehouses' (e.g. remote servers, data centres, etc.) and offers a new map of the structure and interactions in urban life.

This new digital technology application is often also coined internet geography or cyber-geography (Batty, 2012; Leamer and Storper, 2001; Malecki, 2002; Storper and Venables, 2004; Tranos and Nijkamp, 2013b). This information incorporated in these – often real-time – databases is increasingly used in social media and location-based services, for example Foursquare and Facebook are able to inform others on the spatial imprint of daily urban activity behaviour of residents or visitors, and opens new ways for digital geography and even psycho-geography (in relation to spatial mental maps (see Kourtit et al., 2015c)). In the public domain this type of information can also be used for geocentric incident management and urban or regional crowd management (see also Arribas-Bel et al., 2015; Boyd and Crawford, 2012). In the next subsection, we will illustrate the potential of digital technology for urban governance by means of an application of a recently developed tool, coined 'Urban Facebook' (see Kourtit and Nijkamp, 2013d,e).

5.2 Urban Facebook

The 'urban facebook' approach is a new tool that is extensively supported by high-quality visual assessment and is the base for methods aiming to map novel redevelopment initiatives, in order to be able to identify and understand specific local needs and necessary spatial developments (see Kourtit and Nijkamp, 2013d, p.4381). It offers a basis for interventions that tackle present and future urban problems, foundations, challenges and consequences (in combination with urban scenarios, which are essentially strategic future image experiments based on, for example, the imagining of future smart cities' positions) designed to achieve the desired goals related to urban strategic visions, while, in addition, this approach may encourage the urban economy to stay (internationally) competitive (see Kourtit and Nijkamp, 2013d, p.4381).

This stakeholder-oriented bottom-up approach is, inter alia, based on information collected during interviews from different stakeholders with a wide range of interests in relation to the area concerned, followed by the use of a strength–weakness–opportunities–threats (SWOT) analysis methodology using social media (viz. a Facebook tool) and visual support tools (e.g. three-dimensional pictures, movies). A novel element is the use of visual decision support tools – based on future images and photographs – in order to elicit preferences of stakeholders on various aspects of these future alternatives. This interactive approach helps to transform the current area into a new creative hotspot (Fusco Girard et al., 2014, p. 4). Thus, the framework is a direct action platform that offers social utilities to connect various people who work and live together, supported by high-quality visual assessment tools, for mapping intelligent, novel, redevelopment initiatives for the area under consideration.

This approach was carried out for different cases in Europe, for instance in and around the Nederlandsche Dok en Scheepsbouw Maatschappij (NDSM)-area – a former dockyard with a rich socio-economic and logistic history in Amsterdam – and in the Italian cities Torre Annunziata, Palermo, Naples and Venice (see Kourtit and Nijkamp, 2013d, p.4382). These case studies were undertaken in the context of an enhancement of the attractiveness and promotion of these areas or cities, so as to highlight new urban perspectives and alternatives, and to favour transitional urban systems for sustainable urban development from a forward-looking, long-term strategic policy perspective (a combination of backcasting and forecasting approaches), and to addresses the concerns, values and preferences of their various users, where vision and strategy have to fit well with their environment and its (new) functionality (Kourtit, 2014b, p.194). The evaluation of various development options of these areas and cities is based on a multidimensional analysis of relevant aspects supported by digital information tools, and aims to design a forward-fitting policy for the area or city concerned. The relevant governance evaluation criteria were extracted from interactive stakeholder experiments (Kourtit, 2014b). These case studies appear to offer a refreshing conceptual, methodological and applied policy perspective on the future role of historical areas and cities.

However, it is apparently a great challenge to monitor a complex urban management system and to trace whether the different actors involved are still on course (Kourtit, 2014a, pp. 161–162; Kourtit et al., 2015a). An intelligent and smart approach supported by ICT may become a critical complementary vehicle for proactive strategic urban policy and planning that is better grounded in empirical realities in a global urban environment (see also Boyer, 1983; Hall, 1988; Kourtit, 2014a, pp. 161–162; Ward, 1994). Using new comparable data and results supported by intelligent systems – for instance, the so-called 'urban i-dashboard' – helps to identify important patterns and trends. This intelligence approach may provide a convincing case for a novel view on a set of quantitative assessment instruments to map out the drivers of the urban performance in the 'century of cities' (Kourtit, 2014a, pp. 161–162; Kourtit and Nijkamp, 2015; Kourtit, 2014b,c).

5.3 Policy Monitor Dashboard

Cities are not crafted in stone, but are living organisms. They are evolving systems driven by a multiplicity of actors and stakeholders. It goes without saying that cities have many 'faces'; they are not uniform or identical. The management and governance of these modern, complex and ever-rising urban agglomerations calls for effective and focused decision-making tools. There is a general awareness that traditional urban planning tools (models, stakeholder analysis and consultation methods) are no longer able to cope with the multiplicity of challenges faced by cities in an open world, driven by digital technologies (Arribas-Bel et al., 2015, p. 2).

It is increasingly recognized that advanced ICT use in an urban setting may drastically change the organization of smart cities (see also Kourtit and Nijkamp, 2015). A review of the various opportunities created by ICT services in the context of urban social capital can be found in Cohen-Blankshtain and Nijkamp (2004). In recent years, much interest has arisen in operational Strategic Performance Measurement Systems (SPMS) dashboards for smart cities and urban areas; their use by local authorities has increased in recent years (Kourtit et al., 2015a, p. 15). A dashboard includes big digital data in the form of a set of balanced critical performance predictors (key performance indicators (KPIs)) related to urban or regional performance; together they form a 'digital dashboard'. In this context, a 'dashboard' is defined as a process tool of fundamental and genuine strategic choice(s) between different viable performance predictors, where steering and stimulating the development of a city takes place through critical performance handles, so that decision makers (e.g. responsible representatives, politicians, stakeholders and other actors) are able to take corrective or proactive actions to influence the (regional) constellation of cities' socio-economic characteristics (Kourtit et al., 2015a, p. 15).

5.4 Retrospect

It is clear that ICT adds a new dimension to social capital in the city, as introduced by Bourdieu (1986), amongst others. In particular, digital technology offers a low-cost, high-frequency and user-friendly addition to local social capital, for instance through digital opportunities such as Facebook, Twitter or text messages. This, combined with recent advances in the field of statistical and machine learning, opens an entirely new range of possibilities in terms of sensing and measuring many of the urban phenomena that Jane Jacobs described in her seminal book *The Death and Life of Great American Cities* (Jacobs, 1961) and that are at the heart of managing cities. ICT may be highly beneficial to smart cities, not only from an efficiency perspective, but also from a social cohesion perspective (cf. Arribas-Bel et al., 2015, p. 2; Lewis, 2008; Ratcliffe and Newman, 2011; Sadler, 2005; Westlund, 2015). It should be noted at the end that a critical success factor for such an urban intelligence is to exploit all cognitive and technological opportunities offered by ICT, and in particular the use of digital technologies. Cyberspace may create seemingly invisible but virtually interconnected cities and will have a decisive impact on the urban future in a globalizing world (see also Kourtit and Nijkamp, 2015).

6. PROSPECT

The rise of digital technologies has exerted an unprecedented impact on human activities in cities. The traditional scale and agglomeration advantages in cities were not reduced by the 'death of distance', but were reinforced by the digitization of human life. This digitization reached its highest benefits in urban agglomerations with the consequence that – contrary to the hypothesis of the 'death of distance' – large urban agglomerations were able to grow even faster. Especially the overarching connectivity potential (not only local, but also global) prompted a further rise in urbanization.

Modern social media were able to create new forms of social capital in urban areas, thanks to Twitter, YouTube, Flickr and many other computing and technological advances. This has also prompted a new boost in geo-science, for instance the proliferation of local-based services for traffic incident management, three-dimensional organization of urban space or contingency management based on urban imaginaries. Modern smart cities are likely to turn into open cyber-places that may strengthen contemporaneous urbanization trends. Knowledge and informative acquisition and discovery – as tools for proactive urban planning – will become a great challenge in the 'new urban century', in which data mining and machine learning will reinforce the established planning models machinery. Urban science – aiming at creating smart cities in the future – will most likely become a blend of many disciplines, such as economics, sociology, statistics, geography, informatics and demography.

ACKNOWLEDGEMENT

This contribution of Ana Maria Bonomi Barufi had the financial support of the Brazilian government through the National Council for Scientific and Technological Development (CNPq) – Process 229708/2013-7 and the Coordination for the Improvement of Higher Education Personnel – Process BEX 2501/14-7.

REFERENCES

Akman, I., Yazici, A., Mishrae, A., Arifoglu, A. (2005), E-government, *Government Information Quarterly*, Vol. 22, No. 2, pp. 239–257.

Arribas-Bel, D., Kourtit, K., Nijkamp, P., Steenbruggen, J. (2015), Cyber Cities: The Digital Basis of Social Buzz in Smart Cities, *Applied Spatial Analysis and Policy* (forthcoming).

Arrow, K., Debreu, G. (1954), Existence of an Equilibrium for a Competitive Economy, *Econometrica*, Vol. 22, pp. 265–290.

Barabási, A.-L. (2009), We Are at the Threshold of Understanding Complexity, *12 Scientists on the 21st Century*, World Science Forum, Budapest, pp. 19–26.

Batty, M. (2012), Building a Science of Cities, *Cities*, Vol. 29, pp. S9–S16.

Batty, M., Axhausen, K.W., Gianoth, F., Poednaoukhov, A., Bazzani, A., Wackowicz, M., Portugali, Y. (2012), Smart Cities of the Future, *European Physical Journal*, Vol. 214, No.1, pp. 481–518.

Beaudry, C., Schiffauerova, A. (2009), Who's Right, Marshall or Jacobs? The Localization versus Urbanization Debate, *Research Policy*, Vol. 38, pp. 318–337.

Boschma, R.A. (2005), Proximity and Innovation: A Critical Assessment, *Regional Studies*, Vol. 39, No. 1, pp. 61–74.

Bourdieu, P. (1986), The Forms of Capital. In Richardson, J.G. (ed.), *Handbook of Theory and Research for the Sociology of Education*, New York, Westport, CT and London: Greenwich Press, pp. 241–258.

Boyd, D., Crawford, K. (2012), Critical Questions for Big Data, *Information Communication & Society*, Vol. 15, No. 15, pp. 662–679.

Boyer, C. (1983), *Dreaming the Rational City*, Cambridge, MA: MIT Press.

Brakman, S., Garretsen, H., van Marrewijk, C. (2009), *The New Introduction to Geographical Economics*, Cambridge, UK: Cambridge University Press.
Cairncross, F. (2001), *The Death of Distance 2.0*, London: Texere Publishing Limited.
Camagni, R., Capello, R. (2009), Knowledge-based Economy and Knowledge Creation: The Role of Space. In Fratesi, U., Senn, L. (eds), *Growth and Innovation of Competitive Regions: The Role of Internal and External Connections*, Berlin Heidelberg: Springer-Verlag, pp. 145–165.
Capello, R. (2014), Proximity and Regional Innovation Processes: Is There Space for New Reflections? In Torre, A., Wallet, F. (eds), *Regional Development and Proximity Relations*, Cheltenham, UK and Northampton, MA, USA: Edward Elgar Publishing, pp. 163–194.
Capello, R., Nijkamp, P. (2009), Introduction: Regional Growth and Development Theories in the Twenty-First Century – Recent Theoretical Advances and Future Challenges. In Capello, R., Nijkamp, P. (eds), *Handbook of Regional Growth and Development Theories*, Cheltenham, UK and Northampton, MA, USA: Edward Elgar Publishing, pp. 1–16.
Caragliu, A., Del Bo, C., Nijkamp, P. (2011), Smart Cities in Europe, *Journal of Urban Technology*, Vol. 18, No. 2, pp. 65–82.
Caragliu, A., Del Bo, C., Kourtit, K., Nijkamp, P. (2014), Smart Cities, *International Encyclopedia of Social and Behavioral Sciences* (accepted).
Castells, M. (1998), *The Information Age: Economy, Society and Culture*, Oxford: Blackwell.
Cohen, G., Salomon, I., Nijkamp, P. (2002), Information-Communications Technologies (ICT) and Transport: Does Knowledge Underpin Policy? *Telecommunications Policy*, Vol. 26, pp. 31–52.
Cohen-Blankshtain, G., Nijkamp, P. (2004), The Appreciative System of Urban ICT Policies: An Analysis of Perceptions of Urban Policy Makers, *Growth and Change*, Vol. 35, pp. 166–197.
Cohen-Blankshtain, G., Nijkamp, P., Montfort, K.V. (2004), Modelling ICT Perceptions and Views of Urban Front-Liners, *Urban Studies*, Vol. 41, pp. 2647–2667.
Combes, P.P., Mayer, T., Thisse, J.F. (2008), *Economic Geography*, Princeton, NJ: Princeton University Press.
Combes, P., Duranton, G., Gobillon, L., Puga, D., Roux, S. (2012), The Productivity Advantages of Large Cities, *Econometrica*, Vol. 80, No. 9, pp. 2543–2594.
De Groot, H.L.F, Poot, J., Smit, M.J. (2009), Agglomeration Externalities, Innovation and Regional Growth: Theoretical Perspectives and Meta-Analysis. In Capello, R., Nijkamp, P. (eds), *Handbook of Regional Growth and Development Theories*, Cheltenham, UK and Northampton, MA, USA: Edward Elgar Publishing, pp. 256–281.
Deakin, M. (ed.) (2014), *Smart Cities*, London: Routledge.
Drobniak, A., Brandenburg, H. (eds) (2012), Urban Economic Resilience – New Concept for Post-Industrial City Transition, *Journal of Economics and Management*, Vol. 10, pp. 85–105.
Duranton, G., Puga, D. (2004), Micro-Foundations of Urban Agglomeration Economies. In Henderson, J.V., Thisse, J.F. (eds), *Handbook of Regional and Urban Economics*, Vol. 4, Amsterdam: North-Holland, pp. 2063–2117.
Duranton, G., Puga, D. (2014), The Growth of Cities. In Aghion, P., Durlauf,

S.N. (eds), *Handbook of Economic Growth*, Oxford: Elsevier, 1st edition, Vol. 2, pp. 781–785.
Fragkias, M., Lobo, J., Strumsky, D., Seto, K.C. (2013), Does Size Matter? Scaling of CO_2 Emissions and U.S. Urban Areas, *PLoS ONE*, Vol. 8, No. 6, e64727, pp. 1–8.
Fujita, M., Thisse, J.F. (2012), *Economics of Agglomeration: Cities, Industrial Location and Regional Growth*, 2nd edition, Cambridge, UK: Cambridge University Press.
Fusco Girard, L., Kourtit, K., Nijkamp, P. (2014), Waterfront Areas as Hotspots of Sustainable and Creative Development of Cities, *Sustainability*, Vol. 6, No. 7, pp. 4580–4586.
Giffinger, R., Fertner, C., Kramar, H., Kalasek, R., Pichler-Milanovic, N., Meijers, E. (2007), *Smart Cities – Ranking of European Medium-Sized Cities*, Vienna, UT: Centre of Regional Science From: http://www.smart-cities.eu. Retrieved 18 December 2012.
Glaeser, E.L. (1998), Are Cities Dying? *Journal of Economic Perspectives*, Vol. 12, No. 2, pp. 139–160.
Glaeser, E.L. (2011), *Triumph of the City: How Our Greatest Invention Makes Us Richer, Smarter, Greener, Healthier, and Happier*, London: Macmillan.
Glaeser, E.L., Maré, D.C. (2001), Cities and Skills, *Journal of Labour Economics*, Vol. 19, No. 2, pp. 316–342.
Glaeser, E.L., Gottlieb, J.D. (2009), The Wealth of Cities: Agglomeration Economies and Spatial Equilibrium in the United States, NBER Working Paper 14806.
Glaeser, E.L., Kallal, H.D., Scheinkman, J.A., Shleifer, A. (1992), Growth in Cities, *Journal of Political Economy*, Vol. 100, pp. 1126–1152.
Gordon, I.A., McCann, P. (2000), Industrial Clusters: Complexes, Agglomerations and/or Social Networks? *Urban Studies*, Vol. 37, No. 3, pp. 513–532.
Graham, S., Marvin, S. (1996), *Telecommunications and the City*, London and New York: Routledge.
Hall, P. (1988), *Cities of Tomorrow*, Oxford: Blackwell.
Henderson, J.V. (2010), Cities and Development, *Journal of Regional Science*, Vol. 50, No. 1, pp. 514–540.
Hollands, R.G. (2008), Will the Real Smart City Please Stand Up? *City*, Vol. 12, No. 3, pp. 303–320.
Howells, J.R.L. (2002), Tacit Knowledge, Innovation and Economic Geography, *Urban Studies*, Vol. 39, Nos. 5–6, pp. 871–884.
Jacobs, J. (1969), *The Economy of Cities*, New York: Vintage.
Komninos, N. (2006), The Architecture of Intelligent Cities: Integrating Human, Collective and Artificial Intelligence to Enhance Knowledge and Innovation. Intelligent Environments IE 06, 2nd IET International Conference on Intelligent Environments, pp. 53–61.
Kourtit, K. (2014a), *Competitiveness in Urban Systems – Studies on the 'Urban Century'*, Amsterdam: VU University.
Kourtit, K. (2014b), *The 'New Urban World' – Economic-Geographical Studies on the Performance of Urban Systems*, Poznań, Poland: Adam Mickiewicz University.
Kourtit, K. (2014c), Planet of Cities, by Shlomo Angel. 2012. Cambridge, MA: Lincoln Institute of Land Policy, *Journal of Regional Science*, Vol. 54, pp. 161–162.

Kourtit, K., Nijkamp, P. (2013a), In Praise of Megacities in a Global World. *Regional Science Policy and Practice*, Vol. 5, pp. 167–182.
Kourtit, K., Nijkamp, P. (2013b), Introduction: Regional Innovation Hotspots and Spatial Development, *Journal of Regional Science*, Vol. 53, pp. 745–748.
Kourtit, K., Nijkamp, P. (2013c), The New Urban World – The Challenge of Cities in Decline, *Romanian Journal of Regional Science*, Vol. 7, No. 2, pp. 9–28.
Kourtit, K., Nijkamp, P. (2013d), The Use of Visual Decision Support Tools in an Interactive Stakeholder Analysis—Old Ports as New Magnets for Creative Urban Development, *Sustainability*, Vol. 5, No. 9, pp. 3895–3905.
Kourtit, K., Nijkamp, P. (2013e), Creative Buzz Districts in Smart Cities: Urban Retro-Fitting and Urban Forward-Fitting Plans, *Romanian Journal of Regional Science*, Vol. 7, No. 2, pp. 37–57.
Kourtit, K., Nijkamp, P. (2015), Invisible Cities: The End of the Urban Century? *Italian Journal of Regional Science* (accepted).
Kourtit, K., Nijkamp, P., Partridge, M. (2013a), The New Urban World, *European Planning Studies*, Vol. 21, No. 3, pp. 285–290.
Kourtit, K., Nijkamp, P., Partridge, M. (eds) (2013b), The New Urban World – Opportunity Meets Challenge, *Regional Science Policy and Practice*, Vol. 5, No. 2, pp. 149–151.
Kourtit, K., Nijkamp, P., Franklin, R.S., Rodríguez-Pose, A. (2014), A Blueprint for Strategic Urban Research: The 'Urban Piazza', *Town Planning Review*, Vol. 85, No. 1, pp. 97–126.
Kourtit, K., Nijkamp, P., Partridge, M. (2015a), Challenges of the New Urban World, *Applied Spatial Analysis and Policy* (accepted).
Kourtit, K., Nijkamp, P., Scholten, H. (2015b), The Future of the New Urban World, *International Planning Studies* (accepted).
Kourtit, K., Nijkamp, P., Steenbruggen, J. (2015c), The Significance of Cyber Space for Urban Agglomerations – A Review of Impacts of Digital Data Systems on Smart Cities (unpublished paper).
Krugman, P. (2009), The Increasing Returns Revolution in Trade and Geography, *The American Economic Review*, Vol. 99, No. 3, pp. 561–571.
Leamer, E.E., Storper, M. (2001), The Economic Geography of the Internet Age, *Journal of International Business Studies*, Vol. 32, No. 4, pp. 641–666.
Lewis, P.M. (2008), *Promoting Social Cohesion, The Role of Community Media, Media and Information Society Division*, Directorate General of Human Rights and Legal Affairs, Council of Europe: http://www.amarc.org/conference_europe/document/Promoting_Social_Cohesion_The_Role_of_Communit_Media.pdf.
Malecki, E.J. (2002), The Economic Geography of the Internet's Infrastructure, *Economic Geography*, Vol. 78, pp. 399–424.
Marshall, A. (1890), *The Principles of Economics*, London: Macmillan.
Melody, W.H. (1996), Towards a Framework for Resigning Information Society Policies, *Telecommunication Policy*, Vol. 24, pp. 243–259.
Morgan, K. (2004), The Exaggerated Death of Geography: Learning, Proximity and Territorial Innovation Stems, *Journal of Economic Geography*, Vol. 4, pp. 3–21.
Nam, T., Pardo, T.A. (2011), Conceptualizing Smart City with Dimensions of Technology, People and Institutions, *Proceedings of the 12th Annual Digital Government Research Conference*, ACM, pp. 282–291.
Nijkamp, P. (2008), XXQ Factors for Sustainable Urban Development, *Romanian Journal of Regional Science*, Vol. 2, pp. 1–34.

Nijkamp, P., Kourtit, K. (eds) (2011), *Urban Europe Scoping Document*, Joint Programming Initiative, Urban Europe, Amsterdam: VU University.
Nijkamp, P., Kourtit, K. (2012), The 'New Urban Europe': Global Challenges and Local Responses in the Urban Century, *European Planning Studies*, Vol. 21, No. 3, pp. 291–315.
Nijkamp, P., Kourtit, K. (2013), Cities: A Blessing in Disguise, New Urban World Future Challenges: What Model of Development for the Moroccan City? Rabat, Morocco, 1–2 October, 2012, Royal Institute for Strategic Studies (IRES), Rabat, pp. 44–52.
Nixon, P., Koutrakou, V.N. (2007), *E-Government in Europe*, London: Routledge.
Paskaleva, K. (2013), Smart Cities: A Nexus for Open Innovation. In Deakin, M. (ed.), *Smart Cities: Governing, Modelling and Analyzing the Transition*, London: Routledge, pp. 111–133.
Pentland, A. (2009), Reality Mining of Mobile Communications. In Dutta, S., Mia, I. (eds), *Mobility in a Networked World*, Paris: World Economic Forum/ INSEAD, pp. 75–80.
Pessoa, A. (2014), Agglomeration and Regional Growth Policy: Externalities versus Comparative Advantages, *The Annals of Regional Science*, Vol. 53, No. 1, pp. 1–27.
Porter, M.E. (1990), *The Competitive Advantage of Nations*, Houndmills, UK: Macmillan.
Puga, D. (2010), The Magnitude and Causes of Agglomeration Economies, *Journal of Regional Science*, Vol. 50, No. 1, pp. 203–219.
Ratcliffe, P., Newman, I. (eds) (2011), *Promoting Social Cohesion: Implications for Policy and Evaluation*, Bristol: Policy Press.
Roche, S. (2014), Geographic Information Science I: Why Does a Smart City Need to be Spatially Enabled? *Progress in Human Geography*, Vol. 38, No. 5, pp. 703–711.
Rosenthal, S.S., Strange, W.C. (2004), Evidence on the Nature and Sources of Agglomeration Economies. In Henderson, J.V., Thisse, J.F. (eds), *Handbook of Regional and Urban Economics*, Volume 4. Amsterdam: North-Holland, pp. 2119–2171.
Sadler, S. (2005), *Archigram: Architecture without Architecture*, Cambridge: MIT Press.
Schaffers, H., Komninos, N., Pallot, M., Trousse, B., Nilsson, M., Oliveira, A. (2011), Smart Cities and the Future of Internet: Towards Cooperation Frameworks for Open Innovation. In J. Domingue et al. (eds), *Future Internet Assembly*, LNCS 6656, Berlin, Heidelberg: Springer-Verlag, pp. 431–446.
Starrett, D. (1978), Market Allocations of Location Choice in a Model with Free Mobility, *Journal of Economic Theory*, Vol. 17, pp. 21–37.
Stimson, R.J. (2014), Proximity and Endogenous Regional Development. In Torre, A., Wallet, F. (eds), *Regional Development and Proximity Relations*, Cheltenham, UK and Northampton, MA, USA: Edward Elgar Publishing, pp. 47–93.
Storper, M., Venables, A.J. (2004), Buzz: Face-to-Face Contact and the Urban Economy, *Journal of Economic Geography*, Vol. 4, No. 4, pp. 351–370
Torre, A., Rallet, A. (2005), Proximity and Localization, *Regional Studies*, Vol. 39, No. 1, pp. 47–59.
Tranos, E., Nijkamp, P. (2013a), The Death of Distance Revisited: Cyberspace, Physical and Relational Proximities, *Journal of Regional Science*, Vol. 53, No. 5, pp. 855–873.

Tranos, E., Nijkamp, P. (2013b), Urban and Regional Analysis and the Digital Revolution, *Research Memorandum, 2013–14*, FEWEB, VU University, Amsterdam.
UNFPA (2007), *State of World Population 2007: Unleashing the Potential of Urban Growth*, New York: UNFPA.
Van Geenhuizen, M. and Nijkamp, P. (2012), Can Creative Knowledge Cities Be Created? *European Financial Review*, 3 August.
Van Oort, F.G., Lambooy, J.G. (2014), Cities, Knowledge and Innovation. In Fischer, M.M., Nijkamp, P. (eds), *Handbook of Regional Science*, Berlin Heidelberg: Springer-Verlag, pp. 475–488.
Ward, S.V. (1994), *Planning and Urban Change*, London: Paul Chapman Publishing.
Westlund, H. (2015), Urban Futures in Planning, Policy and Regional Science: Are We Entering a Post-Urban World? *Built Environment* (forthcoming).

3. Smart Specialization Strategies and Smart Cities: an evidence-based assessment of European Union policies*

Andrea Caragliu and Chiara F. Del Bo

1. INTRODUCTION AND MOTIVATION

Recently, the European economy has undergone severe stress. After a decade of stable prices, cheap borrowing, and the progress of the process of enlargement (pushing the European Union (EU) to 28 member countries and about half a billion inhabitants), the European economy entered a stage of economic distress which has so far not yet been fully solved.

The crisis which began in 2008 has had several manifestations. Unemployment has constantly increased in several EU countries, with a particular burden on the younger generations and with a constant rise in long-term rates (European Commission, 2013). The cost of financing public debt has notoriously risen, in particular in Mediterranean countries and in a few new Member States. In addition, the insufficient degree to which the challenging targets in terms of science and innovation set first by the Lisbon Agenda (European Commission, 2000) and then by the EU2020 follow-up (European Commission, 2010) are being met seems to cast doubts on the long-term possibilities to structurally regenerate the EU economy and truly make it more innovative, and, thus, more competitive.

For these reasons, several EU policies aimed at stimulating the innovation rate of the EU territory have recently been promoted. Inspired by the development of information and communication technologies (henceforth, ICTs) and their pervasive role in the growth of productivity registered in the United States in the 2000s, two novel policy concepts have been developed. First, the notion of Smart City emerged as a panacea for urban

* This chapter has been presented at the Tinbergen Institute Workshop on "Dynamics in the New Urban World: Creativity, Culture, Economy and Governance", held in Amsterdam, May 27–28, 2013.

development. Next, along with the Barca Report (Barca, 2009), the notion of Smart Specialization has been proposed as a new policy instrument for EU regional development.

Apparently, these two concepts have little – if anything – in common. Many critiques, in particular of the concept of a Smart City, have emerged, mostly revolving around the fact that they would represent an empty box, with the "smart" label as their only common feature.

However, on a closer inspection, these two policy concepts share much more than a buzzword. Both have been inspired by the impressive impact of the diffusion of ICTs on US productivity growth; both started out as an industry-based concept, yet both evolved to a more space-specific concept, with the local characteristics of a region, or city, impacting on their effectiveness. Finally, they have both been discussed at length, and such discussion caused an evolution of their definitions towards a higher complexity, and the inclusion of several other dimensions of urban and regional development, beyond the simple diffusion of ICTs.

The commitment of EU and national policymakers to these two forms of policies notwithstanding, so far the academic literature has never inspected whether indeed these two concepts share something more than a buzzword, and whether the outcomes of one policy may positively impact the effectiveness of the other. In this chapter we aim to contribute to this debate by formalizing the possible relationship between Smart Specialization and Smart City policies, and discuss an empirical test of the impact of the former on the latter. In order to reach this goal, we first provide a critical review of the relatively scant literature that so far has emerged on these two issues (Section 2). Next, Section 3 presents the theoretical model formalizing a possible relationship between the Smart Specialization and Smart City concepts. In Section 4 the data set assembled and the methodology adopted (including the indicators of Urban Smartness and Smart Specialization calculated for this analysis) for testing the theoretical model are discussed. Section 5 shows the empirical estimates of the model. Finally, Section 6 concludes and summarizes the possible policy implications of this work.

2. LITERATURE REVIEW

2.1 Smart Specialization Strategies

In this section, some highlights of the (so far, relatively scarce) literature on Smart Specialization are presented.[1] The concept is first framed in the

[1] A recent critical overview of the concept is presented in Capello (2014).

historical context in which it was first proposed. Next, the ways in which it has recently been adapted to the changing (macro) economic conditions are discussed. The rationale of this section is in fact to lay down a bridge between this concept and that of the Smart City, as well as to set the foundations for the Smart Specialization index adopted in this work.

The 2000s debate on the so called "Transatlantic productivity gap" (van Ark et al., 2008) highlighted a halt in the process of productivity convergence across the Atlantic Ocean, between the EU and the United States. Countries belonging to the former EU15,[2] which had experienced fast rates of productivity growth in the 1980s and 1990s, were suddenly found to have developed a gap with respect to the United States, where figures suggested that the growth of gross domestic product (GDP) per hour worked averaged 2.3 per cent per year between 1995 and 2006 (van Ark et al., 2008). The reasons for this productivity slowdown in European regions has often been identified in a "slower rate of adoption of investment in information and communication technology in Europe, the relatively small share of technology-producing industries in Europe, and slower multifactor productivity growth" (van Ark et al., 2008, p. 25).

A "Knowledge for growth" experts' group[3] was subsequently created, in 2005, by the former EU commissioner Janez Potočnik, with the mission of finding plausible remedies for the growing US–EU productivity gap; in this context, the notion of Smart Specialization Strategy (henceforth, S3) emerged. S3 has been described in a series of policy documents ("Knowledge economists policy briefs").[4] Initially, most productivity studies attributed a prominent role to ICTs in determining the US–EU gap. In Europe, an insufficient adoption of ICTs was held responsible for this gap with respect to the United States; this is also the story told in Hall and Mairesse (2009) and Foray et al. (2009).[5] The S3 concept, therefore, has focused, at least initially, mainly on research and development (R&D) functions. However, this idea shifted gradually towards the "institutional and governance issues relating to science, and finally towards technological specialisation based on the adoption, dissemination and adaptation of General Purpose Technologies GPTs, primarily understood as ICTs, across a wide range of sectors" (McCann and Ortega-Argilés, 2011, p. 7).

Recently, the economic crisis in Europe highlighted the need to restructure public finances and spatially concentrate the money spent on R&D

[2] That is, belonging to the EU before the 2004–2007 enlargements.

[3] http://ec.europa.eu/invest-in-research/monitoring/knowledge_en.htm.

[4] Downloadable at http://ec.europa.eu/invest-in-research/index_en.htm.

[5] "There are fewer ICT firms in Europe, and ICT is very R&D-intensive, which explains a large share of the differences in business-funded R&D shares" (Hall and Mairesse, 2009, p. 11).

activities, in order to maximize the returns from research expenditure, minimize the risk of overlapping research lines, and stimulate the best from each typology of region. The EU provided an answer to this need with two fundamental policy documents (the Europe 2020 Flagship Initiative and the EU Budget Review), both requiring national and regional governments to "develop smart specialization strategies to maximise the impact of Regional Policy in combination with other Union policies" (European Commission, 2010, p. 6).

This evolution of the S3 concept, from a mainly academic idea, towards an explicitly policy-oriented concept, has been underlined in two recent contributions which pave the way for a more concrete approach to Smart Specialization, amenable to empirical validation and measurement. In McCann and Ortega-Argilés (2011) the challenging shift from an industrial to a regional concept has been described. In Camagni and Capello (2013), however, a new regional typology has been proposed, with the aim to meet the EU challenge for S3, and typify regions according to their innovative skills. The aim of this contribution is to break down the one-size-fits-all spell marking EU innovation policies before the EU2020 agenda was formalized. Both these works share the idea that S3 must go beyond the pure industrial and R&D characteristics of EU regions, and identify, typically with a bottom-up approach, the *competitive advantages* of each EU region.

In fact, given the insufficiently developed regional R&D systems in several areas that are lagging behind, it would be simply inconceivable to suggest a generalized adoption of science-intensive activities, nor would it be feasible to accept the lags registered in peripheral areas. In light of these considerations, we believe that, as it stands, the literature on S3 presents the need to take a further step forward now in the following directions:

- The regional geography of innovation is way more complex than the typical dichotomous classification between core and peripheral areas. Smart Specialization has therefore to be assessed on a continuum of innovation modes and intensities, capable of capturing the often subtle differences across EU areas.
- S3 must somehow go beyond its traditional focus on ICTs, and encompass other elements granting EU regions the label "smartly specialized".
- Any translation of the S3 concept into empirical work must thus involve an element of competitive advantage, suggesting that EU regional growth can be stimulated by extracting from each area its best, and thus not only focusing on the core "European Research

Area" (Camagni and Capello, 2013). In addition, any empirical application of S3 would need to stimulate the *technological diversification* of EU regions, in order to prevent technological lock-in phenomena (McCann and Ortega-Argilés, 2011).

- Finally, S3 has been insufficiently measured.[6] Whilst a call for a bottom-up approach of technological discovery of regional production talents, driven by local entrepreneurs, sounds like a sensible strategy, there is a clear need for sound but straightforward indicators of the S3 process in EU regions.

This chapter tackles these relevant questions by suggesting a novel indicator of regional Smart Specialization. In addition, the link – if any – between the concept of Smart Specialization and that of Smart City (two commonly used words in the recent EU policy jargon) is discussed in an empirical model, subject to econometric testing. Before discussing the S3 indicator in detail, and how Smart Specialization relates to Smart Cities, a few relevant highlights of the literature on Smart Cities are discussed in Section 2.2.

2.2 The Smart City Concept

The label Smart City has emerged in recent years as both a policy and a business concept, and is also increasingly evolving into a full-fledged research topic. Initial characterizations of this policy construct mainly focused on ICTs (exactly as in the case of S3) as the main pillar around which a city should build its smart pathway. Earlier references to the concept include the "wired city" (Dutton et al., 1987) in which the focus was on networking the urban space per se and the "intelligent city" (Komninos, 2002 and 2009) which expands this idea by also considering the cognitive element of a digital city and the relationship between individual cognitive skills and the information system. Equating smartness to the availability, development and use of ICTs is based on the idea that in order to thrive, cities and their inhabitants must be interconnected and create large data flows. The focus on information technologies and data availability is linked to a policy shift from mainly top-down to increasingly more bottom-up approaches (again, analogously to the Smart Specialization case), which strengthen the importance of citizens' participation. This aspect is further stressed by considering the importance of e-government in the creation of a Smart City (Deakin et al., 2011). This in turn suggests an important role for the human capital component of cities (see below) and might also give

[6] Among the few such examples, see Barca and McCann (2011) (methodological note) and Borbon-Galvez (2011).

rise to concerns related to the availability, management and privacy issues related to "big data" (Batty, 2012). This vision of ICT-focused smartness eventually spurred several academic projects and research.[7]

A recent evolution of the Smart City policy concept, especially in the EU, is increasingly characterized by a more specific focus on environmental sustainability and clean energy issues and linked to the overall sustainability goals of the EU2020 framework (de Luca, 2012). In a broader perspective, the focus on environmental sustainability is incorporated in the concept of "resilient city" (Newman et al., 2009). This further characterization has also given rise to a specific strand in the academic literature exploring the need, development and impact of smart solutions in energy creation and consumption. Examples include, for instance, the analysis of smart meters and smart grids at the residential and industrial level and the implications of their adoption on energy bills and consumption patterns (Gans et al., 2013; Clastres, 2011).

Both these takes on the policy issue are paralleled in the business and consultancy sector, where the interest for the Smart City concept is related to the development of software solutions and applications and management models related to both ICTs and energy.[8] The blurred boundaries between a policy concept and a business model, focused on profit maximization, can give rise to semantic confusion and, more relevant, to ethical issues. In what follows we focus on the policy and academic vision of the concept, as we believe that urban planning should be governed and implemented in a public policy arena, with the participation of private actors as citizens, for reasons that are not purely commercial.

From a research, academic viewpoint, a city is deemed "smart" in relation to its human capital component and potential (Berry and Glaeser, 2005; Shapiro, 2006; Winters, 2011). Berry and Glaeser (2005) show that cities with an initially high percentage of educated labor force tend to grow faster. Shapiro (2008) shows that human capital in cities contributes to urban growth directly through productivity gains, and indirectly through the increase in urban amenities. Winters (2011) shows that Smart Cities, that is, those characterized by a high share of college educated population, are growing faster than other cities. This is due to the fact that Smart Cities are able to attract qualified in-migration of students enrolling in higher education and that these students, post-graduation, tend to remain in the metropolitan area, contributing to urban growth.

7 Recent examples include the Smart Cities and Communities European Innovation Partnership (http://ec.europa.eu/energy/technology/initiatives/smart_implementation/technology-roadmap/european-initiative-on-smart-cities), to cite two.

8 Examples of private companies involved in the creation of smart business models and solutions for cities include, but are not limited to, IBM, Cisco and Siemens.

The interest in the subject, in the policy, business and academic worlds, briefly documented above, has given rise to several attempts of providing a definition of the concept and developing rankings of Smart Cities around the world. With respect to the first issue, given the different perspectives from which the subject has been examined, a first attempt to provide a comprehensive and operational definition can be found in Caragliu et al. (2011), based on the work by Giffinger et al. (2007). The advantage of this definition is twofold. On the one hand, it is based on an urban production function perspective, in which smartness is seen as a multidimensional input and precondition to urban economic performance and growth. This clear distinction between inputs and outputs suggests that smartness can be seen as an intermediate step towards the goal of smart and sustainable urban growth. On the other, it breaks down the concept in six dimensions or axes, each amenable to measurement and estimation using data from official statistical sources and as such provides a broad and operational definition of an otherwise fuzzy concept. This is the basis for our empirical analysis and is used to build the Smart City indicator in Section 4.3.

3. A MODEL FOR SMART DEVELOPMENT

From what was critically reviewed in Section 2, a need to bring together two otherwise separate policy concepts such as that of Smart City and the notion of Smart Specialization Strategies emerges. In this chapter we aim to offer an empirical approach to such a need, which firstly requires a general overview of how the two concepts fit together in a regional perspective. In this section we provide a simple formal model that brings together, in a common conceptual framework, the notion of Smart City and Smart Specialization Strategies.

In fact, the literature summarized in Section 2 suggests that the economic performance of regions and countries is also determined by the emergence of Smart Cities, in the sense of the definition provided in Caragliu et al. (2011). Smart Cities can be thought of as also emerging because of a virtuous process of Smart Specialization, as summarized in Figure 3.1.

The model presented here provides a framework for the empirical estimates discussed later in Section 5.

Suppose that, at the beginning of each time period, each region presents a given level of competitive advantage (i.e. a higher-, or lower-than-average productivity growth with regard to the EU). It then can either specialize, or de-specialize, in the economic activity (-ies) presenting positive growth of competitive advantage. This may come as a

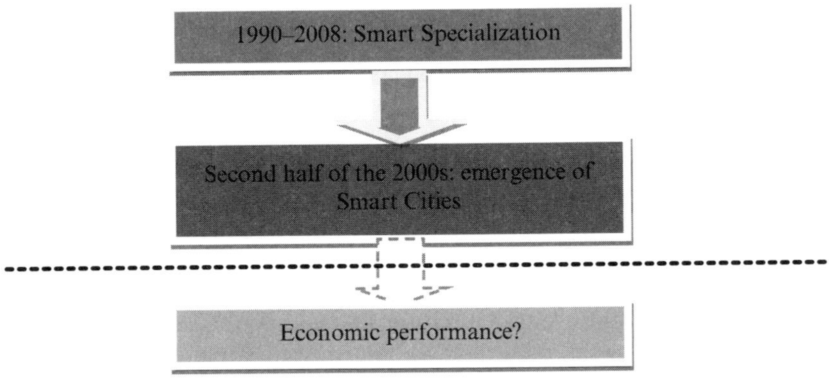

Figure 3.1 A conceptual framework for the emergence of Smart Cities as a consequence of Smart Specialization Strategies

result of either individual, non-coordinated firm activity (entrepreneurs looking for better economic opportunities), or else because of a centrally-coordinated policy initiative (e.g. economic incentives to open production facilities active in the industries where the region presents growth of competitive advantage).

Let us define as i all regions, $i=1,\ldots,m$, j all the industries, $j=1,\ldots,n$, and time indices 0, t and T as three time periods. Finally, let us define $CA_{i,j,t}$, the competitive advantage of region i at time t in sector j, as the difference in a region's industry-specific growth of labor productivity with regard to the average EU27 labor productivity growth. In other words, if $VA_{i,j,t}$ is value added produced in industry j in region i at time t, $VA_{EU,j,t}$ is value added produced in industry j in the EU at time t, $L_{i,j,t}$ is employment in industry j in region i at time t, and $L_{EU,j,t}$ is employment in industry j in the EU at time t, then $CA_{i,j,t}=(VA_{i,j,t}/L_{i,j,t}-(VA_{EU,j,t}/L_{EU,j,t}))$. In dynamic terms, this implies that the process of industrial structural change for each region-industry can be defined as

$$\Delta CA_{i,j,t-0} = \Delta[(VA_{i,j,t}/L_{i,j,t}) - (VA_{EU,j,t}/L_{EU,j,t})] \quad (3.1)$$

The assumption behind this model (and, correspondingly, to the way an indicator of Smart Specialization can be calculated – see Section 4.2 for further details) is that *regions can be defined as smartly specializing if they display a higher-than-average capability to specialize in the industries where they present positive growth of competitive advantage*. The first literature on Smart Specialization traditionally revolved around science-related industries, and, at the origins of this concept, around the so called

"Transatlantic productivity gap" (McCann and Ortega-Argilés, 2011). In this chapter, and, therefore, in our model, we assume, however, that the true source of Smart Specialization is the capability of the regional actors to increase their specialization in industries where they present competitive advantage with regard to other areas, irrespective of the scientific content of the activity involved. In fact, as pointed out in Pontikakis et al. (2009), the one-size-fits-all Innovation Agenda synthesized in the Lisbon Strategy does not properly take into account all the structural differences among EU regions, and the existence of one single innovation target, such as the 3 per cent R&D/GDP expenditure goal, is, in our opinion, not feasible.

The increase over time in the competitive advantage (eq. 3.1) is here used as a market signal that can be received by entrepreneurs and institutions, which can either focus their activity on industries presenting higher-than-average growth of competitive advantage, or instead presenting lags with regard to the EU average. Consequently, let us now define $SPEC_{i,j}$, as the share of employment in region i in industry j: $SPEC_{i,j}=L_{i,j}/L_i$ and $\Delta SPEC_{i,j}$, as the change in regional industrial specialization over the period t–T. We can thus define $S3_{i,,j,T}$ as the degree to which, between periods t and T, the level of specialization in region-industry i-j has been able to grow *more than the EU average* if presenting competitive advantage with regard to the EU27. Following the definition of Smart Specialization processes given above, we can therefore state the following equation which defines our measure of Smart Specialization:

$$S3_{i,j,T} = (\Delta SPEC_{i,j,T-t} - \Delta CA_{i,j,t-0}) \tag{3.2}$$

We are therefore assuming that each region can specialize in an economic activity which presents some degree of competitiveness at the continental level, irrespective of the level of technology embedded in the economic activity.

So far, this definition is industry-specific. At a more aggregate level, each region i presents different industries in which it has been structurally specializing. We can therefore aggregate all eqs. (3.2) to obtain our region-specific measure of Smart Specialization $S3_{i,T}$ as follows:

$$S3_{i,T} = \sum_{j=1}^{n} w_j 3S_{i,j,T} \tag{3.3}$$

where the w_j represent the weights assigned to each industry in the generation of the region-specific Smart Specialization. In fact, the Smart Specialization literature usually revolves around the fact that being specialized in scientific industries would constitute the "real" Smart Specialization

(Foray et al., 2009; McCann and Ortega-Argilés, 2011). Eq. (3.3) allows the testing of this hypothesis, by letting the w_j vary in order to reflect the different weights associated to more research-intensive industries (see also Section 4 below for an empirical test).

Smart Specialization can in turn be related to the emergence of Smart Cities, which thrive on the existence of a set of growth-enhancing urban characteristics as explained in Section 2. For this concept we follow the theoretical definition laid down in Caragliu et al. (2011), and work out a model whereby the concepts of Smart Specialization and Smart City are interrelated. This is done as follows. We assume that the probability of region i to cradle the emergence of a Smart City, π_i, will obey the following functional form:

$$\pi_{i,T} = \alpha_1 + \beta_1 S3_{i,T} + \gamma Z_i + \eta_1 \quad (3.4)$$

where $\eta_1 \sim i.i.d.(0,1)$, while Z_i is a matrix of region-specific controls. Since the real probability of the existence of a Smart City within each region is not known *ex ante*, we resort to calculating an indicator of smartness for each city, and then aggregate city-specific indicators at the regional level using city population levels as weights (see Section 5 for further details).

Eq. (3.4) represents a reduced form which can be estimated, provided all the above-mentioned assumptions are met. This equation will therefore represent the baseline model for all the empirical analyses carried out in Section 5.

4. THE DATA SET AND THE METHODOLOGY

This section presents the data needed both for calculating the S3 and urban smartness indicators, as well as for the empirical analyses carried out in Section 5. Because of the structure of the empirical estimates, the data for calculating the urban smartness indicator present a time lag with respect to Smart Specialization data, so as to minimize the risk of endogeneity in the empirical analyses.

4.1 The Data Set

Because of the wide array of urban and regional characteristics summarized in the concepts of Smart Specialization and Smart City, any empirical analysis requires a relevant amount of data. Raw data entering the calculations are summarized in Table 3.1; further details on each block can be found, respectively, in Sections 4.2, 4.3 and 5, and in Appendix 1.

Table 3.1 The data set

Logical step	Raw data	Source	Available years
1. Smart Specialization indicator	Sectoral data (15 NACE 2-digit industries) on: • Value added in constant 2000 prices • Labour force	Cambridge Econometrics	1990–2008
2. Urban smartness indicator	Human capital Social capital Transport infrastructure ICT infrastructure Natural resources E-government	Urban Audit	2004–2011
3. Control variables in the main regression	Per capita GDP in constant 2000 prices	Eurostat	1999–2001
	Agglomerated/urban/rural typology	ESPON 1.1.1	–
	R&D/GDP	Eurostat	1999–2001
	Regional trust	EVS	2000

Notes: NACE = Statistical classification of economic activities in the European Community; EVS = European Values Study.

4.2 An Indicator of Regional Smart Specialization in the EU

Following the model of Smart Specialization discussed in Section 3, our empirical analysis needs to be complemented by an indicator of Smart Specialization which meets the following criteria:

- transparency;
- ease of calculation;
- comparability across different regions;
- inclusion of ways to test the relevance of scientific sectors in assessing the smartness of specialization processes.

On the basis of eq. (3.3), data on industry specialization and labor productivity have been collected for the period 1990–2008 for 279 EU NUTS (Nomenclature of Territorial Units for Statistics), two regions and 15 NACE 2-digit industries.[9]

[9] Raw data on industry GDP and labor force are based on the Cambridge Econometrics data base. A full list of the industries used in the calculation of this indicator is instead presented in Table 3.A2 in Appendix 2.

Table 3.2 Estimates of the ancillary regression for regional Smart Specialization

Dependent variable	Change in regional industrial specialization 1990–2008
Constant term	−0.38***
	(0.01)
Initial level of competitive advantage	1.83*
	(1.18)
R^2	0.12
Joint F test	133.21***
Number of observations	4,185
Industry fixed effects	Yes
Robust standard errors	Yes

Notes: ***, **, *: significance at 10, 5 and one per cent, respectively.
Robust standard errors in brackets.

Empirically, we regress the change in regional industry specialization between 1990 and 2008 on the initial level of competitive advantage, that is, the difference between regional labor productivity and the average level of labor productivity at the EU27 level for each industry, plus a full battery of industry fixed effects, to rule out structural differences across industries. Formally, we estimate an ancillary regression of the form:

$$\Delta SPEC_{i,j,T-t} = \alpha_0 + \beta_0 \sum_{j=1}^{n} w_j \Delta CA_{i,j,T-t} + \beta_j \eta_j + \varepsilon_0 \quad (3.5)$$

where $\varepsilon_0 \sim i.i.d.(0,1)$, and the η_j are the industry fixed effects. The results of estimating eq. (3.5) are presented in Table 3.2.

The regression presented in Table 3.2 divides a hypothetical chart (Figure 3.2), showing a scatterplot of competitive advantage on the X-axis, and the subsequent change of industrial specialization on the Y-axis, in two areas:

- regions specializing more than the average in industries initially presenting competitive advantage;
- regions specializing less than the average in industries initially presenting competitive advantage.

In Figure 3.2, these areas are identified with the regression line whose estimated equation is shown in Table 3.1.

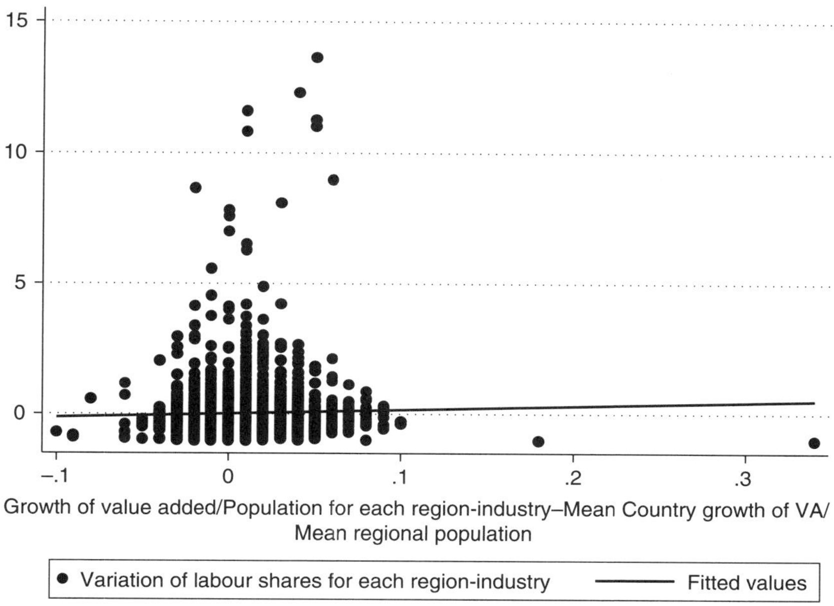

Source: Authors' elaboration.

Figure 3.2 Regional Smart Specialization

As a final step, our Smart Specialization indicator is defined as the residual of this regression, that is, as the vertical distance between the regression line and the Y-axis coordinates, indicating regional specialization (Figure 3.2). Formally, this implies calculating the fitted residuals $\hat{\varepsilon}$ in eq. (3.5), and aggregating them at the regional level. This indicator therefore measures the potential of a region to specialize in industries presenting competitive advantage more than the EU average.

In addition, this indicator allows a full analysis of the implied major relevance of science and science-related industries in the process of Smart Specialization. As should be clear now from the theoretical sections, the literature on Smart Specialization stresses the relevance of innovation and science as sources of long-run competitive advantage. In fact, the ways in which individual industries' contributions to the regional Smart Specialization index are weighted can reflect such relevance, by attributing higher weights to science-based industries, and then testing whether the empirical results of the baseline model hold (see Section 5.2).

4.3 An Indicator of Urban Smartness in the EU

Following the definition in Caragliu et al. (2011), we propose an urban smartness indicator for 309 EU cities based on data along the following six dimensions: human capital, social capital, transport infrastructure, ICTs, natural resources and e-government. For each axis, which we ultimately see as inputs to an urban production function, four individual vectors were considered and further reduced by means of Principal Component Analysis (PCA), leading to six indicators corresponding to the six axes. The final aggregate measure is the un-weighted average of the six indicators and represents the overall urban smartness indicator. Table 3.A1 summarizes the underlying variables used in the analysis for each indicator, taken from the Urban Audit database and integrated with data from the ESPON FOCI project (Lennert et al., 2010) and Eurostat. In order to increase data availability, we have considered the mean value for the period 2008–2012, thus making use of three waves of data. We dealt with missing data by interpolation.

For the human capital dimension, we consider the broad definition provided in Caragliu et al. (2012) and focus on the formal education component (measured by the number of students in tertiary education per 1,000 inhabitants); the sectoral employment component (measured by the proportion of employment in skill-intensive industries); and the functional urban hierarchy component (measured by the number of listed companies with headquarters in the city). The resulting aggregate indicator will better reflect the multifaceted nature of urban human capital.

Social capital is measured by taking into account the crime rate in the city (car thefts, burglaries and crimes per 1,000 inhabitants) and the number of elected representatives. As documented by, for example, Putnam (2001), social capital levels can be inferred and predicted by looking at crime rates at different levels of spatial aggregation, as the two phenomena are negatively correlated. The link between social capital and civic participation, including involvement in local elections, has been recognized since the work of Coleman (1988). Building on this literature, we include a measure of the number of elected representatives at the city level as an additional positive correlate of social capital (Putnam et al., 1993).

The overall availability of the local transport infrastructure system is considered by using information on the length of the public transport network and the size of the urban fleet, while the quality of the network is measured by observing the proportion of restricted bus lanes over the total and the number of stops per 1,000 inhabitants (on these issues see, for example, Geurs and van Wee, 2004).

The ICT component accounts for both a demand and supply side perspective, as advocated by the Organisation for Economic Co-operation and Development (OECD, 2005). On the demand side, household internet access is considered, while, for the supply side, the production of ICT products, services and web contents is used.

The natural resources component encompasses the management of solid urban waste (measured by the percentage waste which is recycled), the amount of public green space to which the citizens have access (proportion of area in green space) and pollution (measured by the annual average concentration of PM10 and NO_2), as discussed in Tajima (2003).

Finally, e-government is measured by the interaction of citizens with public authorities on the internet (measured by the percentage of users who interacted with and downloaded documents from public authorities) and by the number of administrative forms which can be submitted and downloaded electronically at the country level, following an established literature in public administration studies (see for example, Welch et al., 2005).

For each axis presented in Table 3.A1 we identify one principal component (PC) by selecting those which are associated to greater than unity Eigenvalues (Kaiser, 1961) and for which the factor loadings are reasonable (Dunteman, 1989). With respect to this latter issue, the crime element in the social capital component should be negatively related to the resulting PC, as it should be in the case of pollution in the natural resources axis. The six PCs are then aggregated, by means of a simple un-weighted average, in an aggregate indicator of urban smartness. Table 3.3 presents the first 20 cities in the corresponding ranking.

Figure 3.3 provides a visual representation of the levels of the Smart City indicator in the EU cities in our sample. The first comment is London's role as a clear outlier, with respect to other cities in the sample, and as such it has been excluded from the empirical analyses in the following sections. In general, there is a high level of variability, only partly explained by country effects. In Italy, for example, some cities, mainly, but not exclusively, located in the north, are characterized by a positive indicator (e.g. Milano, North; and Reggio di Calabria, South), while others by negative values (Verona, North; and Palermo, South). It is also clear that size is not the main factor driving the ranking, as relatively smaller cities (e.g. Graz, Austria, 300,002 inhabitants) rank higher than larger, even capital, cities (e.g. Helsinki, Finland, with an urban population of 1,159,211).

Table 3.3 Urban smartness ranking

Rank	City	Country
1	London	UK
2	Aarhus	DK
3	Arnhem	NL
4	Aberdeen	UK
5	Cambridge	UK
6	Darmstadt	DE
7	Krakow	PL
8	Tampere	FI
9	Innsbruck	AT
10	Wien	AT
11	Manchester	UK
12	Lille	FR
13	Aalborg	DK
14	Salzburg	AT
15	Leeuwarden	NL
16	Nijmegen	NL
17	København	DK
18	Groningen	NL
19	Mainz	DE
20	Lisboa	PT

Source: Authors' elaboration.

5. SMART CITIES AND SMART REGIONS: AN EMPIRICAL ANALYSIS

Following the conceptual model of smart development set out in Section 3, we present the results of the empirical analysis which is aimed at exploring the links between Smart Specialization Strategies and the emergence of Smart Cities at the regional level. The Smart City indicator derived in Section 4.3 is used as the basis for the regional smartness indicator. For each region, the urban smartness indicator is multiplied by the share of each city's population over total urban population in the region. This regional smartness indicator is first treated as a continuous variable and is then transformed into a categorical variable, divided into five classes according to the quantiles of the distribution. The categorical variable is used to link the empirical model to its theoretical counterpart (eq. 3.4) in terms of probability. For each region in our sample, the level and extent of its Smart Specialization Strategies between 1990 and 2008 are

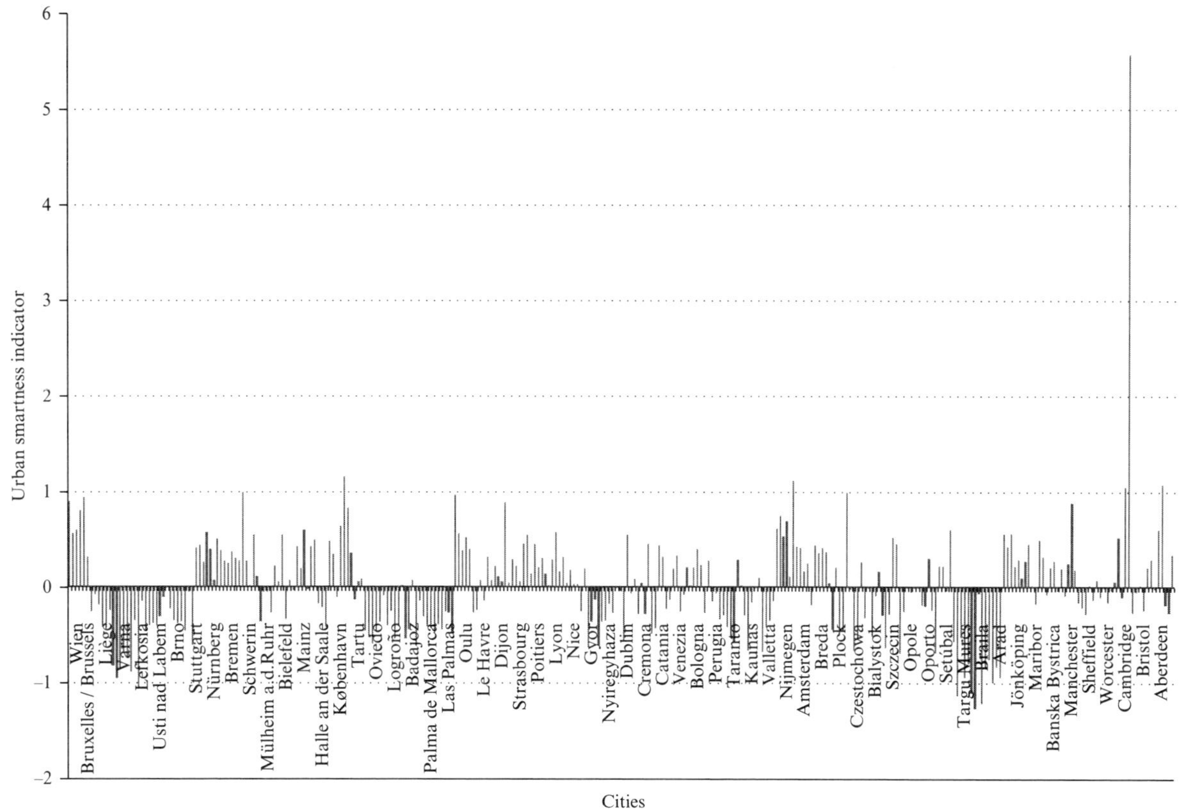

Source: Authors' calculations.

Figure 3.3 Urban smartness indicator

summarized by the indicator presented in Section 4.2, which aggregates, at the regional level, the residuals of eq. 3.5 and indicates whether each region is specializing in industries presenting competitive advantage with respect to the EU average. In Section 5.2 this indicator is modified to account for differences between high-tech sectors (following the Pavitt, 1984 classification) and those with a lower innovative content. To explore the relationship between regional Smart Specialization and the probability of hosting a Smart City, the following empirical model is estimated (eq. 3.6), by means of ordinary least squares (OLS), with robust standard errors, when the dependent variable is continuous and with ordered logit and probit models, with robust standard errors, when it is expressed as a categorical variable.

$$Smart_{i,T} = \alpha_1 + \beta_1 3S_{i,T} + \gamma_i Z_i + \eta_1 \tag{3.6}$$

The matrix Z includes the following region-specific regressors: the log of per capita GDP, dummy variables that reflect the regions' settlement structure, specifically urban and rural, with agglomeration as the omitted category, the log of R&D expenditures over GDP, the log of average trust and a dummy variable for regions belonging to East European States.

5.1 Baseline Estimates

Table 3.4 presents results of the estimation of eq. 3.6. In the first column, we focus on smartness as a continuous variable, and estimate the model with OLS. In columns 2 and 3, respectively, we use the categorical dependent variable and the main equation is estimated by logit and probit models.

Starting from the OLS regression and focusing on our main explanatory variable of interest, the indicator of regional Smart Specialization Strategies between 1990 and 2008 (Table 3.4, column 1), suggests the existence of a positive and statistically significant relationship with the presence of Smart Cities in the region.

The estimated coefficient suggests that for a one unit increase in the regional Smart Specialization indicator there is a .3 unit increase in urban smartness, aggregated at the regional level. A region which has been specializing, in past years, in sectors and activities in which it presents competitive advantage with respect to the EU, is also more likely to host, within its boundaries, one or more Smart Cities. This finding hints at the existence of a positive relationship between the two "smart" EU policy concepts, which are operationalized according to the definitions and procedures laid out in the previous sections. Since our Smart Specialization

Table 3.4 Smartness and Smart Specialization (baseline estimates)

Dependent variable: regional smartness indicator			
Model	(1)	(2)	(3)
Constant term	−0.74**	No constant term is shown for discrete models. However, marginal effects for the highest dependent variable class are provided	
	(0.35)		
Regional smart specialization	0.29**	0.36**	0.40***
	(0.13)	(0.14)	(0.15)
Log per capita GDP	0.42***	0.29***	0.31***
	(0.09)	(0.09)	(0.08)
Urban region	0.09	0.09*	0.09*
	(0.06)	(0.05)	(0.05)
Rural region	0.19**	0.26***	0.25***
	(0.08)	(0.10)	(0.10)
Log R&D/GDP	0.11**	0.14***	0.15***
	(0.05)	(0.04)	(0.04)
Log average trust	0.08	0.01	0.01
	(0.07)	(0.05)	(0.05)
Dummy for regions located in NMS	0.36***	0.31	0.32*
	(0.13)	(0.20)	(0.17)
Estimator	OLS	Ordered logit	Ordered probit
Robust standard errors	Yes	Yes	Yes
Number of obs.	200	200	200
(Pseudo) R^2	0.43	0.17	0.17
Joint F test	25.77***	–	–
Wald Chi square test	–	80.07***	83.29***

Notes:
***, **, *: significance at 10, 5 and one per cent, respectively.
NMS = New Member States.
Robust standard errors in brackets.

indicator is built considering all sectors and without differentiating according to the innovative content of the industries in which the region is specialized, this result also suggests that there exists a broad correlation between potential success of smart policies at the urban and regional levels, even without narrowing the analysis to innovative, high-tech sectors and accounting for the presence of competitive advantage in more traditional sectors and activities (for a further discussion of this issue, see Section 5.2).

Despite the complexity of the issue being analyzed, the levels of fit identified in the estimates are rather high. OLS estimates (Table 3.4, column 1) are associated with a .4 R^2, while count estimates (columns 2 and 3) display a .17 McFadden's pseudo-R^2. The identified Pseudo-R^2s are not far from the .2 threshold indicated in McFadden (1974) as suggesting an "excellent model fit".

Despite our general definition of Smart Specialization, we wish to control for the regions' innovative potential and to this end we include a measure of regional R&D expenditures over GDP. The estimated coefficient is positive and statistically significant (with a value of 0.11) and suggests that regions which spend relatively more on R&D are indeed more likely to host a Smart City within their boundaries.

As expected, a region's economic wealth (GDP per capita) is positively correlated with the regional urban smartness indicator. In fact, the availability of funds and resources is likely to increase the possibility of investing in Smart City policies in resource-intensive sectors such as, for example, transport infrastructure or environmental protection programs.

Reciprocal, interpersonal trust at the regional level, however, does not seem to be significantly related to urban smartness at the regional level.

Finally, the role of the regions' settlement structure in terms of population density (urban, rural or agglomerated regions as defined by ESPON project 1.1.1[10]) and the influence of belonging to New Member States (NMS)[11] are analyzed by means of dummy variables. With respect to the urbanization structure, regions which are predominantly rural appear to be associated with a higher presence of Smart Cities, compared to agglomerated regions. No statistically significant result is found when considering highly urbanized regions (although the estimated coefficient is positive). Rural regions might be characterized by smaller and maybe less networked and urbanistically defined cities, with respect to the agglomerated regions. These cities might not be affected by negative congestion externalities and might benefit more, in terms of smart policy success, from the implementation of a set of policy measures aimed at creating Smart Cities. Cities in

[10] *Agglomerated* regions are defined as those regions hosting a city of more than 300,000 inhabitants and a population density higher than 300 inhabitants/sq. km. or with a population density between 150 and 300 inhabitants/sq. km. *Urban* regions are defined as hosting a city between 150,000 and 300,000 inhabitants and a population density between 150 and 300 inhabitants/sq. km. (or a smaller population density – between 100 and 150 inhabitants/sq. km. but with a bigger center, with more than 300,000 inhabitants) or a population density between 100 and 150 inhabitants/sq. km. Finally, *rural* regions are those areas with a population density lower than 100 inhabitants/sq. km. and a center with more than 125,000 inhabitants, or a population density lower than 100 inhabitants/sq. km. with a center smaller than 125,000 inhabitants. See also Capello and Chizzolini (2008).

[11] New Member States (NMS) are: Bulgaria, Czech Republic, Cyprus, Estonia, Latvia, Lithuania, Poland, Romania, Slovak Republic, Slovenia.

agglomerated regions might also be further along a defined development and urban structure trajectory and as such be less amenable to further positive changes in the direction of urban smartness.

Considering instead the east dummy variable, regions belonging to NMS appear, on average, to be associated with higher levels of urban smartness. This finding might suggest the existence of an overall catching-up process, with cities in Eastern European countries actively investing in the upgrade of their urban fabric which is conducive to the emergence of Smart Cities as defined in the previous sections.

In probability terms, looking at results from the probit regression (which is characterized by a slightly higher log-likelihood with respect to the logit specification), the average marginal effect for the highest dependent variable class of 0.40 (Table 3.4, column 3) suggests that the probability of a region scoring high in the aggregate urban smartness indicator increases with regional Smart Specialization.

The transition from the continuous specification of the urban smartness indicators towards a specification in terms of probability, for a region, of being in a higher class of urban smartness, smooths out some heterogeneity and allows for a more general analysis. Interestingly, the sign and significance of the estimated parameters, with respect to OLS regressions (Table 3.4, column 1) are the same, but some differences emerge. In particular, the relative importance of regional wealth, as summarized by per capita GDP, with respect to regional specialization, is reversed. While in the OLS specification the coefficient for GDP was higher than that of Smart Specialization, the reverse is true in the probit (and logit) model, providing evidence of a strong link, once smoothing has occurred, of the two smart policy concepts. The other difference is related to the loss of significance, when moving to probit (and logit) models of the NMS dummy variable, suggesting that the importance of belonging to this set of countries may be overrated in the OLS model. Further research is, however, needed to confirm or dismiss these hypotheses.

For a visual analysis of the relationship between urban smartness and Smart Specialization, in Figure 3.4 the probability of being in the highest class of urban smartness is plotted against the Smart Specialization index with corresponding confidence intervals after the regression as in Table 3.4, column 2. The positively (and increasingly so) sloped curve confirms the positive association between the two smart policies documented by commenting on estimated coefficients from the regression analysis.

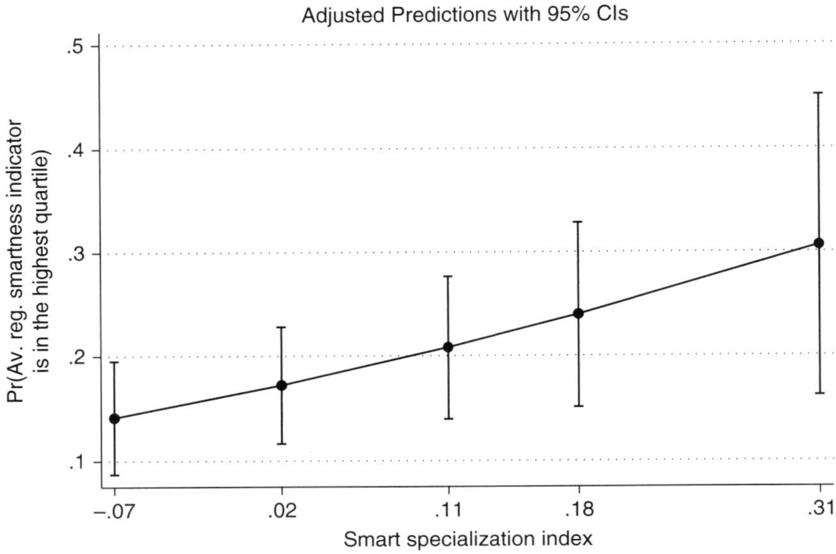

Source: Authors' elaboration.

Figure 3.4 Marginal effects (logit model) for different outcomes of the regional smartness parameter

5.2 Consistency Checks: The Relevance of Science-based Industries

In order to link our S3 indicator more closely to the relevant literature (see, for example, Foray et al., 2009), in this section we explicitly take into account the innovative content of sectors and define two alternative Smart Specialization indices. In the first case, we assign a higher weight to industries which can be considered as high-tech and innovative, following the Pavitt (1984) classification. Specifically, the following group of sectors (NACE Rev2 sectors DF–DH; DL; J and K) are considered as innovative and, as a group, are assigned twice the weight assigned to the group of more traditional sectors.[12] This amounts to estimating the empirical counterpart of the following equation, based on equation 3.3 with different weights, *w*. In particular, the formulation in equation 3.7 implies that the S3 indicator is multiplied by 0.125 for each sector belonging to the innovative group and by 0.045 if it belongs to a traditional sector.

[12] Equal weights are assigned to Pavitt versus non-Pavitt groups of sectors. The values shown in equation 3.7 are obtained by then assigning equal weight to the sectors in the Pavitt and non-Pavitt group (respectively, 5 and 11 sectors).

$$3S_{i,T} = \sum_{j \in Pavitt} 0.125*3S_{i,j,T} + \sum_{j \notin Pavitt} 0.045*3S_{i,j,T} \tag{3.7}$$

Results of OLS estimation are presented in Table 3.5, column 1. In this case, the estimated coefficient associated with the newly defined S3 indicator which gives more weight to Smart Specialization in high-tech industries is not statistically significant, suggesting that the emergence of Smart Cities is not necessarily driven by regional specialization in innovative sectors.[13] This result is further corroborated by inspection of Table 3.5, column 4, where the specialization index assigns a positive weight only to Pavitt sectors (equation 3.8).

$$3S_{i,T} = \sum_{j \in Pavitt} 3S_{i,j,T} \tag{3.8}$$

These results are confirmed, albeit with some qualifications, when estimating the logit and probit models (Table 3.5, columns 2 and 3, 5 and 6) and suggest interesting policy implications. The estimation based on equation 3.7 (i.e. the one which accounts for specialization in both innovative and traditional sectors, but giving more weight to the former) suggests that the emergence of Smart Cities and Smart Specialization are positively related, although both the estimated coefficient and statistical significance are lower with respect to the results in Table 3.4, columns 2 and 3, suggesting that the association is weaker. The estimated parameters of the other regressors, however, retain similar values. Considering Smart Specialization Strategies only in high-tech sectors, as in Table 3.5, columns 5 and 6, leads instead to insignificant results, as in the OLS specification, suggesting that the narrowest definition of Smart Specialization does not seem to be related at all to the Smart City concept and policy results. To conclude, while regional Smart Specialization, defined in broad terms, and Smart City policies are positively related, a narrower definition of Smart Specialization, which is centered more around the innovative sectors, is unrelated to the emergence of Smart Cities. Regions which present a competitive advantage, and thus specialize in traditional, non-high-tech sectors are still potential candidates for successful Smart City policies and are not necessarily confined to a secondary role in the urban EU arena.

[13] The sign and significance of estimated coefficients of the other regressors is qualitatively and quantitatively similar to results in Table 3.4, to which the interested reader is directed.

Table 3.5 Smartness and Smart Specialization (the role of high-tech industries)

Dependent variable: regional smartness indicator						
Weights used	Pavit industries weight twice as normal sectors			Only Pavitt industries are used for the regional smartness indicator		
Model	(1)	(2)	(3)	(4)	(5)	(6)
Constant term	−0.85** (0.37)	No constant term is shown for discrete models. However, marginal effects for the highest dependent variable class are provided		−0.96** (0.38)	No constant term is shown for discrete models. However, marginal effects for the highest dependent variable class are provided	
Regional Smart Specialization	0.13 (0.08)	0.22** (0.10)	0.25** (0.11)	0.12 (0.17)	0.31 (0.21)	0.32 (0.22)
Log per capita GDP	0.45*** (0.09)	0.31*** (0.09)	0.33*** (0.08)	0.48*** (0.07)	0.32*** (0.09)	0.36*** (0.09)
Urban region	0.08 (0.05)	0.09* (0.05)	0.08 (0.05)	0.06 (0.06)	0.08 (0.05)	0.07 (0.05)
Rural region	0.18** (0.08)	0.25** (0.10)	0.24** (0.10)	0.17** (0.08)	0.22** (0.10)	0.21** (0.09)
Log R&D/GDP	0.11** (0.05)	0.14*** (0.04)	0.15*** (0.04)	0.11** (0.05)	0.14*** (0.04)	0.16*** (0.05)
Log average trust	0.07 (0.07)	0.00 (0.05)	0.00 (0.05)	0.05 (0.07)	0.00 (0.05)	0.00 (0.05)
Dummy for regions located in NMS	0.37*** (0.13)	0.33 (0.21)	0.34* (0.18)	0.38*** (0.14)	0.32 (0.21)	0.33* (0.17)
Estimator	OLS	Ordered logit	Ordered probit	OLS	Ordered logit	Ordered probit
Robust standard errors	Yes	Yes	Yes	Yes	Yes	Yes
Number of observations	200	200	200	200	200	200
(Pseudo) R^2	0.42	0.16	0.16	0.42	0.16	0.16
Joint F test	26.99***	–	–	27.66***	–	–
Wald Chi square test	–	76.10***	79.13***	–	75.54***	80.60***

Notes:
***, **, *: significance at 10, 5 and one per cent, respectively.
Robust standard errors in brackets.

6. CONCLUSIONS

EU policy objectives strategies are increasingly being framed around the aim of achieving smart, sustainable and inclusive growth (see for example the EU2020 website)[14] for all EU Member States and several specific provisions and initiatives cite these concepts widely. In this chapter, we have focused on one of these policy "buzzwords" and provided a conceptually grounded and rigorous empirical analysis of the relationship between two popular policy concepts revolving around "smart".

Specifically, we have framed the concept of Smart Specialization and Smart City on common theoretical grounds and examined the possible links between specific policy interventions in these areas. After providing an empirical measure of both policy constructs in the EU, econometric analysis suggests a significant and positive correlation between regional Smart Specialization Strategies and successful Smart City initiatives.

However, our results are amenable to more complex interpretations, with potentially important policy implications. Building from the academic and policy-oriented literature, we have provided more general, and in our view, more complete characterizations of both policy measures, moving beyond the focus on ICTs, for Smart City, and the focus only on high-tech and innovative sectors, for Smart Specialization. While we by no means underestimate the importance of both factors in defining the two constructs, we also believe both concepts should be examined with a broader perspective.

Both concepts are referred to frequently at the academic, policy and, in the case of Smart City, also at the business level. The underlying definitions, however, albeit often not explicitly stated, appear to change in the different contexts and according to different strands of thought and literature, suggesting that the boundaries of both policy measures are quite extended. To overcome this issue, we have developed two empirical methodologies, based on official statistics for EU regions and cities, which are easily implementable and which allow us to quantify and assess the levels of Smart Specialization Strategies and the degree of urban smartness in the EU. The first finding suggests that EU regions are indeed following a Smart Specialization path, and this is true for both innovative and more traditional sectors. Smart Cities are also identified in both western and eastern EU Member States, and do not appear to be univocally related to size or economic wealth. Once again, the Smart City measure is broadly defined and encompasses, along with the presence, development and use of ICTs, different dimensions which ultimately can be thought of as urban growth determinants.

[14] http://ec.europa.eu/europe2020/services/faqs/index_en.htm.

The empirical analysis of the determinants of urban smartness, at the regional level, including Smart Specialization Strategies, also allows us to conclude that the two concepts are positively related, in that regions showing a certain degree of industrial change dynamics also tend to be more likely to develop cities with a higher degree of "smartness". The fact that both our empirical measures include, but do not rely solely on new technologies and science, can also be read in terms of which direction policy interventions should follow. Should regions, both those at the technological frontier and the more traditionally-oriented ones that lag behind, all invest in innovative activities in high-tech sectors? We believe the answer to be negative and suggest that not all regions enjoy the same industrial pattern (e.g. some are focusing on services, some others on primary activities), while R&D is typical mostly of large manufacturing companies, and not all regions and countries have reached the same development stage. Regions in the south and east of Europe are further away from the frontier, and thus may find it more difficult to achieve a common R&D target; thus, lagging regions may best focus on industries in which they have competitive advantage. The results presented here, while suggesting that this may indeed be the case, would ideally benefit from further work on this issue, in particular in the assessment of the further causal link between smart EU policies and regional economic performance.

REFERENCES

Barca, F. (2009). "Barca Report". Retrieved online on April 8, 2015 at http://ec.europa.eu/regional_policy/archive/policy/future/barca_en.htm.

Barca, F., and McCann, P. (2011). "Methodological note: outcome indicators and targets – towards a performance oriented EU cohesion policy". Retrieved online on May 21, 2013 at http://ec.europa.eu/regional_policy/sources/docgener/evaluation/doc/performance/improve_inno_resear_en.pdf.

Batty, M. (2012). "Smart cities, big data", *Environment and Planning B: Planning and Design*, 39 (2): 191–193.

Berry, C.R., and Glaeser, E.L. (2005). "The divergence of human capital levels across cities", *Papers in Regional Science*, 84 (3): 407–444.

Borbon-Galvez, Y. (2011). "Evolution of sectoral specialization of EU regions: fuzzy logic and panel logistic model analyses", Paper presented at the 6th International Seminar on Regional Innovation Policies, Lund (SE), October 13–14, 2011.

Camagni, R., and Capello, R. (2013). "Regional innovation patterns and the EU regional policy reform: towards smart innovation policies", *Growth and Change*, 44 (2): 355–389.

Capello, R. (2014). "Smart specialisation strategy and the New EU cohesion policy reform: introductory remarks", *Scienze Regionali – The Italian Journal of Regional Science*, 13 (1): 5–14.

Capello, R., and Chizzolini, B. (2008). "The estimation procedure: data and results", in Capello, R., Camagni, R., Chizzolini, B., and Fratesi, U. (eds), *Modelling Regional Scenarios for the Enlarged Europe*, Berlin (DE): Springer Verlag.

Caragliu, A., Del Bo, C.F., and Nijkamp, P. (2011). "Smart cities in Europe", *Journal of Urban Technology*, 18 (2): 65–82.

Caragliu, A., Del Bo, C., and Nijkamp, P. (2012). "A map of human capital in European cities", in Van Geenhuizen, M., and Nijkamp, P. (eds), *Creative Knowledge Cities: Myths, Visions and Realities*, Cheltenham, UK and Northampton, MA, USA: Edward Elgar Publishing.

Clastres, C. (2011). "Smart grids: another step towards competition, energy security and climate change objectives", *Energy Policy*, 39 (9): 5399–5408.

Coleman, J.S. (1988). "Social capital in the creation of human capital", *American Journal of Sociology*, 94, Supplement: Organizations and Institutions: Sociological and Economic Approaches to the Analysis of Social Structure, S95–S120.

de Luca, A. (2012). "Come (ri) pensare la smart city", *Eyesreg*, 2 (6): 143–146.

Deakin, M., Lombardi, P., and Cooper, I. (2011). "The IntelCities community of practice: the capacity-building, co-design, evaluation and monitoring of eGov services", *Journal of Urban Technology*, 18 (2): 13–38.

Dunteman, G. (1989). *Principal Components Analysis*, Thousand Oaks (CA): Sage.

Dutton, W.H., Blumler, J.G., and Kraemer, K.L. (1987). *Wired Cities: Shaping the Future of Communications*, Washington (DC): Annenberg School of Communications.

European Commission (2000). "Lisbon European Council 23 and 24 March 2000: Presidency conclusions". Retrieved online on April 8, 2015 at http://www.europarl.europa.eu/summits/lis1_en.htm.

European Commission (2010). "Regional policy contributing to smart growth in Europe 2020", COM(2010) 553 final. Retrieved online on May 20, 2013 at http://ec.europa.eu/regional_policy/sources/docoffic/official/communic/smart_growth/comm2010_553_en.pdf.

European Commission (2013). "Labour market developments in Europe 2013". Retrieved online on April 8, 2015 at http://ec.europa.eu/economy_finance/publications/european_economy/2013/ee6_en.htm.

Foray, D., David, P., and Hall, B. (2009). "Smart specialization – the concept", *Knowledge Economists Policy Brief 9*, June.

Gans, W., Alberini, A., and Longo, A. (2013). "Smart meter devices and the effect of feedback on residential electricity consumption: evidence from a natural experiment in Northern Ireland", *Energy Economics*, 36: 729–743.

Geurs, K.T., and van Wee, B. (2004). "Accessibility evaluation of land-use and transport strategies: review and research directions", *Journal of Transport Geography*, 12 (2): 127–140.

Giffinger, R., Fertner, C., Kramar, H., Kalasek, R., Pichler-Milanović, N., and Meijers E. (2007). "Smart cities. Ranking of European medium-sized cities", Centre of Regional Science of Vienna, www.smart-cities.eu.

Hall, B.H., and Mairesse, J. (2009). "Corporate R&D returns", *Knowledge Economists Policy Brief 6*. Retrieved online on April 8, 2015 at http://ec.europa.eu/invest-in-research/pdf/download_en/kfg_report_no6.pdf.

Kaiser, H.F. (1961). "A note on Guttman's lower bound for the number of common factors", *British Journal of Mathematical and Statistical Psychology*, 33 (2): 233–236.

Komninos, N. (2002). *Intelligent Cities: Innovation, Knowledge Systems and Digital Spaces*, London (UK): Routledge.
Komninos, N. (2009). "Intelligent cities: towards interactive and global innovation environments", *International Journal of Innovation and Regional Development*, 1 (4): 337–355.
Lennert, M. et al. (2010). "FOCI – Future Orientations for Cities Final Report". Retrieved online on April 8, 2015 at http://www.espon.eu/export/sites/default/Documents/Projects/AppliedResearch/FOCI/FOCI_final_report_20110111.pdf.
McCann, P., and Ortega-Argilés, R. (2011). "Smart specialisation, regional growth and applications to the EU", Working paper, accessed May 13, 2013 from http://dialnet.unirioja.es/servlet/articulo?codigo=3693537.
McFadden, D. (1974). "Conditional logit analysis of qualitative choice behavior", in Zarembka, P. (ed.), *Frontiers in Econometrics*, New York: Academic Press, pp. 105–142.
Newman, P., Beatley, T., and Boyer, H. (2009). *Resilient Cities: Responding to Peak Oil and Climate Change*, Washington (DC): Island Press.
OECD (2005). "Guide to measuring the information society". Working Party on Indicators for the Information Society, www.oecd.org/dataoecd/41/12/36177203.pdf.
Pavitt, K. (1984). "Sectoral patterns of technical change: towards a taxonomy and a theory", *Research Policy*, 13 (6): 343–373.
Pontikakis, D., Chorafakis, G., and Kyriakou, D. (2009). "R&D specialization in Europe: from stylized observations to evidence-based policy", in Pontikakis, D., Kyriakou, D., and van Bavel, R. (eds), *The Question of R&D Specialization*", Brussels: JRC, European Commission, Directoral General for Research, pp. 71–84.
Putnam, R.D. (2001). "Social capital: measurement and consequences", *Canadian Journal of Policy Research*, 2 (1): 41–51.
Putnam, R.D., Leonardi, R., and Nanetti, R.Y. (1993). *Making Democracy Work: Civic Traditions in Modern Italy*, Princeton, NJ: Princeton University Press.
Shapiro, J.M. (2006). "Smart cities: quality of life, productivity, and the growth effects of human capital", *Review of Economics and Statistics*, 88 (2): 324–335.
Shapiro, J.M. (2008). "Smart cities: quality of life, productivity, and the growth effects of human capital", *The Review of Economics and Statistics*, 88 (2): 324–335.
Tajima, K. (2003). "New estimates of the demand for urban green space: implications for valuing the environmental benefits of Boston's big dig project", *Journal of Urban Affairs*, 5 (5): 641–655.
van Ark, B., O'Mahony, M., and Timmer, M.P. (2008). "The productivity gap between Europe and the United States: trends and causes", *Journal of Economic Perspectives*, 22 (1): 25–44.
Welch, E.W., Hinnant, C., and Jae Moon, M. (2005). "Linking citizen satisfaction with e-government and trust in government", *Journal of Public Administration Research and Theory*, 15 (3): 371–391.
Winters, J.V. (2011). "Why are smart cities growing? Who moves and who stays", *Journal of Regional Science*, 51 (2): 253–270.

APPENDIX 1

The six axes in the urban smartness definition are measured with the following indicators (Table 3.A1).

Table 3.A1 Indicators for the six axes of the Smart City definition

Urban smartness axis	Raw data
1. Human capital	Proportion of population aged 15–64 qualified at tertiary level (ISCED 5–6) living in Urban Audit cities – percentage
	Students in tertiary education (ISCED 5–6) living in Urban Audit cities – number of students per 1,000 inhabitants
	Proportion of employment in financial intermediation – business activities
	Proportion of employment public administration – health education
	Sum of the previous two
	Number of companies with headquarters in the city quoted on the national stock market
2. Social capital	Car thefts per 1,000 population
	Burglaries per 1,000 population
	Crimes per 1,000 population
	Number of elected city representatives
3. Transport infrastructure	Length of public transport network per inhabitant
	Share of restricted bus lanes from public transport network
	Number of buses (or bus equivalents) operating in the public transport per 1,000 population
	Number of stops of public transport per 1,000 population
4. ICT infrastructure	Percentage of families with internet access at home
	Number of local units producing ICT products
	Number of local units producing ICT-related services
	Number of local units producing web content
5. Natural resources	Proportion of solid waste arising within the boundary processed by recycling
	Proportion of the area in green space
	Green space (in sq. m) to which the public has access, per capita
	Annual average concentration of PM10
	Annual average concentration of NO_2

Table 3.A1 (continued)

Urban smartness axis	Raw data
6. E-government	Percentage of internet users who interacted via internet with the public authorities in the last 12 months (country data) Percentage of internet users who sent filled forms to public authorities in the last 12 months (country data) Number of administrative forms available for download from official website Number of administrative forms which can be submitted electronically

APPENDIX 2

The 15 NACE 2–digit industries used for the calculation of the Smart Specialization indicator are shown in Table 3.A2.

Table 3.A2 List of industries used for the calculation of the Smart Specialization indicator

NACE industry code	Full industry name
A+B	Agriculture
C+E	Mining, quarrying and energy supply
DA	Food, beverages and tobacco
DB+DC	Textiles and leather etc.
DF+DG+DH	Coke, refined petroleum, nuclear fuel and chemicals etc.
DL	Electrical and optical equipment
DM	Transport equipment
DD+DE+DN+DI+DJ+DK	Other manufacturing
F	Construction
G	Distribution
H	Hotels and restaurants
I	Transport, storage and communications
J	Financial intermediation
K	Real estate, renting and business activities
L+M+N+O+P	Non-market services

4. Agglomeration economies in large versus small cities: similar laws, high specifities

Roberto Camagni, Roberta Capello and Andrea Caragliu

1. INTRODUCTION

During the 1970s, the debate on agglomeration economies was strongly in favour of a natural law valid for all cities, leading to the existence of an "optimal" city size; based on a number of empirical studies, agglomeration advantages were said to exist up to a certain size, after which decreasing returns emerged, leading to one single "optimal" city size, achieved by all cities when marginal location costs equal marginal location benefits.[1]

However, many criticisms arose against the optimal city size theory, starting with the author who contributed most to the popularity of the optimal urban size concept, namely William Alonso (1971). These criticisms include the observations that cities perform different functions, are characterized by different specializations and consequently operate with different production functions (Henderson, 1974, 1996). In the words of Richardson: "we may expect the efficient range of city sizes to vary, possibly dramatically, according to the functions and the structure of the cities in question" (1972, p. 30). In the real world, one would never expect the optimal position for each and every firm to occur at the same level of output; so why should one expect the optimal point in different cities to be identified at the same population level? In this literature, the opposite view that each city operates on its own cost and production curves is assumed, defining a specific optimal size for each city.

In Camagni et al. (2013), the ideas that one single optimal city size does exist, as well as the opposite, too simplistic view that infinite optimal city sizes exist, are abandoned. Cities are assumed to be comparable, as

[1] Among many examples of this burgeoning literature, see Shefer (1973), Carlino (1980) and Sveikauskas et al. (1988).

they share common cost and benefit functions with heterogeneous cost and benefit factors, thereby allowing cross-sectional empirical analyses. Each city maintains its own specificity and unicity, and consequently is attributed its own "equilibrium" size through an econometric model which derives the "equilibrium size" by directly equating marginal costs and benefits to urban size.

Analogously, in this work the aim is to show that if average (net) urban benefits assume an inverted U-shaped form, this is true for both large and small cities; the difference between large and small cities lies in the fact that the latter turn into diseconomies of scale at a smaller size. The starting point is the acknowledgement of the existence of different city size classes (small, medium, large) and the consideration of each class as encompassing structurally similar cities. Large cities are de-specialized in terms of activity sectors, host high-level functions and labour professions; medium-sized cities are generally more specialized and highly performing in the specialization sectors; small cities mainly host low-level skills and activities (Conti and Dematteis, 1995). This way of reasoning is in line with the central place theory (Christaller, 1933), which attributes higher functions to cities of higher rank, able to host functions of their size with functions typical of smaller cities. As we will see later on, unlike Christaller, our approach does not link urban ranks to urban size, opening up the possibility that cities of the same size perform different functions.

In a simplified view, agglomeration economies are taken for granted in small and medium-sized cities and only in large cities should the problem of a downturn in urban returns to scale eventually emerge. On the other hand, assuming a more comprehensive view, the theoretical conjecture of this chapter is that the exploitation of agglomeration economies is relatively smooth inside the three/four traditional size intervals, implying, however, the presence of some specific limiting/enabling factors when cities approach some critical instability point, that is, a situation determined by a critical size turning increasing returns into decreasing ones. Therefore, cities may experience a halt in their growth path and even a decline irrespective of their size class, in the absence of these conditional factors. These factors are not quantitative, but rather qualitative in nature and a quantum leap in their endowment is needed at specific intervals if agglomeration economies are to fully generate their beneficial effects. The quality of activities and production factors hosted, the density of external linkages and cooperation networks, the quality of urban infrastructure – in internal and external mobility, in education, in public services – are all enabling factors allowing a long-term "structural dynamics" process (in the language of dynamic modelling) through what may be called a process of urban innovation in each urban rank.

The focus of the analysis is no more the identification of the behaviour of single cities, but rather the behaviour of the individual categories of cities, sharing common size features, and their differentiation. Thus, the explanation of a relatively good urban economic efficiency and therefore a relatively higher urban dynamics based on higher urban attractiveness is not mechanically linked to the existence of agglomeration economies; instead, this work highlights under which conditions agglomeration economies appear and are exploited inside each urban size class.

This work has important theoretical, conceptual and normative implications. The concepts of agglomeration economies/diseconomies are no longer generically applied to the whole spectrum of city sizes, but linked to the presence of specific context conditions which are typical of each urban size class. In each size class similar laws govern the evolutionary paths of cities. For instance, in order to avoid decreasing returns, cities need to innovate at some critical stage; however, these laws operate at different size scales.

The empirical analysis supports this statement. The explanation of agglomeration economies is not simply linked to city size. On the contrary, specific urban features, like the presence of high level functions and cooperation networks among cities, are identified as the main drivers of increasing returns, and explicitly disentangled from physical size. In addition, the role of these urban features in explaining increasing returns recalls that the nature of agglomeration economies is found in territorial characteristics of an area, rather than in pecuniary externalities generated by market interaction among firms which individually exploit internal economies of scale when a new firm enters the market (Krugman, 1991). This chapter also provides empirical evidence about the validity of the theoretical concept of "borrowed size" (Alonso, 1973), whereby small cities manage to achieve increasing returns even in the absence, or insufficient endowment, of local enhancing factors, by borrowing functions and networks from higher order cities located nearby.

The chapter is structured as follows. Section 2 briefly presents the recent analyses that still link urban growth patterns to agglomeration economies, and highlights the existing conceptual toolbox that allows the traditional view of the role of agglomeration economies in urban growth to be superseded. Section 3 presents the rich database behind the empirical analysis on 136 European cities of different size. Section 4 contains the interpretative econometric analysis, while section 5 concludes.

2. DETERMINANTS OF URBAN GROWTH PATTERNS: BEYOND AGGLOMERATION ECONOMIES

The interest in the role of cities in explaining national economic performance is not new and has always been at the basis of urban economics theory and economic geography studies. In the 1990s, thanks to seminal contributions (Glaeser et al., 1992), a resurgence of interest in cities and in their role in national economic performance was registered, followed by more recent studies especially for the North American reality (Sassen, 2002; Rosenthal and Strange, 2004; Glaeser, 2008).

This revival of interest in the role of cities in explaining national economic performance is not just driven by an academic fashion (Henderson, 2010), but finds concrete evidence of real changes in the role of large cities in driving national economies (Nijkamp and Kourtit, 2011, 2012). In the period 1980–2000, large (mostly, but not only) European cities benefitted from two main favourable exogenous factors enhancing their performance: the emergence and consolidation of the information and communications technology (ICT) paradigm, quickly utilized to re-launch urban activities after the previous de-industrialization, and the launching of the European Single Market project by Jacques Delors in 1985, which determined a large inflow of foreign direct investment (FDI) into large gateway cities in all European countries. On the other hand, recently the economic crisis mostly hit large and capital cities, natural loci of most economic and financial activities, leaving small cities the role of being the most resilient areas to economic downturn in advanced economies.

Agglomeration economies have been recently highlighted as the main reason for the success of small cities on national economic growth; while large cities experience decreasing returns drastically limiting their growth rates, small cities enjoy agglomeration economies, and therefore cumulative growth rates (Dijkstra et al., 2013). This explanation is not convincing, and risks an *ex post* circular reasoning: a structural break – namely the limit between economies and diseconomies – is used to explain cyclical economic phenomena, with no interpretation of why it takes place exactly at a specific moment and in a particular place. Apparently, two problems are mixed together: a structural and a cyclical one. The former takes into consideration the existence of a theoretical explanation concerning the way and conditions for the different city size classes to exploit increasing returns to urban scale (the how problem); the latter problem concerns the question of whether different classes of urban size are differentially impacted by expansion or crisis periods (the when problem). The how issue is logically more interesting than the when issue, as descriptive evidence shows that there are some large cities still able to play a role in their national economies, and some small cities still lagging behind, showing that, for the same urban size, agglomeration economies seem to play a positive role for some cities and not for others (Camagni et al., 2014).

Some relevant theoretical interpretations concerning increasing returns to urban scale – going beyond the use of a single function for the entire spectrum of city sizes, interpreting the capacity of cities to exploit agglomeration economies – are already available in urban economic theory, and deserve empirical demonstration.

The first explanation for the capacity of a city to overcome diseconomies of scale is provided by the SOUDY (Supply Oriented Urban DYnamics) model (Camagni et al., 1986). The model assumes that an "efficient" city size interval exists for each hierarchical rank, associated with rank-specific economic functions. For each economic function characterized by a specific demand threshold and a minimum production size, a minimum and a maximum city size exists beyond which urban location diseconomies overcome production benefits typical of that function.

As Figure 4.1 shows, under these conditions for each economic function and each associated urban rank, a minimum and a maximum city

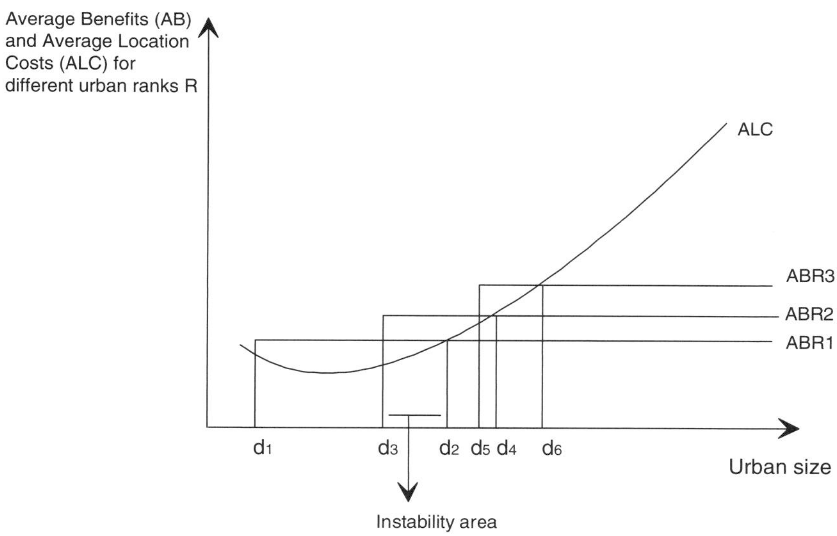

Source: Camagni et al. (1986).

Figure 4.1 Efficient city size for different urban functions

size can be defined, and in this interval the city operates under efficiency conditions (i.e. with net positive gains) (d_1–d_2 for the function – and centre – of rank 1; d_3–d_4 for the function – and centre – of rank 2). The higher the production benefits (profits) of the single functions (increasing with rank), the higher the efficient urban size interval associated with such function.

As each centre grows, approaching the maximum size compatible with its rank ("constrained dynamics"), it enters an instability area (e.g. in d_3–d_2 in Figure 4.1) where it becomes a potentially suitable location for higher order functions, thanks to the achievement of a critical demand size. In dynamic terms, each city's long-term growth depends on its ability to move to higher urban ranks, developing or attracting new higher-order functions ("structural dynamics"). This "jump" is not mechanically attained: it represents a true urban innovation and is treated as a stochastic process in the dynamic model.

The interest of this model resides in the fact that it overcomes some of the limits of the "optimal" city size theory, by suggesting:

- the need to replace "optimal" size by an "interval" within which the city size is "efficient",[2] that is, where average production benefits exceed average location costs;
- the need to allow different "efficient" urban intervals according to the functions actually performed by the cities;
- the possibility of separating urban ranks from urban size. Unlike Christaller's approach, two cities of the same size (for example, size d_2 in Figure 4.1) can belong to two ranks (1 and 2 in the example), depending on their capacity to attract/develop higher functions.

This approach to urban evolution could be easily applied to a simplified urban hierarchy, defined by common-sense urban size classes (small, medium, large), showing that a smooth process of growth, based on multiplier effects and agglomeration economies, may work for each size class inside its specific size interval, but that a further expansion process is subject to a constraint, a bifurcation in the development path, a stochastic "jump" over new and more advanced activities and functions (Figure 4.2). All this is obtained, however, without being able to explain the width of the interval (for which size the city in each class reaches its maximum point),

[2] Richardson (1972) suggests replacing the concept of optimal city size with an efficient interval of urban size in which urban marginal benefits are greater than marginal location costs.

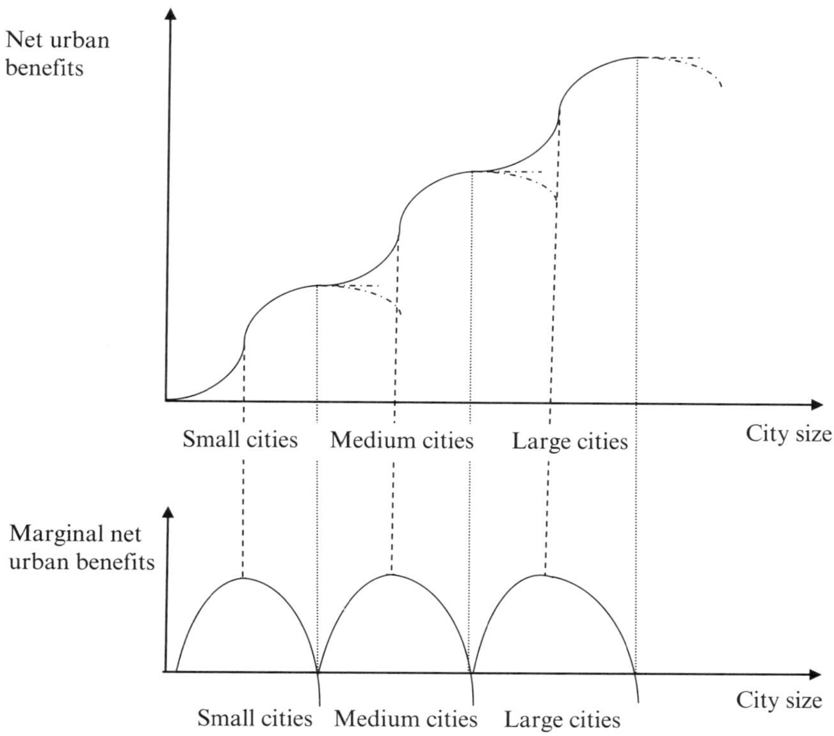

Source: Authors' elaboration.

Figure 4.2 Urban evolution in a simplified urban hierarchy. Total and marginal net urban benefits by city size classes

as well as the speed with which the maximum size is achieved (the slope of the urban benefits logistic curve).

The second theory helpful in explaining the determinants of agglomeration economies going beyond urban size is the city network theory. Born in the field of industrial economics (Williamson, 1985; Chesnais, 1988), the concept of network behaviour – namely a cooperative organizational form, intermediate between internal and external growth of the firm, between "make" or "buy" – was transferred into urban economics providing a successful theoretical framework to overcome the limiting interpretative power of the traditional central-place model (Camagni, 1993; for a review of the concept, see Capello and Rietveld, 1998). In fact, real city-systems in advanced countries have departed from the abstract

Christaller pattern of a nested hierarchy of centres and markets, showing (Camagni, 1993):

- processes of city specialization and presence of higher order functions in centres of lower order;
- horizontal linkages between similar cities, not allowed in the traditional model: for example, the financial and headquarter networks among top world cities, or the art cities linked through tourist "itineraries" (so called "synergy networks"); the systems of specialized cities exploiting the advantages of the division of labour, like the Dutch Randstad or the network of medium-size cities in the Veneto region ("complementarity networks") (Camagni and Capello, 2004).

The city-network model allows single cities to upgrade their economic functions without necessarily increasing their individual size. Therefore, cities of intermediate size are being increasingly looked upon as the places that could well host the growth of the years to come: a limited city size, in fact, facilitates environmental equilibrium, efficiency of the mobility system and the possibility for citizens to withhold a sense of identity, provided that a superior economic efficiency is reached through external cooperation with other cities, located in the same regions or distant but well connected.

In the new logic, other elements come to the fore – economies of vertical and horizontal integration, and network externalities similar to those emerging from "club goods". These elements provide the possibility for cities to reach increasing returns and scale economies through a network integration – in the economic, logistic and organizational fields – with other cities. In this sense, the concept of city networks recalls that of "borrowed size", which was launched by Alonso (1973) to explain a disconnection between size and function of smaller cities that were part of a megalopolitan urban complex: "[t]he concept of a system of cities has many facets, but one of particular interest . . . is the concept of borrowed size, whereby a small city or metropolitan area exhibits some of the characteristics of a larger one if it is near other population concentrations" (Alonso, 1973, p. 200).

Small cities can in fact "borrow" size from proximate large cities. In fact, "small firms can locate in smaller settlements and yet access specialized labour and informational external economies of nearby larger urban areas" (Phelps et al., 2001, p. 613). This implies that individuals, firms and institutions located in small and medium-sized cities, but not far from large metro areas, may reap the benefits of a central location (i.e. being located in a large and diversified metropolitan area), without incurring, however, in scale diseconomies (congestion, crime and so forth) typically associated with large cities. This alternative explanation is also empirically tested in this chapter, as an alternative way to understand how small cities achieved agglomeration economies and outperformed large ones.

An important difference exists between the concept of borrowed size and that of city networks. The concept of city networks adds to that of "borrowed size" the idea that size can be borrowed not only thanks to physical proximity to larger centres, but thanks to relationships and flows of a mainly horizontal and non-hierarchical nature among complementary or similar centres, located far from each other, with the aim to achieve network externalities (Camagni, 1993; Capello, 2000; Camagni and Capello, 2004).

Urban productivity has been empirically found to be more closely related to urban connectivity – a concept similar to urban network relations – than to urban scale (McCann and Acs, 2011), thus supporting the global city argument but also the medium-size cities' potentials.

The joint application of the SOUDY model and the city-network paradigm has relevant implications for urban efficiency and growth: size and agglomeration economies are not the only determinants of factor productivity and urban performance. The presence of high-order functions and integration inside city-networks are also extremely important elements in the explanation of the competitive advantage of cities, allowing productivity to be boosted even in presence of limited urban size.

We do not expect increasing returns to be associated only with large cities, but that the best performing cities (from the economic point of view) of all sizes are those characterized by agglomeration economies. Moreover, we expect that the increasing returns to size depend on high value functions and city networks. Again, this is irrespective of the size of cities.

Our research hypotheses are therefore the following:

a. a single function valid for the entire spectrum of city sizes does not correctly interpret the existence of increasing and decreasing returns in net urban benefits to urban size;
b. an asymptotic level of net urban benefits is reached inside each size class of cities (in this case: first and second-order cities, or large and medium cities), as in Figure 4.2, indicating the existence of an equilibrium city size in each size class;
c. the best performing cities in each class are able to postpone and overcome the appearance of decreasing returns, independently from their class size, thus being able to fully exploit increasing returns to urban scale;

d. this capability to exploit increasing returns depends on the development of higher valued functions and external cooperation networks, for both small and large cities.

Similar laws concerning the existence of increasing/decreasing returns are expected to work in both large and medium-sized cities, the size of each city being constrained by structural elements and not by a unique agglomeration function. The size at which agglomeration economies turn into diseconomies is expected to be different for the different classes of cities, as well as the intensity of functions and networks.

3. THE MODEL AND THE DATA DESCRIPTION

3.1 The Estimated Model

The above-mentioned research questions are addressed by estimating an aggregate urban production function in the traditional neoclassical form of average location benefits (henceforth, ALB). ALB depend on city size, measured as the absolute number of inhabitants, as in the classical literature (Sveikauskas et al., 1988; Catin, 1991). In order to distinguish between increasing and decreasing returns to scale, a quadratic form is imposed for the ALB with the introduction of the squared population term in the empirical model. Networks and functions act on ALB as they achieve a critical population mass; this is captured by the interaction term between networks and functions, on the one hand, and population, on the other.

The basic estimated model reads as follows:

$$ALB = const + \beta_1 Pop + \beta_2 Pop^2 + \beta_3 Pop{*}Functions + \beta_4 Pop{*}Networks + \varepsilon \tag{4.1}$$

where ALB stands for average location benefits, and Pop stands for population.

The indicator of net urban advantage used here is urban rent, measured through house prices per square metre (see, e.g. Capello, 2002).[3] The use of this indicator is based on a crucial underlying hypothesis, namely that the differences in house prices between large and small cities measure

[3] Urban rent is usually interpreted as the rent paid to the house owner. However, house prices represent the capitalized rent over time, and for this reason may be chosen as a proxy for urban rent.

their relative attractiveness (and thus their net localization advantage), as a result of an evaluation made by the market of the "value" of these locations. Analogously, the dynamics of urban house prices capture the changes in attractiveness of each location, and thus the dynamics of urban net advantage.

According to this logic, urban rent is a useful indicator of advantages and costs of different urban sizes, and of the existence of an optimal city size. This latter is the size which allows the achievement of the maximum net agglomeration advantages, estimated by the market as an *equilibrium rent level*. For urban areas larger than the optimal size, scale diseconomies would prevail, causing a relocation of residential and production activities, a decrease in city size and a consequent decrease in urban rent. In the same way, a city which is smaller than the optimal size would be characterized by suboptimal rent levels, which would attract production and residential activities, causing an increase in city size and consequently an increase in urban rent.

The basic model is estimated for the all cities, split into two "uniform categories" of large and small cities, treated as archetypes of different urban categories; uniformity is expected to depend on the physical size, as usually done in the economic geography literature. Large cities are in fact defined as those cities (larger urban zones (LUZ) areas, in Eurostat's definition) that are characterized by more than 1 million inhabitants. Small cities are instead identified as those LUZ areas with a number of inhabitants in a range from 1 million to 200,000 inhabitants. In both cases, data used to define the classes refer to 2011. The proposed classification of city size classes may be questionable, but in the absence of a commonly agreed typology this organization of the existing size information represents a neutral starting point for the empirical analyses.[4]

Separate estimates for the two groups were required, since no significant results were obtained for the whole sample. This is already an interesting result, suggesting that small-class cities are different in nature than large-class ones.

Within each group, the outperforming cities with respect to the national average have been identified, and two dummies created for, respectively, large- and small-class outperforming cities. In order to analyse the specificities of the outperforming cities with respect to the average behaviour, the basic model has been estimated again by introducing the interaction terms between the independent variables and the outperforming city dummies, as follows:

[4] The distribution of LUZ populations used for the identification of the three classes is shown in Figure 4.A1 in the Technical Appendix.

$$ALB = const + \beta_1 Pop + \beta_2 Pop^2 + \beta_3 Pop^*Functions + \beta_4 Pop^*networks$$
$$+ \beta_5 Pop^*D_1 + \beta_6 Pop^{2*}D_1 + \beta_7 Pop^*Functions^*D_1$$
$$+ \beta_8 Pop^*Networks^*D_1 + \beta_9 D_1 + \varepsilon \quad (4.2)$$

$$ALB = const + \beta_1 Pop + \beta_2 Pop^2 + \beta_3 Pop^*Functions + \beta_4 Pop^*networks$$
$$+ \beta_5 Pop^*D_2 + \beta_6 Pop^{2*}D_2 + \beta_7 Pop^*Functions^*D_2$$
$$+ \beta_8 Pop^*Networks^*D_2 + \beta_9 D_2 + \varepsilon \quad (4.3)$$

Eqs (4.2) and (4.3) contain the interaction terms with D_1 and D_2, which represent the relatively best performing cities compared to the national average, respectively for large- and small-class cities (see also Section 4). Before entering the estimation procedure, the database on which the model is estimated is first presented (Section 3.2), in order to explain the choice of the period and the identification of the dummies for the best performing cities.

For small-class cities, an alternative version of model eq. (4.3) entails the use of a measure of borrowed size, that aims at capturing the possibility that small-class cities may have in fact borrowed the use of high-level urban functions and long-distance connectivity from large metro areas, irrespective of their own (relatively) small size. This implies that the alternative model entails the estimation of the following equation, where functions and networks are substituted by borrowed size:

$$ALB = const + \beta_1 Pop + \beta_2 Pop^2 + \beta_3 D + \beta_4 D^*Pop + \beta_5 D^*Pop^2$$
$$+ \beta_6 Borrowedsize + \beta_7 D^*Borrowedsize + \varepsilon \quad (4.4)$$

3.2 The Database

In order to empirically test both research questions stated in Section 2, a novel data set has been assembled, which exploits the relatively recent release of metro area data from Eurostat. Table 4.1 summarizes the main sources of the data set assembled for the present analysis.

Eurostat provides a detailed definition of metropolitan statistical areas in Europe. Data on metro regions are based on an aggregation of NUTS3 administrative regions, and the process of aggregation aims at maximizing the overlapping of such regions with functional urban areas (LUZ). In fact, the aim of this statistical classification is to "correct the distortions created by commuting" by "including the commuter belt around a city" (Dijkstra, 2009, p. 1).

Table 4.1 The data set

Data	Indicator	Source of raw data	Years available
GDP	Constant 2005 € GDP	Eurostat	1995–2009
Population	Average yearly metro area population	Eurostat	1995–2009
Land rent	Prices of an average apartment in the city's CBD	Eurostat/ Urban Audit, author's integration[1]	2004, 2011
High urban functions	Share of high skilled occupations over total population[2]	Labour Force Survey	1995–2007 (average 1998–2002 and 2002–2006 have been calculated)
City networks	Number of Framework Programme 5 and 6 co-participations	CORDIS	1998–2002 (FP5) 2002–2006 (FP6)

Notes:

1. House prices data have been integrated through single national sources.
2. High level functions are defined as the International Standard Classification of Occupations (ISCO) 88 class 1, encompassing "legislators, senior officials and managers". Micro data have been aggregated at Nomenclature of Territorial Units for Statistics (NUTS) 2 level, and the value of the NUTS2 region is assigned to the metro area. A full list of ISCO professions is available at the URL http://laborsta.ilo.org/applv8/data/isco88e.html.

Source: Authors' elaboration.

For these regions, data on gross domestic product (henceforth, GDP) in current prices and population from 1995 to 2009 have been collected. Because the early years (1995–2000) were missing from the data set, population in the NUTS3 regions forming metropolitan areas has been aggregated following the official Eurostat classification. GDP data has been deflated with the Eurostat country-specific deflator, to obtain GDP in constant 2005 prices (net of within-country price variations, which cannot at the present state being fully eliminated).

The data on GDP and population have been used to identify those cities that over- or under-performed with respect to the country average (i.e. whose productivity defined as GDP/population grew faster than the country average in each selected time period).

Next, the data necessary to estimate the models presented in eqs (4.2) and (4.3) have been collected. As explained in Section 3.1, urban land rent represents the measure of average urban location benefits. Land rent is measured here with the price per square metre of an average quality apartment located in the central business district (CBD) of each city in the sample. Data, collected for the years 2004 and 2011 (see below for details), have also been deflated with the country deflator.

Finally, urban functions have been measured with the share of high skills professionals over total population (source: micro database of Eurostat's labour force survey, aggregated at the NUTS2 level; see Table 4.1 for details). In order to measure urban networks, the approach used in Camagni et al. (2013) has been followed and urban networks are measured by the number of Framework Programmes (henceforth, FPs) 5 and 6 to which institutions of each surveyed city participated. "FPs constitute the main planning instruments and funding sources for R&D policies in the EU, their mission being to respond to the challenges of the integration process by investigating the socio-economic, technological, industrial and cultural aspects of the EU" (Basile et al., 2012, p. 710). As such, they represent a good proxy for the capability of a city to engage in long-distance networks aiming to foster scientific cooperation, and represent a comprehensive measure of the quality and thickness of external urban networks.

Finally, as a proxy for borrowed size (viz. the accessibility of small-class cities to functions and networks typical of large urban areas), for each small-class city we calculated a spatially-lagged value of population in large-class urban areas. Borrowed size is therefore defined as:

$$Borrowedsize_i = W\overline{pop} = \sum_{j=1}^{n} pop_j w_j, \ \forall j \neq i \tag{4.5}$$

where i and j represent respectively large- and small-class cities, W is an nXn distance weight matrix between large- and small-class cities (each entry in the matrix is equal to 0 if the two cities are large- and small-class cities and equal to the inverse of the geographical distance in kilometres if the two cities are one second class and one first class), and $\overline{pop}$ represents the vector of first class city populations.[5]

[5] The bar notation indicates a vector.

4. AN INTERPRETATIVE MODEL OF URBAN STRUCTURAL DYNAMICS: FIRST VERSUS SECOND CLASS CITIES

4.1 Outperforming Cities: Do Increasing Returns Play a Role?

Table 4.2 reports the estimated results for the basic model, and for eqs (4.2) and (4.3). The first two columns show that an estimate based on the full sample of cities (including both class 1 and class 2 cities) is in stark contrast with the theoretical expectations based on the classical literature on the existence of a maximum for the ALB function. This suggests the need to analyse this phenomenon more in-depth, by separating cities of class 1 and 2, which evidently present different characteristics. Columns 3 through 8 show random effects estimates for class 1 (columns 3 through 5) and class 2 (columns 6 through 8), respectively. Ordinary Least Squares (OLS) estimates did not provide good results, while fixed effects for single cities are conceptually excluded in this exercise; peculiarities for single cities in exploiting agglomeration advantages not depending on size, functions and networks neither exist, nor are expected to play a role. The choice of random effects estimates is also justified by the standard Breusch–Pagan test, suggesting that random effects estimates are indeed to be preferred to standard OLS ones.

Results in columns 1–3 suggest the counterintuitive existence of a U-shaped form of the ALB curve, with a negative population coefficient, and a positive coefficient for square population. These results underline the existence of unlimited agglomeration economies, for the entire sample and for large cities, when specific interpretative variables are not introduced to explain these economies, other than physical size.

When the specific advantages of large size are controlled for, namely high-value functions and networks (column 5), the shape of ALB with respect to urban size turns into a inverse U-shaped curve, as suggested by the theoretical literature, capturing the disadvantage deriving from a (excessively) large size and therefore providing empirical evidence about the structural differences between first and second class cities.

Column 5 shows that the coefficients have the expected signs and turn out to be significant, with the exception of networks, which are not found significant in explaining urban location benefits. The (overall) R^2 of this model is equal to 0.51.

The results for second-class cities are presented in columns 6–8. A first important result is that the model does not fit for the whole sample of second-class cities, but only for Western European second-class cities, suggesting that second-class cities in Central and Eastern European Countries

Table 4.2 Estimation results

Dependent variable	Average urban benefits (Log urban rent)							
Sub-sample	All cities		Class 1 cities			Class 2 cities		
Model	(1)	(2)	(3)	(4)	(5)	(6)	(7)	(8)
Constant term	25.19***	23.65***	30.24**	−8.38	−21.70	−1.45	−46.51	−40.42
	(7.32)	(7.48)	(13.21)	(16.12)	(14.50)	(27.52)	(38.10)	(35.19)
Metro area population	−2.80***	−2.78**	−3.38*	1.80	3.72*	1.09	7.84	7.06*
	(1.04)	(1.06)	(1.81)	(2.21)	(1.97)	(4.06)	(5.63)	(5.20)
Square metro area population	0.11***	0.08**	0.13**	−0.05	−0.12*	−0.03	−0.28	−0.26*
	(0.04)	(0.04)	(0.06)	(0.08)	(0.07)	(0.15)	(0.21)	(0.19)
Dummy urban performance (the city outperformed the country)	–	−6.69	–	–	–	–	–	–
		(14.29)						
Dummy urban performance * metro area population	–	0.72	–	–	–	–	–	–
		(2.02)						
Dummy urban performance * square metro area population	–	−0.02	–	–	–	–	–	–
		(0.07)						
Dummy outperforming class 1 cities	–	–	–	77.76***	106.63***	–	–	–
				(28.90)	(27.54)			
Dummy outperforming class 1 cities * metro area population	–	–	–	−10.63***	−14.61***	–	–	–
				(4.03)	(3.82)			
Dummy outperforming class 1 cities * square metro area population	–	–	–	0.36**	0.50***	–	–	–
				(0.14)	(0.13)			
Dummy outperforming class 2 cities	–	–	–	–	–	–	55.79*	51.29*
							(36.75)	(32.99)
Dummy outperforming class 2 cities * metro area population	–	–	–	–	–	–	−8.47*	−7.76*
							(5.43)	(4.88)
Dummy outperforming class 2 cities * square metro area population	–	–	–	–	–	–	0.32*	0.30*
							(0.20)	(0.18)

High urban functions * metro population	–	0.02***	–	–	0.02***	–	–	0.02***
		(0.00)			(0.001)			(0.001)
City networks * metro population	–	0.01***	–	–	0.01*	–	–	0.003*
		(0.00)			(0.00)			(0.00)
Dummy outperforming class 1 cities * high urban functions * metro population	–	0.01*	–	–	0.02*	–	–	–
		(0.005)			(0.01)			
Dummy outperforming class 1 cities * city networks * metro population	–	−0.12**	–	–	0.00	–	–	–
		(0.05)			(0.00)			
Dummy outperforming class 2 cities * high urban functions * metro population	–		–	–	–	–	–	0.01*
								(0.00)
Dummy outperforming class 2 cities * city networks * metro population	–		–	–	–	–	–	−0.004
								(0.003)
Number of obs.	314	314	72	72	72	158	158	158
Joint F-test / Wald χ^2 test	38.36***	32.17***	20.59***	45.88***	180.78***	5.24***	4.16***	43.05***
Breusch–Pagan Test (OLS vs random effects)	–	–	10.85***	11.36***	6.93***	15.50***	16.78***	7.01***
R^2	0.14	0.38	0.20	0.25	0.51	0.04	0.07	0.42
Within			0.38	0.19	0.38	0.25	0.13	0.37
Between			0.23	0.26	0.54	0.05	0.06	0.44
Estimation method	OLS	OLS	RE	RE	RE	RE	RE	RE
Robust standard errors	Yes	Yes	Yes	Yes	Yes	Yes	Yes	Yes

Notes:
All variables are in log. *, **,*** imply significance at 10, 5 and 1 per cent, respectively.
Standard errors in parentheses.
OLS= Ordinary Least Squares estimates; RE= Random Effects estimates.

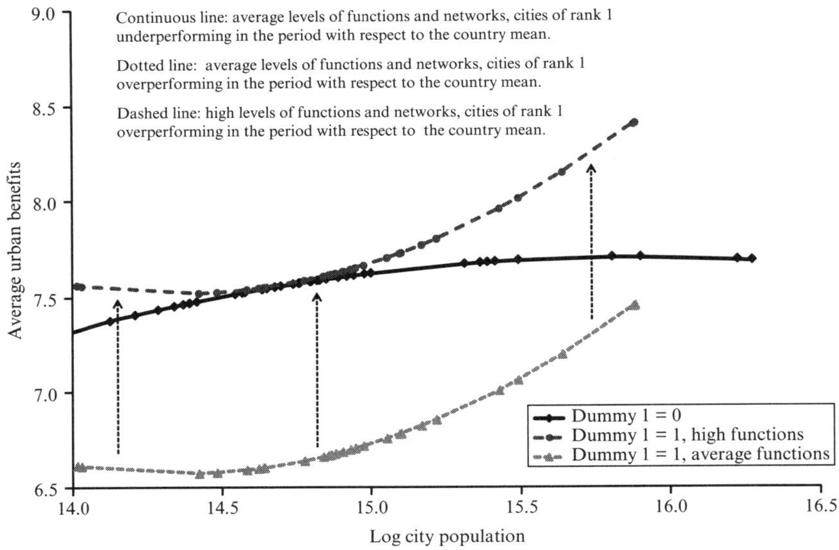

Source: Authors' elaboration.

Figure 4.3 Average urban location benefit curve for first-class cities

(CEECs) maintain a very peculiar dynamic that has no similarity to those of advanced ones.

On the basis of these results, it is worth emphasizing that the simultaneous validity of similar laws across the two size classes, as evidenced by the high level of fit of the estimates presented in columns 5 and 8, does not deny the relevance of the high specificities that make these two typologies remarkably different. As will be argued below, these results point out the need of analyses differentiated between these two classes, so that no single optimal city size across the whole urban world is sought, while instead class-specific optimality can be identified.

Figures 4.3 and 4.4 report the average location benefit curve for size, respectively for first- (Figure 4.3) and second- (Figure 4.4) class cities. Many interesting messages are contained in these figures, namely:

- for underperforming cities, the curve shows an inverted U-shape (the continuous curve in the figures);
- when only outperforming cities of both categories are analyzed (dotted line in Figures 4.3 and 4.4), the average location benefit

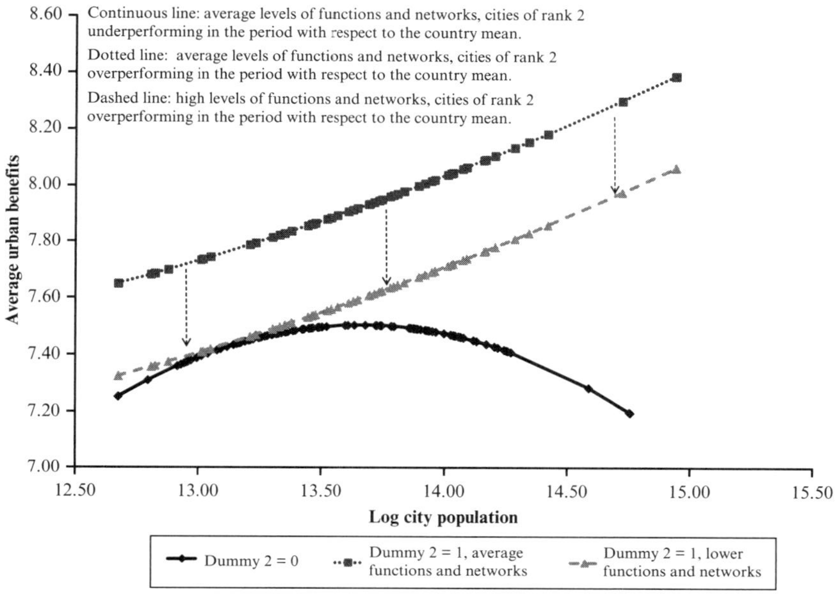

Source: Authors' elaboration.

Figure 4.4 Average urban location benefit curve for second-class cities

curve has a U-shaped form, showing that increasing returns in size are associated with best performing cities;

- the above statement is true for both first- and second-class cities, supporting the idea that the form of the ALB does not depend on city size;
- a higher level of high-value functions shifts the average location curve upwards (dashed line in Figure 4.3), that is, higher functions produce, *ceteris paribus*, higher location advantages, and this is true for both categories of cities. This result also witnesses, that unlike Christaller's approach, in the real world two cities of the same size can belong to two classes, depending on their capacity to attract/develop higher functions;
- Figures 4.3 and 4.4 show that second-class outperforming cities manage to achieve the bifurcation point from the underperforming cities at lower levels of functions compared to first-class cities (dashed line).

The similarities of the trends between second- and first-class cities suggest that the laws of structural dynamics are similar between the two

Table 4.3 *Optimal city size, critical size and level of functions for first- and second-class cities*

	First-class cities	Second-class cities
Optimal city size (number of inhabitants) (maximum point of the benefit curve function)	7,275,332	714,973
Critical size of outperforming cities turning diseconomies into economies of agglomeration (minimum point of the benefit curve function of outperforming cities)	1,794,075	296,559
Share of advanced functions and critical size necessary for outperforming cities to achieve the same level of urban benefit as the other cities	29% at a size of 2,250,000	7.5% at a size of 545,000

Source: Authors' elaboration.

urban archetypes. However, the last statement pertaining to the level of functions required to achieve the bifurcation point induces some reflections on the specificities in the way the laws of structural dynamics manifest themselves in the two categories of cities.

Table 4.3 reports the optimal city size, the critical size at which (for outperforming cities) diseconomies turn into economies and the level of high functions necessary to achieve the same level of urban benefits of other cities.

Specificities emerge, in that second-class cities achieve decreasing returns for a much lower city size than first-class ones; optimal second-class city size is achieved at around 700,000 inhabitants, while for first-class cities the maximum is around 7 million. By the same token, first-class outperforming cities require a size of around 1,700,000 inhabitants to turn diseconomies into economies of scale; while second-class outperforming cities require a critical size of about 300,000 inhabitants.

Specificities of the two categories of cities also emerge in the share of high-level functions required by outperforming cities in order to achieve the same level of urban benefits; first-class cities require 29 per cent of high-value functions and a size of 2,250,000 inhabitants, while second-class cities need 7.5 per cent of employment in high-level functions and a size of 545,000 inhabitants. Therefore, smaller cities require a lower intensity of high-level functions and a lower size to gain increasing returns, as the SOUDY model theoretically explained.

Our first three assumptions have been proved. A single urban benefit function, valid for all cities, and able to interpret the existence of agglomeration economies linked to urban size, does not exist. An asymptotic level of urban ALB may be achieved in each class; however, this holds for underperforming cities, unable to avoid or postpone the emergence of decreasing returns, independent of their city size. On the contrary, outperforming cities show increasing returns, and this holds for both first- and second-class cities.

This common law holds for both second- and first-class cities, but with specificities characterizing each single class: decreasing returns are achieved for lower city sizes in second-class cities than in first-class cities. The level of functions allowing diseconomies to turn into economies is lower for smaller than for larger cities.

4.2 Exploitation of Agglomeration Economies: Do Functions Play a Role?

The aim of this second analysis is to highlight the determinants of agglomeration economies. In addition to city size, higher urban functions are expected to play a role in explaining increasing returns.

Figure 4.5 shows the way in which marginal location benefits change by increasing the high-value functions. Especially for first-class cities (Figure 4.5a), this result is evident. Marginal location benefits are

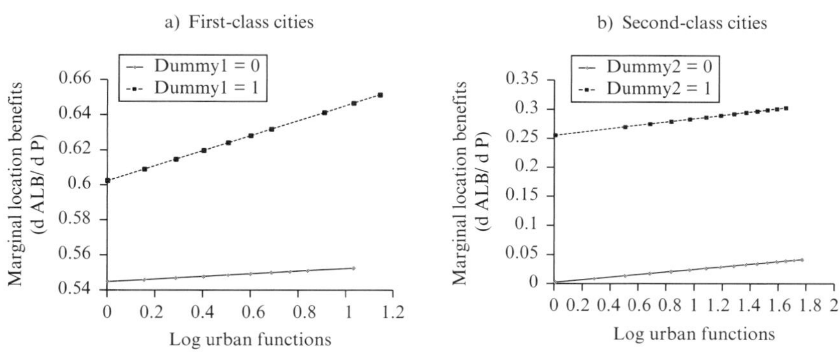

Source: Authors' elaboration.

Figure 4.5 Marginal urban benefits at different levels of high-value urban functions

positively related to the level of value-added functions; for an average level of functions, the marginal benefit of outperforming cities is 13 per cent higher than the one obtained by the whole sample. However, the increase is limited when the average city sample is taken into consideration, while it shows a positive slope for outperforming first-class cities; for second-class outperforming cities the impact of functions on the marginal urban benefits are high, but the effect remains constant as the intensity of functions increases. All these results also apply for the best performing second-class cities (Figure 4.5b), although the slope of the estimated marginal location benefits–functions relation is less steeply inclined.

These results explain the effects of pure physical size through the lens of the determinants and nature of agglomeration economies, highly dependent on urban characteristics, more than on the existence of pecuniary externalities related to market interactions of firms enjoying increasing returns, which is assumed with imperfect competition.

4.3 Exploitation of Agglomeration Economies: Does Borrowed Size Play a Role?

In this section the empirical analyses above are complemented with a specific analysis of the role of cities' capability to borrow size from nearby large metro areas in fostering agglomeration economies. As anticipated in Section 3, borrowed size is measured with the spatially lagged values of population dwelling in other cities. Table 4.4 shows the estimates of the baseline model, which, for convenience, is repeated in column 1, and of the model in eq. (4.4), which encompasses borrowed size (column 2) and the interaction term between borrowed size and the dummy for outperforming second-class cities (column 3).

As anticipated in Section 4, Table 4.4 presents results where high-level urban functions and city networks are substituted by borrowed size. The results suggest that, after controlling for the other main determinants of location benefits, while borrowed size does not suffice per se to allow higher benefits, it acts as a catalyst for second-class cities that outperformed compared to the country mean. Thus, the hypothesis is that such cities can actually borrow functions and networks located in large urban areas, but without incurring the costs typically associated with locations in large urban areas.

Table 4.4 Estimated borrowed size

Model	(1)	(2)	(3)
Constant term	−46.51	−59.32*	−49.95
	(29.62)	(31.48)	(31.03)
Metro area population	7.84*	9.48**	8.27*
	(4.36)	(4.54)	(4.49)
Square metro area population	−0.28*	−0.34**	−0.30*
	(0.16)	(0.17)	(0.16)
Dummy class 2 city outperformed the country	55.78*	62.10*	44.09*
	(33.05)	(33.09)	(30.13)
Dummy class 2 city outperformed the country * metro area population	−8.47*	−9.40*	−7.24*
	(4.86)	(84.87)	(4.50)
Dummy class 2 city outperformed the country * square metro area population	0.32*	0.36**	0.28*
	(0.18)	(0.18)	(0.16)
Borrowed size	–	0.12	0.04
		(0.11)	(0.10)
Class 2 city outperformed the country * borrowed size	–		0.25*
			(0.15)
Number of obs.	158	158	158
Wald χ^2 test	4.16***	30.15***	36.19***
Breusch-Pagan test (OLS vs. RE)	16.78***	16.90***	18.01***
	(0.00)	(0.00)	(0.00)
R squared	0.07	0.07	0.07
Within	0.13	0.15	0.18
Between	0.06	0.06	0.06
Robust standard errors	Yes	Yes	Yes
Estimation technique	RE	RE	RE

Notes:
All variables are in log. *, **,*** imply significance at 10, 5 and 1 per cent, respectively.
Dependent variable: average urban benefits (log urban rent).
RE: Random Effects estimates.

5. CONCLUSIONS

This chapter shows that the existence of agglomeration economies and the risk of agglomeration diseconomies are undeniable. However, this general law holds for both small and large cities; there are large cities able to (re)gain economies of agglomeration, despite their large size, as well as small cities that show decreasing returns when they achieve a very small size. The explanation of this apparent contradiction is that cities are able to overcome diseconomies of scale either through innovating in the functions that they perform, or in the organization of activities with other cities, through city networking.

Our empirical study shows that outperforming cities are those enjoying economies of scale, and that these economies of scale are related to the level of functions and networks in cities. These laws of structural dynamics are similar for both second- and first-class cities; however, the way in which these laws appear are specific for each city class.

These results are able to highlight the real nature of agglomeration economies, disentangling specific urban characteristics impacting on increasing returns from pure urban size, and showing that increasing returns, in the form of pecuniary externalities, exploited by firms in their market interactions are only part of the story.

These results have important urban policy implications. Against the recent issue of whether policymakers should concentrate their limited resources in larger cities in order to exploit agglomeration economies, or spread their investment in a larger set of cities during a crisis period, the reply comes logically from the results of this exercise. Investment should be devoted to cities in order to make any of them, despite their size, able to turn their risk of decreasing returns into agglomeration economies, by investing in revitalizing their functions and their ways of cooperation.

REFERENCES

Alonso, W. (1971). "The economics of urban size", *Papers and Proceedings of the Regional Science Association*, 26: 67–83.

Alonso, W. (1973). "Urban zero population growth", *Daedalus*, 102 (4): 191–206.

Basile, R., Capello, R., and Caragliu, A. (2012). "Technological interdependence and regional growth in Europe: proximity and synergy in knowledge spillovers", *Papers in Regional Science*, 91 (4): 697–722.

Camagni, R. (1993). "From city hierarchy to city networks: reflection about an emerging paradigm", in Lakshmanan, T. and Nijkamp, P. (eds), *Structure and change in the space economy: festschrifts in honour of Martin Beckmann*, Berlin: Springer Verlag, pp. 66–87.

Camagni, R. and Capello, R. (2004). "The city network paradigm: theory and empirical evidence", in Capello, R. and Nijkamp, P. (eds), *Urban dynamics and growth: advances in urban economics*, Amsterdam: Elsevier, pp. 495–532.

Camagni, R., Diappi, L., and Leonardi, G. (1986). "Urban growth and decline in a hierarchical system: a supply-oriented dynamic approach", *Regional Science and Urban Economics*, 16 (1): 145–160.

Camagni, R., Capello, R., and Caragliu, A. (2013). "One or infinite optimal city sizes? In search of an equilibrium size for cities", *The Annals of Regional Science*, 51 (2): 309–341.

Camagni, R., Capello, R., and Caragliu, A. (2014). "The rise of second class

cities: what role for agglomeration economies?" *European Planning Studies*, DOI 10.1080/09654313.2014.904999.
Capello, R. (2000). "The city network paradigm: measuring urban network externalities", *Urban Studies*, 37 (11): 1925–1945.
Capello, R. (2002). "Urban rent and urban dynamics: the determinants of urban development in Italy", *The Annals of Regional Science*, 36 (4): 593–611.
Capello, R. and Rietveld, P. (1998). "The concept of network synergy in economic theory: policy implications", in Button, K., Nijkamp, P. and Priemus, H. (eds), *Transport networks in Europe*, Cheltenham, UK and Northampton, MA, USA: Edward Elgar Publishing, pp. 57–83.
Carlino, G. (1980). "Contrast in agglomeration: New York and Pittsburgh reconsidered", *Urban Studies*, 17 (3): 343–351.
Catin, M. (1991). "Économies d'agglomération et gains de productivité", *Revue d'Économie Régionale et Urbaine*, 5: 565–598.
Chesnais, F. (1988). Technical co-operation agreements between firms, *STI Review*, Vol. 4, Paris: OECD.
Christaller, W. (1933). *Die zentralen Orte in Suddeutschland*, Jena, Germany: Gustav Fischer.
Conti, S. and Dematteis, G. (1995). "Entreprises, systems and network dynamics: the challenge of complexity", in Conti, S., Malecki, E. and Oinas, P. (eds), *The industrial enterprise and its environment: spatial perspectives*, Aldershot: Avebury, pp. 217–242.
Dijkstra, L. (2009). "Metropolitan regions in the EU", *Regional Focus*, 1: 1–9.
Dijkstra, L., Garcilazo, E., and McCann, P. (2013). "The economic performance of European cities and city regions: myths and realities", *European Planning Studies*, 21 (3): 334–354.
Glaeser, E.L. (2008). *Cities, agglomeration and spatial equilibrium*, Oxford: Oxford University Press.
Glaeser, E.L., Kallal, H., Scheinkman, J.A., and Shleifer, A. (1992). "Growth in cities", *Journal of Political Economy*, 100 (6): 1126–1152.
Henderson, J. (1974). "The sizes and types of cities", *The American Economic Review*, 64: 640–656.
Henderson, J. (1996). "Ways to think about urban concentration: neoclassical urban systems vs. the new economic geography", *International Regional Science Review*, 19 (1/2): 31–36.
Henderson, J. (2010). "Cities and development", *Journal of Regional Science*, 50 (1): 515–540.
Krugman, P. (1991). *Geography and trade*, Cambridge, MA: Cambridge University Press.
McCann, P. and Acs, Z.J. (2011). "Globalization: countries, cities and multinationals", *Regional Studies*, 45 (1): 17–32.
Nijkamp, P. and Kourtit, K. (2011). "New urban Europe: a place 4 all", *Urban Governance in the EU Current Challenges and Future Prospects*, Committee of the Regions, European Commission, DG RTD, Brussels, pp. 61–76.
Nijkamp, P. and Kourtit, K. (2012). "The new urban Europe: global challenges and local responses in the urban century", *European Planning Studies*, 21 (3): 291–315.
Phelps, N.A., Fallon, R.J., and Williams, C.L. (2001). "Small firms, borrowed size and the urban-rural shift", *Regional Studies*, 35 (7): 613–624.

Richardson, H. (1972). "Optimality in city size, systems of cities and urban policy: a sceptic's view", *Urban Studies*, 9 (1): 29–47.

Rosenthal, S.S. and Strange, W.C. (2004). "Evidence on the nature and sources of agglomeration economies", in Henderson, J.V. and Thisse, J.-F. (eds), *Handbook of regional and urban economics*, Vol. 4 "Cities and geography", Amsterdam: Elsevier, pp. 2119–2171.

Sassen, S. (ed.) (2002). *Global networks, linked cities*, New York: Routledge.

Shefer, D. (1973). "Localization economies in SMSA's: a production function analysis", *Journal of Regional Science*, 13 (1): 55–64.

Sveikauskas, L., Gowdy, J., and Funk, M. (1988). "Urban productivity: city size or industry size", *Journal of Regional Science*, 28 (2): 185–202.

Williamson, O.E. (1985). *The Economic Institution of Capitalism*, New York: The Free Press.

TECHNICAL APPENDIX: DEFINITION OF THE URBAN SIZE CLASSES

The choice of the threshold values over which the three urban classes used in the empirical section are defined is by nature arbitrary. As shown in Figure 4.A1, the statistical distribution of LUZ populations in European Union cities (in this case, 2011 data are represented) is a continuum that presents no clear threshold between any possible class division.

However, at two points in the distribution (corresponding to about 200,000 inhabitants and 1 million inhabitants), the percentage growth of population between the city to the right-hand side and the left-hand side of the threshold value is nil (and, more precisely, equal to 0.000 per cent).

Interestingly, the typology used in this chapter, which is, as previously discussed, based only on population levels, is highly correlated with an analogous definition provided within the European Observation Network for Territorial Development and Cohesion (ESPON) 1.1.1 project.

In that case the universe of regions in Europe has been defined as encompassing three typologies of regions: agglomerated regions, that is, those regions hosting a centre of at least 300,000 inhabitants and a population density higher than 300 inhabitants/sq. km, or a population density between 150 and 300 inhabitants/sq. km; urban regions, hosting a centre between 150,000 and 300,000 inhabitants and a population density between 150 and 300 inhabitants/sq. km, or a lower population density, between 100 and 150 inhabitants/sq. km with a larger centre (with more than 300,000 inhabitants), or a population density between 100 and 150 inhabitants/sq. km; and, finally, rural regions, with a population density lower than 100/sq. km and a centre larger than 125,000 inhabitants, or a population density lower than 100 inhabitants sq. km with a centre smaller than 125,000 inhabitants.

The two typologies, that is, the one used in our empirical analyses, correlate at the 43 per cent level (significant at all conventional values).

When reviewing the two typologies (Table 4.A1), it is clear that the two classifications present relevant similarities. In particular, regions classified as belonging to the first class as used in this chapter and also being agglomerated in the ESPON classification are 43 out of the total of 61 in the ESPON sample (equal to 70 per cent); a relatively larger difference emerges from the second class/urban classes, which overlap in 62 per cent of all cases.

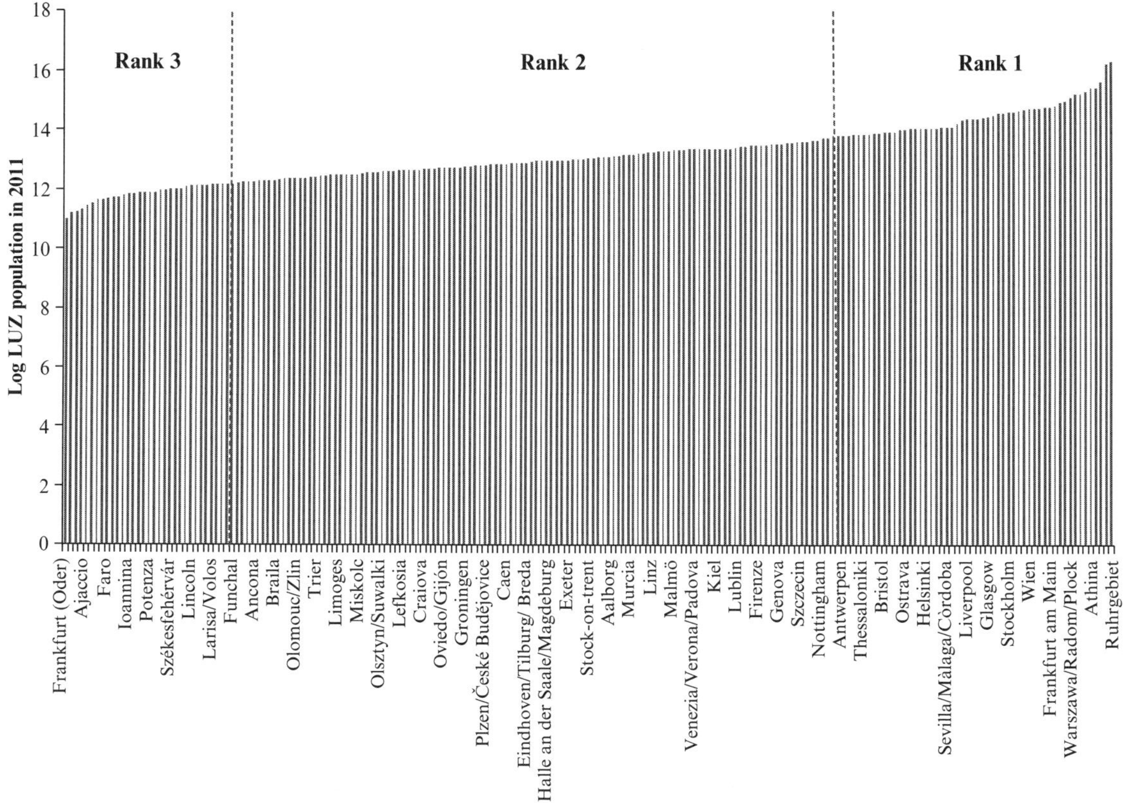

Source: Authors' elaboration.

Figure 4.A1 LUZ population levels in 2011 and definitions of urban class

Table 4.A1 Tabulation of EU27 NUTS2 regions classified according to the typology used in this chapter, and the ESPON typology (project 1.1.1)

Typology used in this chapter	ESPON typology			Total
	Agglom	Urban	Rural	
Class 1	43	17	1	61
Class 2	21	73	24	118
Class 3	18	37	36	91
Total	82	127	61	270

Source: Authors' elaboration and ESPON database.

PART 2

Cities, innovation and productivity

5. Multi-actor analysis of metropolitan performance indicators*

Karima Kourtit, Miruna Mazurencu Marinescu and Peter Nijkamp

1. INTRODUCTION

Our society lives in the 'urban century'. Massive urbanization trends are increasingly seen as one of the hottest fields of research and policy, as these megatrends are decisive for the sustainable future of our planet. The development of urban systems and metropolitan areas is indeed critically dependent on various spatial-demographic forces of a global nature. First, the change in the world population will likely amount to approximately 2–3 percent growth per annum in the decades to come (see United Nations 2011). Consequently, the earth will most likely have to be the habitat for at least 9 billion people by the year 2050 (Kourtit 2014).

A second megatrend is the likely unequal spread of these rising numbers of people. It is forecasted that there will likely be an increasing geographic skewness in the spatial distribution of the world population, with a rapid rate of increase in major regions like Latin America, Africa and Asia, accompanied by a modest rate of increase, and even stable development, in other parts of the world (in particular, Europe). Some countries like Japan or France may even show a considerable reduction in absolute population size (Kourtit 2014).

A third megatrend is likely to be a rise in urbanization rates, especially in those countries that may face a fast population rise. Worldwide, we observe that more and more people tend to migrate to urban agglomerations, to the extent that, for the first time in human history, more than 50 percent of the world population is now living in urban areas (see Kourtit 2013). But these urbanization rates show an increasing diversity, which is rapidly rising in

* A previous and partial analysis of the database in this chapter can be found in Kourtit et al. 2014). Various material used in this chapter display close similarities with one other article by the co-authors (Kourtit et al. 2014), which was developed in parallel at the time of the publication of the present article.

megacities (with more than 10 million inhabitants) and in metropolises (in general, urban agglomerations, with more than 1 million inhabitants) (see Angotti 1995; McNeill 1999; Kourtit 2014). The future of our planet will likely be an urban future.

We observe nowadays an increasing interest in the development of metropolitan areas. Metropolises tend to become the common settlement pattern all over the world, ranging from small agglomerations (e.g., Brussels) to megacities (e.g., São Paulo) (see Turok 2004). It should be added that in many cases such metropolises are not isolated islands, but are often part of a broader network of interconnected metropolitan agglomerations. Joining forces among such urban regions reinforces the agglomeration benefits that are at the heart of any city formation (see Docherty et al. 2004; Ewen and Hebbert 2007; Kern and Bulkeley 2009; Neal 2012). Such intra- and inter-metropolitan externalities may be related to knowledge creation and transfer, innovative milieus, open and flexible labour markets, effective environmental and energy policy, joint marketing efforts, cultural performance, and so on.

> Being a Parisian is not about being born in Paris, it is about being reborn there. (Anne Hidalgo, Mayor of Paris)

A variety of contemporaneous developments can be observed in polynuclear urban developments, with a satellite system of suburban areas (as opposed to a 'star' pattern that characterizes older metropolises), edge cities and new towns around a central core area (Ile de France, Los Angeles, etc.). All such geographically and functionally integrated settlement patterns serve to increase the efficiency and productivity – and hence the growth and competition potential – of urban agglomerations. But it is an as yet unanswered question which metropolises in our world are to be seen as the most successful ones; in other words, which ones would generate the highest performance, and why? This calls for a solid and empirical comparison of performance indicators – and their background factors – of major cities in our world.

This chapter aims to advance knowledge on critical performance conditions of metropolises in our world by carrying out a statistical analysis of performance indicators for about 35 world cities. Extensive databases for these cities are derived from the so-called Global Power City Index (GPCI) database constructed by the Institute of Urban Research of the Japanese Mori Memorial Foundation (2013). After an econometric analysis of the interest profiles of multiple stakeholders in these cities, some policy conclusions will be formulated.

2. LITERATURE REVIEW AND HYPOTHESES

Our world has turned into a complex spatial-economic system. Scale advantages are the *raison d'être* of growing business firms, and form the cornerstone for contemporary global business developments. 'Big size' of corporate organizations is perhaps as such not a human ideal, but more an economic necessity to survive in a competitive environment. Increased productivity – supported by innovative behaviour – is (or represents) the critical success factor to gain a strong competitive position in business life, and propels a permanent drive to do things better and to expand markets and market shares. The space-economy forms here an important action platform.

The above neo-Schumpeterian interpretation of entrepreneurial dynamics also essentially holds for the life of cities. Cities are born and may grow, in population, in attractiveness or in wealth. Some cities conquer a stable position – sometimes even at a structurally low welfare level – others may shrink – sometimes on a temporary basis as a result of unfavourable headwinds (Detroit, for example) – and again others may gain an increasingly strong profile. The latter category is on a rising edge. Many cities in our world grow in population size, and several also in prosperity. But irrespective of urban economic welfare, most cities on our planet appear to grow in population numbers. They are transformed into large urban agglomerations (metropolises), while many of these big cities – especially in the developing world – grow into megacities. Our planet is gradually moving towards an urban planet (see Sassen 1991), and many planners talk about 'the urban century'.

But the emerging urbanization rates do not show a uniform pattern. City growth all over the world is rather heterogeneous. To some extent, one may compare the evolution of cities with that of business firms. The laws of competition stipulate that firms try to achieve an increasingly larger share of their relevant markets, and may exhibit fluctuating growth patterns. This strategy is also valid for cities in an open world. Such cities have to acquire and retain the patronage of (potential and actual) residents, visitors and business life. They have to attract various (selected) classes of important economic agents to their territory. Consequently, a successful city is a city that is able to attract a prominent share of the international market of urban agents and stakeholders. Thus, urban evolution calls for an endogenous explanation of the driving forces of city evolution, both the impact of available urban attractiveness indicators and the implementation of appropriate urban governance measures (Kourtit 2013). The scientific, mainly quantitative estimation and evaluation of the various factors that determine the socio-economic performance of large cities, is called metropolitan performance analysis (MPA).

MPA is not a single and unambiguous research tool, but mainly a set of quantitative assessment instruments to depict the drivers of the performance of urban agglomerations. An overview of several of these tools can be found in a study by Kourtit (2013), which offers an empirical illustration of the relevance of several assessment tools, such as: self-organizing mapping models, data envelopment analysis (DEA) models, rough set analysis and multi-criteria analysis.

The information needed to carry out a comparative benchmark analysis for several cities may originate from several statistical sources, in particular:

- generally accessible statistical data on cities;
- specific survey-based indicators on urban performance;
- perceptions of stakeholders on relevant urban features;
- quantitative assessments of urban attractiveness from expert opinions.

The recent literature on urban studies offers a wealth of contributions on comparable experiments regarding the economic, social, entrepreneurial, innovative or creative profile of cities. There is a rising interest in urban benchmark studies. This has led to a variety of general ranking studies of global cities, world cities, metropolitan agglomerations, and so on, while various sectoral or functional ranking studies have also been performed, for example on tourist cities, business cities, financial cities, artistic cities and the like.

A noteworthy study was undertaken by Grosveld (2000) who applied the concept of Porter's (1990) competitive advantage theory to a comparison of leading cities in the world. His study is based on an extensive analysis of perceptions of 'city makers', from different socio-economic clusters: hospitality, real estate and architecture, corporate services, academia, performing arts, museums, international trade and transport, international organizations, media, finance and multinationals. The information on these perceptions stems from an extensive and focussed survey questionnaire approach among some 85 leading world cities: 31 in Europe, 19 in North America, 16 in Asia, 19 in Latin America, 35 in Asia+, and 19 in other continents. His findings offer a wealth of detailed insights into the functional-sectoral rank order of various cities in our world. Such research results prompt the need for a solid and quantitative causal analysis.

An important question – after the great many exploratory studies in the past decades – is, therefore, whether an explanatory model can be designed that would offer a valid scientific linkage from a set of explanatory background factors to a set of relevant performance indicator(s) of a given city or a set of cities. This would call for an econometric-statistical analysis of detailed and standardized data covering a large number of cities, while taking into account the specific geographic characteristics of such cities (e.g., developed versus developing world, choice of continent, city size class, etc.). Fortunately, in the framework of our study, we had access to a rather comprehensive and very detailed, multilevel database relating to 35 metropolises of our world, that is, the above-mentioned GPCI database.

3. MULTI-ACTOR MODELLING RESULTS

The current literature on urban developments is vast. It is widely accepted that cities are magnets of economic power, but also hubs in global networks. They are complementary to each other, but are also each other's competitors. The merger of internal strength and external orientation determines the performance and economic profile of cities (see Neal 2012).

Cities operate in an international playing field and, hence, their socio-economic performance may show much variation. The question is then: why do some cities outperform others? This idea formed the basis of the creation of the above-mentioned GPCI database to be used for our MPA. This database contains extensive information – in standardized and comparative quantitative form – of many world cities which are evaluated and ranked according to their 'magnetism', that is, their competitive power to attract visitors, creative people and business enterprises from all over the world. This open access database is carefully validated through field visits and in-depth assessment reports. It contains a wealth of multi-annual data on major critical indicators – and a very detailed list of sub-indicators – for economic strength of the relevant cities contained in the database. At present, this data system has accurate information on 35 world cities ranging from New York to Istanbul, and from Tokyo to Geneva. This extensive GPCI database also offers the possibility for a benchmarking of each individual city, in terms of strength and weakness regarding each individual performance indicator.

Thus, the GPCI aims to offer systematic and comparative information on the comprehensive economic position of major cities in the world, and it does so by focussing on a wide variety of functions performed by the cities under consideration. For each individual city, six main classes of functions were carefully mapped out and numerically assessed, namely, economy (EC), research and development (RD), cultural integration (CI), liveability (Liv), environment (Env) and accessibility (Acc). In addition, the importance of these indicators was carefully assessed by five distinct groups of stakeholders, namely, managers, researchers, artists, visitors and residents.

The purpose of this chapter is now to address these above-mentioned substantive research questions by using a multilevel modelling approach. Multilevel analysis (or modelling) is a term used to describe a set of analyses sometimes also referred to as multilevel random coefficient models (Bryk and Raudenbush 1992; Kreft and De Leeuw 1998; Snijders and Bosker 1999; Bliese 2013, p. 5).

Usually, the definition of multilevel modelling reflects a wide range of interrelated multilevel features (see also Klein and Kozlowski 2000), like within-group agreement and reliability, contextual ordinary least squares (OLS) models, covariance theorem decomposition, random coefficient modelling and random group resampling (Bliese 2013, p. 25). For the purpose of the current chapter, we will restrict our analysis to the application of multilevel random coefficient models by using the GPCI data set gathered from the Mori Memorial Foundation database for a five-year period ranging from 2009 to 2013.

The general model specification is based on the aim to explain the perception of the performance (or importance) of a given city for each of the five classes of stakeholders on the basis of the six background factors. The general model has the following expression (formulated as a fixed effects model):

$$y_{it} = \alpha + X'_{it}\beta + \nu_{it} \tag{5.1}$$

where y_{it} is the dependent variable, X_{it} is a matrix of explanatory or moderator variables, and ν_{it} is an $\sim IID(0,\sigma^2_\nu)$ error term; the index *i* refers to a city *i*, while the index *t* refers to the time period. In our statistical analysis, PROC MIXED in SAS software was used in order to determine which of the various groups of city functions are statistically significant for the various stakeholder classes: managers, researchers, artists, visitors and residents.

To pursue this, model (1) was successively estimated having as the dependent variable the score assigned by the various actors (managers, researchers, artists, visitors and residents). The database refers – as mentioned – to the years 2009–2013. (Detailed statistical test results are available from the authors.)

An analysis of the results of Table 5.1 shows that the only coefficients that are statistically significant are related to the factors/dimensions economy and accessibility, a result which was to be expected for the class of managers, as these factors are generally decisive for entrepreneurial performance. The results confirm the business model that firms have a main interest in economic background factors and efficiency-enhancing factors (accessibility), and less interest in other factors.

For the class of researchers, we find that the coefficients for research and

Table 5.1 *Urban performance assessment by managers (fixed effects)*

Solution for fixed effects					
Effect	Estimate	Standard error	Degrees of freedom	1.1.1. t value	1.1.2. Pr > |t|
Intercept	17,3492	7,3564	4	2,36	0,0778
EC	0,1178	0,01597	164	7,38	<.0001
RD	−0,0074	0,02011	164	−0,37	0,7141
CI	0,00947	0,01372	164	0,69	0,4913
Liv	0,02022	0,02134	164	0,95	0,3449
Env	−0,0014	0,01984	164	−0,07	0,9453
Acc	0,04711	0,02048	164	2,3	0,0227

Table 5.2 *Urban performance assessment by researchers (fixed effects)*

Solution for fixed effects					
Effect	Estimate	Standard error	DF	t value	Pr > |t|
Intercept	5,7727	6,7235	4	0,86	0,439
EC	−0,0104	0,0177	164	−0,59	0,5578
RD	0,2994	0,02231	164	13,42	<.0001
CI	0,01999	0,01522	164	1,31	0,1911
Liv	0,06098	0,0235	164	2,59	0,0103
Env	0,01182	0,02201	164	0,54	0,592
Acc	−0,0204	0,02272	164	−0,9	0,3701

development (R&D) and liveability are statistically significant at a 5 percent significance level (see Table 5.2). This is again a plausible result, as the seedbed conditions for research are often R&D profiles and quality of life.

Researchers are clearly interest in a well-developed R&D infrastructure, as well as in a good local quality of life.

Next, for the group of artists, the driving forces economy, R&D, cultural integration, liveability and accessibility appear to be statistically significant at a 5 percent significance level, with livability being even more important than cultural integration (see Table 5.3).

Artists appear to attach a high value to conditions of cultural integration and liveability. This group seems to flourish better in less competitive and less logistically connected urban space.

These statistical findings are partly in accordance with our expectations. It is noteworthy that economy and accessibility turn out to be statistically

Table 5.3 Urban performance assessment by artists (fixed effects)

Solution for fixed effects					
Effect	Estimate	Standard error	DF	t value	Pr > |t|
Intercept	13,0929	5,8328	4	2,24	0,0882
1.1.3. Economy	−0,0535	0,01923	164	−2,78	0,006
RD	0,08552	0,02429	164	3,52	0,0006
CI	0,1188	0,01658	164	7,16	<.0001
Liv	0,156	0,02523	164	6,18	<.0001
Env	−0,0221	0,02396	164	−0,92	0,3578
Acc	−0,0683	0,02474	164	−2,76	0,0064

Table 5.4 Urban performance assessment by visitors (fixed effects)

Solution for fixed effects					
Effect	Estimate	Standard error	Degrees of freedom	t value	Pr > |t|
Intercept	18,5004	6,2764	4	2,95	0,0421
Economy	0,00947	0,01994	164	0,48	0,6353
RD	0,05156	0,02518	164	2,05	0,0422
CI	0,0612	0,01718	164	3,56	0,0005
Liv	0,08615	0,02622	164	3,29	0,0012
Env	−0,0773	0,02484	164	−3,11	0,0022
Acc	0,04195	0,02564	164	1,64	0,1038

significant, but the sign is negative. This suggests some validity of the JacobsFlorida hypothesis that culture may flourish in a somewhat stressful situation, in which the economy and the accessibility are not necessarily well organized. But this finding needs more careful examination.

The results in Table 5.4 indicate that visitors highly value liveability and cultural integration, followed by R&D. These factors are the only positively significant ones at a 5 percent significance level and confirm our prior expectations. The environment exerts apparently a negative influence; this may be due to the fact that various environmental indicators are seen as more structurally important for residents than for temporary visitors.

Finally, for the residents, liveability matters most, but also R&D and environment appear to exert a statistically significant effect, at a 5 percent significance level (see Table 5.5). The results are rather plausible: residents prefer a good atmosphere in which to live and work, while R&D offers a good platform for skilled people and talent in the city.

Table 5.5 *Urban performance assessment by residents (fixed effects)*

Solution for fixed effects					
Effect	Estimate	Standard Error	Degrees of freedom	t value	Pr > |t|
Intercept	9,8702	10,7314	4	0,92	0,4098
Economy	0,00238	0,01691	164	0,14	0,888
RD	0,1225	0,02127	164	5,76	<.0001
CI	−0,0041	0,01451	164	−0,28	0,7807
Liv	0,1502	0,02274	164	6,61	<.0001
Env	0,04761	0,02098	164	2,27	0,0245
Acc	0,03105	0,02166	164	1,43	0,1535

4. FURTHER STATISTICAL ANALYSIS

The GPCI data set is rich in nature, as it depicts in a multilevel form the various relevant characteristics of all 35 cities under consideration. The time span of this database is unfortunately rather short (2009–2013), but it is still important to map out the short-term trend over the relevant time span of the data. With the data representation in univariate form, it is also possible to visually examine whether or not there are identifiable patterns between time and the performance outcome (total city score). The software commands below use the Lattice Package in R to produce the plot of all 35 cities (see Figure 5.1) (see also Bliese 2013, p. 70). R is user-friendly, open-source software that is flexible in using and amending standard software packages (such as Statistical Package for the Social Sciences (SPSS)). A disadvantage is the use of rather complicated statements and commands. The horizontal axis in Figure 5.1 represents the time axis, while the vertical axis measures the city scores for each of the cities under consideration.

```
> library(lattice)
> xyplot(MULTDV~TIME|as.factor(city), data= univ.dateorase [1:63,],
type=c("p", "r", "g"), col="blue", col.line="black", xlab="TIME", ylab="Score")
```

This technical sequence from the R software produces Figure 5.1 depicting the evolution in time, 2009–2013, of the cities' total scores.

From this plot, we observe that there is variability in both levels of the total score and in the way it varies over time. The goal in our growth modelling exercise is now to determine whether or not there are consistent patterns in the relationship between time and the dependent variable (DV), which is the total city score. This will be highlighted in the subsequent subsections (see also Bliese 2013, p. 71). The general observation from the benchmarking exercise in Figure 5.1 is that there is a high score of variability in the growth performance of the cities concerned. These are several degrees of growth performance. An exception appears to be Moscow.

4.1 Examination of the Total City Score

The first step in our multilevel growth modelling is to analyse the features of the dependent variable, that is, total city score. As in classical multilevel modelling, we start by estimating a null model and calculating next the intraclass correlation coefficient (ICC),[1] represented in R (see also Bliese 2013, p. 71).

```
> null.model<-lme(MULTDV~1, random=~1|city, data=univ.dateorase, na.
action=na.omit, control=list(opt="optim"))
> VarCorr(null.model)
city = pdLogChol(1)
```

The summary output of the null model is depicted in Table 5.6, again denoted in R.

From the variances obtained in Table 5.6 we can calculate the ICC.

```
>8.406391e+00/(8.406391e+00+1.428285e+05)
[1] 5.885307e-05
```

Table 5.6 The null model

	Variance	Standard deviation
(Intercept)	8.41	2.899378
1.1.4. Residual	143000	377.926541

[1] The intraclass correlation (or the intraclass correlation coefficient), is a descriptive statistic that can be used when quantitative measurements are made on units that are organized into groups. It describes how strongly units in the same group resemble each other (see for details Satchel 2013, p. 105; another source is: https://www.boundless.com/statistics/correlation-and-regression/correlation/other-types-of-correlation-coefficients/).

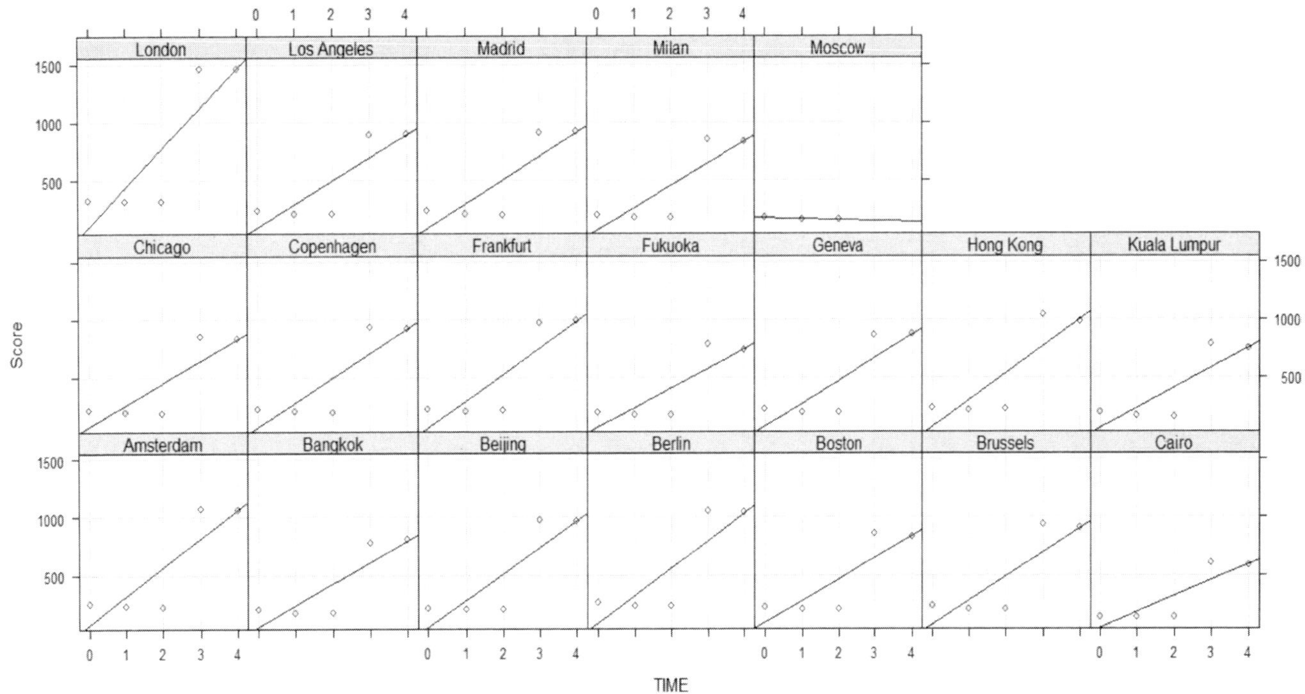

Figure 5.1 City variability across time

The ICC associated with the total score appears to be very small. This indicates that very little of the variance in any city score can be explained by the intrinsic properties of the city itself.

4.2 Modelling of Time Dependency

The second step involves modelling the relationship between time and the dependent variable. We shall begin by modelling a linear relationship and add progressively more complicated relationships such as a quadratic form, a cubic form, and so on. In order to test whether a linear relationship exists between time and the total city score, we regress the total score in a given time in the model with a random intercept, which we call model.2 (see also Bliese 2013, p. 71).

```
>model.2<-lme(MULTDV~TIME, random=~1|city, data=univ.dateorase, na.
action=na.omit, control=list(opt="optim"))
>summary(model.2)$tTable
```

These results are given in Table 5.7.

An examination of the fixed effects indicates that there is a significant linear relationship between time and the total city score, such that the total score increases by 214.65 in each time period. Since in our approach the first time period was coded as 0, the intercept value in this model then represents the average level of the total score in the first time period. Specifically, in the first time period the average city total score was found to be equal to 78.55.

Clearly, more complicated time functions can be included in various ways, either through raising the time variable to various power levels, or by converting time into power polynomials (see also Bliese 2013, p. 72). Below, the results of some of these techniques are represented. model.2b includes quadratic trend.

Table 5.7 Results of model.2

Value	Value	Standard error	1.1.5. Degrees of freedom	1.1.6. t value	1.1.7. p value
(Intercept)	78.55487	29.58726	139	2.655023	8.855996e-08
TIME	214.65069	11.89783	139	18.041169	3.094869e-38

Table 5.8 Results of model.2b

1.1.8. Value	1.1.9. Value	1.1.10. Standard error	1.1.11. Degrees of freedom	1.1.12. t value	1.1.13. p value
(Intercept)	186.355	32.93	138	5.65	0.000
TIME	−0.951	37.49	138	−0.025	0.000
I(TIME^2)	53.900	8.98	138	5.997	0.000

Table 5.9 Results of model.2c

Value	Value	Standard error	Degrees of freedom	t value	p value
(Intercept)	507.8562	17.58	138	28.87	0.000
poly(TIME, 2)1	4015.74	198.95	138	20.18	0.000
poly(TIME, 2)2	1193.1397	198.95	138	5.99	0.000

```
> model.2b<-lme(MULTDV~TIME+I(TIME^2), random=~1|city, data=univ.
dateorase, na.action=na.omit, control=list(opt="optim"))
> summary(model.2b)$tTable
```

The results are depicted in Table 5.8.

While model.2c includes time as a power polynomial (Table 5.9).

```
>model.2c<-lme(MULTDV~poly(TIME,2), random=~1|city, data=univ.dateor-
ase, na.action=na.omit, control=list(opt="optim"))
> summary(model.2c)$tTable
```

Both models clearly show that there is a significant quadratic trend. We can thus conclude that time tends to have a quadratic relationship with the total city score.

4.3 Model Slope Variability

A potential limitation which is inherent in model.2 is that it takes for granted that the relationship between time and total city score is constant for all cities. Specifically, it assumes that each city score increases on average by 214.65 in each time period.

Table 5.10 Results of contrasting model.2 and model.3c

Model	Degrees of freedom	AIC	BIC	logLik	Test
model.2	4	2383.21	2395.82	−1187.65	
model.3c	9	2386.41	2414.79	−1184.207	1 vs. 2
	L.Ratio	p value			
	6.79	0.23			

Notes:
AIC = Akaike information criterion; BIC = Bayesian information criterion; logLik = Log-Likelihood method – a R software function that returns the log-Likelihood of a VAR, level-VECM, SVAR or SVEC object; L.Ratio = log likelihood ratio test.

An alternative model that needs now to be tested is one that allows the slopes to vary randomly. Given the degree of variability in Figure 5.1, a random slope model seems quite a plausible assumption in the light of the current data. The random slope model is tested here next by adding the quadratic effect for time as a random effect in our model. This will be called model.3.

Consequently, we will now update our previous model (2) by adding a different random effect component and next contrast model.2 and model.3c (see also Bliese 2013, p. 72).

```
> model.3c<-update(model.2, random=~TIME+I(TIME^2)|city)
> anova(model.2, model.3c)
```

The results are shown in Table 5.10.

The results clearly indicate that a model that allows the slope between time and total city score to vary randomly does not fit the data better than a model that fixes the slope to a constant value for all cities. As we have progressively redone the calculations from a three-year to five-year database, we can draw the following conclusion: the longer the time horizon, the more the tendency appears to be in favour of a model that fixes the slope to a constant value for all cities.

4.4 Modelling Error Structures

The fourth step in developing the level-1 model involves assessing the error structures of the model. It is important to carefully scrutinize the level-1 error structures, because significance tests may be dramatically affected, if error structures are not properly specified. The purpose of this step is to

Table 5.11 Results of contrasting model.3c and model.4a

Model	Degrees of freedom	AIC	BIC	logLik	Test
model.3c	9	2386.413	2414.793	−1184.207	
model.4a	10	2350.887	2382.42	−1165.444	1 vs. 2
	L.Ratio	p value			
	37.5259	<.0001			

Table 5.12 Test for variance homogeneity

0	1	2	3	4
1799.609	1857.982	2035.171	39123.376	38257,354

determine whether the model fit improves by incorporating (a) an autoregressive structure with serial correlations and (b) heterogeneity in error structures. This will be called model.4.

Tests for an autoregressive structure (autocorrelation) are conducted here by including the correlation option in lme. We shall therefore update model.3c above and include a lag 1 autocorrelation as follows (see Bliese 2013, pp.72–73):

```
> model.4a<-update(model.3c, correlation =corAR1())
> anova(model.3c, model.4a)
```

The results are depicted in Table 5.11.

It appears that a model that allows for autocorrelation fits the data better than a model that assumes no autocorrelation.

A summary of model.4a reveals that the autocorrelation estimate is −0.758622 (known as Phi coefficient).

We can further examine the degree to which the variance of the responses of stakeholders changes over time. A test of variance homogeneity is conducted by examining the variance of the total city score at each time point using the Tapply Command (Table 5.12; for details see Bliese 2013, p. 73).

```
> tapply(univ.dateorase$MULTDV, univ.dateorase$TIME, var, na.rm=T)
```

The analysis of the results from Table 5.12 suggests that the variance of the total city score is increasing over time.

5. CONCLUSIONS

The application of multilevel models to competitive urban performance analysis is rather novel, to the best of our knowledge. R software appears to be an appropriate tool for examining the growth profiles of a series of competitive cities.

The statistical-econometric analysis in our study has brought to light important research findings. Firstly, we have tested which city functions are statistically significant for the various stakeholders/actors – managers, researchers, artists, visitors and residents – by using a fixed effect model operated in SAS software. For the managers, the dimensions economy and accessibility are statistically significant; for the researchers, the coefficients for R&D and liveability are statistically significant at a 5 percent significance level; for artists, liveability and cultural integration matter most; visitors value more liveability, cultural integration followed by R&D.

Secondly, in order to extend the analysis, growth models from a multilevel modelling methodology have been applied. The results indicate that exceptionally tiny variance in any city score can be explained by the properties of the city itself.

A further examination of the fixed effects results indicates that there is a significant linear relationship between time and the total city score, such that the total score increases by 214.65 in each time period. Since the first time period was coded as 0, the intercept value in this model consequently represents the average level of the total score in the first time period. Specifically, in the first time period the average total city score was found to be equal to 78.55. We can also conclude that time has a quadratic relationship with total score (see also Bliese 2013, p. 72).

In addition, the results clearly indicate that a model that allows the slope between time and the total city score to vary randomly does not fit the data better than a model that fixes the slope to a constant value for all cities from our sample.

Finally, a model that allows for autocorrelation does offer a better fit than a model that assumes no autocorrelation (see Bliese 2013, p. 72).

These preliminary findings will lead to better articulate metropolitan development policies in order to increase the cities' total score. The combined effect of the perception of stakeholders and the strength of the performance profile of the cities concerned offer important handles for focussed urban policies. Thus, these cities will become more appealing to various stakeholders, while at the same time maintaining their competitive advantage.

Unfortunately, in our MPA we have limited observation waves (observations collected at several moments in time), but the current research is sufficiently promising to be further extended once we gain access to more data.

As we have undertaken various waves of calculations, we may conclude that various results remained consistent over time: for instance, the most significant dimension for managers is economy and for researchers is R&D, while other aspects may change over time. For instance, for three repeated measures (three years) a model that allowed the slope between time and the total city score to vary randomly fits the data better, while for five repeated measures a model that fixes the slope to a constant value for all cities fits the data better.

This current study has also intended to offer an illustration of how R software can be used in the niche of multilevel models for assessing metropolitan performance analysis. R is a very powerful programming language that performs complex data analyses and can help investigate complex data structures such as the GPCI database created by the Institute of Urban Research of the Japanese Mori Memorial Foundation. Clearly, this exercise is only the start of a more comprehensive research programme.

BIBLIOGRAPHY

Angotti, T., 1995, The Metropolis Revisited. *Futures*, 27 (6), 627–639.

Bliese, P., 2013, Multilevel Modeling in R (2.5): A Brief Introduction to R, the multilevel package and the nlme package, March 28, 2013, http://cran.r-project.org/doc/contrib/Bliese_Multilevel.pdf.

Bryk, A.S., and Raudenbush, S.W., 1992, *Hierarchical Linear Models: Applications and Data Analysis Methods*. Sage, Newbury Park, CA.

Docherty, I., Gulliver, S., and Drake, P., 2004, Exploring the Potential Benefits of City Collaboration. *Regional Studies*, 38 (4), 445–456.

Ewen, S., and Herbert, M., 2007, European Cities in a Networked World during the Long 20th Century. *Environment and Planning C: Government and Policy*, 25, 327–340.

Grosveld, H., 2000, *The Leading Cities of the World and their Competitive Advantages*. Thela Thesis, Amsterdam.

Institute for Digital Research and Education, UCLA (n.d.) Statistical Computing Seminars, Repeated Measures Analysis with R. Available at http://www.ats.ucla.edu/stat/R/seminars/Repeated_Measures/repeated_measures.htm.

Institute of Urban Research of the Japanese Mori Memorial Foundation, 2013, *Global Power City Index*. The Mori Memorial Foundation, Tokyo.

Kern, K., and Bulkeley, H., 2009, Cities, Europeanization and Multi-level Governance: Governing Climate Change through Transnational Municipal Networks. *Journal of Common Market Studies*, 47 (2), 309–322.

Kourtit, K., 2013, *The New Urban World*. Ph.D Thesis, VU University, Amsterdam.
Kourtit, K., 2014, Book Review: Planet of Cities, by Shlomo Angel. *Journal of Regional Science*, 54 (1), 161–162.
Kourtit, K., Mazurencu Marinescu, M., and Nijkamp, P., 2014, Growth Modelling of Metropolitan Performance Indicators – An Application by Means of R Software. *Procedia Economics and Finance*, 10, 314–323.
Kozlowski, S.W.J., and Klein, K.J., 2000, A Multilevel Approach to Theory and Research in Organizations: Contextual, Temporal, and Emergent Processes, in K.J. Klein and S.W.J. Kozlowski (eds), *Multilevel Theory, Research and Methods in Organizations: Foundations, Extensions, and New Directions* (pp. 3–90). Jossey-Bass, San Francisco, CA.
Kreft, I.G., and De Leeuw, J., 1998, *Introducing Multilevel Modeling*. Sage, London.
Mazurencu Marinescu, M., and Pele, D.T., 2012, Applying Multilevel Modelling for Assessing Business Performance in Software: Case Study – The Companies Operating in Romania's ICT sector. *Journal of International Business and Economics*, 12 (3), 99–102.
McNeill, D., 1999, Globalization and the European City. *Cities*, 16 (3), 143–147.
Neal, Z., 2012, *The Connected City: How Networks are Shaping the Modern Metropolis*. Routledge, New York.
Porter, M., 1990, *The Competitive Advantage of Nations*. Macmillan, London.
Sassen, S., 1991, *The Global City*. Princeton University Press, Princeton.
Satchel, R.M., 2013, *Burn, Boil & Eat: An Intersectional Analysis of Stereotypes in the Most Influential Films of All Time*. Graduate Faculty of the Louisiana State University and Agricultural and Mechanical College, USA.
Singer, J.D., 1998, Using SAS Proc Mixed to Fit Multilevel Models, Hierarchical Models, and Individual Growth Models. *Journal of Educational and Behavioral Statistics*, 24, 323–355.
Singer, J.D., and Willett, J.B., 2003, *Applied Longitudinal Data Analysis*. Oxford University Press, New York.
Snijders, T.A.B., and Bosker, R.J., 1999, *Multilevel Analysis: An Introduction to Basic and Advanced Multilevel Modeling*. Sage Publications, London.
Snijders, T.A.B., and Bosker, R.J., 2012, *Multilevel Analysis: An Introduction to Basic and Advanced Multilevel Modeling*, 2nd edn. Sage Publications, London.
Turok, I., 2004, Cities, Regions and Competitiveness. *Regional Studies*, 38 (9), 1069–1083.
United Nations, Department of Economic and Social Affairs, Population Division, 2011, *World Urbanization Prospects: The 2011 Revision*, New York (Extended Dataset on CD-ROM, ST/ESA/SER. A/308, Sales No. 11 XIII.7).

6. Entrepreneurial governance for local growth

Amy Rader Olsson, Hans Westlund and Johan P. Larsson

INTRODUCTION

In Sweden, as elsewhere, local governments address not only local service provision but also development, although local development is largely a function of economic forces at the regional, national and global levels. Few local governments have the resources to make the kinds of capital investments often required to significantly improve development potential. Therefore, local development initiatives often require investment and policies coordinated with other local governments, regional authorities and national agencies as well as private firms. The planning literature therefore emphasizes the importance of local institutional capacity for innovation and collaboration with a range of public and private partners (Cars et al. 2002, Rader Olsson 2009.)

Some have described the phenomenon of local government efforts to actively foster expansion and economic development as entrepreneurial behavior (Wilks-Heeg et al. 2003).[1] However, the insights from the literature on entrepreneurship have not been brought to bear in the planning and governance literature. This chapter therefore explores the concept of entrepreneurship as applied to the efforts of local governments to promote development in new ways and in new forms. Can tools and metrics developed within entrepreneurship research be useful in understanding how municipalities approach local development challenges? To address these questions, we used a questionnaire including both standard questions and ample opportunity for spontaneous responses to try to find examples

[1] This reference refers primarily to urban municipalities and "urban entrepreneurialism." We share with Wilks-Heeg et al. (2003) an interest in the way in which local public authorities now actively engage in development oriented initiatives, though our survey sample includes a large number of rural municipalities.

of municipalities that seem to take an entrepreneurial approach to local development.

The remainder of this introductory section introduces existing conceptualizations of entrepreneurship from several dimensions and as an individual or collective phenomenon. The sections that follow review the results of our survey. Concluding sections discuss the implications of our findings for the study of entrepreneurship.

Entrepreneurship: A Multidimensional Phenomenon

The mainstream of empirical entrepreneurship research has confined itself to relatively simple and robust definitions of the concept: the starting up of new businesses or being self-employed. Many general definitions of entrepreneurship are centered on the discovery (or creation) of business opportunities and the gathering of resources to exploit them. Nevertheless, a growing body of literature is investigating the phenomenon of entrepreneurship outside the business sphere. There is now a relatively developed field of research on social entrepreneurship (see e.g. Boschee 1995, Leadbetter 1997, Peredo and McLean 2006), civil/civic entrepreneurship (Henton et al. 1997, Banuri et al. 2002, Gawell 2006), academic entrepreneurship (Klofsten and Jones-Evans 2000, Powers and McDougall 2005, Wright et al. 2007), innovative entrepreneurship (in contrast to replicative entrepreneurship; see Wennekers and Thurik 1999, Piergiovanni and Santarelli 2006, Baumol 2010) and political entrepreneurship within or connected to the public sector (Buchanan and Badham 1999, Harris and Kinney 2004, Chatterjee and Lakshmanan 2009). From a traditional view of entrepreneurship, this "multidimensional" use of the concept can be questioned. It can be argued that the use of the entrepreneurship concept should be restricted to the business field and that the other, abovementioned phenomena should have other denominations and not seek to find favor by exploiting the popularity of the entrepreneurship concept. On the other hand, it can be claimed that the increasing use of the concept outside the business world reflects a recognition that entrepreneurial behavior does exist in other spheres of society, and that this behavior can be analyzed within the same theoretical framework as traditional entrepreneurship.[2] This chapter takes this latter perspective as its starting point.

[2] This discussion strongly resembles the discussion of whether social capital should be denominated capital or not. As shown in Westlund (2006), using the term capital for social capital does not have any support in traditional capital theory and it is thus a matter of taste whether the concept should be used or not. If fact, it can be argued that the multidimensional use of the entrepreneurship concept has a stronger theoretical support than the denomination "capital" for social capital.

Perspectives on Entrepreneurship

As the notion of entrepreneurship as a multidimensional phenomenon has become more accepted, some have sought to provide unifying definitions of entrepreneurship. Among these, one of the most often cited is the definition of entrepreneurship as involving several distinct but interrelated processes of discovery/creation, resource mobilization and exploitation of new opportunities (Shane 2003). Hindle (2010) builds on earlier research from Blackman and Hindle (2008), Klyver (2005) and Davidsson (2004) that describes entrepreneurship as either related to the creation of new organizations (an emergence perspective) or new relationships that can include new links between existing organizations (an opportunity perspective) (Blackmen and Hindle, Klyver, Davidsson in Hindle 2010). These admittedly broad definitions would seem to leave room for the definition of local government development efforts as entrepreneurial if they involve the creation of new institutions of governance, new links between existing institutions or actors or new ways of exploiting opportunities.

Can Entrepreneurial Behavior be a Collective Phenomenon?

There is an emerging consensus in the literature that entrepreneurs can be found within firms, civil society organizations and in both the public and private sectors. But can entrepreneurial behavior describe a collective phenomenon or is it reserved for a description of individual behavior? The entrepreneurship literature has hitherto reflected an overwhelming emphasis on the individual entrepreneur. However, more recent contributions reflect a growing sense that the individual entrepreneur requires a network of supporters, and moreover, the idea that entrepreneurship involves mobilizing a support community. As noted earlier, this may be the result of an ongoing dialogue between scholars of entrepreneurship, social capital and institutional change. Followers of this approach refer to the work of Shane and Venkataraman (2000) and others who underscore that entrepreneurship requires both entrepreneurial individuals and an environment offering lucrative opportunities (Shane and Venkataraman 2000, Shane 2003; for a review see also Hindle 2010). We find a particular reliance on this approach in studies of policy and political entrepreneurship. Pozen (2008) for example notes that policy-related entrepreneurship by definition involves the process or mobilizing support from a variety of different stakeholders and decisionmakers. Therefore, qualities such as networking and brokering are critical to the success of the policy entrepreneur. In other words, policy entrepreneurs—and indeed all entrepreneurs—must navigate existing structures of stakeholders, rules and resources. Westlund and Bolton (2003) introduce the concept of "entrepreneurial social capital" based on Johannisson's (2000) contention that entrepreneurship is a collective phenomenon and earlier references to "community entrepreneurs" (Johannisson and Nilsson 1989). Johannisson and Nilsson refer to individuals who act as change agents and facilitators for a range of other entrepreneurial activities including within existing organizations, public, private and intermediate. But as we learn more about the role of social capital we can ask whether or not it is possible to disassociate the actions of the individual from that of the collective. In other words can groups be entrepreneurs or, better yet, engage in entrepreneurial behavior?

We suggest that if local governments work to discover new development opportunities, mobilize resources to achieve them and exploit them actively, then we can describe such activities as "entrepreneurial." This does not negate the complex and important phenomena describing how individual change agents build support for and diffuse new ideas to a broader audience. Rather, we are simply interested in another piece of the puzzle; less the who and how of entrepreneurial behavior within local governments and more the *what*: what is actually attempted and why.

Entrepreneurship and Institutions

The evolving literature on policy-related entrepreneurship has a strong institutional flavor. Kalantaridis and Fletcher (2012) describe institutional entrepreneurship as involving the process by which individual agents diffuse ideas and practices across a wider network. In describing the critical and necessary community context for entrepreneurship, Björkman and Sundgren (2005) describe political entrepreneurship in contrast to economic entrepreneurship: economic entrepreneurship is exploiting market opportunities and political entrepreneurship is exploiting opportunities within an organization. This organization-internal view on entrepreneurship links it to the literature on intrapreneurship (Pinchot and Pinchot 1978, Pinchot 1985, Stough and Haynes 2009). Related definitions of political entrepreneurship focus even more explicitly on political entrepreneurship as creating new organizations or new institutions (norms and rules) or working outside the boundaries of existing institutions (Thornton 1999, Kropp and Zolin 2008).These can be compared with definitions and studies of institutional entrepreneurship as "the endogenous transformation of institutional environments" (Pacheco et al. 2010, McMullen 2010). Scheingate (2003) offers a definition of political entrepreneurship as entrepreneurial innovation: "a speculative act of creative recombination that, when successful, transforms the institutional boundaries of authority" that can include non-market relations with external actors. This perspective is developed in Chatterjee and Lakshmanan (2009) who describe political entrepreneurs as nodes, linking social and economic entrepreneurs. These authors, and many others, underscore that instable institutional frameworks or local conditions (such as economic downturns) can create opportunities for political entrepreneurs to develop new institutions for collective action.

MEASURING ENTREPRENEURIAL BEHAVIOR IN LOCAL GOVERNMENTS

We describe municipal efforts to promote local development using new types of initiatives, partnerships and institutions as "entrepreneurial governance."[3] We measure activities designed to be productive or developmental in character rather than activities designed to influence policies for the purpose of rent seeking. We focus on the local (municipal) level of government, a scale we argue that has been largely ignored in the literature (but see Schneider and Teske 1992). One reason for this focus is that in Sweden, a large share of income taxes accrue to municipalities[4] and they are responsible for many local services that have the potential to benefit from innovative service provision initiatives. Likewise, this study is more interested in entrepreneurial governance as a reflection of municipal capacity for innovation related to local economic development than in identifying individual political or policy entrepreneurs.

Few studies address the issue of how to measure entrepreneurship within local governments. Those that do, develop metrics of rather different character. Schneider and Teske (1992) are concerned with the motivation of the (individual) political entrepreneur to affect the direction of local policy. They classify local government expenditures in the U.S. as allocational ("housekeeping" expenditures such as overheads related to government administration but also public safety), redistributive (welfare, urban renewal and hospitals) or developmental (generally related to the provision of infrastructure such as transport, sewage, water and energy). Using Peterson's (1981) contention that allocational expenditures are those least subject to political limits and other rigid institutional structures,

[3] A more detailed explanation of why we have chosen to use the term "entrepreneurial governance" to describe this phenomenon in local government is offered in the discussion section of the chapter.

[4] The local municipal revenue base is comprised of income from municipal income taxes (roughly 20–25 percent) plus/minus redistributive contributions to other municipalities, as well as local fees for some services. The municipal level has among others responsibility and authority for child care, schools, elderly care, local land use planning and local sector development (environment, energy etc.).

they argue that allocational expenditures offer political entrepreneurs the greatest opportunity for profit. They test this hypothesis by comparing the share of allocational expenditures to the number of observed political entrepreneurs, based on a survey of municipal clerks asked to identify individuals with entrepreneurial characteristics. The political entrepreneurs identified were mostly mayors or politicians (almost 70 percent) but also city managers, bureau chiefs and private businessmen. Probit estimates of the likelihood of finding a political entrepreneur based on the levels of various types of expenditures (as well as other local conditions) show that allocational expenditures have a significant and positive effect on the probability of finding local political entrepreneurs, while redistributive and developmental expenditures are associated with a somewhat reduced likelihood of finding political entrepreneurs.

While the results of Schneider and Teske's (1992) analysis are compelling, their reliance on a rather simple taxonomy of budget expenditures raises some questions. Welfare expenditures, defined here as "redistributive," could include innovative social welfare initiatives that involve new partnerships with other public or private actors (which we would define as entrepreneurial activity). Likewise, allocative expenditures may well be tied to very rigid municipal charters that restrain innovation in governance and public administration. For example, many municipal charters in the U.S. require that the community maintains its own fire or police department, which restrains local governments from entering into partnerships with other communities to achieve scale economies.

We offer a third approach that is more focused on observing entrepreneurial communities than on finding and measuring the incidence of individual policy-oriented entrepreneurs. Compared to the aforementioned studies, our survey is measuring something different; not the incidence of entrepreneurs who can profit individually from opportunities offered by different institutional and environmental contexts, but rather entrepreneurial municipal governments that exhibit a capacity for experimentation and innovation in the pursuit of developmental goals. We seek to measure *collective capacity* for exploiting opportunities for innovation in local government activity rather than *individual capacity* for exploiting opportunities for personal gain within the constraints of local government activity.

SURVEY METHOD AND DATA

Following Shane (2003, p. 4) we constructed a survey based on the idea that "Entrepreneurship is an activity that includes the discovery, evaluation and exploitation of opportunities to introduce new goods and services, ways of organizing, markets, processes, and raw materials, through organizing efforts that previously had not existed." A growing literature has taken this opportunity approach as a starting point for applying the entrepreneurship concept in fields of society outside the business sphere.

Our study uses new empirical data from a survey of Swedish municipalities who responded to open-ended and multiple choice questions designed to capture municipalities' own examples of the ways in which local governments create/discover, evaluate opportunities, mobilize resources and exploit opportunities for local development.

Swedish Municipal Classifications

The Swedish Board of Agriculture has developed a classification system for municipalities in Sweden that reflects not only population size and density, but functional relationship with neighboring communities. Municipalities are classified as four municipal types (MT): (MT 1) metropolitan areas (N=46), (MT 2) urban areas (N=47), (MT 3) rural areas/countryside (N=164), and (MT 4) sparsely populated rural areas (N=33). The four types of areas are defined as follows. Metropolitan areas (MT 1): Includes municipalities where 100 percent of the population lives within cities or within a 30 km distance from the cities. Using this definition, there are three metropolitan areas in Sweden: Stockholm, Gothenburg and Malmo. Urban areas (MT 2): Municipalities with a population of at least 30000 inhabitants and where the largest city has a population of 25000 people or more. Smaller municipalities neighboring these urban municipalities are included in a local urban area if more than 50 percent of the labour force in the smaller municipality commutes to a neighbor municipality. In this way, a functional-region perspective is adopted. In practice, this group of municipalities is comprised of regional centers and the suburban municipalities surrounding them. Rural areas/countryside (MT 3): Municipalities not meeting the criteria for metropolitan areas and urban areas are classified as rural areas/countryside, given they have a population density of at least five people per square kilometer. Sparsely populated rural areas (MT 4) are those municipalities not included in the three categories above and with less than five people per square kilometer.

Survey Data

To capture municipal activities that can be described in terms of entrepreneurial governance, we developed a questionnaire addressed to municipal directors. The rationale for using municipal directors as respondents is similar to that of Schneider and Teske (1992), namely that local civil

Table 6.1 Numbers and response rates for each municipal category

	Missing	Response	Sum	Response %
Metro	11	35	46	76%
Urban	8	39	47	83%
Rural	25	139	164	85%
Sparse	8	25	33	76%
Total	52	238	290	82%

servants possess an overview of local political and governance activities that makes them credible respondents.[5] In our case, however, the municipal directors were asked to describe activities rather than nominate individuals. The web survey was sent out in June 2009 to all 290 municipal directors in Sweden and was followed up by telephone interviews. The response rate was 82 percent. Table 6.1 shows the number of responding municipalities and the response rate in each category.[6]

The survey was comprised of over 30 questions regarding a range of activities generally outside the scope of "everyday" municipal business. Such activities include new forms of cooperation with business and with other municipalities to attract new business or new residents, participation in marketing, tourism and benchmarking initiatives, and participation in European Union (EU) projects related to local development. These questions capture and measure the (essentially positive) initiatives of communities that seek to experiment with new ways of working to achieve local development goals. The survey sought to capture entrepreneurial activities in various stages: discovery or creation and evaluation of opportunities, resource mobilization and exploitation of these opportunities (see Shane 2003). Thus, the following types of activities were measured:

- Creating, discovering and evaluating new opportunities ("Identify"): Benchmarking, marketing, learning and competence development activities and strengthening local business climate. (Maximum points: 10 of total 55.)
- Mobilizing resources ("Mobilize"): Includes co-financing of development projects with local industry, project cooperation with

[5] Schenider and Teske (1992) use municipal clerks as respondents, while we used city managers/city directors. Both types of respondents possess a good overview of municipal policy and are closely involved in the creation of new agreements, contracts and other innovative institutions for partnership.

[6] Only the municipalities that answered all questions in the survey are counted as having responded.

other municipalities, and development projects co-financed by EU and national agencies. (Maximum points: 12 of 55.)

- Exploiting opportunities ("Exploit"): Measures for promoting industrial development, for example improving cooperation with local industry. (Maximum points: 33 of total 55.)

The distribution of points among the three stages was based on an assumption that most points should be available in the third, "executive" stage. Note that the category labels above were not given in the survey. Instead, multiple choice questions were presented individually and there was also additional information from text boxes that could be used for further explanation and the follow-up telephone interviews. For example municipalities were asked to what extent they work together with local industry and then to elaborate on the character of this type of cooperation.

Scores

In the first stage, responses in each category were scored and tabulated. Taken together, the three categories produced a potential score range of 0–55 points, an average of 28 points, and a maximum and minimum of 43 and nine points respectively. In other words, the 238 municipalities that answered all questions represent a wide range of observed entrepreneurship activities. Table 6.2 shows descriptive statistics for the three categories of the survey.

Results were documented for each individual municipality but also by spatial type, using the division of geographic types described above. To help compare smaller and larger communities of the same general type (urban, rural) we call the larger areas "higher order" and the smaller areas "lower order" (Table 6.3). Metropolitan areas have the lowest scores for entrepreneurial governance but the highest rankings for economic entrepreneurship (startups/capita), here measured as startup firms per 10000 population. Sparse rural and rural municipalities have high scores for

Table 6.2 Descriptive statistics

Category	Observations	Mean	Standard Deviation	Minimum	Maximum
Identify	238	4.76	1.36	0	7
Mobilize	238	8.67	2.14	2	13
Exploit	238	14.64	4.63	4	25
Total Index	238	28.06	6.46	9	43

Table 6.3 Entrepreneurial governance scores, indexed to national averages

Municipal type	Economic entrepreneurship (annual rate of new firms per 10 000 population)	Entrepreneurial governance
Metro/urban municipalities		
Metropolitan (higher order)	132	90
Urban (lower order)	100	105
Rural municipalities		
Rural (higher order)	91	100
Sparse rural (lower order)	99	105
National average	100	100

Table 6.4 Average scores of the three entrepreneurial stages for the four municipal types

	Identify	Mobilize	Exploit	Sum
Metro	4.97	7.89	12.63	25.49
Urban	5.18	8.38	15.90	29.46
Rural	4.66	8.79	14.63	28.08
Sparse	4.36	9.52	15.56	29.44
Total	4.76	8.67	14.64	28.07

entrepreneurial governance and lower rates of startup firms (economic entrepreneurship).[7]

Table 6.4 shows the average scores of the three entrepreneurial stages for the four municipal types. Some observations can be made. The low total score for the metropolitan municipalities is due to lower scores for resource mobilization and exploitation of opportunities. The urban municipalities have the highest totals thanks to high scores in identifying/creating and in exploiting opportunities. The sparse rural municipalities have the lowest score for identifying opportunities but the highest for mobilizing resources.

[7] However, some studies have found equally high startup rates in rural and urban areas when they are defined in a way other than that defined in this chapter; see, for example, Eliasson and Westlund (2013).

The former can probably be explained by the fact that these are the smallest municipalities that lack resources for strategic analysis and planning, while the latter probably reflects the fact that this group has the best access to EU structural funds and other regional development resources. Metro and urban municipalities score highest for identifying opportunities but lowest for mobilizing resources. Regarding exploitation it is the "little brothers" of each municipal category, the urban and sparsely settled areas, that score highest.

SURVEY RESULTS

This section summarizes the results from the survey questions and interviews. As noted, respondents were invited to provide additional comments to their answers given to standard questions and were also contacted for follow-up interviews by telephone. These results provide a deeper understanding of the character and motivation for various types of entrepreneurial governance activity. All answers from text boxes and from interviews were documented and used to better understand responses to the standard questions. For example, more detailed responses to questions regarding whether or not municipalities invested in activities to strengthen the local business climate revealed that these activities included everything from production of information brochures, to the formation of business councils to discuss local land use plans, to municipal administrative reforms regarding business permits.

Identifying, Creating and Evaluating New Opportunities

We classified activities as being related to this category if they could be said to improve the preconditions for development. There is a strong emphasis on learning and capacity building activities both within the local government and in the community in general, as well as marketing campaigns meant to attract new residents or business.

Measures for strengthening the local business climate

Measures and activities for strengthening the local business climate include sponsoring projects supporting new startups for specific groups such as immigrants or women (84 percent), support for education and cluster development (65 percent) and marketing activities to attract new business (76 percent). Examples of activities municipalities use to strengthen the local business climate include producing information brochures, forming business councils to discuss local land use plans, and municipal administrative reforms to speed the approval of business-related permits. Almost half report investing in business incubators and a quarter invest in science parks. Other business development measures reported include investments in transport infrastructure, including owning or co-financing railroads and airports. Here again, detailed responses reveal a high incidence of informal meetings but also the creation of new companies and organizations for business development, marketing, logistics and goods handling, or to guide the implementation of large projects such as new housing developments. Several also note initiatives within local government to offer training programs for civil servants in "customer-oriented" public service.

Benchmarking, learning and competence development activities

Three quarters (75.6 percent) of municipalities invest in surveys and related activities that measure local opinion among residents or businesses and/or benchmark results against that of other communities. Participating in formal benchmarking studies such as the "municipal compass," a benchmarking tool offered by the Swedish Society of Municipalities and County Councils since 2002, is reported by 67.6 percent. Almost as many (66.4 percent) also produce surveys among municipal staff or develop other forms for stimulating and implementing "bottom-up" ideas for new development initiatives or increasing efficiency in public administration. Such activities can be important starting points for entrepreneurial activities, representing the phases in which background material is gathered and opportunities recognized.

Marketing

Municipal representatives were asked to what extent the local government, alone or in association with other actors, had tried to create or strengthen an identity or image for the municipality. A majority responded that they had engaged in this type of city marketing, "to a very great extent" or "to a relatively great extent." About one quarter (27 percent) had used city/municipality marketing programs relatively little and 8.4 percent not at all. A review of the descriptions of the profiles and images used to market local communities reveals striking similarities. About one third include an "entrepreneurial attitude," a "land of opportunity" or a community that is in general friendly to business. At least as many underscore the community's responsiveness to residents' concerns and a "customer focus." Others highlight specific sectors or business profiles such as tourism, lean production techniques or small business. A good quality of life and a safe or clean environment is a common theme.

Over 90 percent had taken specific promotional initiatives between

2006 and 2009, and one third report establishing a marketing company to produce ongoing programs (alone or in partnership with other actors). Examples of marketing initiatives include setting up citizen and employee panels, marketing campaigns targeted to tourists and property buyers from specific countries such as the Netherlands and Germany, or participation in international conventions. Many initiatives are related to new or improved/refurbished infrastructure such as retail centers, central area redevelopment, specialized schools or new housing developments. Many report initiatives to make attractive parcels of land available to developers, which may require changes in formal and informal institutions governing zoning or permitting processes. In some cases improving attractiveness has meant adding staff, such as tourist managers, and in other cases reducing staff to cut administrative cost.

Although the scope and ambition level of local marketing initiatives vary widely, it is in this context that many respondents noted the creation of cooperative initiatives with other actors. These include neighboring communities, communities along a major transport corridor, regional market development companies, and a range of business partners including developers. Some, though not all, of these initiatives have created new institutions for partnership.

Mobilizing Resources

We chose to focus on the ways in which local governments mobilize resources outside local government resource and capital mobilization processes (taxation, borrowing, etc.). In other words, we focused on resource mobilization activities that involved co-financing with other communities or with local firms, which is sometimes also a way to attract grants and subsidies from other sources such as the EU. In other words we are interested in what municipalities do to reduce their individual financing share of public or semi-public goods, to capitalize on scale economies or to access additional public revenue (through subsidies).

Development projects (co-financed by EU and national agencies)

Survey respondents reported frequent participation in development projects co-financed by the EU and national development agencies. The highest share (41.7 percent) participated in one to five European projects in the period between 2006 and 1009, and almost a third (30.4 percent) participated in between six and ten projects. Also notable is that one fifth (20 percent) participated in more than 15 development projects co-financed from sources external to the community. About 60 percent participated in one to five projects co-financed by national development

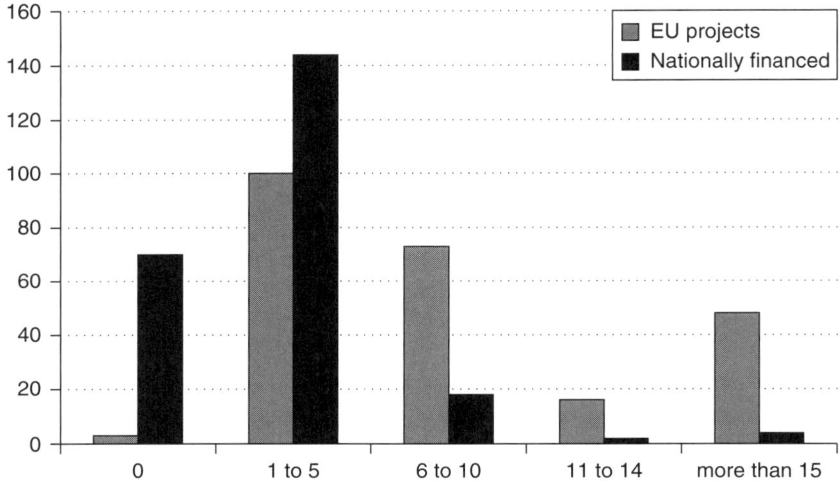

Figure 6.1 Number of municipalities and number of development projects funded or co-funded by national or international agencies, 2006–2009, responding Swedish municipalities

agencies during the same period, but almost a third (29.4 percent) had no nationally financed projects (Figure 6.1).

These projects represented a total contribution to the local community that ranged from a few million kronor (about 200 000 euro) to 4.5 million euro. This is a significant increase of local development resources to municipal coffers and can be said to represent a profit from municipal entrepreneurship, though these contributions often require co-financing from local authorities; most had contributed about 20 000–80 000 euro. A particular source of development funds for Swedish municipalities is the EU LEADER+ program for small business development in rural areas. Several noted that experience with LEADER+ projects helps mobilize resources for other projects, both from within the community and from other EU programs. LEADER projects also created networks and other institutions for cooperation among local businesses and between small business startups and the local government authorities. In this sense they fit the criteria for political entrepreneurship as related to institutional change and activity outside traditional institutional boundaries. LEADER and other European programs have also led to institutional change within local authorities: 57 percent of municipalities report having a dedicated coordinator for European proposals and programs.

Co-financing of projects with local industry

Municipal representatives were asked how many projects the local government had co-financed with industry in the three year period between 2006 and 2009. Almost half (45 percent) reported two to four projects and over a quarter had five to nine projects. About 13 percent had no projects or one project, and roughly the same number had more than ten. Notably, 7 percent reported more than 15 unique projects co-financed with local industry during the three year period. Detailed responses, however, reveal a wide range including single events (such as co-produced meetings or congresses, or producing a brochure) but also major multi-year initiatives for urban development or training. The latter include the creation of new institutes and in some cases new infrastructure, such as a new motorsports stadium, biofuel facility or training center. Many larger projects and associated investments are linked to development projects co-funded through national development programs or the EU's structural funds.

Exploiting Opportunities

This category included several questions asking communities how they go about forming new cooperative ventures for promoting industrial development by improving cooperation with local industry. We asked local government representatives to be as specific as possible about the types of activities they engage in to capitalize on opportunities for local development together with firms or other communities. Some activities self-reported by municipalities may fill several functions, for example a regular series of dialogues with local industry leaders may help to discover new opportunities but also to exploit them.

Cooperation with local industry

Municipalities cooperate with local industry on a wide range of initiatives. Almost all municipalities meet with industry representatives in the context of information meetings, industry breakfasts and the like—and indeed, the extent to which such activities in and of themselves represent entrepreneurship can be debated. More interesting is the high incidence (over 80 percent) of municipalities that report common projects with industry, including developing new infrastructure such as district heating systems, startup firm incubators and science parks. Many of these projects have necessitated the creation of new organizations and institutions of governance such as commonly owned business development corporations. Admittedly, few of these initiatives are radical in the sense that they are "new to the world," to use a distinction often used in the literature on entrepreneurship (see, for example, Baumol's (2010) distinction between innovative and replicative entrepreneurship) but they are often new to the local political context. Half of the responding municipalities noted that local business policies are developed in close dialogue with industrial leaders and that this has led to the creation of new networks between the municipality and businesses, but also among businesses and among municipalities.

Cooperation with other municipalities

Three quarters of responding municipalities reported cooperating with other municipalities to attract new residents and companies and almost all (94 percent) cooperate with neighboring communities to attract visitors. It bears noting that, in Sweden, income taxes accrue to local governments but business taxes do not, so communities profit directly from new residents whereas businesses are valuable if they create jobs for local residents or provide goods and services that attract or retain residents. Municipalities in the same region often compete for residents (and, less often, businesses), but can also pool resources to try to attract more households or firms to the region. Of the municipalities reporting cooperating with other local governments in the same county (96 percent), about one quarter cooperated with local governments in nearby counties, but only 3.4 percent with other Swedish communities. However, 9.5 percent report cooperating with local governments in other countries to attract new residents, and 5.6 percent to attract new business, which may be an effect of structural funds providing resources for cross-border cooperation. As such they may represent instances where political entrepreneurship was necessary to produce institutional change.

Empirical Results—Conclusion

The main finding from the descriptive statistics reported above is that a vast majority of Swedish municipalities can be classified as engaging in entrepreneurial governance in a number of various fields. As shown in Table 6.4, emphasis on the various stages of the entrepreneurial process varies somewhat by municipal type. Possible explanations for this phenomenon are discussed in the next section.

ANALYSIS AND DISCUSSION

Entrepreneurial Governance as a Strategy to Reduce Risk and Cost

In one of the most comprehensive reviews of concepts of entrepreneurship, Pozen (2008) attempts to tease out the key differences among concepts defined as "entrepreneurial." He argues that economic entrepreneurs (who he calls capitalist entrepreneurs) are in general more willing and able to bear risk in the pursuit of their goals. Indeed, economic entrepreneurs typically assess the profit potential of their new venture in relation to the risk of failure in the market. Pozen (2008) notes that other types of entrepreneurs, such as policy, social or civil entrepreneurs, do not incur similar levels of personal risk. Our study suggests that for the municipalities we surveyed, this distinction can be taken even further. Those municipalities with higher survey scores seemed to be those that actively seek new partnerships with industry, or initiate common projects with other municipalities, as a way of significantly reducing risk and cost. A higher proportion of municipal initiatives were projects or temporary partnerships than new companies, public–private partnerships or long term ventures. This can also be seen as a lower-risk strategy when experimenting with new ideas.

In other words, the potential to reduce risk associated with development initiatives is in itself the motivation for testing new ideas and ways of working. The high incidence of investments in benchmarking and marketing studies can also be seen as a way of reducing risk by helping municipalities to better estimate the potential impact of introducing new ideas or investing in new initiatives or infrastructure.

On the other hand we found the highest scores among the "little brother" municipalities: those with a relatively less powerful strategic position. Sparse rural communities had higher scores than other rural communities, and smaller urban centers had higher scores than metropolises. This may reflect the weaker relative position of small cities relative to larger agglomerations, and of sparse rural areas relative to other rural areas, as they compete for households and firms. In this sense, "little brother" municipalities are strongly motivated to seek new ways to improve their competitive position and may be more willing to act as political entrepreneurs. The two concepts need not be mutually exclusive; smaller rural communities and smaller cities are more motivated to take risks but are also resource-poor relative to their larger neighbors. They must introduce new initiatives (which is usually associated with some risk), but they can only control costs (which may be difficult to estimate for new initiatives) by spreading risk, by working together with industry, with the EU or with other municipalities.

This perspective finds support in recent contributions to the literature on entrepreneurship focusing on why entrepreneurs make the choices to organize as firms (or not). A 2007 special issue of the *Journal of Management Studies* brought together scholars of entrepreneurship and of the theories of firm formation to investigate these issues. In their introduction to the special issue, Alvarez and Barney (2007) note that the question of the organization of governance institutions for entrepreneurship is under-studied and suggest that it is associated with what we know about how economic actors make choices regarding the organization of their activities (as firms, through alliances, etc.). Although theories of the firm (using transaction cost and contract approaches) do a good job of explaining some firm formation, they assume that the risks and rewards for various alternative governance structures can be estimated, at least as probabilities. In entrepreneurial settings, they argue, it may be impossible to assess risks and rewards. They therefore use the term "entrepreneurial governance" to describe how and why entrepreneurs may adopt different institutions of governance than traditional firms.

The results of our survey suggest that a similar phenomenon occurs as local governments assess the risks (political and economic) and potential development benefits associated with new development initiatives. We have therefore borrowed the concept of entrepreneurial governance as a way of describing the particular phenomenon of local governments creating, mobilizing and exploiting new opportunities for local growth. We use this term because it was coined to describe the choices made by entrepreneurs regarding the character of governance institutions—with a focus on the ways in which decisions to organize new institutions are related to the risk associated with new development ventures.

Entrepreneurial Governance and New Institutions

Our approach follows the emphasis in the literature in entrepreneurship regarding the creation of new institutions, and also the definition of institutional entrepreneurship as endogenous institutional change. Indeed, this is what makes entrepreneurial behavior among municipalities somewhat unique. Municipal governments are highly constrained by their embeddedness in a range of higher-level institutions such as regional or national regulations. Just as important, local municipal charters typically define strict procedural institutions that often imply significant constraints to innovative behavior. Municipalities with 12-year land use planning horizons—and a host of other interdependent policymaking institutions based on this time frame—may find it difficult to capitalize on an opportunity to cooperate with municipalities with shorter or longer planning horizons. It may be nearly impossible to quickly mobilize local budget resources required to co-finance capital investments due to municipal institutions demanding local referenda, harmonization with budget cycles, and so on. Therefore, we describe political entrepreneurship as involving the creation of new institutions for development, without necessarily changing or reforming existing institutions. Rather, municipal entrepreneurship—in our study—is defined as new institutions layered onto an existing institutional structure. As such, our definition of political entrepreneurship closely follows Scheingate (2003) in its emphasis on "creative recombination that, when successful, transforms the institutional boundaries of authority" but we underscore that these new institutions may be temporary and may not imply transformation of the underlying institutional framework governing municipal behavior.

Earlier in this chapter we related our concept of political entrepreneurship to the conceptual traditions introduced by Kingdon (1984), Mintrom and Norman (2009) and others. However, our survey results indicate that we may be measuring something rather different, and that this may have important implications when developing metrics and searching for patterns of behavior among municipalities. Policy entrepreneurship focuses on producing changes in laws, rules or in the allocation of resources to existing initiatives. Policies are principles that govern a range of other decisions that follow. We are by contrast measuring experiments and research into new ways of working, resource mobilization and partnership that, according to our findings, are constructed specifically because they can promote local development without necessitating changes in local (or regional or national) policy.

The importance of this distinction becomes clearer when considering how new ideas are diffused among municipalities of different types. Shipan and Volden (2008) studied patterns of policy diffusion among U.S. cities and found that larger cities are more likely to adopt new policies, and are more likely to learn from other cities than smaller cities, but less likely to imitate the policies of other cities. Our survey results indicate that lower order municipalities (sparse rural municipalities and regional centers) are more likely to engage in learning and competency building activities, and are more likely to initiate new development initiatives than their larger counterparts. Are these results in conflict?

Perhaps not. Perhaps higher order municipalities (metropolises, and rural municipalities that are larger than the peripheral communities around them), do have a greater capacity to learn from other communities and adopt new policies. However, it may be the lower order municipalities that most actively seek to improve their own capacity and that are attracted to initiatives that can be tested within existing policy frameworks and with fewer municipal contributions. Instead of leading by enacting new municipal policies, these types of communities seek partnerships and temporary projects that can leverage sparse local resources. This implies that policy entrepreneurship and political entrepreneurship (as defined in this study) measure very different phenomena. Moreover, it suggests that there are important differences in the way that larger and smaller communities in local markets introduce new ideas.

With this in mind we may want to consider local government efforts to work outside the confines of local politics and governance institutions when searching for new ways to approach local development as the creation of new institutional fields rather than new institutions per se. Kalantaridis and Fletcher (2012) make a clear distinction between changes in the interactions among the various actors involved in entrepreneurship, distinguishing between changes to institutions (changing the existing rules within which actors must operate) and institutional fields (within which sets of rules meet, and whose power derives from the fact that actors seeking support and legitimacy must conform to other modes, rules and ways of working). Importantly, they argue that the creation of institutional fields may include both new and existing institutions. The results of our survey, which emphasize the temporary and special arrangements formed with other communities or with firms without dismantling existing local government institutions, could be argued to be the creation of new institutional fields. However, more study is needed to articulate the character of institutional fields in this context.

CONCLUDING REMARKS

This study is a contribution to the very limited literature on entrepreneurship related to local development at the municipal level and offers new empirical data regarding the ways in which Swedish municipalities approach local development in new ways and with new partners. The survey results support the notion that what we can call "entrepreneurial governance" is occurring in a wide variety of municipalities; it is not a phenomenon exclusive to only urban or high-growth municipalities. While our survey employed a fairly broad definition of entrepreneurship, a close examination of results reveals a high incidence of new institutions created to support development at the municipal level. These include formal agreements such as public–private partnerships or co-financing agreements with other municipalities, but also new forums for informal exchanges of knowledge and dialogue. Municipalities are immobile and often have rigid procedural institutions, not least to ensure democratic process and transparency; in other words local bureaucrats or politicians cannot decide to radically transform their own institutions. This may well be why our survey noted many instances of municipalities creating space for innovation by participating in cooperative projects (which often can be governed by institutions that don't need to follow municipal procedures).

Importantly, most of these new institutions were created to govern specific projects or studies. Many were of a temporary character or new organizations were created that were not under the direct authority of any one municipality. This type of temporary partnering with other public and private authorities—often in the context of planning new strategic development investments—may have afforded individual municipalities a degree of freedom to experiment with new ideas and approaches without fear of reprisal and without hindrance from procedural institutions. This implies that partnering and other forms of cooperation between municipalities and other public and private actors may not only reflect resource constraints or recognition that the relevant economic geography comprised an area larger than the municipal borders. Rather, collaboration and cooperation may be an efficient strategy to experiment with new ideas without the transaction costs—and risk—involved in reforming municipal institutions. The fact that our entrepreneurship scores were higher among lower order municipal types, who are arguably most vulnerable to competition from larger neighboring higher order communities, may reflect the challenge of "doing more with less;" introducing new ideas and initiatives without the transaction cost or pecuniary investment involved with acting alone or with introducing new policies. It could be useful, in further studies, to track the progression of important local policy initiatives from short term project or pilot project to formal policy change.

In sum, we find that municipal development initiatives can be described as a form of entrepreneurial behavior because they involve seizing opportunities for reaching development goals by creating new institutions—or perhaps institutional fields—that can steward new ideas and encourage experimentation. On the other hand, they may be distinguished from other types of social, civil or policy entrepreneurship in that they tend to layer temporary or limited collaborative institutions onto existing municipal institutions of governance rather than transforming existing institutions. We conclude that the types of municipal development initiatives we studied can be analyzed as a form of entrepreneurship and compared to other types of entrepreneurship such as policy-related entrepreneurship and institutional entrepreneurship. Just as institutional entrepreneurship has been argued to address a "blind spot" in institutional theory by integrating notions of individual change agents, we attempt to fill a gap in the entrepreneurship literature. Specifically, the literature on entrepreneurship now reflects an interest in the ways in which entrepreneurs are dependent on the resources (social, economic, environmental) of communities, but not how the process of building those community resources is in itself an entrepreneurial enterprise.

The results of this study have also highlighted some issues regarding the way in which statistics are collected for various types of municipalities. Growing interest in functional relationships as a determining factor in defining municipalities as urban or rural has led to the development of new taxonomies that still offer only crude divisions between, for example, urban and rural municipalities. It may be that for the purposes of this type of analysis, using municipal statistics grouped by labor market region would yield different results.

A final question is whether or not the results of this study can be generalized to most other western countries or if Sweden might constitute a special case. Sweden has only 290 municipalities (compared with, for example, ca. 8100 in Italy and 12000 in Germany). Municipalities have taxation authority and are responsible for a wide range of local services. The average municipal tax rate in 2014 is 20.65 percent of taxable incomes. This indicates that Sweden might be a special case because the municipal level has relatively high discretion and resources compared the regional or national levels. On the other hand, it is not primarily size or access to resources that determines whether or not an organization acts in an entrepreneurial manner or not. Rather, municipal propensity to engage in entrepreneurial governance activities depends on the existence of supportive formal and informal institutions, the latter including local social capital. It is beyond the scope of this chapter to make an international comparative analysis of this issue, but this is an important topic for future research on entrepreneurial governance.

ACKNOWLEDGEMENTS

The chapter has been partly financed by the national research council Formas, grant No 2009-1192. The authors are indebted to Marie Lidbom for assistance with data collection. Discussions with Per Frankelius contributed to the forming of the questionnaire on political entrepreneurship in local government.

REFERENCES

Alvarez, Sharon and Jay B. Barney (2007) The entrepreneurial theory of the firm (guest editors introduction). *Journal of Management Studies* 44(7): 1057–1063.

Banuri, T., A. Najam and N. Odeh (eds) (2002) *Civic Entrepreneurship: A Civil Society Perspective on Sustainable Development*. Islamabad, Pakistan: Gandhara Academy Press.

Baumol, W.J. (2010) *The Microtheory of Innovative Entrepreneurship*. Princeton, NJ: Princeton University Press.

Björkman, H. and M. Sundgren (2005) Political entrepreneurship in action research: learning from two cases. *Journal of Organizational Change Management* 18(5): 399–415.
Blackman, D. and K. Hindle (2008) Would using the psychological contract increase entrepreneurial business development potential? In Barrett, R. and Mayson, S. (eds) *International Handbook of Entrepreneurship and HRM*. Cheltenham, UK and Northampton, MA, USA: Edward Elgar Publishing, Chapter 19, pp. 382–397.
Boschee, J. (1995) Social entrepreneurship. *Across the Board* 32(3): 20–23.
Buchanan, D. and R. Badham (1999) *Power, Politics and Organizational Change: Winning the Turf Game*. London: Sage.
Cars, Goran, P. Healey, A. Madanipour and C. de Magalhaes (eds) (2002) *Urban Governance, Institutional Capacity and Social Milieux*. Aldershot, UK: Ashgate.
Chatterjee, L. and T.R. Lakshmanan (2009) The fashioning of competitive dynamic advantage of entrepreneurial cities: role of social and political entrepreneurship. In Karlsson, C., Andersson, Å.E., Cheshire, P.C. and Stough, R.R. (eds) *New Directions in Regional Economic Development*. Berlin, Heidelberg, New York: Springer, pp. 107–120.
Davidsson, P. (2004) *Researching Entrepreneurship*. New York: Springer.
Eliasson, K. and H. Westlund (2013) Attributes influencing enterprise propensity in urban and rural Sweden. *Annals of Regional Science* 50(2): 479–514.
Gawell, M. (2006) *Activist Entrepreneurship: Attac'ing Norms and Articulating Disclosive Stories*. Stockholm: Stockholm University School of Business.
Harris, M. and R. Kinney (2004) *Innovation and Entrepreneurship in State and Local Government*. Lanham, MD: Lexington Books.
Henton, D., J. Melville and K. Walesh (1997) The age of the civic entrepreneur: restoring civil society and building economic community. *National Civic Review* 86: 149–156.
Hindle, Kevin (2010) How community context affects entrepreneurial process: a diagnostic framework. *Entrepreneurship and Regional Development: An International Journal* 22(7–8): 599–647.
Johannisson, Bengt (2000) Modernizing the industrial district—rejuvenation or managerial colonization. In Taylor, M. and Vatne, E. (eds) *The Networked Firm in a Global World: Small Firms in New Environments*. Aldershot, UK: Ashgate, Chapter 12.
Johannisson, B. and A. Nilsson (1989) Community entrepreneurs: networking for local development. *Entrepreneurship and Regional Development* 1(1): 3–19.
Kalantaridis, Christos and Denise Fletcher (2012) Entrepreneurship and institutional change: a research agenda. *Entrepreneurship and Regional Development: An International Journal* 24(3–4): 199–214.
Kingdon, John W. (1984) *Agendas, Alternatives, and Public Policies* (second edition). Boston, MA: Little, Brown & Company.
Klofsten, M. and D. Jones-Evans (2000) Comparing academic entrepreneurship in Europe – the case of Sweden and Ireland. *Small Business Economics* 14: 299–309.
Klyver, K. (2005) Entrepreneurship and social network development: a life cycle approach. PhD dissertation, University of Southern Denmark.
Kropp, Fredric and Roxanne Zolin (2008) US Federal Government entrepreneurship: new enterprise structures. *Journal of Small Business and Enterprise Development* 15(3): 595–605.
Leadbetter, C. (1997) *The Rise of the Social Entrepreneur*. London: Demos.

McMullen, Jefferey (2010) Delineating the domain of development entrepreneurship: a market based approach to facilitating inclusive economic growth. Working paper, Kelly School of Business, Indiana University.

Mintrom, Michael and Philippa Norman (2009) Policy entrepreneurship and policy change. *The Policy Studies Journal* 37(4): 649–667.

Pacheco, D.F., J.G. York, T.J. Dean and S. D. Sarasvathy (2010) The coevolution of institutional entrepreneurship: a tale of two theories. *Journal of Management* 36: 974–1010.

Peredo, A.M. and M. McLean (2006) Social entrepreneurship: a critical review of the concept. *Journal of World Business* 41(1): 56–65.

Peterson, Paul E. (1981) *City Limits*. Chicago, IL: University of Chicago Press.

Piergiovanni, R. and E. Santarelli (2006) What is the best policy for innovative entrepreneurship? In Santarelli, E. (ed.) *Entrepreneurship, Growth, and Innovation: The Dynamics of Firms and Industries*. Berlin, Heidelberg, New York: Springer.

Pinchot, G. (1985) *Intrapreneuring: Why You Don't Have to Leave the Corporation to Become an Entrepreneur*. New York: Harper & Row.

Pinchot, G. and E. Pinchot (1978) Intra-corporate entrepreneurship, Tarrytown School for Entrepreneurs. http://www.intrapreneur.com/MainPages/History/IntraCorp.html (2010-01-28).

Powers, J.P. and P.P. McDougall (2005) University start-up formation and technology licensing with firms that go public: a resource-based view of academic entrepreneurship. *Journal of Business Venturing* 20: 291–311.

Pozen, David E. (2008) We are all entrepreneurs now. *Wake Forest Law Review* 43: 283–340.

Rader Olsson, Amy (2009) Relational rewards and communicative planning: understanding actor motivation. *Planning Theory* 8(3): 263–281.

Scheingate, Adam D. (2003) Political entrepreneurship, institutional change and American political development. *Studies in American Political Development* 17: 185–203.

Schneider, Mark and Paul Teske (1992) Toward a theory of the political entrepreneur: evidence from local government. *The American Political Science Review* 86(3): 737–747.

Shane, S. (2003) *A General Theory of Entrepreneurship: The Individual-Opportunity Nexus*. Cheltenham, UK and Northampton, MA, USA: Edward Elgar Publishing.

Shane, S. and S. Venkataraman (2000) The promise of entrepreneurship as a field of research. *Academy of Management Review* 25: 217–221.

Shipan, Charles R. and Craig Volden (2008) The mechanics of policy diffusion. *American Journal of Political Science* 52(4): 840–857.

Stough, R. and K. Haynes (2009) Intrapreneurship in the public sector. In Shockley, G., Frank, P. and Stough, R. (eds) *Non-market Entrepreneurship, Interdisciplinary Approaches*. Cheltenham, UK and Northampton, MA, USA: Edward Elgar Publishing, pp. 127–142.

Thornton, Patricia H. (1999) The sociology of entrepreneurship. *Annual Review of Sociology* 25: 19–46.

Wennekers, S. and R. Thurik (1999) Linking entrepreneurship and economic growth. *Small Business Economics* 13: 27–55.

Westlund, H. (2006) *Social Capital in the Knowledge Economy: Theory and Empirics*. Berlin, Heidelberg, New York: Springer.

Westlund, Hans and Roger Bolton (2003) Local social capital and entrepreneurship. *Small Business Economics* 21: 77–113.
Wilks-Heeg, S., B. Perry and A. Harding (2003) Metropolitan regions in the face of the European dimension: regimes, re-scaling or repositioning? In Salet, W., Thornley A. and Kreukels, A. (eds) *Metropolitan Governance and Spatial Planning*. London: Spon Press.
Wright, M., B. Clarysse, P. Mustar and A. Lockett (2007) *Academic Entrepreneurship in Europe*. Cheltenham, UK and Northampton, MA, USA: Edward Elgar.

7. Cities as seedbeds of responsible innovation

Marina van Geenhuizen and Qing Ye

1. RESPONSIBLE INNOVATION

The concept of 'responsible innovation' has been introduced quite recently in innovation studies. Originating in ethics, science philosophy and policy-making on science and innovation (von Schomberg, 2012; Owen et al., 2012; van den Hoven et al., 2013; Stilgoe et al., 2013) and preceded by attention mainly for responsible entrepreneurship (EC, 2003; Sanford, 2011), the concept of 'responsible innovation' is now being elaborated and translated into empirical research. Responsible research and innovation can be described as follows: '. . . a transparent, interactive process by which societal actors and innovators become mutually responsive to each other with a view to the (ethical) acceptability, sustainability and societal desirability of the innovation process and its marketable products' (von Schomberg, 2012). This definition has an emphasis on the type of application of new products, processes and so on, but also on the processes involved, mainly on the interaction between science and society (see, van den Hoven et al., 2012; Owen et al., 2012; van den Hoven, 2013). Using a normative perspective, new and concrete ideas should be turned into products and services that create jobs and prosperity, but at the same time accommodate moral and public values. Such an approach would enable the avoidance of innovations that turn out to be contested, and to focus on fields concerning societal needs that have not been focused on to date and continue innovations based on societal needs that have already been recognized, such as certain green technologies (van den Hoven et al., 2013).

The concept of responsible innovation is broader compared to that of sustainability innovation, in that it not only encompasses new solutions concerning renewable resources (e.g. energy), it also includes quality improvement of certain societal systems while keeping them affordable (e.g. the medical system and transport) and it has a stronger emphasis on moral and public values. This can be illustrated with wind energy solutions which are sustainable, but sometimes morally objectionable and not responsible, if people living close to wind turbines suffer from noise annoyance. Likewise, in the introduction of the electronic patient register (EPR) – although it may improve efficiency and quality of medical care – an emphasis is put on the protection of the privacy of patients, as privacy is seen as a strong moral value.

To gear the innovation process to societal (sustainability) needs or to see sustainability as a driver of innovation is not new, and questions on the desirability of particular new technologies 'among the public', as emphasized in responsible innovation, have already been raised (Roome and Winn, 1993; Hall and Vredenburg, 2003; Leydesdorff and Etzkowitz, 2003). However, the emphasis today on responsible innovation is much stronger than in previous times, particularly in many high-level policy and strategy European Union (EU) documents, while the technologies involved are more comprehensive, including for example those that could make health care and safety more affordable and effective, such as information technology. We mention the EU Innovation 2020 strategy to create smart growth and the Horizon 2020 programme that defines Societal Challenges as one of the main priorities (EC, 2011).

An interesting question is whether responsible innovation could ever lead to products/services being profitable. We could assume that in the case of consumer products/services, first, no profit can be made because the product is too expensive and/or user value is relatively low, but after improvements in user value and price, 'crossing the chasm' and entering the mass market, profitability can be gained in the same way as any other technology product (Mohr et al., 2010). As an example, we could mention electric vehicles.

Remarkably, in studies on transitions towards higher sustainability within society, the quality of space (place) has received scarce attention (Schot and Geels, 2007). Rather, the focus in transition studies has been on the national innovation system (e.g. Coenen et al., 2012; Truffer and Coenen, 2012; Hansen and Coenen, 2013) thereby overlooking local/regional specificities that enhance or block developments towards transitions. However, spatially oriented studies are quickly increasing in number today (e.g. Bulkeley et al., 2010; Quitzau et al., 2012; Brachert et al., 2013; Klitkou and Coenen, 2013; see also the literature overview by Hansen and Coenen, 2013). From various perspectives it can be reasoned that specific qualities of regions and cities make a difference in potentials for sustainability innovation, be it transformative forms of spatial planning as niche management, localized assets in research and testing sites such as wind tunnels and medical-nuclear facilities, a strong development of local civic society and sustainability pressure groups, or local potentials for networking with other regions (Quitzau et al., 2012).

2. THE ROLE OF URBAN PLACES

There is a knowledge gap in understanding which (urban) places hold privileged positions in sustainability assets and networks (Hodson and Marvin, 2010) – including technology, actors, resources and institutions – and how these are strategically coupled with the needs/interests of trans-local actors, in multi-scalar networks. With regard to urban places, the following four broad theoretical perspectives can be mentioned:

- Agglomeration theory, with the aim to understand the impact of scale effects on transitions due to sheer city size (critical mass) and/or diversity in economic sectors. Central is the idea that innovation benefits from a high density of knowledge spill overs in cities (Audretsch, 1998; Karlsson, 2008). On the micro level of firms, agglomeration advantages are derived through mechanisms such as sharing, matching and learning (Duranton and Puga, 2004). This refers both to firms as a site benefiting from localized assets in cities and to firms as being embedded in innovative networks at different spatial scales (Bunnell and Coe, 2001).
- Creative knowledge city approaches, with the aim to understand the role of the creative class and the role of specific local knowledge (Storper 1997; Florida, 2005). Due to its high level of economic and cultural capital, the 'new middle class' is thought to be bearer and driver of the consumption- and culture-driven urban economic sectors, a vision which can easily be extended to cover 'sustainability-driven' urban economic activity, in which a 'civic' university and its researchers play an increasingly important and responsible role while connecting with local pressure groups and communities and, virtually, also with global ones (Deakin, 2009; Goddard and Vallance, 2013).
- Evolutionary approaches, to understand the city/region as a selection environment for sustainability technologies and the mechanisms involved (Safarzynska and van den Bergh, 2008; Brachert et al., 2013). Aside from a spatial perspective these approaches also include an important historical perspective, particularly in the understanding of historical path dependencies for future spatial development paths, to be more precise, the combination of historical contingency and the rise of self-reinforcing effects steering a technology (or industry) along one path rather than another (Martin, 2010; De Laurentis, 2013).
- Urban policy approaches, to understand generic policies that are more or less in favour of applying sustainability solutions in urban

problem areas (van Geenhuizen and Nijkamp, 2012), and more specific ones. The latter may include: nurturing community culture and initiatives susceptible to sustainability goals; enhancing urban industry specialization in one of the sustainability energy areas, such as the photovoltaic and fuel cell industries; and, taking initiatives to bring multiple stakeholders together in living labs for co-creation between researchers and users (Nevens et al., 2013; van Geenhuizen, 2014) and in niches for learning, protection and empowering of sustainability solutions (Cooke, 2009; Coenen et al., 2012; Smith and Raven, 2012).

The chapter has a focus on spin-off firms from universities because these can be viewed as a major channel of technology transfer (interaction) between universities and the economy and society (Shane, 2004). Although there are other channels for technology transfer, such as licensing and direct university–business collaboration, spin-off firms are thought to be among the most important ones for impact on the local/regional small business infrastructure, direct and indirect employment gains, and a further diffusion of inventions. However, most university spin-offs are facing a shortage in resources, particularly knowledge of the market, marketing skills, management capability and financial capital, often preventing them from moving into the next growth stage (Vohora et al., 2004; van Geenhuizen and Soetanto, 2009). More importantly, if responsible innovation or sustainability is a major *driver* of innovation among them, a higher level of complexity and uncertainty emerges in their learning network, and as a consequence more resources are needed (Barney and Clark, 2007; Hall and Vredenburg, 2003; Sweet et al., 2003). These networks include a wider diversity of partners, such as public authorities, pressure groups, and customer groups aside from the conventional ones, calling for additional skills and (managerial) competences.

The approach in this chapter is that of agglomeration theory, including cities as the origin and seedbed of new sustainability (or responsible) technologies and applications. Accordingly, responsible spin-off firms in two contrasting cities will be compared in an exploration of their growth and in a case study analysis concerning local urban assets and important firm networks. The assumption is that, on the basis of various agglomeration benefits in metropolitan areas, sustainability (responsible) spin-offs tend to grow quicker in this environment.

To our knowledge there are no studies to date that have addressed sustainability and (responsible) innovation among university spin-off firms in relation to the city of location. As indicated earlier, cities have seldom been associated with creating and nurturing important sustainability technologies and paths to transition. However, there is a need for more nuance in this context:

1. Cities have been and are increasingly associated with the application of sustainable technologies, such as in the 'green' city and 'smart city' movements. There are many key contributions in the literature referring to urban sustainability in infrastructure, housing construction and low-carbon cities, this for example within the need to 'retrofit' existing buildings and the built environment in response to long term challenges of climate change and resource constraints, eventually calling for 'urban transitions' (Eames et al., 2013).
2. Cities have, however, seldom been considered as seedbeds and nurturers of sustainability inventions and as contributors to comprehensive socio-technical transitions concerning sustainability (Geels, 2004; Geels and Schot, 2007; Smith et al., 2010; Coenen et al., 2012; Truffer and Coenen, 2012). Accordingly, there are still few contributions addressing the city as a creator of new sustainability technology, as a seedbed for such technology, as protective niches, and as nodes of powerful stakeholder networks that can push the technology along the path to higher levels of sustainability and socio-technical transition, thereby also affecting the infrastructure and institutions necessary for such transitions.

We take a micro-level approach to firms and draw on a sample of 105 spin-off firms – of which we label 59 as being involved in responsible innovation – and on six case studies in answering the following questions: (1) To what extent does urban location matter in the growth of spin-off firms engaged in responsible innovation; and (2) What are the key assets of large cities and what are the key profiles of networks that enhance the growth of these firms and potential moves on paths towards higher levels of sustainability?

3. RESPONSIBLE INNOVATION IN PRACTICE

The sample used in this study is a data set from two universities, Delft University of Technology (TU Delft, the Netherlands) and the Norwegian University of Science and Technology (NTNU) (Trondheim, Norway). No differences are assumed in national innovation systems between the two countries involved – the Netherlands and Norway – as both share a somewhat risk-avoiding entrepreneurship culture (GEM, 2010), show similar scores on the main innovation scoreboard indicators (GEM, 2010;

ProInno Europe, 2011), and have a relatively small domestic market. There is one exception to this, namely, Norway has a supportive national policy towards wind energy; the Netherlands has not or not anymore, but this country – through its research programme on high-tech automotive engineering – has been supportive in the development of electric vehicles.

The population of spin-offs at the two universities satisfied important conditions: survived to 2006/7 for between two and 15 years. With an overall response rate of 70 per cent (105 spin-offs), in 2006/7, data were collected using a semi-structured questionnaire in face-to-face interviews with the principal manager, focusing on company characteristics, particularly the product/service and profiles of the networks in terms of type of partners and level of openness. In 2011, data were collected on the status of the company, size (employment and turnover) and changes in product/services. In addition, six spin-off firms served as in-depth case studies to explore the type of cities and the networks involved.

Given the updated data set of 105 firms, we determined which of the spin-offs could be labelled as active in responsible innovation. To that end we used the product/process description provided in their interview and we triangulated this information with their website and with branch journals, such as on solar energy and medical applications. Accordingly, we have labelled them as responsible innovation if they deal with sustainable energy production and use; quality and efficiency improvements in the medical sector, such as in elderly care; energy efficiency in industrial processes and in waste treatment; vehicle technology to apply sustainable energy sources and/or to use fuel more efficiently; buildings made of sustainable material and energy-efficient buildings. Sustainability inventions concerning food production fell beyond our analysis as none of the sampled spin-offs was engaged in that. We did not assign the label of responsible innovation in cases of software for recreational games, software for invitation and subscription to meetings, and technical innovation to extend oil exploration and exploitation. It would be wrong to say that these innovations are not responsible, but they fall beyond the scope of the category of responsible innovation.

However, translating the concept of responsible innovation into measurable indicators of business activity is not that easy. First, the conceptualization of 'ethical acceptability', 'unattended social fields' and 'contested innovations' in a business context is still somewhat weak. This means that our approach has been pragmatic in selecting those spin-offs that are engaged in product/services that satisfy broad criteria of sustainability, safety and health. Second, and particularly true for this study, we can only partially grasp the process characteristics of the way the innovations come into being, thereby potentially missing urban factors such as policy forces

Table 7.1 Application area of responsible innovators

	Absolute number	%
Sustainable energy[a]	17	28.8
Sustainable mobility, vehicle technology	14	23.8
Medical care and cure	11	18.6
Efficient industrial processes	6	10.2
Efficient waste treatment (recycling)	6	10.2
Sustainable buildings and safety	5	8.5
Totals (spin-offs)	59	

Source: Adapted from van Geenhuizen and Ye (2014).

Note: [a] Including energy efficiency.

in enhancing innovation through financial incentives and through the organization of living labs as innovation tools.

A small majority of the firms in the sample (56 per cent) is involved in responsible innovation in 2010, while a good 40 per cent is not. Most of the former have a full involvement meaning that all activities deal with responsible innovation. The largest area of application is sustainable energy, at 28.8 per cent (Table 7.1). This is followed by sustainable mobility and vehicle technology, at 23.8 per cent, and medical care and cure at 18.6 per cent. All other areas of application in our sample are substantially smaller.

In detail, sustainable energy, as a category, includes new types of solar cells, improved batteries for storage, improved windmills (rotor blades and body), improved turbines (stability for deep-sea use), but also energy saving in the use of refrigerators and cooling systems. The medical sector includes design of instruments for minimal invasive surgery, ergonomic furniture, and practical help in daily care of the elderly, as well as new medicines.

4. TRENDS IN GROWTH

4.1 Contrasting Cities

We first discuss differences between the two cities of investigation: Delft and Trondheim. TU Delft is in Delft, a medium-sized city with 96,800 inhabitants (in 2010) (Statistics Netherlands, 2012) in the Randstad metropolitan area in the western part of the Netherlands. The Netherlands Organization for Applied Scientific Research (TNO; applied sciences) is also in Delft. Unlike many other metropolitan areas, the Randstad does not consist of one large core city. Instead, it is composed of several relatively large cities that are connected to each other, that is, it is a polycentric urban system. The area includes four large cities: Amsterdam, Rotterdam, The Hague and Utrecht. Two of these cities are in the province of South Holland at approximately 10 km distance from Delft: The Hague, with a population of 488,600 in 2010 (municipal level), home of the national government and many international organizations on justice, and Rotterdam with 605,500 inhabitants in 2010 (Statistics Netherlands, 2012), a world centre of seaport activity, (petro)chemical industry, and logistics and trading. The city of Delft is between The Hague and Rotterdam, with the other larger cities, that is, Amsterdam and Utrecht, each with their own universities at approximately 50 km distance.

NTNU is in the city of Trondheim in the middle of Norway, with a population of 170,900 inhabitants in 2010 (municipality; Statistics Norway, 2012). Trondheim is a single city at a considerable distance from large cities, for example the distance from Trondheim to Oslo and Bergen is approximately 400 km and to Stockholm (Sweden) is approximately 600 km. Entrepreneurs in Trondheim have to spend much longer travelling to get to other large cities than firms in Delft even if air transport is used. Also, due to a smaller number of inhabitants and firms, local customers for the launching of products/services tend to be relatively scarce in Trondheim. Although Trondheim (unlike Delft) is located in a non-metropolitan area, it has received an important task in the national innovation system. Besides being the third largest city in Norway after Oslo and Bergen, Trondheim has the function of 'knowledge capital' of Norway with various government research institutes, such as SINTEF. Trondheim is the centre of the Trøndelag region with a population of slightly more than 420,000 inhabitants (2010; Statistics Norway, 2012). By contrast, the province of South Holland hosts 3.5 million inhabitants, clearly indicating a difference in 'mass'. Such a difference is also evidenced by the size of the regional economy, South Holland's economy, in terms of gross domestic product is almost seven times larger than the one in Trøndelag.

4.2 Growth of Spin-off Firms

The responsible innovators in our database are equally distributed over the two cities, 29 in Delft and 30 in Trondheim. With regard to employment, spin-offs involved in responsible innovation in Delft tend to grow more quickly than their counterparts in Trondheim. Average annual growth of jobs (in full-time equivalent) tends to be higher in Delft at a rate of 1.8 compared to 0.6 in Trondheim, a difference that is significant at $p=0.05$ level (Table 7.2). Unlike employment growth, turnover growth is measured

Table 7.2 Job growth among spin-offs in responsible innovation (start-up to 2010)

Job growth (fte)[a]	Total sample	Delft	Trondheim
Average annual growth (s.d.)	1.2 (0.30)	1.8 (0.54)	0.6 (0.22)
Number of spin-offs	59	29	30
t-test		2.03**	

Notes:
** $p<0.05$.
[a] fte = full time equivalent.

Table 7.3 Turnover among spin-offs in responsible innovation in 2010

Turnover (euro)	Delft	%	Trondheim	%
No turnover	1	3.5	3	10.0
<100,000	3	10.3	6	20.0
100,000–300,000	5	17.2	4	13.3
>300,000	20	69.0	17	56.7
Total	29	100	30	100

Note: Pearson $Chi^2=2.34$, $p=0.51$.

as a rank variable. The broad pattern of employment growth is also true for turnover – Delft shows a stronger presence of higher growth classes, witness 86.2 per cent versus 70.0 per cent in Trondheim (Table 7.3). In line with our expectations, these trends indicate stronger potentials for university spin-off firms in developing responsible innovations in Delft compared to Trondheim.

As the previous analysis is a rather simple one, we explore as a next step a growth model at the firm level, in which both urban location and various networking (openness) variables are included, in addition to a set of control variables.

4.3 Exploration of a Growth Model

University spin-off firms as responsible innovators are typically in need of external resources, for example to deal with uncertainty and to 'bridge' a period of experimentation if the innovation is radical and infrastructure and institutions need to be adapted, and assets need to be accessed that are not locally available. However, at the same time, these firms have limited experience in searching for and establishing networks and are short of resources in monitoring and management to fully benefit from networks, leading to varying degrees of openness in their knowledge networks with a different influence on growth (Barge-Gil, 2010; Dahlander and Gann, 2010; Drechsler and Natter, 2012; van Geenhuizen and Ye, 2014).

We measure openness in knowledge networks by using two dimensions, that is, openness size and openness diversity. The networks could be identified on the basis of the interview data from 2006/7 (see section 3). Openness 'size' refers to the external knowledge pool as measured as a variable derived from breadth and depth (Laursen and Salter, 2006) (see Appendix A). Breadth, number of different types of knowledge acquired, and depth, tie strength (strength of the relationship) between the firm and its partners, constitute the knowledge pool that is actually accessed. The mathematical modelling assigns weights to the strength variables, using the entropy-weight method. This measures the effective amount of information of the data and better reflects reality. Further, openness diversity describes the heterogeneity of partners' social background, including spatial orientation (local versus non-local). A distinction is made between partners from large companies and from small ones, government representatives at a high level, university professors, lead customers, family and friends, and so on. As control variables we use the growth ambition of managers at start-up, indicating whether they really intend to grow and push their innovation to a large (international) market thereby bringing a transition closer, or just want to stay small; age of the spin-off at the time of the survey, a greater age indicating increasing potentials for growth derived from accumulated learning in dealing with risks and overcoming the 'liability of newness'; and size of the spin-off at start-up.

Growth is measured as average annual job growth. We follow a stepwise approach in first inserting the control variables and urban location, followed by each of the network variables separately. Among the network variables, we also explore a moderating effect, namely of urban location with network characteristics (Table 7.4). The model power reaches a level of 0.22 (R^2) if only the control variables and urban location are inserted (Model 1), with the coefficients of urban location and growth ambition as significant, indicating a positive influence from being located in Delft, and a positive influence from the ambition to grow. Including only the network variables (Model 2) gives a slightly stronger model power of 0.26 with coefficients that are positive and significant for openness diversity and the moderating effect of urban location and openness diversity.

We may conclude so far that networking makes sense in terms of diversity, as a stronger diversity in network partners tends to enhance growth over the lifetime of the spin-off firms. This particularly holds true for

Table 7.4 A simplified model of employment growth (from start-up to 2010)

	Model 1 ß (standard error)	Model 2 ß (standard error)
Control variables		
Growth ambition	0.82 (0.27)***	
Firm age	−0.08 (0.36)	
Firm size (at start-up)	0.31 (0.26)	
City	1.40 (0.56)**	
Network variables		
Openness size (pool)		0.02 (0.27)
Openness diversity (partners)		1.15 (0.30)***
City x openness diversity		10.19 (3.29)***
N	59	59
F	3.90***	6.54***
R^2	0.22	0.26
Root MSE	2.07	2.00

Note: ** p<0.05; *** p<0.01.

spin-offs in Delft, witness the positive and significant beta coefficient of the interaction effect, overall, indicating that metropolitan areas provide not only a better location for responsible innovation but also a better place for benefits from diverse networking.[1]

5. A MICROSCOPIC LOOK INTO CITIES AND NETWORKS

We make use of six case studies to further explore the assets of the cities and the profile of the networks involved, including spatial scales and

[1] In a recent publication (van Geenhuizen and Ye, 2014), we estimated a growth model using the full sample of spin-off firms (N=105) including responsible innovators and other spin-offs, and using a more strict definition of responsible innovators, namely those engaged in responsible products/processes, full-time/part-time, and being innovative at a high level. Also, growth was measured in a different way, namely as growth in the years following the measurement of the networks (2006–10). This approach revealed a trend of negative influence of openness diversity on growth, which may be understood as also being affected by a time effect, namely the 2008 crisis, causing more danger to spin-off firms with high levels of diversity in their network due to monitoring difficulties and management difficulties. In the current chapter, we wanted to avoid including such time effect, therefore we took growth as growth since start of the spin-offs.

diversity. The data are gained from a mix of sources, including an in-depth interview with one of the managers of the spin-off, company websites, newspaper and branch journal coverage, and so on, allowing for triangulation of results. The main descriptive results are in Appendix B.

In terms of linkage of the firms with the city, case study A and case study E illustrate a metropolitan location but also a (partial) relocation to a city adjacent to the metropolitan area and to a more remote area in the Netherlands. Case study B and case study F illustrate a location in a peripheral area lacking some agglomeration advantages while the firms 'compensated' for this by creating access to a specialized cluster abroad and to the national capital city. Case study C and case study D illustrate various agglomeration advantages of their metropolitan location. Furthermore, in terms of technology, the case studies deal with wind energy, battery charging technology for electric vehicles, thin-film production of solar cells, laser-based imaging technology for eye care and privacy protection solutions for medical software concerning e-medicine and the EPR. With regard to networks of the firms and their diversity, a distinction is made between providing financial capital, collaboration with related firms (co-developers, customers, suppliers) and collaboration with large firms that give access to global markets, thereby identifying contrasts between more diverse and relatively one-sided networks.

Before starting the analysis of local assets and networks, we discuss the responsible innovation of the case studies (van Geenhuizen and Ye, 2014). Case study A is involved in wind energy by elaborating a generic technology, called boundary layer suction, and applying it to the optimal shaping of rotor blades in order to increase the efficiency of wind turbines. It is also involved in reshaping the rotor blades aimed at reduction of noise annoyance caused by the turning of the blades. Accordingly, one of the objections against wind energy, particularly its generation on land, noise annoyance, may be reduced on the basis of the solution developed by this firm. Case study B is also involved in wind energy, by focusing on increasing efficiency, namely by applying a gearless drivetrain in larger turbines and solving the problems of stability of the turbine body of large wind turbines which can be used at sea. Wind farms outside coastal waters are a solution for the 'visual' damaging of coastal landscapes, and thus more acceptable, but their construction and maintenance are more expensive.

Case study C is about a charger (hardware and software) for electric vehicles that shortens the charging time significantly without damaging the battery, and accordingly substantially increases the user value of electric vehicles. The main stakeholders that already benefit from the improvement are various airports. In addition, some municipalities in the Netherlands that intend to improve air quality through emission reduction, perceive electric vehicles as part of a solution. Furthermore, electric vehicles produce less noise compared to conventional vehicles, which is the reason why some companies/municipalities consider using electric vehicles to distribute goods (such as beer to pubs and express delivery services of mail/parcels) and to collect waste in the city during the night, thereby relieving the traffic burden during the day. Case study D – active in a small segment of health care, namely eye care – contributes to making eye care more accurate and cheaper through laser-based retinal imaging, which is also more comfortable for patients. Through the mobile character of the equipment and ease of connecting to laptops, the innovation is a good solution for developing countries which use mobile clinics. In particular, the company provides a better diagnosis of retinal damage from diabetes which is increasing worldwide, and thereby adds to the prevention of blindness. Two of the case study firms did not survive. Case study E, a collaboration with TU Delft, developed a new technology (thin films) to produce solar cells without using silicon which could make the cells much cheaper. And finally, Case study F was active in medical software development for e-consult with family doctors and specialists in hospitals which could be a solution for dealing with large distances (Norway). It was particularly involved in developing privacy protection solutions concerning the EPR.

5.1 Case Study A

This spin-off started with the modelling of aerodynamics and air flow and applied it to the shaping of cars and to windmills' rotor blades. It reduced its activity in wind energy a few years ago, due to the decrease in national support and the absence of a large Dutch company in the Netherlands with which the spin-off could collaborate. Accordingly, the spin-off diversified with a broader application of its technology into other markets, such as construction of buildings and the food processing industry, while remaining active in the optimal shaping of vehicles. This situation of a relatively weaker focus tends to exclude the main contribution of the spin-off to the wind energy technology system. Since its start-up in 2005, the spin-off benefited from the specialized knowledge at TU Delft in the Netherlands, its wind tunnel facility, and facilities to nurture entrepreneurship. It relocated a few years later to a city in the south of the country, in the province of North Brabant, where a location subsidy and (soft) venture capital from public–private organizations could be accessed, which at the time was absent in the province of South Holland where Delft is. The company has remained multi-scalar with regard to its networks, including some European car manufacturing cities, but with an increased accent on cities in the Netherlands and increased one-sidedness in the sense of being mainly a customer/co-developer network.

In terms of the relation with agglomeration advantages, case study A illustrates that city size in itself is important for incubation but less important for nurturing and growth, because a specialization in wind energy was missing in the metropolitan area, as were attractive financial incentives. Overall, it seems that the diversification of the firm into other markets makes progress in sustainability transition in wind energy less realistic.

5.2 Case Study B

This spin-off firm illustrates a consistent focus on wind energy while benefiting from various types of national support in Norway and actively connecting with the main players in the value chain in Denmark's wind energy cluster, through a subsidiary there. In elaborating a gearless drivetrain and a solution for greater stability of the turbine body (for the largest turbines), the firm in past years attracted national government investment and venture capital from consortia, including support from two national test customers, among others Statoil Hydro, and accordingly could take advantage of niche-like conditions. However, this case study also illustrates a path in which a second generation of the new technology (the gearless drivetrain) had to be developed, causing some delay. Job growth of this firm is clearly larger compared to the previous case study.

In terms of smaller agglomeration advantages, case study B missed important partners in the wind turbine value chain in the area, except for a testing site which was close by (Valsnes). Unlike case study A, the spin-off decided to 'compensate' for missing players in the value chain by opening a subsidiary in a relevant cluster abroad. The networks of the spin-off are more diversified in terms of number of functions, namely financing by public and private parties, co-developers and customers (pilot), and access to main producers along the value chain. At the same time, the national enhancement of Trondheim as a prominent science city has made excellent research facilities available in the city, which is rather unusual for remote areas. Overall, one may expect that this company – despite its location outside a metropolitan area – will contribute relatively strongly to progress in wind energy.

5.3 Case Study C

Case study C seems the most successful in sustainability progress as indicated by a quick growth, namely, nine full-time equivalents (ftes) per year in 2006–10. Since 2008 the networks covered various pilots of fast charging stations, dealing with five different partners: a car manufacturer, electricity company, battery manufacturer, public authorities (for pilot testing) and a multinational energy/electrical installation company. The spin-off also benefited from national subsidies in automotive engineering research and (more indirectly) from a favourable taxation on electrical cars making them cheaper for consumers. The company also benefited from venture capital funding from Vancouver (Canada) by a 'respected' partner in the sector, thereby increasing its international credibility and reputation. In 2012, the company – with a total workforce of 80 people – joined its former multinational collaborator, for reasons of accelerating the process of scaling-up the production and achieving complementary assets, mainly concerning entry to global markets. The multinational perceives itself as world leader in charging equipment due to this acquisition.

This case study straightforwardly illustrates agglomeration advantages. These advantages are concerned with the knowledge that was created at TU Delft, the nurturing circumstances created at the incubator in Delft, the ease of networking with electricity companies and of getting involved in pilots in the area, and, finally, the spatial proximity to the site of the multinational (Rotterdam) with which collaboration started. At the same time, the spin-off connected to complementary networks in the region of Eindhoven, adjacent to the metropolitan area, for collaboration in automotive engineering research and mechatronics.

5.4 Case Study D

The fourth case study illustrates a consistent focus on a relatively small part of the medical sector, that is, eye care and within that segment on a specific diagnostic field. What caused some delay is that market introduction had to wait for approval by the US Food and Drugs Administration (FDA), which occurred in 2011. The firm was successful in a first market introduction, immediately after the FDA approval, and its subsequent success can be attributed to its later networks providing access to national and international venture capital (Switzerland) from the medical sector, improving credibility. Also, the collaboration with a market-focused company in Germany, providing complementary assets concerning market entry, has contributed to growth. A more recent round of capital investment allows the firm to accelerate the global 'roll-out' of its innovation, while at the same time it continues research and development (R&D) on other smart and relatively cheap eye-diagnostic instruments, partly in collaboration with Philips in the adjacent south of the Netherlands. Most recently, the firm started to collaborate with a Japanese multinational company (MNC) for joint sales using the latter's channels, first in European countries and then in Asia, thereby adding to the multi-scalar and diversified network of the firm. The spin-off firm is already substantially contributing to a transition in eye care, namely by making eye diagnostic measurement more accurate but also cheaper and, in particular, affordable in developing countries.

Agglomeration advantages can be described as follows. Part of the R&D (prototypes) took place in collaboration with TU Delft and early venture capital came partly from suppliers in the metropolitan area. The spin-off relocated to The Hague, close to Delft, and developed an international orientation with a subsidiary in Boston (for R&D/testing in the region and for sales) in addition to complementary collaboration in the adjacent area in the south of the Netherlands, concerning its second eye care invention. Successful international networks include Switzerland for venture capital, and various international linkages in Germany, the US and, most recently, Japan, for sales. The European head office of the Japanese MNC is in the city-region of Amsterdam.

5.5 Case Study E

This spin-off clearly illustrates loss of focus, in three ways, namely, products, structure and internal organization. Aside from the production process of thin-film solar cells, it became active in touchscreens and related products. It also established a set of related limited liability companies, and it started the pilot activities (a pilot plant) at a site in the north of the country, approximately three hours travel time by car from Delft. At this site a subsidy of 20 per cent was granted for building the pilot plant.

Case study E illustrates agglomeration advantages in the metropolitan area, mainly through the university where the company in its first years benefited from incubation facilities in the faculty laboratory and from the knowledge creation and application there. Research took place, however, also in collaboration with a research centre in North Holland (ECN). There were no specific financial incentives in the metropolitan area, which is the reason why the company was attracted to a region in the north of the country that provided such incentives. From 2009, the company increasingly felt the impact of the economic crises, as well as competition from solar panel manufacturers in China that were able to use the same thin-film technology (weak patent protection); however, at much lower costs. It seems that this firm, although initially promising, could not contribute to major steps in sustainability transition.

5.6 Case Study F

This company has maintained its focus on medical software supporting e-health, for which the initial knowledge was developed at NTNU in Trondheim. It was successful in introducing the e-consulting software to market, but it stagnated at the point of evaluation of the first market uses. At the same time, the firm was involved in contributing to the EPR, but the major disadvantage experienced in Trondheim was the absence of government players and of larger software companies that could better deal with the somewhat conservative culture and actor complexity in the medical sector, the last from the involvement of patients, medical doctors, hospitals, insurance companies, and so on. The networks of this spin-off have remained national, namely dealing with national health players and dealing with larger software firms in similar fields. The awareness of being too small for introducing further inventions to market made the spin-off decide to join its main collaborator in the Oslo region, in 2006, seven years after its foundation.

In terms of available/missing agglomeration advantages, though the firm benefited from the knowledge available at NTNU in Trondheim, it was facing disadvantages from 'isolation' from the main players in the Oslo metropolitan area in the years following incubation.

The results are summarized in Table 7.5, in which we also included those urban assets that enhance speed of bringing the specific responsible innovations to market. Four case studies illustrate the metropolitan area as a site of incubation of the technology solution, but the peripheral city in this study – due to its prominent national science position – acts in the same way. In addition, two case studies illustrate the metropolitan area providing easy access to international venture capital through national network linkages (knowledge spillovers) and to international market access opportunities through the presence of European offices of MNCs, but the same case studies illustrate at the same time strong complementary networking with an adjacent cluster specialized in mechatronics, (medical) instruments and automotive engineering in the Netherlands.

What was missing in the metropolitan area in the Netherlands at the time, however, was a set of specific financial incentives, which were offered in other regions. In addition, the results indicate that remote cities can also contribute to sustainability gains if the firms compensate for what is missing through networks with clusters over larger distances and if they are engaged in a specialization for which natural assets are locally available, such as the windy seashores of empty islands. Overall, we identify five important local urban assets in metropolitan areas of which three seem

Table 7.5 Main lines in the case study analysis outcomes

Four case studies	Metropolitan local assets: • Invention and fostering of entrepreneurship • National government offices[a] • Access to international venture capital[a] • Access to MNCs • Cities' interest in undertaking pilot studies[a]	Reason for relocation to and collaboration in (adjacent) clusters: • Financial incentives • Specialist knowledge in manufacturing • Cities' interest in undertaking pilot studies
Two case studies	Remote city local assets: • Invention and fostering of entrepreneurship (if national policy) • Natural testing sites (windy shorelines)[a]	Reason for relocation to and collaboration in metropolitan area/specialist cluster: • Specialist knowledge in manufacturing • Launching customer (services) • Segments of manufacturing value chains

Note: [a] = more important for responsible innovation.

to be strongly associated with relatively stiff barriers faced in responsible innovation: proximity to national authorities (concerning issues of regulation), easy access to international venture capital (providing credibility to small spin-offs) and the willingness of city authorities to conduct supportive pilot studies, the last, however, are also found outside metropolitan areas.

The results from a *firm* perspective make us tentatively conclude that the chance of market introduction and increase in sustainability tends to be large if the firms maintain a tight product-market focus, adapt their location or networks to be present in major clusters, and connect with partners – locally and globally – covering different essential functions. The last development reflects the positive influence of openness diversity on the growth of the firms since their establishment. Nevertheless, there are two influences that need to be mentioned that originate beyond the city and firms' strategic choice, and these are national support policies for sustainability technologies which may be different between countries (such as wind energy in Norway and the Netherlands) and also between periods, and decrease in demand due to influence from economic crises and price competition from abroad.

6. CONCLUDING REMARKS

This chapter addresses the question as to whether urban location matters in the growth of university spin-off firms involved in responsible innovation, what the key assets of large cities are and which key profiles of firm networks enhance growth and potential moves towards higher levels of acceptance. A database of 59 university spin-off firms was used, representing responsible innovation, which is conceived in this chapter as broader than sustainability innovation, namely including medical care/cure, sustainable energy, sustainable mobility, waste treatment, safety, and so on. A growth model was explored and six case studies were analysed from the perspective of urban agglomeration advantages and network diversity.

The results of the modelling indicated that spin-off firms' growth benefits from a location in a metropolitan area and from openness in networks, the latter mainly through diversity of partners. The preliminary outcomes of the case studies can be summarized as follows. The metropolitan area acts as a site of incubation for inventions and new firms but remote cities may act similarly provided that they have a favoured position in the national university system. The metropolitan area also provides access to international venture capital and market opportunities, the last through the presence of foreign MNCs. In addition, the case studies indicate the lack of presence of all required assets in one and the same metropolitan area; rather there is strong complementary networking of the metropolitan area with an adjacent cluster specialized in mechatronics, (medical) instruments and automotive engineering, allowing both regions to contribute to higher levels of sustainability.

Also, the case study analysis indicates that peripheral cities can equally contribute to sustainability gains if the firms established here compensate what is missing locally through networks with clusters over larger distances and are engaged in a specialization for which unique natural assets are locally available. From a firm and management perspective, we have come to the following preliminary conclusions. The chance of market introduction tends to be large if the firms maintain a tight product-market focus, are present in major clusters, and connect with diverse local and global partners. However, the best conditions specific to responsible innovation seem available in metropolitan areas, due to proximity to national regulatory authorities, easier access to international venture capital – through knowledge spillovers – and a larger willingness among public authorities to conduct pilot studies.

Despite the interesting results, this study is faced with some limitations. As previously indicated, the first lies in the limited approach to responsible innovation because of the currently still weak conceptualization of responsible innovation and from the nature of the database used. The major challenge is to elaborate responsible innovation conceptually and, in empirical research, to picture and characterize activity and interaction of firms with societal actors on their path towards market introduction and increased sustainability. A second limitation originates from the countries where the sample of university spin-off companies was drawn, that is, the Netherlands and Norway, and the limitation of two cities. The results tend to be generalizable to a small number of regions given a similar context under the EU framework and similarity with regional economies oriented towards maritime and energy activity, namely, in Denmark and northern UK (e.g. Scotland). The variety in regional economies and in city size could be increased in future research.

One of the preliminary outcomes is that limited agglomeration advantages in peripheral regions can be compensated for by connecting to specialized clusters. However, particular shortages in metropolitan areas also need to be compensated for by networking with other places. This situation means that the ability of university spin-offs to network is crucial, including searching, negotiation, monitoring and creating benefits from networks or partnerships, while most progress tends to be made through multi-scalar and diversified networks. In our network analysis, working with a small sample, we could not identify optimal levels of networks, beyond which the returns decrease, and how that may change with the age and experience of the firms. The use of social network analysis tools specifically designed to combine with paths to higher levels of sustainability (Hermans et al., 2013) may be helpful in characterizing the networks and identifying optimal networks in future research.

REFERENCES

Audretsch, D.B. (1998) Agglomeration and the Location of Innovative Activity, *Oxford Review of Economic Policy*, Vol. 14, No. 2, pp. 18–29.

Barge-Gil, A. (2010) Open, Semi-Open and Closed Innovators: Towards an Explanation of Degree of Openness, *Industry and Innovation*, Vol. 17, No. 6, pp. 577–607.

Barney, J.B., Clark, D.N. (2007) *Resource-Based Theory: Creating and Sustaining Competitive Advantage*. New York, Oxford University Press.

Brachert, M., Hornych, C., Franz, P. (2013) Regions as Selection Environments? The Emergence of the Solar Industry in Germany from 1992 to 2008, *European Planning Studies* (published online).

Bulkeley, H., Castan-Broto, V., Hodson, M., Marvin, S. (eds) (2010) *Cities and Low Carbon Transitions*. London, Routledge.

Bunnell, T.G., Coe, N.M. (2001) Spaces and Scales of Innovation, *Progress in Human Geography*, Vol. 25, No. 4, pp. 569–589.

Coenen, L., Benneworth, P., Truffer, B. (2012) Toward a Spatial Perspective on Sustainability Transitions, *Research Policy*, Vol. 41, No. 6, pp. 968–979.
Cooke, P. (2009) Transition regions: green innovation and economic development, Druid Summer Conference Copenhagen.
Dahlander, L., Gann, D.M. (2010) How Open is Innovation? *Research Policy*, Vol. 39, No. 6, pp. 699–709.
Deakin, M. (2009) Towards a Community-based Approach to Sustainable Urban Regeneration, *Journal of Urban Technology*, Vol. 16, No.1, pp. 91–112.
De Laurentis, C. (2013) Innovation and Policy for Bioenergy in the UK: A Co-evolutionary Perspective, *Regional Studies*, DOI: 10.1080/00343404.2013.834320, pp. 1–15.
Drechsler, W., Natter, M. (2012) Understanding a Firm's Openness Decisions in Innovation, *Journal of Business Research*, Vol. 65, No. 3, pp. 438–445.
Duranton, G., Puga, D. (2004) The Micro-foundations of Urban Agglomeration Economies, in: Henderson, J.V., Thisse, J.F. (eds). *Handbook of Regional and Urban Economics*, pp. 2063–2117. North-Holland, Elsevier.
Eames, M., Dixon, T., May, T., Hunt, M. (2013) City Futures, Exploring Urban Retrofit and Sustainable Transitions, *Building Research and Information*, Vol. 41, No. 5, pp. 504–516.
EC (European Commission) (2003) Responsible entrepreneurship. A collection of good practice cases among small and medium-sized enterprises across Europe. Brussels: EC Directorate General for Enterprises.
EC (European Commission) (2011) Horizon 2020. The Framework Programme for Research and Innovation. Communication from the Commission. Brussels.
Farla, J., Markard, J., Raven, R., Coenen, L. (2012) Sustainable Transitions in the Making: A Closer Look at Actors, Strategies and Resources, *Technological Forecasting & Social Change*, Vol. 79, pp. 991–998.
Florida, R. (2005) *Cities and the Creative Class*. New York/London, Routledge.
Geels, F.W. (2004) From Sectoral Systems of Innovations to Socio-Technical Systems. Insights about Dynamics and Change from Sociology and Institutional Theory, *Research Policy*, Vol. 33, pp. 897–920.
Geels, F.W., Schot, J. (2007) Typology of Sociotechnical Transition Pathways, *Research Policy*, Vol. 36, pp. 399–417.
Geenhuizen, M. van (2014) Critical Success Factors in Health Innovation in Cities: From Ivory Tower to Living Labs, *International Journal of Global Environmental Issues*, Vol. 13, No. 2–4, pp. 258–280.
Geenhuizen, M. van, Soetanto, D.P. (2009) Academic Spin-Offs at Different Ages: A Case Study in Search of Key Obstacles to Growth, *Technovation*, Vol. 29, No. 10, pp. 671–681.
Geenhuizen, M. van, Nijkamp, P. (eds) (2012) *Creative Knowledge Cities: Myths, Visions and Realities*. Cheltenham, UK and Northampton, MA, USA, Edward Elgar Publishing.
Geenhuizen, M. van, Ye, Q. (2014) Responsible Innovators: Open Networks on the Way to Sustainability Transitions, *Technological Forecasting & Social Change*, Vol. 87, pp. 28–40.
GEM (2010) www.gemconsortium.org/docs/266/gem-2010-global-report.
Goddard, J., Vallance, P. (2013) *The University and the City*. London, Routledge.
Hall, J., Vredenburg, H. (2003) The Challenges of Innovating for Sustainable Development, *MIT Sloan Management Review*, Vol. 45, No. 1, pp. 61–68.

Hansen, T., Coenen, L. (2013) The Geography of Sustainability Transitions: A Literature Review, Lund University, CIRCLE Working Papers 2013/39.

Hermans, F., Apeldoorn, D. van, Stuiver, M., Kok, K. (2013) Niches and Networks: Explaining Network Evolution through Niche Formation Processes, *Research Policy*, Vol. 42, pp. 613–623.

Hodson, M., Marvin, S. (2010) Can Cities Shape Socio-Technical Transitions and How Would We Know If They Were? *Research Policy*, Vol. 39, pp. 477–485.

Hoven, M.J. van den (2013) Value Sensitive Design and Responsible Innovation, in: Owen, R., Bessant, J., Heintz, M. (eds). *Responsible Innovation: Managing the Responsible Emergence of Science and Innovation in Society*, pp. 75–84. New York, Wiley.

Hoven, M.J. van den, Wildschut, E., Bakker, E. (2012) Responsible Innovation at Port Cities, *BDC*, Vol. 12, No. 1, pp. 765–770.

Hoven, J. van den, Jacob, K., Nielsen, L., Roure, F., Rudze, L., Stilgoe, J. (2013) Options for Strengthening Responsible Research and Innovation. Expert Group Report.

Karlsson, C. (ed.) (2008) *Handbook of Research on Innovation and Clusters: Cases and Policies*. Cheltenham, UK and Northampton, MA, USA, Edward Elgar Publishing.

Klitkou, A., Coenen, L. (2013) The Emergence of the Norwegian Solar Photovoltaic Industry in a Regional Perspective, *European Planning Studies*, Vol. 21, No. 11, pp. 1–24.

Laursen, K., Salter, A. (2006) Open for Innovation: The Role of Openness in Explaining Innovation Performance among U.K. Manufacturing Firms, *Strategic Management Journal*, Vol. 27, No. 2, pp. 131–150.

Leydesdorff, L., Etzkowitz, H. (2003) Can 'the Public' be Considered as a Fourth Helix in University-Industry-Government Relations? Report on the Fourth Triple Helix Conference, 2002, *Science and Public Policy*, Vol. 30, No. 1, pp. 55–61.

Martin, R. (2010) Roepke Lecture in Economic Geography – Rethinking Regional Path Dependence: Beyond Lock-in to Evolution, *Economic Geography*, Vol. 86, pp. 1–27.

Mohr, J., Sengupta, S., Slater, S. (2010) *Marketing of High-technology Products and Innovations*. Upper Saddle River, Pearson/Prentice Hall.

Nevens, F., Frantzeskaki, N., Gorissen, L., Loorbach, D. (2013) Urban Transition Labs: Co-Creating Transformative Action for Sustainable Cities, *Journal of Cleaner Production*, Vol. 50, pp. 111–122.

Owen, R., Macnaghten, P., Stilgoe, J. (2012) Responsible Research and Innovation: From Science in Society to Science for Society, with Society, *Science and Public Policy*, Vol. 39, No. 6, pp. 751–760.

ProInno Europe (2011) www.proinno-europe.eu/inno-metrics/page/innovation-union-scoreboard-2011.

Quitzau, M.B, Hoffmann, B., Elle, M. (2012) Local Niche Planning and Its Strategic Implications for Implementation of Energy-Efficient Technology, *Technological Forecasting and Social Change*, Vol. 79, pp. 1049–1058.

Roome, N., Winn, S. (1993) R&D Management Responses to the Environment: Current Theory and the Implications to Practice and Research, *R&D Management*, Vol. 23, No. 2, pp. 147–160.

Sanford, C. (2011) *The Responsible Business: Reimaging Sustainability and Success*. San Francisco, Jossey-Bass.

Safarzynska, K. and Van den Bergh, J.C.J.M (2008) Evolutionary Modelling in Economics: A Survey of Methods and Building Blocks, *Papers on Economics and Evolution*, No. 0806, Philipps University Marburg, Department of Geography.
Schomberg, R. von (2012) www.fondazionebassetti.org (accessed 30 December 2012).
Schot, J., Geels, F.W. (2007) Niches in Evolutionary Theories of Technical Change, *Journal of Evolutionary Economics*, Vol. 17, pp. 605–622.
Shane, S. (2004) Academic Entrepreneurship: University Spin-offs and Wealth Creation, in: Venkataraman, S. (ed.). *New Horizons in Entrepreneurship*. Cheltenham, UK and Northampton, MA, USA, Edward Elgar Publishing.
Smith, A., Raven, R. (2012) What is Protective Space? Reconsidering Niches in Transitions to Sustainability, *Research Policy*, Vol. 41, pp. 1025–1036.
Smith, A., Vos, J.P., Grin, J. (2010) Sustainability Transitions: The Allure of the Multilevel Perspective, and Its Challenges, *Research Policy*, Vol. 39, pp. 435–448.
Statistics Netherlands (2012) www.statline.cbs.nl.
Statistics Norway (2012) www.ssb.no/en.
Stilgoe, J., Owen, R., Macnaghten, P. (2013) Developing a Framework for Responsible Innovation, *Research Policy*, Vol. 42, pp. 1568–1580.
Storper, M. (1997) *The Regional World. Territorial Development in a Global Economy*. New York, The Guilford Press.
Sweet, P., Roome, N., Sweet, S. (2003) Corporate Environmental Management and Sustainable Enterprise: The Influence of Information Processing and Decision Styles, *Business Strategy and the Environment*, Vol. 12, No. 4, pp. 265–277.
Truffer, B., Coenen, L. (2012) Environmental Innovation and Sustainability Transitions in Regional Studies, *Regional Studies*, Vol. 46, pp. 1–21.
Vohora, A., Wright, M., Lockett, A. (2004) Critical Junctures in the Development of University High-Tech Spin-Out Companies, *Research Policy*, Vol. 33, No. 1, pp. 147–175.

APPENDIX A

The value of openness size was calculated as:

$$Size = \sum_{i=1}^{n} (B_i \times D_i) \tag{7.1}$$

where n is the number of types of external knowledge, such as market, technology, and so on. The breadth B_i is the number of partners within a type of knowledge. There are B_i partners within the knowledge content i, each has a 'depth' as $d_j (j = 1 \ldots N)$, which is a composite variable derived from frequency of interaction (r), duration of relationship (u), and the entrepreneurs' assessment of closeness of the relationship (c, M-rank categorical variable) calculated as:

$$\begin{cases} r_j = r \times l \\ u_j = \ln(u + 1) \\ c_j = \dfrac{c}{M} \end{cases} \tag{7.2}$$

where r_j, u_j and c_j are the frequency of interaction, duration of relationship and the entrepreneurs' assessment of closeness of the relationship to the partner, j. $r \times l$ can be seen as 'frequency-distance product', which is intended to eliminate the distance as a factor of frequency of interaction. These variables will be further normalized (for each variable, min: 0; max: 1). Next, a weighting method is used derived from thermodynamic theories. Entropy is a measure of the degree of disorder, uncertainty or randomness of a probabilistic system, while information entropy can also measure the effective amount of information in the data. If there are m criterions and n objects which need to be evaluated, the entropy of the ith criterion is defined as Hi:

$$H_i = -k \sum_{j=1}^{n} f_{ij} \ln(f_{ij}) \; (i = 1,2,\ldots,m) \tag{7.3}$$

where $f_{ij} = \frac{r_{ij}}{\sum_{j=1}^{n} r_{ij}}$, and $k = \frac{1}{\ln(n)}$. And we assume that when $f_{ij} = 0$, $f_{ij} \ln(f_{ij}) = 0$.

Basically, the larger the entropy H_i, the less information it is possible to provide. For instance, if most of the partners are judged as very close to the entrepreneurs, the assessment of closeness (r) would not be an efficient indicator for the tie strength, since it cannot provide enough information or distinction to differentiate various strengths of tie. Therefore, the entropy weight of the ith criterion can be calculated by:

$$w_i = (1 - H_i) / \left(m - \sum_{i=1}^{m} H_i \right) \tag{7.4}$$

The entropy weights for the three indicators of tie strength can now be calculated, as $w_u = 0.30$, $w_r = 0.38$, $w_c = 0.32$. And the formula for the tie strength is as follows:

$$D_j = w_u u_j^* + w_r r_j^* + w_c c_j^* \quad (7.5)$$

where for D_j, a higher value indicates a relatively tighter relationship, thus a greater 'depth' (min: 0; max: 1).

Openness diversity describes the heterogeneity of the partners' socio-economic backgrounds, including spatial orientation. The knowledge partner diversity is calculated as:

$$Der = \left(1 + \frac{El}{2}\right) \times Hs \quad (7.6)$$

where $Hs = 1 - \sum_{k=1}^{8} (\frac{a_k}{N})^2$, and (7.7)

where a_k is the number of partners with a different social background, $k = 1$(*large or medium business*), 2(*government*), 3(*university*), 4(*small business*), 5(*family/friends*), 6(*venture capitalists*), 7(*lead customers*), 8(*others*).

N is the total number of partners a firm interacts with, with a higher value indicating a higher level of social background difference (min: 0; max: 1). Further, *EI* is calculated as

$$EI = \frac{E_p - I_p}{E_p + I_p} \quad (7.8)$$

where E_p is the number of external, non-local, partners, reached within a one hour car drive, and I_p is the number of local partners ($E_p + I_p = N$). A high value indicates a relatively strong external orientation (min: −1; max: 1).

APPENDIX B CITIES AND NETWORKS OF CASE STUDIES A TO F

Company, city and network pattern	Localized assets and function of networks
Spin-off A (2005) Air flow dynamics (wind energy) (annual growth of 1.3 fte in 2006–10)	
Cities: Delft followed by Breda (NL)	• TU Delft: Technology, wind tunnel facility and strong entrepreneurship building (particularly at Faculty of Aerospace) • Breda: North-Brabant (Province) provides location incentives (subsidy) and 'soft' venture capital
Early network: Modena (Italy), Ingolstadt (Germany) and Utrecht (NL) Current network: various additional cities in the Netherlands, and Brussels 'Multi-scalar'	• Car industry as customer/co-developer and rail industry as customer/co-developer • Additional: Different industries, e.g. food process industry, construction sector, as customers/co-developer 'Relatively poor networks (functionality)'
Spin-off B (2006) Turbine technology (wind energy) (annual growth of 3.8 fte in 2006–10)	
Cities: Trondheim and Valsnes (Norway,) with second site in Silkeborg (Denmark), and representation office in Hong Kong (China)	• NTNU: Technology, wind tunnel facility, and testing space in Valsnes; collaboration with university of Bath (UK) • Silkeborg: Access to value chain in wind turbine cluster • Hong Kong: Access to Chinese suppliers and customers
Network: Focus, including Trondheim, Stavanger and Oslo (partially 'within' company network) 'National, but increasingly multi-scalar'	• Venture capital, partly from government, oil industry, and environmental funds • Governmental organization and oil company as (test) customer (pilots) • Various value chain producers 'Diversified network'
Spin-off C (2005) Battery charging technology (growth of 9.0 fte in 2006–10)	

Company, city and network pattern	Localized assets and function of networks
Cities: Delft (NL) with second site in Eindhoven (NL)	• TU Delft: Technology and important incubation facility • Eindhoven in adjacent cluster as 'the place to be', with access to mechatronics/automotive engineering cluster
Early network: consumer electronics Later: various larger, international cities, such as Amsterdam and Rotterdam (NL), Vancouver (Canada), Zurich (Switzerland), and Taipei (Taiwan), and various smaller cities in the Netherlands, such as Leeuwarden and Den Bosch 'Multi-scalar'	• Venture capital, mainly from the sector, abroad • Pilot of public charging stations in various cities, mainly Rotterdam and Leeuwarden (a protective niche), also supported by energy companies and launching customer • Joined Swiss MNC to access manufacturing of hardware and customer markets abroad (complementary assets) 'Diversified network'
Spin-off D (2006) Laser – based retinal imaging technology (growth of 7.5 fte in 2006–10)	
Cities: Delft followed by The Hague (NL) and Boston (US)	• TU Delft: Technology; The Hague for a spacious place • Later: Subsidiary in Boston (US) for part of the scientific network (hospitals) and sales organization
Early network: national and international Later network: Zug (Switzerland), Uitgeest and Venlo (NL), Essen (Germany), Boston area (US), Eindhoven (NL) 'Multi-scalar'	• Early stage: Grants (from US) • Venture capital, national and sector abroad (Switzerland) • Suppliers (mainly hardware) • Research collaboration with Dutch MNC in adjacent cluster • Sales organization in Germany and US • Most recently: Sales collaboration with Japanese MNC 'Diversified network'
Spin-off E (1999) Thin-film technology –photovoltaic (bankruptcy in 2011)	
Cities: Delft (Bleiswijk) and later on partial relocation to Leeuwarden (NL) for pilot plant construction	• TU Delft: Technology, incubation within the faculty, followed by a small R&D factory close to Delft; Leeuwarden:

Company, city and network pattern	Localized assets and function of networks
	Province of Friesland (NOM) provides 20% of construction costs of pilot plant
Network: Petten (North Holland),The Hague, Rotterdam, Leeuwarden (NL), Langen (Germany)	• Early network: Collaboration with energy research centre in North Holland (ECN) • Ministry of Economic Affairs (subsidy), investment fund • Sales partner (SolarTotal)
'Somewhat international'	• Province of Friesland, city of Leeuwarden (NOM) (pilot plant) • Germany (Langen): Agreement on marketing touchscreen 'Diversified network due to focus on touchscreens'
Spin-off F (1999) Medical (e-health) software (integrated in larger firm in 2007)	
Cities: Trondheim	• NTNU: Technology; collaboration with Tromsø University Institute of Telemedicine
Network: Tromsø, Oslo	• Oslo: Launching customer (software firm) and national decisionmaking units in medical sector
'National'	• Joined this larger software firm in Oslo to better access markets 'Relatively poor networks (functionality)'

8. Innovation capacity, workforce diversity and intra-industrial externalities: a study of German establishments*

Stephan Brunow and Valentina Miersch

1. INTRODUCTION

Knowledge-based economies focusing on production and services need to be innovative in the long-run in order to secure long-term welfare. In a global world where countries compete to create and produce the latest market-leading products, the innovation capacity of a country's domestic industry is of particular importance. There are various types of innovation, namely the introduction of products new to the market, the improvement of the quality of existing products or the adoption of new technologies (Grossman and Helpman, 1991). In order to remain competitive in the long-run it seems beneficial to consider all of these areas. However, innovation is costly and there is uncertainty regarding its success. According to existing literature, workforce diversity with respect to age, cultural background, human capital and occupations may improve the innovative capacity of an establishment (Van der Vegt and Janssen, 2003, Ozgen et al., 2011a, Østergaard et al., 2011, Brunow and Stockinger, 2013). Then fewer resources are required to achieve more innovation. In this chapter we investigate in particular what kinds of establishments are relatively more innovative and undertake more than one type of innovation. For this purpose an ordered logit model is estimated using German survey and administrative data. We consider establishment characteristics, the diversity of the workforce employed and possible regional spillover effects within industries as a proxy for regional innovation systems (Griliches, 1979, Camagni and Capello, 2013). In addition, industry- and region-specific effects are taken into account. We provide evidence that

* This research is part of the 'Migrant Diversity and Regional Disparities in Europe' research project (MIDI-REDIE). Financial support by NORFACE is gratefully acknowledged.

(i) workforce diversity matters, (ii) spillover effects are present, (iii) the probability of innovating does not depend on the location and (iv) the marginal effects are strongest for performing two types of innovation, which means that establishments tend to spread their innovation capacity across various innovation types.

The chapter is structured as follows. Section 2 provides a theoretical outline of innovation processes and considers relevant variables from a theoretical perspective. Section 3 reviews related empirical work. In Section 4 the data basis and the variables included are introduced, while in Section 5 the estimation issues are discussed and the results presented and interpreted. Finally, Section 6 concludes.

2. THEORETICAL BACKGROUND

Theoretical and empirical literature on innovation has been well examined, as innovation is seen as an important driver of economic growth. Individuals' or firms' motives for becoming innovative can be related to various theories. From an individual perspective, the creation of a new product or service may enable a person to become self-employed and to secure their income in the future. It may also provide an opportunity to leave unemployment. More frequently, however, innovation is explained from a firm perspective. Starting with the theory of Schumpeter's 'creative destruction', innovation is both a result and a key driver of the profit-seeking behavior of individual firms. Firms compete in a market and the firm that offers the newest product, or the one of the best quality, will enjoy relatively higher profits. Being the market leader demands product innovation and especially improvement. Another motive for firms to be innovative is also based on profit-seeking: namely entry into new markets. Offering products that are new to the market provides firms with the opportunity of a monopoly rent, which can be seen as an additional premium over marginal costs, at least in the short-run and possibly also in the long-run. The theoretical models typically relate to a horizontal product market with an expanding variety of products (Romer, 1990). In the light of profit-seeking and long-run firm success, Teece et al. (1997) argue that a firm's capability and especially the within-firm specific dynamic knowledge creation process is a requisite for such success.

Both of these reasons for firms seeking to innovate are likely to require more intensive research and development (R&D). A third strategy aimed at boosting profits and improving the firm's own product is the adoption of other technologies. This may involve imitating competitors' products or may be the introduction of technologies from firms in 'unrelated' sectors. All the concepts are discussed in the theoretical literature (see e.g. Grossman and Helpman, 1991) and research or innovative activities are typically assumed to be relevant. Thus, innovation inputs can be linked to innovation outcomes, as suggested by Griliches (1979). Griliches develops the concept of the knowledge production function. In this function, typically human-capital-related inputs H_i of the ith research unit as well as factors external to the research unit X_i are introduced, as shown in equation (8.1):

$$Q_i = AH_i^{\alpha}K_i^{\beta}X_i^{\gamma} \tag{8.1}$$

In this equation Q_i relates to the innovative outcome and A relates to overall labor productivity of the research unit. All other inputs K_i describe other factors relevant to the knowledge production process. The positive parameters α, β and γ do not necessarily add up to 1, such that increasing or diminishing returns are theoretically possible.

The external factors X_i are intended to control for possible spillover effects because some parts of 'innovative capital' and knowledge, which are external to the firm, are observable and therefore have characteristics of a public good. These external factors make innovation less costly because relatively less H_i and K_i is needed to produce the same amount, Q_i. Being located in an innovative environment then reduces the overall cost of innovation, which ultimately makes innovation more likely. In such a regional innovation system (Asheim et al., 2011, Capello, 2014) various theories serve as explanations for an innovative milieu: it is closely linked to evolutionary economics (Nelson and Winter, 2009), institutional economics (Nelson, 1993), new regional economics (Storper, 1993) learning economics (Foray and Lundvall, 1996), and network theory (Håkansson, 1987). Camagni and Capello (2013) show how complex such a regional innovation system is. They put particular emphasis on the regional network and innovation patterns and the necessity of smart policies for a sustainable innovation region. However, the external factors are limited with some respect: not every firm necessarily gains from this possible positive externality. This is the case when the firm's absorptive capacity (Cohen and Levinthal, 1990, Zahra and George, 2002) does not allow the evaluation of the value of new, external resources.

From the knowledge production function it becomes obvious that cost of innovation depends on wages for H_i and the cost of the other inputs, K_i. In accordance with the knowledge production function, applied studies, as introduced in the following section, use conventional R&D inputs as explanatory variables, such as the stock or proportion of university graduates in the workforce but also information on the cost of innovation such as wages or R&D expenditures. These variables serve to explain the innovation outcome, Q_i, measured by the number of patents or the overall likelihood of being innovative.

We have so far introduced motives for being innovative and factors that might be relevant for innovative activities. We now turn to the decision to become innovative: On the one hand innovation may lead to future profits; on the other hand innovation is costly and the probability of success might be small. Especially the uncertainty of the innovative success makes companies less likely to be innovative when the company is rather risk-averse which might particularly be the case for sole traders and partnership companies. Becoming innovative therefore depends on balancing the expected profits and the expected costs. Theoretical literature, such as Grossman and Helpman (1991) or Baldwin (1999), frequently relates this trade-off to the concept of Tobin's Q (Tobin, 1969): If the expected discounted profit exceeds the costs of innovation, innovation is performed. Thus, for a given cost, which can be expressed by means of the knowledge-production function, the higher the expected profit, the greater the likelihood of being innovative. From an empirical point of view the unobservable future profit is not available. However, the theoretical results obtained in a general equilibrium setting offer some insights: the expected discounted profit may be expressed in terms of the current profit and parameters that influence the discounting of future profits. These are the depreciation rate, the (long-run) interest rate on capital and possibly the growth rates of the capital or knowledge stock (see e.g. Baldwin and Forslid, 1997, Baldwin, 1999, Baldwin et al., 2001). Thus, in an empirical assessment current profit might be a weak but valid proxy for expected future profits.

The theoretical outline provides important and relevant variables for explaining innovation in general. According to the knowledge production function, human capital variables, productivity and cost-related variables as well as variables describing the regional environment should be included in a regression. Profit-related measures control for the likelihood of becoming innovative and therefore also for the trade-off between costs and profits as stated by Tobin's Q.

3. LITERATURE REVIEW

The theoretical section highlights variables relevant to innovation processes. In the following literature review we consider mainly empirical work on the coherence between innovation, productivity and spillover effects from a higher level of aggregation, such as the region. Among others, Cameron (1996) supports the theoretical literature and shows that innovation raises growth and productivity. Cainelli et al. (2006) observed that investment in information and communication technologies (ICT) in particular has an impact on growth and productivity. The study by Koellinger (2008) examines the relationship between innovation in internet-based technologies and firm performance. The results show that all types of innovation, such as internet-enabled and non-internet-enabled product or process innovation, have a positive effect on turnover and employment growth. Crépon et al. (1998) provide evidence of a positive relationship between firm productivity and innovation output, even when keeping both the skill composition of labor and physical capital intensity constant. Thus, more productive firms tend to be more innovative.

In a cross-country comparison of France, Germany, Spain and the UK, Griffith et al. (2006) analyze the impact of innovation on productivity and obtain mixed results with respect to different types of innovation. For most countries, product innovation yields productivity gains.

Cassiman et al. (2010) state that a positive effect of exports on productivity found in the empirical studies is linked to firms' innovation decisions. Their analyses for Spanish manufacturing firms provide strong evidence that product innovation raises firms' productivity significantly, but process innovation does not, and, as a consequence of product innovation, small firms without export activities become more likely to enter the export market. This line of argumentation is in line with the theoretical explanation of the Melitz (2003) model. For German companies operating in the service sector, however, Ebling and Janz (1999) provide evidence that export activities do not intensify innovation.

As suggested by the knowledge-production function theory, further studies demonstrate that firm innovation is positively influenced by R&D activities (Acs et al., 1994, Thornhill 2006, Hall et al., 2009). The study conducted by Hall et al. (2009) for Italy shows that R&D intensity, firm size and investment in equipment raise the probability of performing process and product innovation. Although both types of innovation are positively related to firms' productivity, they find that process innovation has a greater effect.

Simmie et al. (2002) analyze the relationship between the function of a city/region and innovation behavior. They find that in 'regional cities', such as Stuttgart or Milan, innovations are more closely linked to their regional and national economies than they are in 'global cities' such as Paris and London. This is related to knowledge spillovers in space and regional clusters. In regions where firms are more closely connected to the local economy, innovation boosts local productivity. On the other hand, innovations affect more than the local economy when firms are integrated in global markets and are located in 'global cities'. Other empirical work conducted by Duranton and Puga (2001) and Feldman and Audretsch (1999) takes into account the role of diversity and city size on innovation. They find that larger, more diverse cities and regions are typically more innovative, which is in line with the evidence of Simmie et al. (2002). In addition, Feldman and Audretsch (1999) find that the degree of local competition fosters innovative activity more than a local monopoly does. Duranton and Puga (2001) and de Groot et al. (2007) show at the regional level that regional growth measured by means of innovative outcomes is higher when the local economy gains from agglomeration effects and especially local diversity (urbanization effects, Jacobs externalities). The work of Basile et al. (2012) analyzes regional knowledge spillovers on productivity growth and they find a significant influence of relational, social and technological proximity.

From a regional European perspective, Ozgen et al. (2011a) consider patent applications as innovative outcomes and find significant effects of the regional economic environment, supporting Griliches' (1979) theory of knowledge-production. Pfirrmann (1994) focuses on regional innovation disparities in former West Germany while analyzing small and medium-sized firms: firm-specific factors have a greater effect on innovation efforts than factors associated with the regional environment. This evidence corresponds with that obtained by Sternberg and Arndt (2001), who examine small and medium-sized European firms and find that firm-level factors have a greater effect on the level of innovation activity than region-specific and external factors. The effect of the regional environment variables on firms' incentives to be more innovative, however, supports the theory, launched by Griliches (1979), that knowledge/human capital spillover is a driving force of long-run economic growth (e.g. Romer, 1990). Capello and Lenzi (2014) provide empirical evidence of the importance of scientific knowledge available in the region on local scientific knowledge-creation processes. This, however, is context related and depends on the regional innovation pattern.

The study by Almeida and Kogut (1997) uses patent data to examine the innovative ability of small firms in the semiconductor industry by focusing on their technological diversity and their integration within local knowledge networks. By comparing the innovation activity of start-ups and larger firms it is shown that small firms innovate in less 'crowded' areas when exploring new technological fields. They also observe that small firms have a stronger link to regional knowledge networks than large firms. Thus, the number of firms in a location may serve as an explanatory variable to capture network activities of cooperating firms. Related to this, the study by Baptista and Swann (1998) analyzes the effect of industrial regions on firms' innovation activities for the UK. By observing 248 manufacturing firms during the period from 1975 to 1982, they show that rising employment in a firm's own sector and region leads to an increase in the firm's own innovation activities. Regarding firm size, Blundell et al. (1999) show that larger firms tend to be more innovative than smaller competitors not just because of size effects but also simply because they may lose relatively more when they are not innovative.

The study conducted by Thornhill (2006) demonstrates that firm performance is affected by firm knowledge, industry dynamism and innovation. More specifically, while highly skilled labor is most profitable for a company's performance in dynamic environments, stable production industries profit more from investments in training. Zucker et al. (1998) show for the USA that the presence and availability of intellectual human capital, measured as 'star' bio-technology scientists, is the reason for newly founded firms in the field of bio-technology in the particular region. This study concludes that localized intellectual human capital plays a key role in the development of the bio-tech industry. Therefore, industry-specific knowledge and its availability lead, first, to innovation which, in a second stage, leads to regional industrial development and firm formation. There are also sector-specific differences: by comparing cost functions and investment levels in the R&D of public and private firms, Nett (1994) finds that private firms are more innovative than public ones. Frenkel et al. (2001) compare Israeli and German industrial firms by analyzing firm characteristics, location and regional innovation. They conclude that firms in high-tech industries are significantly more innovative than those in traditional sectors.

The literature review reveals, first, that industry- and region-specific effects have to be considered and, second, that most of the factors discussed in the theoretical literature have been tested empirically and show the expected signs. A third finding is that there are interdependencies between innovation, productivity and export behavior, which leads to endogeneity concerns. Thus, it is possible to show correlation but not causal effects – a restriction which also exists in this study.

4. DESCRIPTION OF DATA AND VARIABLES

4.1 Data Sources

In the empirical analysis we use German survey data from the IAB Establishment Panel. We link this data basis with a special sample drawn from the IAB Employment History, which was aggregated to the establishment level. This data source is based on administrative data covering the entire population of all employees subject to social security. The self-employed and civil servants cannot therefore be observed. Despite this limitation, the data are highly reliable as they are used for calculating contributions to unemployment insurance. Because the IAB Employment History contains data on the entire population in employment subject to social security, we are able to compute additional measures at the regional level (NUTS 3) and at the industrial level (2-digit, NACE Rev. 1.1). The administrative data is collected at establishment level and not firm level. A firm might operate at one or more establishments. We can only observe individual establishments and we cannot identify establishments belonging to the same firm. This limitation is due to data regulations and we have to accept it. However, it is the only existing data source for Germany that permits this kind of research.

Data on establishment characteristics are taken from the IAB Establishment Panel, which is not recorded on the basis of the social security system. Data on the workforce employed is taken from the IAB Employment History.

4.2 Dependent Variable

Our explanatory variable is derived from survey data for the years 1998, 2001, 2004, and from 2007 until 2010. Establishments were asked whether they had performed innovation activities in the previous year by introducing new products or improving existing products, or whether they had adopted new technologies. In this chapter we do not focus on each binary outcome on its own and ask which variables are relevant for one of the innovation types. Instead, we investigate which establishments are more likely to perform various types of innovation. From the binary outcomes we construct our dependent variable: it is the number of innovation activities at the establishment as a measure of the establishment's innovative capacity within one survey year. It therefore takes values ranging from 0 to 3. Several authors argue that the combination of innovation and imitation yields technological improvements (Benhabib and Spiegel, 1994, Acemoglu et al., 2003, 2006, Vandenbussche et al., 2006). In the light of our dependent variable it would mean that being active in more than one innovative field may improve the overall competitiveness of the establishment and therefore secures long-run entrepreneurial success. In a first step we limit our investigation by not attempting to distinguish between the resulting combinations of innovation types. However, our dependent variable is also limited as it treats all types of innovation equally. Especially the market value of a product introduction will be different from the market value of a product adoption. Thus, the quality–quantity trade-off of various innovation types is not controlled for.

Table 8.1 *Distribution of innovation activities in establishments (percentage)*

	No innovation	Innovation in one area	Innovation in two areas	Innovation in three areas
1998	49.37	25.12	19.91	5.59
2001	53.40	23.56	17.93	5.11
2004	57.93	24.06	14.65	3.36
2007	47.87	23.26	20.66	8.21
2008	51.81	25.81	16.88	5.49
2009	49.38	26.09	18.43	6.10
2010	52.56	24.99	16.81	5.64
Average	51.91	24.66	17.77	5.65
No. obs.*	24,677	11,701	8,273	2,479

Note: * The number of cases varies slightly between models as a result of missing data.

Other types of innovation outcomes have been discussed and applied in the literature (Kleinknecht et al., 2002, Acs et al., 2002). Patent applications may serve as a better proxy but this data cannot be uniquely linked to the establishments and is therefore not available for our investigation. Also, some patents might have a strategic component and have no market value at all. Expenditures on innovation or market shares by imitative and by innovative products are not surveyed and therefore are unavailable. Other measures of innovation outcomes as collected for instance by the Community Innovation Survey (CIS) cannot be linked to the IAB establishments for data security reasons. We therefore stick to our measure of innovation capacity and take its limitations into account.

Table 8.1 shows the distribution of the innovative capacity of individual establishments. It can be seen that on average more than 51 percent of all firms did not innovate at all. About 25 percent of all establishments innovate in one of the three areas, about 17 percent invest in two innovation types and, finally, less than 6 percent on average perform all three types of innovation. Thus, only a small proportion of establishments decide to build up a strong innovation capacity within one year. The distribution of innovation activities is also very constant over time.

The last row reports the number of observations to be used in the model which we consider in the empirical section in more detail. It represents the minimum number of observations. The reported distribution of probabilities remains largely the same if the entire sample is considered.

4.3 Establishment Characteristics as Explanatory Variables

Innovation capacity is explained by various variables. From the IAB Establishment Panel we use information about the legal form of the establishment (Lee and Rodríguez-Pose, 2013). Two dummy indicators are set to 1 if the establishment is a sole trader or a private partnership company. The reference category therefore relates to establishments which are limited companies. Because innovation involves a degree of uncertainty and is therefore risky, sole traders and private partnerships are less likely to be innovative. In both of these cases establishment success is directly related to the owner's income, so risk aversion is higher. Another dummy indicator is set to unity if the establishment has a foreign owner (Castellani and Zanfei, 2003). Foreign owners might have an interest in long-run company success with higher dividend payments. The establishments have to be relatively more innovative in order to secure this success. Thus, one might expect a positive estimate in the empirical assessment. This is supported by Love et al. (1996), Love and Ashcroft (1999) and Michie and Sheehan (2003). Other empirical research shows no significant effect (Bishop and Wiseman, 1999, De Propris, 2000). Finally, some studies observe a negative effect (Love and Roper, 1999, Martínez-Ros, 1999). Table 8.2 provides a descriptive overview of the innovative outcome and establishments' legal form characteristics. As can be seen, about one third of all establishments are sole traders of which two thirds perform no innovative activities. Partnership companies are seldom included in the sample but have a

Table 8.2 Innovation activities and legal status of establishments

			Innovation activities within legal form			
Legal status	No. of cases	No. of cases (%)	No innovation (%)	Innovation in one area (%)	Innovation in two areas (%)	Innovation in three areas (%)
Sole trader	23,617	32.96	66.99	18.60	11.57	2.84
Partnership company	4,921	6.87	56.05	22.94	15.85	5.16
Capital limited company	43,119	60.17	43.74	28.00	21.16	7.11
Foreign ownership						
No	67,888	94.74	53.5	23.99	17.18	5.33
Yes	3,769	5.26	29.74	34.65	25.76	9.84

higher propensity towards innovation. About 60 percent of all establishments are capital limited companies and are typically more innovative by means of this descriptive picture. More than 55 percent of all those companies do innovate and about half of the innovative companies innovate in at least two different fields. Although foreign ownership is seldom – only 5.3 percent of all establishments belong to that group – two thirds of these are innovative in at least one field.

The technical state of the machinery in the production process provides a proxy for productivity. As suggested in the existing work, a higher level of productivity is associated with a higher probability of becoming innovative. A positive effect of the technical state of machinery is shown by Hall et al. (2009) and Bellmann et al. (2013). Because the information about the technical state of the machinery is categorized, we introduce a set of dummy variables that relate to each category; these are: new technology, moderate technology and old technology. The reference group is the newest, state-of-the-art technology.

We also control for the age of the establishments. Sørensen and Stuart (2000) provide evidence that older firms are more successful in the market with their innovation as they are more experienced. On the other hand, older firms might act in their traditional or 'old-fashioned' way and are therefore less innovative or less successful in innovative processes (Freel, 2003). Thus, variables controlling for establishment age can offer any sign, depending on the strength of the contrary effects, as it captures a net effect. There are several concerns regarding an age measure which relates, for example, to the number of years that the establishment has existed. First, the administrative data has been recorded since 1975. There is no information available on West German establishment foundation before 1975. Therefore, the establishment age will be biased for all companies that already existed in 1975. Whereas this might be a relatively small bias, there is a similar problem with regard to establishments located in eastern Germany. There, the earliest data recorded relate to 1991. Some establishments already existed before that year, so the bias in the establishment age becomes more serious. We therefore introduce two dummy indicators, one for an establishment age between five and 14 years and a second one for establishments that have been observed for at least 15 years. The reference category is an establishment age of less than five years. Because our data set starts in 1998, the reference group contains only eastern German establishments that were founded after 1993, when the 'dust of reunification' had partly settled. Those establishments that already existed before the administrative data were collected are therefore included in the second group with an establishment age of 5–14 years, irrespective of whether they may be older. However, it is fair to argue that the change in the organizational structure and the political system in establishments founded in East Germany prior to reunification were strong enough for the restructured establishment to be regarded as a new firm, irrespective of its 'true' age.

In accordance with the theoretical considerations we use the logarithm of the establishment's revenues as a proxy for expected returns and the current ability to invest in innovation. It also serves as a proxy for establishment size. In the literature review it was argued that greater productivity is related to higher exports and that firms have to innovate in order to be competitive in export markets in the long-run. We employ export as a proportion of total sales as another control for such an increase in productivity. The logarithm of the average daily wage paid to workers controls for the cost component. Although wages are assumed to mirror productivity, we expect a negative sign. Consider two 'identical' establishments, which are located in the same region and operate in the same industry and, most importantly, achieve the same level of revenues but pay different wages. Then the establishment which pays higher wages is expected to have higher costs and, therefore, the probability of innovation should be smaller. If, however, the estimates are positive, then it is likely that wages capture unobserved and uncontrolled productivity differences. The work by Van Reenen (1996) and Pianta and Tancioni (2008) considers wages in the light of innovation and demonstrates a significant impact that depends on which sector innovates and who is the innovator (i.e. the company under observation or its competitors). Wages increase in firms that perform innovation activity, but they fall if competing firms innovate. Thus innovation activities affect wages in a way that raises concerns regarding reverse causality. We therefore have to accept the limitation and cannot report causal effects but provide evidence of a correlation when wages have a significant effect on innovation behavior.

4.4 Workforce Diversity

From individual observations from the IAB Employment History we compute the following variables. Human capital as a proportion of the total workforce provides a frequently used variable to describe the capacity of the workforce to be innovative. Our measures of human capital follow an advanced approach that takes into account both characteristics of the occupation and formal qualifications. On the basis of a cluster analysis, occupations are classified into low-skilled or high-skilled depending on the average time spent on routine and non-routine work, the average time spent on manual and analytical work and, third, on the proportion of people holding a university degree within this occupation. The classification on the basis of tasks also takes into consideration under- and over-qualification, which has been shown to exist in the German labor market (Brunow and Hirte, 2009). This is described in detail in Trax et al. (2012). The present study differs from the approach used by Trax et al. (2012): we manually reclassify three occupational groups as low-skilled. These are post office workers, clerks and salespersons. The interpretation of high-skilled depends on occupations and formal qualifications. High-skilled occupations are those with a large amount of non-routine and analytical work and a large proportion of graduates.

Despite the measures already introduced of workforce diversity with respect to education and tasks, other studies also consider diversity with respect to age, gender and ethnicity, which we partly consider as well (Zajac et al., 1991, Watson et al., 1993, Drach-Zahavy and Somech, 2001, Van der Vegt and Janssen, 2003, Laursen et al., 2005, Østergaard et al., 2009). Whenever it was possible, we considered diversity measures separated by the two groups of low- and high-skilled workers to take the 'quality differential' between both groups on innovative processes into account.

The work by Ottaviano and Peri (2005) highlights the importance of cultural diversity for production and consumption. The hypothesis is that the presence of many cultures in a region increases, for example, the availability of different skills, country-specific knowledge, various ways of solving problems or, from a consumption point of view, the range of culture-specific products and services (see also Nathan and Lee, 2011). Cultural diversity leads to higher levels of innovation when different cultures interact and combine their culture-specific skills, and knowledge and problem-solving abilities, thereby increasing efficiency (Osborne, 2000, Drach-Zahavy and Somech, 2001, Hong and Page, 2001, 2004, Fujita and Weber, 2003, Page, 2007, Berliant and Fujita, 2008, Niebuhr, 2010, Ozgen et al., 2011b, Parrotta et al., 2012). However, there can be negative effects as well: language barriers hamper communication and cultural conflicts may also lead to efficiency losses (Zajac et al., 1991, Williams and O'Reilly, 1998). The net effect can therefore be positive or negative. Because innovation is more likely to be related to human capital, we distinguish between low-skilled and high-skilled when controlling for cultural diversity. In existing literature on cultural diversity the effect is frequently split into two parts: the 'baseline' effect controls for the general presence of foreigners. To this end we include the proportion of foreigners, split into skill groups. The second part considers the distribution of the foreigners employed. We use the fractionalization index for this purpose:

$$Frac = 1 - \sum_{i}^{I} s_i^2, \tag{8.2}$$

where s_i is the proportion that the *i*th cultural group constitutes out of *I* cultural groups employed. This measure is zero if all foreigners belong to the same cultural group and reaches its maximum when all the cultural groups employed are similarly distributed. We again split the measures into the two skill groups. When cultural diversity might be related to different skills and abilities, it is worth separating the effect of the specific knowledge required in distinct jobs from the cultural diversity measures.

We use the occupation data as a proxy for job diversity and construct fractionalization measures on occupational diversity within the low- and high-skilled groups. Although the definitions of the low- and high-skilled groups are based on occupations, the classification does not rely on occupational diversity. Thus, occupational diversity focuses on the distribution of occupations performed within each skill group. If there is a large range of occupations, more specific knowledge from various fields and disciplines is available to the establishment and this could raise the capacity for innovation. On the other hand, if the diversity of occupations is larger, then there might be a smaller focus in the production and, especially, the innovation process. Then occupational diversity might be 'bad'.

Another form of workforce diversity is associated with age diversity (Østergaard et al., 2011). Mincer's wage equation approach shows how individual productivity changes during the life cycle. Whereas a young employee possesses the latest knowledge, practical work experience increases with age, which raises productivity. However, at the same time, some knowledge becomes obsolete and individual productivity might also decline. If people of different ages interact within a company, high levels of experience can be combined with the latest knowledge, making innovation processes more efficient. Is, for instance, the obsolescence of knowledge more influential on the individual productivity of older workers than their additional experience, or is the new knowledge of younger workers less relevant for the innovation process? A higher degree of workforce diversity with respect to age might be negative on innovative outcomes, which is found by Østergaard et al. (2011). We therefore control for age diversity, also on the basis of the fractionalization index. We refrain from using the shares of employed age cohorts because they are highly collinear. Because the special sample from the IAB Employment History does not distinguish between different age cohorts, we use the official Linked Employer–Employee Data, IAB LIAB, to construct this variable. However, this data set does not cover all establishments so the overall data set shrinks.

4.5 Intra-industrial Spillover Effects

Two other variables relate to the region and industry and are intended to control for localization economies (Marshall-Arrow-Romer externalities, Glaeser et al., 1992, Combes et al., 2004). Each region corresponds to the NUTS 3 level (German districts or *Kreise*) and the industry classification is based on the two-digit level of the German Classification of Economic Activities, NACE Rev. 1.1 (WZ 2003).

The first variable indicates the number of establishments belonging to the same industry located in the region in which the respective establishment operates. This is intended to control for 'cluster' effects within industries (Storper and Venables, 2004) as well as for competition effects. Higher levels of competition make it even more important to innovate in order to remain competitive (Geroski, 1989, 1990, Harris and Trainor, 1995). However, a larger number of competitors also increases the likelihood of positive spillover effects. Unfortunately, we cannot separate the spillover effects from competition pressure.

The second variable relates to the proportion of human capital employed within an industry in the region as an alternative measure of the region's industry-specific knowledge capacity. This proportion is computed excluding the establishment under consideration to avoid collinearity issues. We also tested for other kinds of externality measures as suggested by Combes et al. (2004), but they were found to be insignificant. We therefore keep to the parsimonious model.

A more detailed description of the construction of the variables under consideration is provided in Table 8.A1 in the appendix. A descriptive overview of the variables under consideration is provided in Table 8.3 and a correlation matrix in Table 8.A2 in the appendix.

5. ESTIMATION ISSUES AND RESULTS

5.1 Estimation Issues

We aim to explore the number of areas in which individual establishments innovate, that is, whether an establishment undertakes no innovation, or at least one, two or three types of innovation. We do not distinguish between different combinations of innovation types. Our dependent variable is ordinal and can take the values 0 to 3. Because there is no constant difference between the four outcomes but there is a clear order, the dependent variable is limited dependent. Given the type of data, the ordered logit approach is appropriate and delivers consistent and unbiased estimates. It

Table 8.3 Descriptive statistics of explanatory variables

Variable	Mean	Standard deviation	Minimum	Maximum
log. revenue	14.457	2.209	6.215	24.119
log. wage	4.147	0.449	0.517	6.008
prop. exports	0.074	0.185	0.000	1.000
prop. high-skilled workers	0.163	0.255	0.000	1.000
D. sole trader	0.324	0.468	0.000	1.000
D. private partnership comp.	0.070	0.255	0.000	1.000
D. foreign owner	0.051	0.220	0.000	1.000
D. new establishment (<5 years)	0.129	0.335	0.000	1.000
D. young establishment (5–14 years)	0.225	0.417	0.000	1.000
D. old establishment (15+ years)	0.647	0.478	0.000	1.000
D. newest equipment	0.187	0.390	0.000	1.000
D. new equipment	0.485	0.500	0.000	1.000
D. moderate equipment	0.291	0.454	0.000	1.000
D. old equipment	0.037	0.188	0.000	1.000
prop. low-skilled foreigners	0.043	0.107	0.000	1.000
frac. low-skilled foreigners	0.137	0.272	0.000	0.962
prop. high-skilled foreigners	0.012	0.068	0.000	1.000
frac. high-skilled foreigners	0.041	0.161	0.000	0.954
frac. low-skilled occupations	0.367	0.294	0.000	0.923
frac. high-skilled occupations	0.230	0.296	0.000	0.887
frac. age diversity	0.623	0.218	0.000	0.833
log. no. competitors in region and industry	5.301	1.800	0.000	9.649
prop. high-skilled workers in region and industry	0.169	0.143	0.000	1.000

Notes:
No. obs. about 58,000.
D. Dummy, prop. proportion, frac. fractionalization index.

is a non-linear model and therefore coefficients have to be interpreted with care: in contrast to Ordinary Least Square (OLS) an estimated positive coefficient does not necessarily mean that the likelihood of being active in, for example, two innovation fields increases. In the ordered logit model only the interpretation of the marginal effects is meaningful (Greene, 2012).

The data set comprises establishments surveyed in different years such that a panel data set results. Although panel analysis controls for unobserved heterogeneity at establishment level, the average number of observations per establishment, at 2.4, is not sufficient to identify such effects. Because of the non-linearity of the econometric model, standard fixed effects techniques and especially within-demeaning cannot be applied. In order to identify establishment fixed effects, for every establishment a dummy indicator has to be estimated; the incidental parameter problem applies from a methodological point of view (Greene, 2012). From a technical point of view, the variance–covariance matrix is near singularity. We therefore use the pooled data and control for heterogeneity by means of region fixed effects, time fixed effects and industry fixed effects. Region fixed effects control for all unobserved regional factors. This has the advantage, for example, that more productive firms tend to settle in specific regions and less productive firms in others. This selectivity of locational choice will bias the results but the problem is reduced considerably by means of fixed effects, as then firms within one region are considered. Therefore, region fixed effects are favored. A disadvantage of the region fixed effects approach is, however, that variation in regional variables is relatively low and the measures are rather time constant, which then yields insignificant results because of the missing within-region variation (Brunow and Blien, 2015).

Different industries have different probabilities of becoming innovative. As was the case with regions, not controlling for industry characteristics would bias the remaining estimates. Finally, time fixed effects control for unobserved shocks in individual years.

There are several sources of endogeneity. Innovative establishments might locate in innovative regions. Such selectivity is controlled for by means of the region fixed effects, where some similar argument holds for the chosen industry. However, there are other intra-establishment issues. There might be for instance the general motive to be one of the innovative market leaders that demand innovation. Therefore the establishment employs, for example, human capital. Then, this measure is endogenous from an intertemporal perspective. Under such conditions lagged values of the endogenous variable as instruments are invalid as they are also correlated with the decision to be one of the market leaders. Therefore, the results relate only to correlations and not to causal effects.

All the fixed effects are represented by means of dummy variables. The estimates of the remaining variables as outlined in the previous section are therefore conditional on the fixed effects included. We estimate various models excluding and including fixed effects. The results suggest that omitting fixed effects yields systematic differences in parameter estimates. Moreover, the fixed effects are jointly significant and therefore improve the results. Thus, excluding fixed effects yields biased estimates. If we estimate a model including only the fixed effects and compare this 'constant-only' model with the alternatives that include relevant variables as outlined in the previous section, the additional variables significantly improve the model fit.

5.2 Results

Table 8.4 reports the estimated coefficients of the ordered logit model including region, industry and time fixed effects. Reported standard errors are clustered at the establishment level and are therefore robust against some misspecification issues. We provide four different models including subsets of variables. Including additional variables has virtually no effect on the estimates of the included variables. The only difference in parameters and significance is between models 3 and 4 for the effect of wages, when workforce age diversity is taken into account. Individual skills and experience change over time and should therefore influence individual wages. Taking age diversity into account controls for wage diversity and absorbs the effect from the average wage, which now becomes insignificant and smaller in magnitude. Because model 4 has the strongest explanatory power, this is the preferred model for interpretation. The signs of the coefficients provide a first picture and they clearly seem to be as expected. However, they have to be interpreted with caution because they relate to a distribution that describes the likelihood of a firm undertaking no innovation, or one, two or three different types of innovation.

A marginal change in the explanatory variables therefore alters the probability of the outcomes. The change can then have the opposite sign to the estimated coefficients presented in Table 8.4.

Table 8.5 shows the average marginal effects of model 4, where all explanatory variables enter as regressors. We also report the averaged probabilities of each outcome, which is more than 50 percent for no innovation, 28.8 percent for at least one of the three types of innovation, 15 percent for two types of innovation and less than 4 percent for all three types of innovation.

An increase in revenues leads to a significant increase in the probability of innovating. As found in other empirical work, exports are positively related to innovation processes in establishments. As argued in theoretical literature (e.g. Melitz, 2003), exporting firms have to compete in global markets and therefore have to innovate. A larger proportion of high-skilled employees increase the likelihood of a firm being innovative. For all variables the marginal effect is strongest for implementing two types of innovation.

The other control variables on establishment characteristics show the expected signs. Sole traders and privately managed companies are more likely not to innovate than limited companies, which reflects their risk

Table 8.4 Estimated coefficients on the number of innovative activities

	(1)	(2)	(3)	(4)
log. revenues	0.235***	0.197***	0.197***	0.196***
	(0.01)	(0.01)	(0.01)	(0.01)
log. wage	−0.100**	−0.112***	−0.113***	−0.069
	(0.04)	(0.04)	(0.04)	(0.05)
prop. exports	0.753***	0.716***	0.711***	0.743***
	(0.07)	(0.07)	(0.07)	(0.08)
prop. high-skilled workers	0.570***	0.487***	0.483***	0.481***
	(0.05)	(0.06)	(0.06)	(0.07)
D. sole trader	−0.159***	−0.142***	−0.144***	−0.133***
	(0.03)	(0.03)	(0.03)	(0.04)
D. private partnership	−0.110**	−0.094**	−0.094**	−0.118**
	(0.04)	(0.04)	(0.04)	(0.05)
D. foreign owner	−0.052	−0.056	−0.059	−0.055
	(0.05)	(0.05)	(0.05)	(0.05)
D. establishment age 5–14 years	−0.185***	−0.186***	−0.188***	−0.186***
	(0.04)	(0.04)	(0.04)	(0.04)
D . establishment age 15+	−0.262***	−0.272***	−0.271***	−0.259***
years	(0.03)	(0.03)	(0.03)	(0.04)
D. new equipment	−0.211***	−0.215***	−0.215***	−0.190***
	(0.03)	(0.03)	(0.03)	(0.03)
D. moderate equipment	−0.430***	−0.439***	−0.438***	−0.402***
	(0.03)	(0.03)	(0.03)	(0.03)
D. oldest equipment	−0.522***	−0.534***	−0.530***	−0.540***
	(0.06)	(0.06)	(0.06)	(0.07)
prop. low-skilled foreigners		−0.250**	−0.246**	−0.262*
		(0.11)	(0.11)	(0.13)
frac. low-skilled foreigners		−0.102*	−0.102*	−0.110*
		(0.05)	(0.05)	(0.06)
prop. high-skilled foreigners		−0.108	−0.100	0.024
		(0.15)	(0.15)	(0.18)
frac. high-skilled foreigners		0.215***	0.209***	0.255***
		(0.07)	(0.07)	(0.08)
frac. low-skill occupations		0.215***	0.217***	0.198***
		(0.05)	(0.05)	(0.06)
frac. high-skill occupations		0.324***	0.313***	0.292***
		(0.06)	(0.06)	(0.06)
frac. age diversity				0.192**
				(0.07)
log. no. competitors			0.057**	0.063**
in region / industry			(0.03)	(0.03)
prop. high-skilled workers			0.144	0.217
in region / industry			(0.16)	(0.18)

Table 8.4 (continued)

	(1)	(2)	(3)	(4)
region, time, industry FE	yes	yes	yes	Yes
cut value 1	2.917***	2.385***	2.643***	3.166***
	(0.23)	(0.24)	(0.27)	(0.30)
cut value 2	4.261***	3.732***	3.989***	4.543***
	(0.23)	(0.24)	(0.27)	(0.30)
cut value 3	6.087***	5.562***	5.820***	6.417***
	(0.23)	(0.24)	(0.27)	(0.31)
pseudo R2	0.098	0.099	0.099	0.108
log-likelihood	−61 376	−61 312	−61 131	−48 163
no. obs.	58 494	58 494	58 326	47 130
no. establishments	25 183	25 183	25 151	19 235

Notes:
Establishment cluster robust s.e. in ().
Significant at * 10%, ** 5%, *** 1%.
D. dummy, prop. proportion, frac. fractionalization index.

aversion. The maturing of establishments and their installed machinery reduces the likelihood of being innovative. Therefore the youngest establishments which also operate with the latest technology are the ones that are most innovative in more areas. Once they mature and do not reinvest in newer technologies, the likelihood of innovation decreases. This reflects the product life cycle but, of course, also causes endogeneity issues. Establishments that have previously innovated are likely to invest in the latest technology. Thus, the decision to innovate is related to having up-to-date machinery and this is a problem of intertemporal reverse causality. However, given our short panel structure with respect to the number of observations for each establishment, we are unable to solve this endogeneity issue.

We now turn to the workforce employed and especially to diversity issues. First, it is surprising that establishments with a larger proportion of foreigners among the low-skilled are less likely to be innovative. Also, the diversity of low-skilled is negatively related to innovation activities of establishments. This contradicts the hypothesis of different problem solving abilities fostering innovation. However, the low-skilled group comprises occupations that are associated with manual tasks and a large degree of routine work. For the US Peri and Sparber (2009) also delivered evidence that low-skilled foreigners are more likely to specialize in manual-routine jobs. If we look at our findings in the light of this argument, it provides an explanation for the negative relationship. Even if

Table 8.5 Average marginal effects for the change in probabilities

	No innovation	Innovation in one area	Innovation in two areas	Innovation in three areas
log. revenues	−0.040***	0.011***	0.020***	0.009***
	(0.00)	(0.00)	(0.00)	(0.00)
log. wage	0.014	−0.004	−0.007	−0.003
	(0.01)	(0.00)	(0.00)	(0.00)
prop. exports	−0.152***	0.043***	0.074***	0.034***
	(0.02)	(0.00)	(0.01)	(0.00)
prop. high-skilled workers	−0.098***	0.028***	0.048***	0.022***
	(0.01)	(0.00)	(0.01)	(0.00)
D. sole trader	0.027***	−0.008***	−0.013***	−0.006***
	(0.01)	(0.00)	(0.00)	(0.00)
D. private partnership	0.024**	−0.007**	−0.012**	−0.005**
	(0.01)	(0.00)	(0.00)	(0.00)
D. foreign owner	0.011	−0.003	−0.005	−0.003
	(0.01)	(0.00)	(0.01)	(0.00)
D. establishment age 5–14 years	0.038***	−0.011***	−0.018***	−0.009***
	(0.01)	(0.00)	(0.00)	(0.00)
D. establishment age 15+ years	0.053***	−0.015***	−0.026***	−0.012***
	(0.01)	(0.00)	(0.00)	(0.00)
D. new equipment	0.039***	−0.011***	−0.019***	−0.009***
	(0.01)	(0.00)	(0.00)	(0.00)
D. moderate equipment	0.082***	−0.023***	−0.040***	−0.019***
	(0.01)	(0.00)	(0.00)	(0.00)
D. oldest equipment	0.110***	−0.031***	−0.054***	−0.025***
	(0.01)	(0.00)	(0.01)	(0.00)
prop. low-skilled foreigners	0.053*	−0.015*	−0.026*	−0.012*
	(0.03)	(0.01)	(0.01)	(0.01)
frac. low-skilled foreigners	0.022*	−0.006*	−0.011*	−0.005*
	(0.01)	(0.00)	(0.01)	(0.00)
prop. high-skilled foreigners	−0.005	0.001	0.002	0.001
	(0.04)	(0.01)	(0.02)	(0.01)
frac. high-skilled foreigners	−0.052***	0.015***	0.025***	0.012***
	(0.02)	(0.00)	(0.01)	(0.00)
frac. low-skill occupations	−0.040***	0.012***	0.020***	0.009***
	(0.01)	(0.00)	(0.01)	(0.00)
frac. high-skill occupations	−0.060***	0.017***	0.029***	0.013***
	(0.01)	(0.00)	(0.01)	(0.00)
frac. age diversity	−0.039**	0.011**	0.019**	0.009**
	(0.02)	(0.00)	(0.01)	(0.00)
log. no. competitors in region / industry	−0.013**	0.004**	0.006**	0.003**
	(0.01)	(0.00)	(0.00)	(0.00)

Table 8.5 (continued)

	No innovation	Innovation in one area	Innovation in two areas	Innovation in three areas
prop. high-skilled workers	−0.044	0.013	0.022	0.010
in region / industry	(0.04)	(0.01)	(0.02)	(0.01)
prob (at means)	0.529	0.288	0.150	0.033

Notes:
Establishment cluster robust s.e. in ().
Significant at * 10%, ** 5%, *** 1%.
D. Dummy, prop. proportion, frac. fractionalization index.

the definition of low-skilled and high-skilled is based upon task-related measures, the 'within' heterogeneity is still present in both skill groups. Then, a larger proportion of low-skilled foreigners is associated with production units with little or no innovation capacity. Unfortunately, the IAB Establishment Panel contains no information about the field in which the establishment specializes, so we cannot distinguish between production units and other 'mixed' establishments comprising production units and innovation departments. These differences are thus then captured by differences in the workforce structure.

The picture of cultural diversity among the low-skilled is mirrored in the group of high-skilled foreigners. First, the proportion is insignificant, indicating that it does not matter whether foreigners or Germans are employed in the high-skilled segment. However, if the high-skilled foreigners are more diverse, the capacity for innovation increases, which supports the skilled hypothesis that different approaches to problem solving, country-specific knowledge and increased cultural diversity have an impact on the innovation outcome. The marginal effect of high-skilled cultural diversity is strongly negative for performing no innovation and has the strongest effect on implementing two types of innovation. Thus, establishments that employ a diverse, highly skilled foreign workforce are the ones that are relatively more innovative.

Another form of workforce diversity is the diversity of occupations within the workforce. In the German apprenticeship system the training is very detailed and focused. Therefore, a greater level of diversity with respect to occupations measures the (occupation-specific) knowledge available to the establishment. One might argue that greater diversity provides a broader range of knowledge and therefore that innovation is more likely. Our evidence supports this hypothesis, as it does for the group of low-skilled occupations, although its magnitude is smaller compared to the diversity of highly skilled employees. Again, the interaction of different knowledge from different occupations and thus, disciplines, raises the innovation capacity and the stock of knowledge within the establishment.

A related concept of diversity is age diversity, which serves as a proxy for the experience structure. Whereas young employees possess the 'latest' knowledge, mature employees are more experienced. The interaction of the two groups again broadens an establishment's knowledge capacity. Unfortunately, we cannot distinguish here between low- and high-skilled employees because the data on the age distribution comes from the IAB LIAB, which cannot be linked with the advanced classification of occupations. However, we still find a positive and significant marginal effect on innovation outcomes. The more diverse the employed workforce becomes in terms of age, the higher the marginal effect for innovating is and the effect is strongest when two different innovation types are performed.

The results obtained on workforce diversity are in line with the argumentation of Griliches' knowledge production function approach. It was argued that workforce diversity measures different kinds of knowledge and therefore increases the knowledge stock. The interaction between workers from different fields within an establishment transfers knowledge more easily, which is an important driver of innovation. It is linked to lower innovation costs, because the overall efficiency increases, not only in the innovation process but also in the establishment itself.

The knowledge production function approach defined by Griliches (1979) also suggests that there are positive spillover effects at the regional level on establishments' innovation capacity. The reason for this is that knowledge has the character of a public good to a certain extent and therefore the regional environment should provide additional efficiency gains the higher the knowledge stock is. Such an argument is also put forward in the literature on growth (e.g. Romer, 1990, Grossman and Helpman, 1991). Most of the regional variation is captured by regional dummy variables. Unfortunately there is little within-region variation, so the majority of the variables tested become insignificant. This does not have to be the case when we consider intra-industry variables. We employ two variables that describe the regional intra-industry environment. The first one is the proportion of human capital employed in all establishments of the respective industry excluding that of the establishment under consideration. Excluding the respective establishment's own contribution is intended to reduce collinearity issues. Surprisingly, the proportion is insignificant, indicating that a larger proportion of human capital employed in all other establishments in the same industry and region does not yield a greater likelihood of innovating in at least one area. Hunt and Gauthier-Loiselle

(2010) show the existence of knowledge spillover effects for the USA for high qualified immigrants on patent rate. Peri (2005) finds comparative results for regional panel data, Chellaraj et al. (2008) for the series data and Le (2008) for cross-country panel data.

The number of competitors, however, is highly significant and positive in its magnitude for performing at least one type of innovation. The marginal effect is negative and significant for not innovating. Thus, concentration within an industry induces or forces establishments to innovate. Higher levels of competition and therefore increased market pressure, as well as agglomeration and spillover effects, make establishments more innovative (Fritsch and Slavtchev, 2010, McCann and Folta, 2011). Jirjahn and Kraft (2011) find that knowledge spillovers from competitors have a positive impact on incremental innovations. This is also in line with the literature on innovative milieus. On the other hand, establishments that have hardly any competitors are less innovative. There is a rational explanation for this, which is related to monopoly power and a resulting 'no-need-to-innovate' strategy. However, this argument only holds for high transport costs within the industry, which protects the local market; a market-crowding argument that can be found in the New Economic Geography literature.

All the estimates obtained and discussed so far are conditional on the region fixed effects. They serve to reduce problems of selectivity for establishments in specific regions and also control for any unobserved regional characteristics. A classification scheme was developed by the Federal Institute for Research on Building, Urban Affairs and Spatial Development (Bundesinstitut für Bau-, Stadt- und Raumforschung – BBSR) which classifies regions into broader district types. This classification is based upon two criteria: the first one relates to centrality, the second one to population density. A region can be classed as an agglomeration area, an urbanized area or a rural area. Within an agglomeration, the region can be a core city, a densely populated area, a populated area or a rural area. This classification therefore permits regional heterogeneity with respect to the general location and its population.

Regional heterogeneity is captured by the region fixed effects, with each region belonging to one of the nine groups as defined by the BBSR and listed in Table 8.6. In this table we show the probabilities of an establishment performing one or more types of innovation depending on the region. For this purpose we predict the innovation likelihood for each establishment and then calculate the average of the respective probabilities for each regional district type. Because the probabilities for the innovation outcomes are conditional on all explanatory variables, it includes all workforce and establishment characteristics.

It can be seen that the average likelihood of not innovating differs

Table 8.6 Average innovation probabilities depending on an establishment's location

	No innovation	Innovation in one area	Innovation in two areas	Innovation in three areas
Agglomeration district				
1. Core cities	0.509	0.257	0.179	0.055
2. Densely populated areas	0.512	0.250	0.179	0.058
3. Populated areas	0.500	0.256	0.186	0.059
4. Rural areas	0.582	0.234	0.144	0.040
Urbanized district				
5. Core cities	0.512	0.259	0.176	0.053
6. Populated areas	0.503	0.250	0.186	0.061
7. Rural areas	0.551	0.242	0.160	0.047
Rural district				
8. Densely populated rural areas	0.533	0.247	0.170	0.051
9. Sparsely populated rural areas	0.602	0.226	0.135	0.037

Note: All reported values relate to proportions not performing innovation or performing one, two or three types of innovation.

between rural areas (55–60 percent) and all other areas (about 50 percent), irrespective of whether the rural area is located in an agglomeration, urbanized or rural district. Interestingly, for the remaining regions the probabilities of innovating do not vary remarkably. Thus, after controlling for a variety of establishment and workforce characteristics, an establishment located in a core city of an agglomerated district, for instance, has almost the same likelihood of performing two distinct types of innovation as an establishment located in a densely populated rural area in a rural district. The innovation capacity of establishments is therefore not necessarily a pure agglomeration aspect. Another implication of this finding is that unobserved heterogeneity which results in locational selectivity of individual establishments is of minor importance. However, as our results suggest, being in a region with a larger number of competitors increases the likelihood of becoming more innovative. This result supports the presence of regional innovation systems and their relevance for innovative processes (Asheim et al., 2011, Fritsch and Slavtchev, 2011). Although the innovation likelihood does not depend on the location, there are gains when the establishment is located in a denser intra-industrial area, which reflects the possible regional innovation milieu.

The findings can be summarized as follows. The likelihood of innovating is less than 50 percent and this probability is virtually unaffected by the location. The only exceptions are establishments in rural regions, which tend to be non-innovative. The variables under consideration show the expected signs and are in line with other existing work. Interestingly, even if the likelihood of innovating in more than one area is relatively low (about 15 percent for two, and just over 3 percent for three types of innovation), a marginal change in the explanatory variables leads to the strongest change in the probabilities of being innovative in two areas. Thus, establishments use a combination of innovation activities in order to remain competitive. We provide evidence of the existence of spillover effects. When the number of establishments within an industry increase then the likelihood of being innovative in more innovation areas increases. Consider two, A and B. A is located in an agglomerated area within the industry and B is not. As shown in Table 8.4, the likelihood of performing innovation does not differ substantially between the regions. Establishment A benefits from the external spillover effect, which means that A needs to employ fewer resources that are positively related to innovation outcomes. B does not gain from such a spillover effect and therefore has to increase its own innovation capacity, for instance by employing more human capital. Because the proportion of human capital within the region and industry is insignificant, positive spillovers seem to be related to links between firms and network effects or pure competition pressure. The results can be generalized to other countries which are similar in their industrial structure to Germany and especially within the European Union where similarities in institutions and the labor market exist.

6. CONCLUSION

This chapter examines the innovation capacity of individual establishments and especially addresses the question of what type of firm is more likely to implement relatively more types of innovation (product introduction, product improvement or adoption of new technologies). Therefore, each establishment can innovate in one, two or three of these areas or not at all.

After controlling for industry- and region-specific effects, establishment characteristics and those of the workforce employed we provide evidence that establishments can benefit from spillover effects emerging at industry level and from workforce diversity. If the workforce employed is more diverse with respect to the availability of different knowledge, measured as the diversity of occupations, the diversity of age cohorts and the diversity of nationalities employed, the innovation capacity increases and, thus, innovation becomes more likely. This is in line with the knowledge-production function hypothesis suggested by Griliches (1979). In addition, the more pronounced the diversity of the workforce employed is, the more likely the establishment is to be innovative in more than one area.

With respect to spillover effects, our results suggest that the number of competitors is a driving force for being more innovative but not the proportion of human capital employed in the other establishments in the same industry and region. With the exception of very rural regions, the likelihood of innovating is quite constant such that selectivity in specific, innovative regions is of minor importance. In the light of the spillovers this means that establishments located in a competitive environment require less innovation capacity of their own in order to achieve the same innovation likelihood. This also suggests that regional networks, which are associated with a wider variety of intra-industry products, lead to more innovation activity.

Future research may investigate the resulting combination of innovation outcomes in order to better understand the innovation patterns of establishments. For instance, are establishments in agglomerated regions more likely to innovate in new products and product improvement whereas establishments in other regions are more likely to adopt new technologies?

REFERENCES

Acemoglu, D., Aghion, P., and Zilibotti, F. (2003). Vertical integration and distance to frontier. *Journal of the European Economic Association*, 1 (2–3), 630–638.

Acemoglu, D., Aghion, P., and Zilibotti, F. (2006). Distance to frontier, selection, and economic growth. *Journal of the European Economic Association*, 4 (1), 37–74.

Acs, Z.J., Audretsch, D.B., and Feldman, M.P. (1994). R&D spillovers and recipient firm size. *The Review of Economics and Statistics*, 76 (2), 336–340.

Acs, Z.J., Anselin, L., and Varga, A. (2002). Patents and innovation counts as measures of regional production of new knowledge. *Research Policy*, 31 (7), 1069–1085.

Almeida, P., and Kogut, B. (1997). The exploration of technological diversity and the geographic localization of innovation: Start-up firms in the semiconductor industry. *Small Business Economics*, 9, 21–31.

Asheim, B.T., Lawton Smith, H., and Oughton, C. (2011). Regional innovation systems: Theory, empirics and policy. *Regional Studies*, 45 (7), 875–891.

Baldwin, R.E. (1999). Agglomeration and endogenous capital. *European Economic Review*, 43 (2), 253–280.

Baldwin, R., and Forslid, R. (1997). Trade liberalization and endogenous growth: A q-theory approach. *Journal of International Economics*, 50, 497–517.

Baldwin, R., Martin, P., and Ottaviano, G. (2001). Global income divergence, trade and industrialization: The geography of growth take-off. *Journal of Economic Growth*, 6, 5–37.

Baptista, R., and Swann, P. (1998). Do firms in clusters innovate more? *Research Policy*, 27, 525–540.

Basile, R., Capello, R., and Caragliu, A. (2012). Technological interdependence and regional growth in Europe: Proximity and synergy in knowledge spillovers. *Papers in Regional Science*, 91 (4), 697–722.

Bellmann, L., Crimmann, A., Evers, K., and Hujer, R. (2013). Regional determinants of establishments' innovation activities: A multi-level approach. Retrieved from http://ftp.iza.org/dp7572.pdf.

Benhabib, J., and Spiegel, M.M. (1994). The role of human capital in economic development evidence from aggregate cross-country data. *Journal of Monetary Economics*, 34 (2), 143–173.

Berliant, M., and Fujita, M. (2008). Knowledge creation as a square dance on the Hilbert cube. *International Economic Review*, 49 (4), 1251–1295.

Bishop, P., and Wiseman, N. (1999). External ownership and innovation in the United Kingdom. *Applied Economics*, 31 (4), 443–450.

Blundell, R., Griffith, R., and van Reenen, J. (1999). Market share, market value and innovation in a panel of British manufacturing firms. *The Review of Economic Studies*, 66 (3), 529–554.

Brunow, S., and Blien, U. (2015). Agglomeration effects on labor productivity: An assessment with microdata. *REGION*, 2 (1), 33–53.

Brunow, S., and Hirte, G. (2009). Regional age pattern of human capital and regional productivity: A spatial econometric study on German regions. *Papers in Regional Science*, 88 (4), 799–823.

Brunow, S., and Stockinger, B. (2013). Establishments' and regions' cultural diversity as a source of innovation: Evidence from Germany (No. 2013022). Norface Research Programme on Migration, Department of Economics, University College London.

Cainelli, G., Evangelista, R., and Savona, M. (2006). Innovation and economic performance in services: A firm-level analysis. *Cambridge Journal of Economics*, 30 (3), 435–458.

Camagni, R., and Capello, R. (2013). Regional innovation patterns and the EU regional policy reform: Toward smart innovation policies. *Growth and Change: A Journal of Urban and Regional Policy*, 44 (2), 355–389.

Cameron, G. (1996). Innovation and Economic Growth, CEPDP, 277, Centre for Economic Performance, London School of Economics and Political Science, London.

Capello, R. (2014). Proximity and regional innovation processes: Is there space for new reflections? In André Torre and Frédéric Wallet (eds), *Regional Development and Proximity Relations*. Cheltenham, UK and Northampton, MA, USA: Edward Elgar Publishing, pp. 163–194.

Capello, R., and Lenzi, C. (2014). Knowledge, innovation and productivity gains across European regions. *Regional Studies*, DOI: 10.1080/00343404.2014.917167.

Cassiman, B., Golovko, E., and Martínez-Ros, E. (2010). Innovation, exports and productivity. *International Journal of Industrial Organization*, 28 (4), 372–376.

Castellani, D., and Zanfei, A. (2003). Technology gaps, absorptive capacity and the impact of inward investments on productivity of European firms. *Economics of Innovation and New Technology*, 12 (6), 555–576.

Chellaraj, G., Maskus, K.E., and Mattoo, A. (2008). The contribution of international graduate students to US innovation. *Review of International Economics*, 16 (3), 444–462.

Cohen, W.M., and Levinthal, D.A. (1990). Absorptive capacity: A new perspective on learning and innovation. *Administrative Science Quarterly*, 35 (1), 128–152.

Combes, P.-P., Magnac, T., and Robin, J.-M. (2004). The dynamics of local employment in France. *Journal of Urban Economics*, 56 (2), 217–243.

Crépon, B., Duguet, E., and Mairesse, J. (1998). Research, innovation and productivity: An econometric analysis at the firm level. *Economics of Innovation and New Technology*, 7 (2), 115–158.

de Groot, H.L.F., Poot, P., and Smit, M.J. (2007). Agglomeration, innovation and regional development: Theoretical perspectives and meta-analysis, Tinbergen Institute Discussion Paper, no. TI 2007-079/3, Amsterdam and Rotterdam.

De Propris, L. (2000). Innovation and inter-firm co-operation: The case of the West Midlands. *Economics of Innovation and New Technology*, 9 (5), 421–446.

Drach-Zahavy, A., and Somech, A. (2001). Understanding team innovation: The role of team processes and structures. *Group Dynamics*, 5, 111–123.

Duranton, G., and Puga, D. (2001). Nursery cities: Urban diversity, process innovation, and the life cycle of products. *The American Economic Review*, 91 (5), 1454–1477.

Ebling, G., and Janz, N. (1999). Export and innovation activities in the German service sector: Empirical evidence at the firm level. Discussion paper / ZEW: Vol. 99, 53. Mannheim.

Feldman, M.P., and Audretsch, D.B. (1999). Innovation in cities: Science-based diversity, specialization and localized competition. *European Economic Review*, 43 (2), 409–429.

Foray, D., and Lundvall, B.-A. (1996). *Employment and Growth in the Knowledge-Based Economy*. Paris: OCDE.

Freel, M.S. (2003). Sectoral patterns of small firm innovation, networking and proximity. *Research Policy*, 32 (5), 751–770.

Frenkel, A., Shefer, D., Koschatzky, K., and Walter, G.H. (2001). Firm characteristics, location and regional innovation: A comparison between Israeli and German industrial firms. *Regional Studies*, 35 (5), 415–429.

Fritsch, M., and Slavtchev, V. (2010). How does industry specialization affect the efficiency of regional innovation systems? *The Annals of Regional Science*, 45 (1), 87–108.

Fritsch, M., and Slavtchev, V. (2011). Determinants of the efficiency of regional innovation systems. *Regional Studies*, 45 (7), 905–918.

Fujita, M., and Weber, S. (2003). Strategic immigration policies and welfare in heterogeneous countries. CORE discussion papers: Vol. 2003,95. Göttingen, Louvain-la-Neuve: Niedersächsische Staats- und Universitätsbibliothek; CORE.

Geroski, P.A. (1989). Entry, innovation and productivity growth. *The Review of Economics and Statistics*, 71 (4), 572–578.

Geroski, P.A. (1990). Innovation, technological opportunity, and market structure. *Oxford Economic Papers*, 42, 586–602.

Glaeser, E.L., Kallal, H.D., Scheinkman, J., and Shleifer, A. (1992). Growth in cities. *Journal of Political Economy*, 100, 1126–1152.

Greene, W.H. (2012). *Econometric Analysis* (7th edn, internat. edn). Boston: Pearson.
Griffith, R., Huergo Orejas, E., Mairesse, J., and Peters, B. (2006). Innovation and productivity across four European countries. *Oxford Review of Economic Policy*, 22 (4), 483–498.
Griliches, Z. (1979). Issues in assessing the contribution of research and development to productivity growth. *The Bell Journal of Economics*, 92–116.
Grossman, G.M., and Helpman, E. (1991). *Innovation and Growth in the Global Economy*. Cambridge, MA: The MIT Press.
Håkansson, H. (1987). *Industrial Technological Development: A Network Approach*. London: Croom Helm.
Hall, B.H., Lotti, F., and Mairesse, J. (2009). Innovation and productivity in SMEs: Empirical evidence for Italy. *Small Business Economics*, 33 (1), 13–33.
Harris, R., and Trainor, M. (1995). Innovations and R&D in Northern Ireland manufacturing: A Schumpeterian approach. *Regional Studies*, 29 (7), 593–604.
Hong, L., and Page, S.E. (2001). Problem solving by heterogeneous agents. *Journal of Economic Theory*, 97 (1), 123–163.
Hong, L., and Page, S.E. (2004). Groups of diverse problem solvers can outperform groups of high ability problem solvers. *Proceedings of the National Academy of Sciences of USA*, 101:16385–16389.
Hunt, J., and Gauthier-Loiselle, M. (2010). How much does immigration boost innovation? *American Economic Journal*, 2 (2), 31–56.
Jirjahn, U., and Kraft, K. (2011). Do spillovers stimulate incremental or drastic product innovations? Evidence from German establishment data. *Oxford Bulletin of Economics and Statistics*, 73 (4), 509–538.
Kleinknecht, A., van Montfort, K., and Brouwer, E. (2002). The non-trivial choice between innovation indicators. *Economics of Innovation and New Technology*, 11 (2), 109–121.
Koellinger, P. (2008). The relationship between technology, innovation, and firm performance: Empirical evidence on e-business in Europe. ERIM report series research in management finance and accounting: Vol. 2008,031. Rotterdam: ERIM.
Laursen, K., Mahnke, V., and Vejrup-Hansen, P. (2005). Do differences make a difference? The impact of human capital diversity, experience and compensation on firm performance in engineering consulting. DRUID working paper: Vol. 2005, 4. Göttingen, Aalborg: Niedersächsische Staats- und Universitätsbibliothek; DRUID.
Le, T. (2008). 'Brain drain' or 'brain circulation': Evidence from OECD's international migration and R&D spillovers. *Scottish Journal of Political Economy*, 55 (5), 618–636.
Lee, N., and Rodríguez-Pose, A. (2013). Creativity, cities and innovation: Evidence from UK SMEs. Retrieved from http://www.nesta.org.uk/publications/creativity-cites-and-innovation-evidence-uk-smes.
Love, J., and Ashcroft, B. (1999). Market versus corporate structure in plant-level innovation performance. *Small Business Economics*, 13, 97–109.
Love, J., and Roper, S. (1999). The determinants of innovation: R&D, technology transfer and networking effects. *Review of Industrial Organization*, 15, 43–64.
Love, J.H., Ashcroft, B., and Dunlop, S. (1996). Corporate structure, ownership and the likelihood of innovation. *Applied Economics*, 28 (6), 737–746.

Martínez-Ros, E. (1999). Explaining the decisions to carry out product and process innovations: The Spanish case. Getafe: Departamento de Economía de la Empresa. Universidad Carlos III de Madrid.
McCann, B.T., and Folta, T.B. (2011). Performance differentials within geographic clusters. *Journal of Business Venturing*, 26 (1), 104–123.
Melitz, M.J. (2003). The impact of trade on intra-industry reallocations and aggregate industry productivity. *Econometrica*, 71 (6), 1695–1725.
Michie, J., and Sheehan, M. (2003). Labour market deregulation, 'flexibility' and innovation. *Cambridge Journal of Economics*, 27 (1), 123–143.
Nathan, M., and Lee, N. (2011). Does cultural diversity help innovation in cities? Evidence from London firms. SERC discussion paper: Vol. 69. London: SERC.
Nelson, R.R. (1993). *National Innovation Systems: A Comparative Analysis*. New York: Oxford University Press.
Nelson, R.R., and Winter, S.G. (2009). *An Evolutionary Theory of Economic Change*. Cambridge, MA: Harvard University Press.
Nett, L. (1994). Why private firms are more innovative than public firms. *European Journal of Political Economy*, 10, 639–653.
Niebuhr, A. (2010). Migration and innovation: Does cultural diversity matter for regional R&D activity? *Papers in Regional Science*, 89 (3), 563–585.
Osborne, E. (2000). The deceptively simple economics of workplace diversity. *Journal of Labor Research*, 21 (3), 463–475.
Østergaard, C.R., Timmermans, B., and Kristinsson, K. (2009). Beyond technological diversification: The impact of employee diversity on innovation. Retrieved from http://www2.druid.dk/conferences/working_papers/41671358816a1c3d5e53450d0c83.pdf.
Østergaard, C.R., Timmermans, B., and Kristinsson, K. (2011). Does a different view create something new? The effect of employee diversity on innovation. *Research Policy*, 40 (3), 500–509.
Ottaviano, G.I.P., and Peri, G. (2005). Cities and cultures. *Journal of Urban Economics*, 58 (2), 304–337.
Ozgen, C., Nijkamp, P., and Poot, J. (2011a). Immigration and innovation in European regions. IZA Discussion Paper: No. 5676. Bonn: IZA.
Ozgen, C., Nijkamp, P., and Poot, J. (2011b). The impact of cultural diversity on innovation: evidence from Dutch firm-level data. IZA Discussion Paper: No. 6000. Bonn: IZA.
Page, S.E. (2007). *The Difference: How the Power of Diversity Creates Better Groups, Firms, Schools, and Societies*. Princeton, NJ: Princeton University Press.
Parrotta, P., Pozzoli, D., and Pytlikova, M. (2012). Does labor diversity affect firm productivity? IZA Discussion Paper: No. 6973. Bonn: IZA.
Peri, G. (2005). Determinants of knowledge flows and their effect on innovation. *The Review of Economics and Statistics*, 87 (2), 308–322.
Peri, G., and Sparber, C. (2009). Task specialization, immigration, and wages. *American Economic Journal*, 1 (3), 135–169.
Pfirrmann, O. (1994). The geography of innovation in small and medium-sized firms in West Germany. *Small Business Economics*, 6 (1), 41–54.
Pianta, M., and Tancioni, M. (2008). Innovations, wages and profits. *Journal of Post-Keynesian Economics*, 31 (1), 101–123.

Romer, P.M. (1990). Endogenous technological change. *The Journal of Political Economy*, 98 (5), S71–S102.
Simmie, J., Sennett, J., Wood, P., and Hart, D. (2002). Innovation in Europe: A tale of networks, knowledge and trade in five cities. *Regional Studies*, 36, 47–64.
Sørensen, J., and Stuart, T. (2000). Aging, obsolescence and organizational innovation. *Administrative Science Quarterly*, 45 (1), 81–112.
Sternberg, R., and Arndt, O. (2001). The firm or the region: What determines the innovation behaviour of European firms? *Economic Geography*, 77 (4), 364–382.
Storper, M. (1993). Regional 'worlds' of production: Learning and innovation in the technology districts of France, Italy and the USA. *Regional Studies*, 27, 433–455.
Storper, M., and Venables, A.J. (2004). Buzz: Face-to-face contact and the urban economy. *Journal of Economic Geography*, 4 (4), 351–370.
Teece, D.J., Pisano, G., and Shuen, A. (1997). Dynamic capabilities and strategic management. *Strategic Management Journal*, 18 (7), 509–533.
Thornhill, S. (2006). Knowledge, innovation and firm performance in high- and low-technology regimes. *Journal of Business Venturing*, 21 (5), 687–703.
Tobin, J. (1969). A general equilibrium approach to monetary theory. *Wachstum und Entwicklung der Wirtschaft*, 1 (1), 15–29.
Trax, M., Brunow, S., and Südekum, J. (2012). Cultural diversity and plant-level productivity. Retrieved from http://hdl.handle.net/10419/67248.
Vandenbussche, J., Aghion, P., and Meghir, C. (2006). Growth, distance to frontier and composition of human capital. *Journal of Economic Growth*, 11 (2), 97–127.
Van der Vegt, G.S., and Janssen, O. (2003). Joint impact of interdependence and group diversity on innovation. *Journal of Management*, 29, 29–51.
Van Reenen, J. (1996). The creation and capture of rents: Wages and innovation in a panel of UK companies. *The Quarterly Journal of Economics*, 111 (1), 195–226.
Watson, W.E., Kumar, K., and Michaelsen, L.K. (1993). Cultural diversity's impact on interaction process and performance: Comparing homogeneous and diverse task groups. *Academy of Management Journal*, 36, 590–602.
Williams, K.Y., and O'Reilly, C.A. (1998). Demography and diversity in organizations: A review of 40 years of research. In B.M. Staw and L.L. Cummings (eds), *Research in Organizational Behavior*. Greenwich, CT: JAI, Vol. 20, pp. 77–140.
Zahra, S.A., and George, G. (2002). Absorptive capacity: A review, reconceptualization, and extension. *Academy of Management Review*, 27 (2), 185–203.
Zajac, E.J., Golden, B.R., and Shortell, S.M. (1991). New organizational forms for enhancing innovation: The case of internal corporate joint ventures. *Management Science*, 37 (2), 170–184.
Zucker, L.G., Darby, M.R., and Brewer, M.B. (1998). Intellectual human capital and the birth of US biotechnology enterprises. *The American Economic Review*, 88 (1), 290–306.

APPENDIX

Table 8.A1 Correlation matrix of the dependent variable with explanatory variables

	(1)	(2)	(3)	(4)	(5)	(6)	(7)	(8)	(9)	(10)	(11)	(12)	(13)
(1) LHS: no. of innovation areas	1.000												
(2) log. revenues	0.312	1.000											
(3) log. wages	0.212	0.633	1.000										
(4) prop. exports	0.259	0.418	0.305	1.000									
(5) prop. high-skilled workers	0.133	0.120	0.309	0.131	1.000								
(6) prop. low-skilled foreigners	0.041	0.163	0.106	0.123	−0.064	1.000							
(7) frac. low-skilled foreigners	0.183	0.554	0.324	0.291	−0.027	0.443	1.000						
(8) prop. high-skilled foreigners	0.046	0.098	0.090	0.097	0.083	0.165	0.136	1.000					
(9) frac. high-skilled foreigners	0.194	0.425	0.281	0.308	0.173	0.154	0.420	0.196	1.000				
(10) frac. low-skilled occupations	0.211	0.604	0.353	0.295	−0.082	0.121	0.344	0.042	0.208	1.000			
(11) frac. high-skilled occupations	0.276	0.695	0.469	0.386	0.282	0.075	0.395	0.083	0.293	0.499	1.000		
(12) frac. age diversity	0.163	0.549	0.395	0.151	−0.002	0.118	0.261	0.059	0.131	0.468	0.365	1.000	
(13) log. no. competitors in region and industry	−0.139	−0.224	−0.102	−0.251	0.011	0.054	−0.033	0.020	−0.061	−0.267	−0.229	−0.108	1.000
(14) prop. high-skilled workers in region and industry	0.145	0.092	0.245	0.133	0.495	−0.013	0.044	0.074	0.150	−0.053	0.184	−0.015	−0.006

Notes:
No. of observations about 58,000.
D. Dummy, prop. proportion, frac. fractionalization index.

Table 8.A2 List and description of establishment characteristics

Variable	Description	Data source
log. revenues	log. of the level of revenues of the establishment	IAB EP
D. foreign owner	Foreign ownership (yes/no)	IAB EP
D. private partnership company	Partnership company (yes/no)	IAB EP
D. sole trader	Sole trade (yes/no)	IAB EP
D. establishment age 5–14 years	Establishment age between 5 and 14 years (Dummy)	IAB EH
D. establishment age 15+ years	Establishment age 15 years or more (Dummy)	IAB EH
D. new equipment	Establishment operates with new equipment (Dummy, reference: newest equipment)	IAB EP
D. moderate equipment	Establishment operates with rather old equipment (Dummy, reference: newest equipment)	IAB EP
D. oldest equipment	Establishment operates with out-of-date equipment (Dummy, reference: newest equipment)	IAB EP
log. wage	Logarithm of average daily wages paid to employees	IAB EH
prop. exports	Proportion of exports on revenues	IAB EP
prop. high skilled workers	Proportion of high-skilled employees	IAB EH
frac. low-skilled occupation frac. high-skilled occupation	Establishment's diversity of employment over occupations employed within the group of low-skilled (high-skilled) employees; computed on the basis of the fractionalization index	IAB EH
prop. low-skilled foreigners prop. high-skilled foreigners	Proportion of low-skilled (high-skilled) foreigners on all employed low-skilled (high-skilled) workers	IAB EH
frac. low-skilled foreigners frac. high-skilled foreigners	Diversity of low-skilled (high-skilled) foreigners over nationalities; computed on the basis of the fractionalization index	IAB EH
frac. age diversity	Diversity over four age groups of employees of an establishment; computed on the basis of the fractionalization index	IAB LIAB

Table 8.A2 (continued)

Variable	Description	Data source
log. no. competitors in region and industry	Logarithm of the number of establishments within the industry located in the same region	IAB EH
prop. high-skilled workers in region and industry	Proportion of high-skilled employees within the industry located in the same region; measured in full-time equivalents, excluding the contribution of the establishment under consideration	IAB EH

Notes: D. Dummy; prop. Proportion; frac. fractionalization index; IAB EP: IAB Establishment Panel (survey data); IAB EH: IAB Employment History (administrative data); IAB LIAB: IAB Linked Employer–Employee data set (administrative data).

PART 3

Urban systems, infrastructure and sustainable development

9. Exploring surface transportation impact on economic output: a panel Granger causality test*

Zhenhua Chen and Kingsley E. Haynes

1. INTRODUCTION

Economic impact analysis of surface transportation infrastructure has long been an important task for policy makers and academic scholars. A valid knowledge of the linkage between surface transportation infrastructure and economic output not only helps researchers to achieve valid economic impact assessment, it also enables decision makers to develop the right infrastructure investment policies so as to generate greater economic benefits. In the past decades, literature on this topic has expanded exponentially since the milestone studies by Aschauer (1989, 1990, 1994), who found that public infrastructure has a strong positive impact on economic output. However, later studies found that actual impact is much less significant or even insignificant (Gramlich, 1994; Harmatuck, 1996; Nadiri and Mamuneas, 1996; Boarnet, 1997; Fernald, 1999; Boarnet and Haughwout, 2000; Gramlich, 2001).

One of the major arguments that question the validity of these studies indicates that many studies are conducted without specifying the causal relationship (identification problem) between infrastructure and economic output (Gramlich, 1994; Kessides, 1993). On the one hand, surface transportation infrastructure enhances connections of regional transportation networks, which subsequently facilitates both freight and passenger movements by reducing the generalized transportation cost. On the other hand, the improvement of economic output may, as a consequence, lead to an increase in the demand of both freight and passenger mobility, which thus requires an expansion of transportation infrastructure capital. Failure to recognize this endogenous issue may jeopardize the outcome of investigation and even lead to an incorrect policy implication. The issue

* An earlier version of this chapter was presented at the VII World Conference of the Spatial Econometrics Association and the International Tinbergen Institute Workshop.

of endogeneity needs to be addressed properly before any concrete impact analysis is attempted.

Economic development theory suggests that a causality test between transportation input and economic output can be used to justify which theory better explains regional economic growth. The neo-classical growth theory holds that economic growth is exogenous (Solow, 1956, 1957). It is the inputs into the economy that lead to long-term economic growth. Such inputs include technological change, capital and labor accumulation (Haines, 2006). The alternative explanation is endogenous growth theory, which holds that long-term economic growth is driven by internal forces (Romer, 1994). Identifying the causality between economic growth and transportation capital accumulation helps to verify which growth theory is preferable in explaining regional economic growth. This is important given its relevance to economic policy (Hartwig, 2009).

Very few studies have addressed the issue of endogeneity between surface transportation input and economic output within the context of the U.S., although international studies are more abundant. Some studies take the existence of endogeneity for granted. Hence, either a simultaneous equation model or a two-stage least square model was adopted (Duffy-Deno and Eberts, 1991; Kemmerling and Stephan, 2002). In other studies, a Granger causality test is carried out at different scales of analysis by using different indicators. For instance, by using a U.S. time-series data between 1925 and 1989, Lau and Sin (1997) found evidence that was not favorable to endogenous growth theory with respect to public infrastructure. Using data from the 48 contiguous states between 1984 and 1997, Jiwattanakulpaisarn et al. (2009) tested the causality between the density of highway lane-miles and the levels of private sector employment. They found that the annual growth of major highways within the same state and all other states positively influenced employment growth.

In terms of international experiences, many causality tests indicate that public transportation has a positive impact on economic output but not vice versa. For example, Queiroz and Gautam (1992) concluded that road infrastructure plays a significant role in economic growth and development after a Granger test. From a Dutch perspective, Sturm et al. (1999) found that transportation infrastructure investment positively Granger causes gross domestic product (GDP) whereas GDP negatively Granger causes transportation investment.

This study focuses on the U.S. northeast megaregion covering the major metropolitan areas from Northern Virginia up to Portland in Maine. The northeast megaregion is regarded as one of the largest agglomerations of people, economic activity and urbanized land in the U.S. (Regional Plan Association, 2007). The surface transportation infrastructure in the northeast megaregion has been so heavily utilized that it has reached its operating capacity due to a rapid population growth and strong economic development over the last two decades. Urban transportation issues such as road and railway corridor congestion have become increasingly difficult to manage. Over the past years, we have conducted a series of studies using spatial econometric estimation (Chen and Haynes, 2014a, 2015b), computable general equilibrium (CGE) estimation (Chen and Haynes, 2013) and the combination of these two methods (Chen and Haynes, 2014b, 2015a) to investigate the economic impact of transportation infrastructure with a focus on this region. Surface transportation infrastructure including highway, public rail and public transit is generally found to have a positive impact on the level of the regional GDP with elasticity values ranging between 0.023 and 0.119.[1] The contribution from highway infrastructure is found to be the highest compared to other modes such as air, public rail and transit. However, the results remain unsatisfactory given the complexities of potential data issues.

The spatial econometric findings of Chen and Haynes (2014a, 2015b) found that transportation investment "Granger caused" the rise in regional GDP and not the reverse. These findings were supported in terms of both the Hausman test and Generalized Method of Moments (GMM) estimation for the U.S. northeast corridor in the 1990–2010 period. However, the authors worried about the robustness or sensitivity of the causality remaining unclear given that only a one-year lag was adopted in the causality testing. The other evidence for suspecting the validity of the endogeneity tests in these previous studies is the adoptions of employment and private fixed asset as control variables. In fact, regional employment has been found to have a causal effect on the capacity of the non-interstate major road network (Jiwattanakulpaisarn, 2008). Without the verification of the causations between the employment and transportation stock variables, the inclusion of employment as a control variable may lead to spurious results.

This study aims to further investigate the causal linkages between regional economic output and surface transportation infrastructure by addressing the aforementioned issues in the following ways. First, the classical panel Granger test is conducted bivariately between the surface transportation variables and economic output variables. The investigation provides a modal comparative perspective by examining the causation between economic output and various modes including

[1] It should be noted that the elasticities are achieved based on different evaluation frameworks and data, thus are not comparable.

highway, public railway and public transit.[2] Such a modal comparison provides disaggregated information on the causality between economic output and different surface transportation modes. This helps policy makers to better understand the merit of investment policies.

The robustness of the Granger causality test is examined through a sensitivity analysis by comparing the results generated from different lags in each pair of Granger causality models. The test also further enables us to understand the short-term versus long-term causality between the economic outputs and the different surface transportation infrastructures options.

2. DATA

Because of data limitations, evaluations of the impact of surface transportation have been challenged, especially when measured in monetary terms. Many studies have relied on proxy variables as alternatives, such as miles of highways, quality of rail lines, numbers of air passengers (Andersson, et al., 1990; Jiwattanakulpaisarn et al., 2009) or numbers of freight rail stations (Blum, 1982), to quantify infrastructure stock. Normally, these proxies are not as accurate as the capital stock in monetized forms, if the purpose is to measure the impact of infrastructure capital investment.

While most of the economic variables are publicly available, it is difficult to find surface transportation capital stock measured in monetary terms. This is even harder for an investigation at a disaggregated level both spatially and by mode. In the U.S., capital stock data are only available at the aggregated from the U.S. Bureau of Economic Analysis (BEA). The most relevant data on transportation capital stock by mode can be found in Transportation Statistics Annual Reports published by the Bureau of Transportation Statistics (BTS).

However, this data is not adopted in this study for two reasons. First, data is only available for the period 1998–2008. The earlier years of data are not included. Second, while the data provides a good view of the aggregated transportation stock including both publicly and privately owned capital stock levels, there is no additional information on public surface transportation capital stock. A further follow-up with officials in BTS and BEA confirmed that it is not possible to separate them from the general dataset. As a result, public rail, highway and transit stock in the

[2] Public rail in this study is defined as railway infrastructure that is constructed, maintained and operated using public money. Despite private railroad companies such as CSX, Norfolk Southern and Pan Am Lines also having invested in railway infrastructure in this corridor, they are excluded from our investigation.

northeast corridor have to be estimated independently based on the annual capital expenditure data collected from the National Railroad Passenger Corporation (Amtrak) and the U.S. Census Bureau.

Surface transportation infrastructure in this study refers to three modes: highway, public railway and public transit. Waterway and pipeline are excluded because their data are not available. More particularly, our investigation only focuses on public infrastructure. In other words, infrastructure capital outlay is from governmental expenditures.

All variables are converted into a per capita form measured in 2005 constant dollars, and are measured at a per capita level instead of at a gross level in order to reduce the size effect of each Metropolitan Statistical Area (MSA). The dataset is constructed cautiously through the following steps. In the first step, data is aggregated or disaggregated to the unified MSA level based on specific indicator weights. Gross Metropolitan Product (GMP) per capita (in 2005 dollars) and employment are collected from BEA.

Transportation infrastructure is measured in monetary terms. Since no disaggregated transportation infrastructure stock data is publicly available, they are estimated manually using the classical perpetual inventory method (PIM) through the following function form:

$$TK_t = (1 - \delta)TK_{t-1} + TI_t \tag{9.1}$$

where TK and TI indicate transportation capital stock and transportation capital expenditure, respectively, while δ denotes the geometric depreciation rate of transportation stock. Given the fact that there is no better approach to estimate capital stock, we followed the literature in this field and selected 4.1 percent as the value for estimation (Hulten and Wykoff, 1981; Holtz-Eakin, 1993; Ozbay et al., 2007) by assuming all the transportation infrastructures experienced the same rate of depreciation.

Given that the raw data of public capital expenditure before 1970 from the data source is not available, the value of surface transportation capital before 1970 is set to zero in the initial year (1990) and the initial capital stock level (TK1990) of each mode is estimated based on the public capital expenditure during the period 1970–90.[3] Despite many difficulties, we have tried to get as close as we could to improve the accuracy of data. Some details in the data refining process are illustrated in Table 9.1.

Next, all stock per capita is converted to real 2005 U.S. dollars to

[3] It should be noted that this approach has a caveat in that it does not fully capture the fact that a few rail infrastructures on the Northeast Corridor such as the Portal Bridge over the Hackensack River in New Jersey have been operated over a hundred years. In fact, given the rate of 4.1 percent, the actual depreciated capital over the 20 years between 1970 and 1990 is around two thirds of its initial level.

Table 9.1 Data refining process

	Original data	Sources	Initial stock	Method
GMP	Real GDP by Metropolitan Area (millions of chained 2005 dollars)	BEA	–	
Employment	CA04 Total Employment (number of jobs)	BEA	–	
Personal income per capita	CA04 Total Employment (2005 Dollars)	BEA	–	
Public rail capital stock	Amtrak NEC Infrastructure Expenditure Amtrak Facts Sheet of States VA, DC, MD, DE,PA,NJ, NY, CT, RI, MA, NH and ME	Amtrak Department of Engineering Department of Public Affairs[1]	Federal Grant to NEC project from 1972 to 1990[2]	PIM, infrastructure expenditure is apportioned by ridership. Capital procurement is based on geographic location
Highway capital stock	Annual Survey of State and Local Government Finances and Census of Governments (1970–2009)[3]	U.S. Census Bureau	PIM estimated based on 1970–90	Aggregated from individual government units based on their jurisdictional locations
Transit capital stock[4]	Annual Survey of State and Local Government Finances and Census of Governments (1970–2009)	U.S. Census Bureau	PIM estimated based on 1970–90	Aggregated from individual government units based on their jurisdictional locations

Notes:

1. Northeast corridor (NEC) capital infrastructure expenditure includes data from 1990 to 2009 for the mainline, and is obtained from the Amtrak Department of Engineering. Data only includes capital expenditures on safety and reliability, and high-speed rail facilities. Data includes federal, state and local government expenditure.
2. The initial railway infrastructure stock of northeast corridor contains two parts. The majority of the corridor assets were purchased from the Consolidated Rail Corporation (Conrail) during 1976–80 as part of the disposition of the Penn Central Transportation Company's assets (U.S. Government Accountability Office, 2004, 7). The second part was formed from the Northeast Corridor Improvement Project from 1976 to 1990 (Federal Railroad Administration, 1998).
3. Data includes federal, state and local government expenditure.
4. Transit modes include bus, commuter rail, light rail and personal transit.

Table 9.2 Descriptive statistics

Variables	Mean	Std. Dev.	Min	Max	Unit
GMP per capita	41,387	9,341	26,408	89,688	2005$
Employment	874,057	1,846,585	41,942	11,023,744	No. of jobs
Personal income per capita	34,656	8,000	22,201	76,154	2005$
Highway capital stock per capita	714	330	108	2,168	2005$
Public rail capital stock per capita	71	103	0	668	2005$
Transit capital stock per capita	281	649	0	3,871	2005$
Total surface transport capital stock per capita	1,161	896	329	5,935	2005$

Note: Total number of observations: 608.

Source: Bureau of Economic Analysis and U.S. Census Bureau.

eliminate the impact of inflation. The World Bank GDP deflator for the U.S. is applied to all transportation stock variables. The descriptive statistics for the distributions of all variables are described in Table 9.2.

The distribution of surface transportation infrastructure in the northeast corridor is quite uneven both geographically and modally. In terms of the modal comparison, highway infrastructure has the highest value of average stock per capita while public rail has the lowest. As regards geographic comparison, regional differences vary substantially. For instance, the highest level of highway stock per capita is $2,168 in Ocean City MSA in New Jersey in 2009.The lowest amount is $108 per capita, which is in the Boston–Cambridge–Quincy MSA in 1991. Trenton–Ewing MSA in New Jersey has the highest amount of public rail stock per capita whereas the amount is zero in MSAs such as Willimantic MicroMSA in Connecticut, Lebanon MSA in Pennsylvania, and Lewiston–Auburn MSA in Maine. Obviously, all these regions have no public rail service. Transit stock has a similar distributional pattern. The New York–Northern New Jersey–Long Island MSA has the highest amount of transit stock per capita while MSAs such as Vineland–Millville–Bridgeton MSA in New Jersey and Willimantic MicroMSA in Connecticut have no public transit stock. The distribution of surface transportation infrastructure in the northeast regions is also quite uneven. This is understandable as most surface modes are clustered in urbanized and population dense MSAs along the northeast corridor main lines including Washington D.C., Baltimore, Philadelphia, New York and Boston.

3. METHODOLOGY

This study adopts the Granger causality test (Granger, 1969) to identify the relationship between surface transportation infrastructure and regional economic output. This approach is a standard way in applied econometrics (Hartwig, 2009) to investigate causal or identification problems among economic variables. For example, Holtz-Eakin et al. (1988) used a vector autoregressive model to conduct the Granger test. The Granger causality test can be used to test the causal relationships between two time-series variables. The process of testing can be simply described under the assumption that all variables are stationary; *Yt* is regressed on its own lags and on lags of *Xt*. If the lags of *Yt* are found to be jointly statistically significant, then the null hypothesis that *Xt* does not Granger cause *Yt* can be rejected (Hartwig, 2009). In the dynamic panel analysis, the Granger causality test is carried out in two steps: In the first step, a pair of dynamic autoregressive models is implemented, as follow:

$$Y_{it} = a_0 + \sum\nolimits_l^m \alpha_l Y_{it-1} + \sum\nolimits_l^m \gamma_l X_{it-1} + \mu_i + \varepsilon_{it} \tag{9.2}$$

$$X_{it} = \beta_0 + \sum\nolimits_l^m \beta_l X_{it-1} + \sum\nolimits_l^m \in_l Y_{it-1} + \delta_i + \theta_{it} \tag{9.3}$$

where Y_{it} and X_{it} denote the economic variables and surface transportation capital stock variables in region *I* in year *t*, respectively. μ_i and δ_i denote MSA-specific individual effects. The disturbances ε_{it} and θ_{it} are assumed to be independently distributed across MSAs with zero means.

The second step is to run Wald tests (F-test) on the coefficients of the X_{it-1} in the equation (9.2) and the coefficients of the Y_{it-1} in the equation (9.3) to check whether they are jointly statistically different from zero.

Since Granger causality tests require all data to be stationary, it is necessary to test the stationarity of each variable before the test. The standard test for stationarity is to check whether a variable has a unit root. The variable is considered as stationary if unit root does not exist. Table 9.3 presents the result of a panel unit root test using both the standard panel unit root test (Levin et al., 2002) and the cross-sectionally augmented Dickey–Fuller (CADF) statistics with consideration of cross-sectional correlation (Pesaran, 2007). The results suggest that all the variables are stationary after logarithmic transformation.

Because the results of a Granger causality test are highly dependent on

Table 9.3 Panel unit root test (32 MSAs, 1991–2009)

	Levin et al.		Pesaran's CADF	
	Stat.	Prob.	Stat.	Prob.
GMP per capita	−9.279	0.000	−4.256	0.000
Employment	−8.502	0.000	−1.519	0.064
Income per capita	−4.853	0.000	−3.100	0.001
Total transport stock per capita	−5.983	0.000	−1.650	0.049
Highway stock per capita	−6.411	0.000	102.196	0.002
Public rail stock per capita	−10.818	0.000	150.847	0.000
Transit stock per capita	−4.372	0.000	343.093	0.000

Notes:
* All variables undergo logarithmic transformation.
Automatic lag length selection based on SIC: 0 to 3.

the specification of lag length, the validity of the results may be debatable due to any arbitrarily selected lag length. In practice, some criteria such as the Akaike information criterion (AIC), Bayesian information criterion (BIC), Hannan–Quinn information criterion, and Schwarz information criterion (SIC) are often utilized to determine the optimal lag length. However, it should be noted that even when the results are estimated based on the optimal lag length, the sensitivity issue of lag term remains. One solution to check the sensitivity of lags for the Granger test can be done by simply repeating the test using different lag lengths. Thus results can be interpreted as either short-term causality when a short lag length is used or long-term causality when a long lag is used. In this study, we adopt one-, two-, three-, four- and five-year lags so that results of both short-term and long-term causality can be captured.

4. EMPIRICAL RESULTS

Since economic output is measured by GMP per capita, employment and income per capita, the tests are implemented in three groups between the three economic variables and the transportation variables. Table 9.4 shows the result of the Granger causality test between the growth of GMP per capita and the growth of surface transportation infrastructure stock. The relationships between GMP per capita and highway, public rail and transit stock per capita are tested. The sensitivity of the tests is examined by comparing the results generated using different lags of variables. The results suggest that, generally, the level of GMP per capita "Granger causes" the

Table 9.4 Results of Granger causality test between GMP per capita and various surface transportation stock per capita

	F-statistic				
Null hypothesis	Lags 1	Lags 2	Lags 3	Lags 4	Lags 5
Highway per capita does not Granger cause GMP per capita	0.193	0.487	0.399	0.377	0.518
GMP per capita does not Granger cause highway per capita	43.768***	1.761	2.884**	5.280***	6.084***
Public rail per capita does not Granger cause GMP per capita	0.494	0.285	0.269	0.212	3.872***
GMPPC does not Granger cause public rail per capita	0.052	1.302	1.109	1.160	2.939**
Transit per capita does not Granger cause GMP per capita	1.072	0.473	0.577	0.427	0.415
GMP per capita does not Granger cause transit per capita	0.623	1.319	0.987	1.388	1.253
Surface transport per capita does not Granger cause GMP per capita	0.686	0.649	0.498	0.400	0.460
GMP per capita does not Granger cause surface transport per capita	27.838***	2.123	1.108	1.053	0.965

Notes:
*, **, *** denote significance at the 10, 5 and 1 percent levels, respectively.
All variables are measured in first order difference.
Total sample size: 608.

level of the total surface transportation stock per capita only when a one-year lag is used. The reverse causality is not found no matter which (one to five year) lag is used. In terms of the modal investigation, the variation of the GMP per capita is found to "Granger cause" the variation of highway stock per capita when one-, three-, four- and five-year lags are used. Both the GMP per capita and the public rail per capita are found to "Granger cause" the variation of each other when five-year lags are used. In general, the results suggest that during the period 1999–2009, surface transportation investment, particularly highway investment in the northeast corridor was primarily driven by the regional economic condition whereas their contributions to GMP per capita are not statistically significant.

The second group of tests investigates the causation between employment and the surface transportation infrastructure. Unlike the previous results, the tests between employment and transportation variables demonstrate some robust findings (see Table 9.5). Firstly, the highway stock per capita does consistently "Granger cause" the employment as the Wald tests are

Table 9.5 Results of Granger causality test between employment and surface transportation stock per capita

	F-statistic				
Null hypothesis	Lags 1	Lags 2	Lags 3	Lags 4	Lags 5
Highway per capita does not Granger cause employment	6.497**	12.207***	10.794***	9.923***	6.199***
Employment does not Granger cause highway per capita	5.814**	1.956	5.125***	5.722***	4.712***
Public rail per capita does not Granger cause employment	4.422**	1.344	0.816	0.765	0.567
GMP per capita does not Granger cause public rail per capita	0.647	0.424	0.352	0.387	0.431
Transit per capita does not Granger cause employment	0.098	1.564	1.414	1.887	1.686
Employment does not Granger cause transit per capita	2.258	2.222	1.529	1.265	1.419
Surface transport per capita does not Granger cause employment	0.120	3.350**	3.581**	3.703***	1.413
Employment does not Granger cause surface transport per capita	39.739***	1.078	1.461	1.211	0.917

Notes:
*, **, *** denote significance at the 10, 5 and 1 percent levels, respectively.
All variables are measured in first order difference.
Total sample size: 608.

statistically significant across one-year to five-year lags. The reserve causality from employment to highway stock per capita is also confirmed when one-, three-, four- and five-year lags are used. Secondly, public rail stock per capita is found to statistically significantly "Granger cause" the level of employment only in the short term (when a one-year lag is used). Thirdly, the total surface transportation capital stock per capita is found to "Granger cause" the variation of employment when the one-year lag is used, but the reverse causation from surface transport per capita to employment is found statistically significant when two-, three and four-year lags are used.

The third group of tests examines the causation between personal income per capita and surface transportation infrastructure. Again, four pairs of tests are implemented between the personal income per capita and the different modes of surface transportation stock per capita (see Table 9.6). The highway stock per capita is found to "Granger cause" the variation of personal income per capita when the three-, four- and five-year lags are used, whereas income per capita is found to "Granger cause" the variation of highway stock per capita when the one-, three-, four-, and

Table 9.6 Results of Granger causality test between personal income per capita and surface transportation stock per capita

	F-statistic				
Null hypothesis	Lags 1	Lags 2	Lags 3	Lags 4	Lags 5
Highway per capita does not Granger cause income per capita	0.820	1.863	5.407***	5.805***	7.073***
Income per capita does not Granger cause highway per capita	42.686***	1.554	6.525***	8.757***	5.225***
Public rail per capita does not Granger cause income per capita	0.588	3.357**	3.002**	2.371*	2.690**
GMP per capita does not Granger cause public rail per capita	0.075	1.302	1.228	1.020	1.453
Transit per capita does not Granger cause income per capita	1.454	1.937	2.149*	1.322	1.410
Income per capita does not Granger cause transit per capita	0.993	0.592	0.490	0.519	0.389
Surface transport per capita does not Granger cause income per capita	0.666	1.946	0.078	0.475	0.589
Income per capita does not Granger cause surface transport per capita	25.432***	0.387	0.450	0.320	0.156

Notes:
*, **, *** denote significance at the 10, 5 and 1 percent levels, respectively.
All variables are measured in first order difference.
Sample size: 608.

five-year lags are used. Next, public rail per capital is found to "Granger cause" the variation of income per capita when two to five-year lags are used, but the reserve causality is not found. The causation from transit stock per capita to the variation of income per capita is found significant only at the 10 percent significance level when the three-year lags are used. In terms of the overall surface transportation capital stock, the income per capita is found to "Granger cause" the variation of the surface transportation stock per capita in the short term when one-year lag is used. Still, the reverse causality from the surface transportation per capita to the income per capita is not found at any significance level.

5. CONCLUSION

By implementing the three sets of Granger causality test between economic variables and surface transportation variables, this study empirically tested the casual linkages between surface transportation infrastructure and regional economic performance. Real GMP per capita, employment and real personal income per capita are selected as the indicators for regional economic output. The major contribution of this study is that the linkages between economic output and surface transportation infrastructure were examined using panel Granger causality by different economic indicators, modes of transportation and different time lags. The analysis provides much rigorous information at the disaggregated level to understand the causal relationships between the different modes of surface transportation infrastructure and economic outputs.

Generally speaking, the study found that the causal relationship between economic output and surface transportation infrastructure varies by economic indicators, modes of transportation and years of lags being considered in the case of northeast corridor during the period 1991–2009. The Granger causality test suggests that the economic outputs have a more immediate causation on the variation of the aggregate surface transportation per capita but not the opposite, as the causations are found significant when only one-year's lag is used. This confirms that fact that surface transportation investment policies in the U.S. that are implemented by the federal, state and local governments are influenced by regional economic condition. One the other hand, the causal influence of the surface transportation per capita is found to be particularly strong on employment and in a relative longer term (when two- to four-years' lags are used). This may reflect the fact that the regional economic impact of surface transportation infrastructure investment may have been achieved through job creation and such lagged effects emerge normally two to four years after the actual policy implementation.

In terms of the modal specific examinations, different causations are found between highway per capita and different economic output variables. For instance, economic output variables including GMP per capita, employment and personal income per capita are found to "Granger cause" the variations of highway stock per capita whereas the only opposite causations from highway per capita to employment and personal income per capita are confirmed. The two-way causations between highway and employment and income per capita suggest the existence of endogenous relationships. This is consistent with the previous study by Jiwattanakulpaisarn et al. (2009), who adopted the density of highway lane-miles as the transportation input variable for the causal assessment. The causations between public rail per capita and economic outputs are not consistent among different economic variables and across the different lagged models, but the general pattern suggests public rail per capita "Granger causes" the level of employment when a one-year lag is used and it "Granger causes" the variation of income per capita when two- to five-year lags are used. While the result might suggest public rail investment is likely to cause the variation of employment and income per capita, given that the public rail infrastructure is still relatively small compared to other surface transportation modes as well as the fact that cities with Amtrak stations are large metropolitan areas that also likely have strong agglomeration economies which were not measured, the causation from public rail to employment and income per capita may approximate for other unmeasured factors.

It should be noted that the caveats related to the data refining process (such as the selection of depreciation rate) and methodologies (such as the endogeniety between lag variables) may jeopardize the research finding and should be further explored in future study. While the sensitivity of the causation among different modes of transportation has been examined using the classical Granger approach based on the temporal lags, the spatial causations related to the directions of potential spillover effects from different transportation infrastructure should be further evaluated. Last but not least, the research findings only apply to the specific regions and periods outlined in this study. Generic implication or comparison to other regions or periods may be problematic.

REFERENCES

Andersson, Åke E., Christer Anderstig, and Björn Hårsman. (1990). "Knowledge and communications infrastructure and regional economic change." *Regional Science and Urban Economics* 20 (3): 359–376.

Aschauer, David Alan. (1989). "Is public expenditure productive?" *Journal of Monetary Economics* 23 (2): 177–200.

Aschauer, David Alan. (1990). *Why is infrastructure important?* Conference Series Proceedings. Federal Reserve Bank of Boston.

Aschauer, David Alan. (1994). "Infrastructure and macroeconomic performance: direct and indirect effects." Paper to OECD Conference on Capital Formation and Employment. Amsterdam.

Blum, Ulrich. (1982). "Effects of transportation investments on regional growth: a theoretical and empirical investigation." *Papers in Regional Science* 49 (1): 169–184.

Boarnet, Marlon G. (1997). "Infrastructure services and the productivity of public capital: the case of streets and highways." *National Tax Journal* 50 (1): 39–57.

Boarnet, Marlon G., and A.F. Haughwout. (2000). "Do highways matter? Evidence and policy implications of highways' influence on metropolitan development." A discussion paper prepared for The Brookings Institution Center on Urban and Metropolitan Policy. Washington D.C.

Chen, Z., and K.E. Haynes. (2013). "Transportation capital in the United States:

a multimodal general equilibrium analysis." *Public Works Management & Policy*.
Chen, Z., and K.E. Haynes. (2014a). "Public surface transportation and regional output: a spatial panel approach." *Papers in Regional Science*.
Chen, Z., and K.E. Haynes. (2014b). "Spatial impact of transportation infrastructure: a spatial econometric CGE approach." In Adam Rose and Peter Nijkamp (eds), *Regional Science Matters – Studies dedicated to Walter Isard*, Springer-Verlag.
Chen, Z., and K.E. Haynes. (2015a). "Multilevel assessment of public transportation infrastructure: a spatial econometric computable general equilibrium approach." *Annals of Regional Science*.
Chen, Z., and K.E. Haynes. (2015b). "Regional impact of public transportation infrastructure: a spatial panel assessment of the U.S. northeast megaregion." *Economic Development Quarterly*.
Duffy-Deno, K.T., and R.W. Eberts. (1991). "Public infrastructure and regional economic development: a simultaneous equations approach." *Journal of Urban Economics* 30 (3): 329–343.
Federal Railroad Administration. (1998). *Privatization of Intercity Rail Passenger Service in the United States*. Washington D.C.: Federal Railroad Administration.
Fernald, John G. (1999). "Roads to prosperity? Assessing the link between public capital and productivity." *The American Economic Review* 89 (3): 619–638.
Gramlich, Edward M. (1994). "Infrastructure investment: a review essay." *Journal of Economic Literature* 32 (3): 1176–1196.
Gramlich, Edward M. (2001). "Infrastructure and economic development." Remarks by Governor Edward M. Gramlich at the Texas Trade Corridors New Economy Conference. San Antonio, Texas, August 3.
Granger, Clive W.J. (1969). "Investigating causal relations by econometric models and cross-spectral methods." *Econometrica* 37 (3): 424–438.
Haines, Joel D., and Nawaz M. Sharif. (2006). "A framework for managing the sophistication of the components of technology for global competition." *Competitiveness Review: An International Business Journal Incorporating Journal of Global Competitiveness* 16 (2): 106–121.
Harmatuck, D.J. (1996). "The influence of transportation infrastructure on economic development." *Logistics and Transportation Review* 32 (1): 63–76.
Hartwig, Jochen. (2009). "A panel Granger-causality test of endogenous vs. exogenous growth." KOF Working Paper 231.
Holtz-Eakin, Douglas, Whitney Newey, and Harvey S. Rosen. (1988). "Estimating vector autoregressions with panel data." *Econometrica* 56 (6): 1371–1395.
Jiwattanakulpaisarn, Piyapong. (2008). "The impact of transport infrastructure investment on regional employment: an empirical investigation." PhD dissertation, Imperial College London.
Jiwattanakulpaisarn, Piyapong, Robert B. Noland, Daniel J. Graham, and John W. Polak. (2009). "Highway infrastructure and state-level employment: a causal spatial analysis." *Papers in Regional Science* 88 (1): 133–159.
Kemmerling, Achim, and Andreas Stephan. (2002). "The contribution of local public infrastructure to private productivity and its political economy: evidence from a panel of large German cities." *Public Choice* 113 (3–4): 403–424.
Kessides, Christine. (1993). "The contributions of infrastructure to economic

development: a review of experience and policy implications." World Bank discussion paper.
Lau, Sau-Him Paul, and Chor-Yiu Sin. (1997). "Public infrastructure and economic growth: time-series properties and evidence." *The Economic Record* 73 (221): 125–135.
Levin, A., C.F. Lin, and C.S.J. Chu. (2002). "Unit root tests in panel data: asymptotic and finite-sample properties." *Journal of Econometrics* 108 (1): 1–24.
Nadiri, M. Ishaq, and Theofanis P. Mamuneas. (1996). "Contribution of highway capital to industry and national productivity growth (No. BAT-94-008)." Report prepared for Apogee Research, Inc., for the Federal Highway Administration Office of Policy Development.
Ozbay, Kaan, Dilruba Ozmen-Ertekin, and Joseph Berechman. (2007). "Contribution of transportation investments to county output." *Transport Policy* 14 (4): 317–329.
Pesaran, M.H. (2007). "A simple panel unit root test in the presence of cross-section dependence." *Journal of Applied Econometrics* 22 (2): 265–312.
Queiroz, Cesar A.V., and Surhid P. Gautam. (1992). "Road infrastructure and economic development: some diagnostic indicators." World Bank policy research working paper 921.
Regional Plan Association. (2007). "Northeast megaregion 2050: a common future." New York: Regional Plan Association.
Romer, Paul M. (1994). "The origins of endogenous growth." *The Journal of Economic Perspectives* 8 (1): 3.
Solow, Robert M. (1956). "A contribution to the theory of economic growth." *The Quarterly Journal of Economics* 70 (1): 65–94.
Solow, Robert M. (1957). "Technical change and the aggregate production function." *The Review of Economics and Statistics* 39 (3): 312–320.
Sturm, Jan-Egbert, Jan Jacobs, and Peter Groote. (1999). "Output effects of infrastructure investment in the Netherlands, 1853–1913." *Journal of Macroeconomics* 21 (2): 355–380.
U.S. Government Accountability Office. (2004). "Intercity passenger rail: Amtrak's management of northeast corridor improvements demonstrates need for applying best practices (No. GAO-04-94)." Washington D.C.: United States General Accounting Office.

APPENDIX 1: METROPOLITAN STATISTICAL AREAS IN THE STUDY

Core Based Statistical Area	Name	Type	ID
10900	Allentown–Bethlehem–Easton, PA–NJ	MSA	17
12100	Atlantic City, NJ	MSA	26
12580	Baltimore–Towson, MD	MSA	31
12700	Barnstable Town, MA	MSA	9
14460	Boston–Cambridge–Quincy, MA–NH	MSA	5
14860	Bridgeport–Stamford–Norwalk, CT	MSA	14
18180	Concord, NH	McSA	2
20100	Dover, DE	MSA	28
25420	Harrisburg–Carlisle, PA	MSA	20
25540	Hartford–West Hartford–East Hartford, CT	MSA	10
28740	Kingston, NY	MSA	7
29540	Lancaster, PA	MSA	24
30140	Lebanon, PA	MSA	21
30340	Lewiston–Auburn, ME	MSA	0
31700	Manchester–Nashua, NH	MSA	3
35300	New Heaven–Milford, CT	MSA	15
35620	New York–Northern New Jersey–Long Island, NY–NJ–PA	MSA	18
35980	Norwich–New London, CT	MSA	13
36140	Ocean City, NJ	MSA	29
37980	Philadelphia–Camden–Wilmington, PA–NJ–DE–MD	MSA	22
38860	Portland–South Portland–Biddeford, ME	MSA	1
39100	Poughkeepsie–Newburgh–Middletown, NY	MSA	8
39300	Providence–New Bedford–Fall River, RI–MA	MSA	16
39740	Reading, PA	MSA	19
42540	Scranton–Wikes–Barre, PA	MSA	12
44140	Springfield, MA	MSA	4
45940	Trenton–Ewing, NJ	MSA	23
47220	Vineland–Millville–Bridgeton, NJ	MSA	27
47900	Washington–Arlington–Alexandria, DC–VA–MD–WV	MSA	30
48740	Willimantic, CT	McSA	11
49340	Worcester, MA	MSA	6
49620	York–Hanover, PA	MSA	25

Note: MSA= Metropolitan Statistical Area, McSA=Micropoltian Statistical Area.

10. An accessibility index for the Metropolitan Region of São Paulo

Renato S. Vieira and Eduardo A. Haddad

1. INTRODUCTION

According to Spiekermann and Neubauer (2002), accessibility is the most important factor in defining the locational advantage of one region over others. As stated by Carruthers and Lawson (1995), urban accessibility is a relevant aspect of population welfare, and the importance of accessibility increases as societies become more urbanized. However, in the metropolitan regions of the developing nations, the poorer households usually settle on the periphery, where they face a lack of opportunities and higher transportation costs (Vasconcellos, 1999).

As the biggest metropolitan area in Brazil, São Paulo is a clear example of this problem. As observed by Villaça (2011), the central southwestern quadrant of the city is inhabited by rich people, and it is also the area with the highest concentration of employment and urban services. On the other hand, the poorer households (the majority of population) reside on the periphery, which are areas with low density of employment, forcing the majority of the population to commute from the city edges (where they live) to downtown São Paulo (where they work). In addition, as stated by Rolnik and Klintowitz (2011), the transport infrastructure of São Paulo privileges the private vehicle mode, with large avenues and urban highways exclusively for cars; meanwhile, the public system was never a priority for city planners. As a result, São Paulo has an inadequate public transportation system. Summing up the accessibility problem, the wealthy live in central areas, very close to their jobs, and use their private vehicles on high speed avenues. On the other hand, the poorer households reside on the periphery, far from their employment and they depend on public transportation, which was historically ignored by urban planners.

As a measurement of locational advantage, accessibility is a common component of hedonic models for housing valuation. However, because of the lack of data, some simple approximations of accessibility are used; for example, Hermann and Haddad (2005) calculate the Euclidian distance to Sé Square, which is the historical landmark of São Paulo located in the region with the highest density of jobs in the metropolitan area; and Gomes et al. (2012) estimate accessibility as the distance to the closest subway station. However, both of these approximations do not consider the total distribution of jobs nor the heterogeneity of transport infrastructure, and that is why this study aims to elaborate a measurement that contemplates both these aspects.

The literature on empirical studies of urban accessibility is abundant. Several studies analyze the patterns and affects of accessibility distribution for a variety of regions, especially in the developing world. However, we are not aware of any such study carried out for any Brazilian metropolitan region.

Geurs et al. (2012) provide an extensive review of the use of accessibility measurements. The authors identify that one important trend of accessibility studies is the analysis of the social impacts of the transport system and transport decision making, which had received considerably less attention from researchers.

2. THE ACCESSIBILITY ISSUE IN THE METROPOLITAN REGION OF SÃO PAULO

In 2010, the Metropolitan Region of São Paulo had 19,683,975 inhabitants, corresponding to 10 percent of Brazil's population, and 14.4 percent of its gross domestic product (GDP) (IBGE, 2011). However, the city reached this size in a relatively short period; in 1890 it had only 65,000 inhabitants, and as a consequence of European immigration and national industrialization, the city received millions of immigrants during the first half of the twentieth century. Till 1950, the transport system was centered on the tram; however, according to Rolnik and Klintowitz (2011), during the 1950s, the core of transport structure changed from rail to road.[1] The city kept growing rapidly until the end of the 1980s, when the total population reached 8.6 million inhabitants,[2] and by this time, the city's economy was already consolidated in the service sector.

According to Nadalin (2010), during the second half of the twentieth century there was a "displacement" of the central business district (CBD), which shifted from the historical downtown to the southwestern quadrant of the city, as shown in Figure 10.1.

1 For a detailed revision of the historical development of São Paulo's transportation network, see Rolnik and Klintowitz (2011).

2 Not counting the other cities of the metropolitan region.

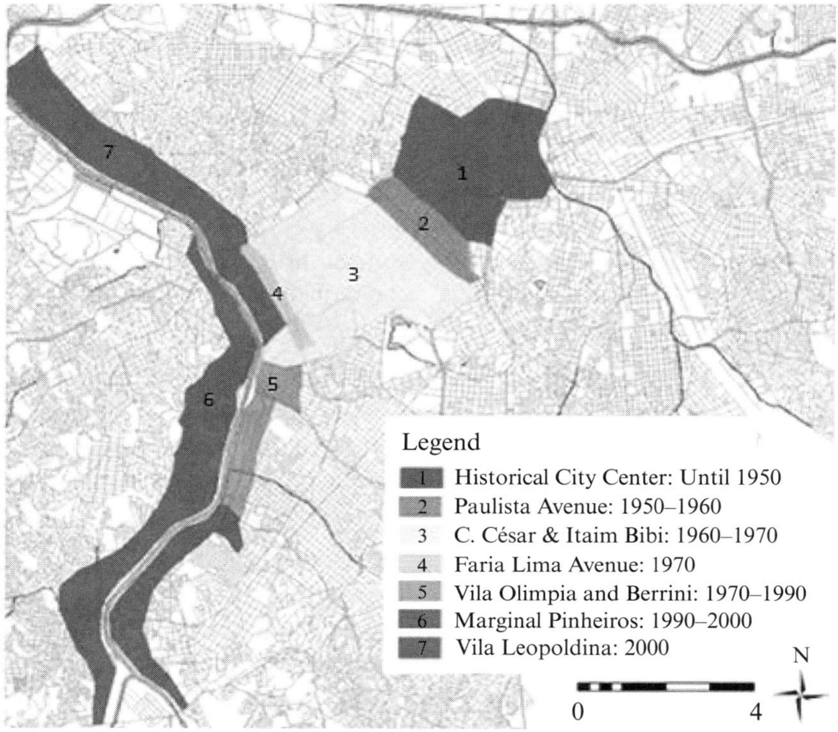

Source: Nadalin (2010).

Figure 10.1 Spatial shift of the CBD

It is difficult to identify nowadays where the CBD is, because there is no central and unique region that has both the highest concentration of employment and companies' headquarters. For instance, although historical downtown has the highest employment density of the urban area, it is neither the most expensive area nor does it have the jobs with higher wages, which instead are concentrated around Faria Lima and Berrini avenues in the southwestern quadrant.

The population of São Paulo is fairly evenly distributed over the urban area, and it is difficult to identify any spatial pattern regarding the population density over the entire metropolitan area. Other variables such as employment, income, and education have a clear spatial pattern, with higher values on central areas; however, while employment distribution is centered downtown, income and tertiary education have the highest values on the southwestern quadrant of the city (see these figures in Appendix 1).

According to Villaça (2011), the spatial distribution of employment and transport infrastructure are the cornerstones of the socioeconomic segregation in São Paulo and other Brazilian cities;[3] the richer households live near their place of employment and take advantage of the road infrastructure, while the poorer households live on the periphery, and are dependent on public transportation. Therefore, when developing a measurement of accessibility, it is relevant to capture these two vectors (distribution of jobs and transport infrastructure).

3. METHODOLOGY

The accessibility index developed in this study is based on Hansen's formulation (Hansen, 1959), which defines accessibility as the potential of opportunities for interaction. According to Du and Mulley (2006), the Hansen gravity-based accessibility measures can be considered the most robust approach to measure accessibility to a certain service, such as employment, as the main advantage of this indicator is the ability to combine the effects of transport and land use. The limitations are: the calibration of the impedance function and the segregation of the effects of separation and attractiveness. Nevertheless, indicators derived from Hansen's model have been widely used for this type of measurement in the literature (Raia, 2000), and its basic formulation is shown below:

$$A_i = \sum_{j=1}^{n} \frac{w_j}{d_{ij}(t)} \tag{10.1}$$

According to this formula, the accessibility A for each region i is given by the summation of opportunities w available at each region j divided by the impedance $d_{ij}(t)$ to go from i to j.

We defined the opportunities w_j as the total employment E in each region j.

$$w_j = E_j \tag{10.2}$$

The values of E_j were extracted from the Origin-Destination (OD) Survey of 2007, in which 30,000 households were interviewed to collect socioeconomic and commuting data on all residents. The Metropolitan Region

[3] For a complete analysis of the historical process of urban organization in Brazil see Villaça (2011).

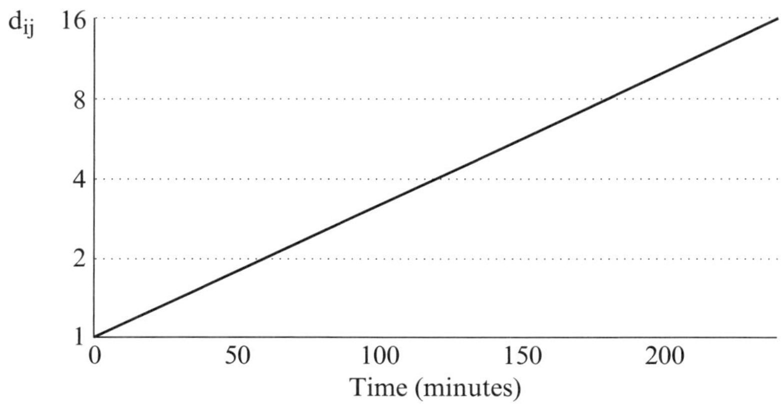

Figure 10.2 Impedance function with $\alpha = 0.01154$

of São Paulo was divided into 460 zones, and applying specific expansion factors, the projected values for each variable were extrapolated to the entire population in each zone. Thus, regions *i* and *j* are defined according to the 460 zones of the OD survey.

We defined the impedance function $d_{ij}(t)$ as an exponential function of travel time between each pair of zones.

$$d_{ij}(t) = e^{\alpha t} \quad (10.3)$$

where α is a calibration parameter, which was defined as:

$$e^{\alpha \times 60} = 2 \rightarrow \alpha = 0.01154 \quad (10.4)$$

From this definition, the impedance function has the characteristic shown in Figure 10.2.

The reason for choosing this specific value for the parameter α is that it provides an intuitive interpretation for the impedance factor. Any job located within zone *i* itself is weighted by 1; a job located 1 hour from zone *i* is weighted by 1/2; a job located 2 hours from zone *i* is weighted by 1/4; 4 hours leads to weight of 1/8; and so on.

It must be noted that the relative value of accessibility over different zones is susceptible to different specifications of α and to different functional forms of the impedance variable. Johansson et al. (2003) show that "willingness to commute" is not linear on commuting time. The authors observe that the frequency of commuting decreases at a slower ratio for destinations located between zero and 45 minutes, it decreases more rapidly

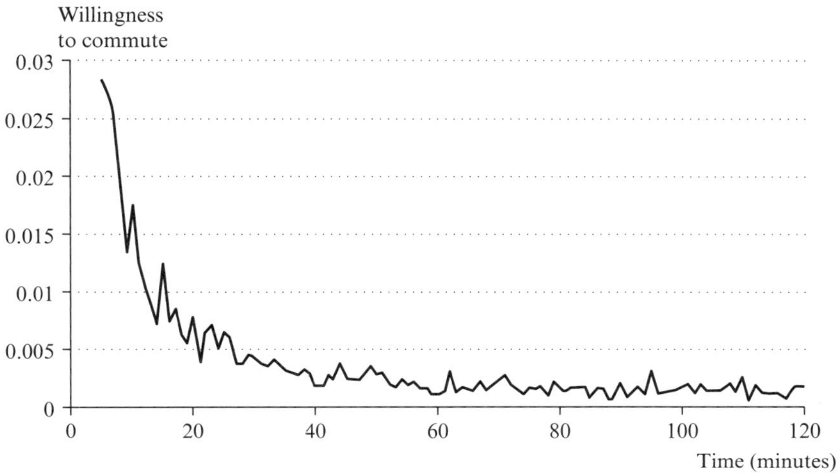

Figure 10.3 Observed willingness to commute over commuting time

for destinations between 45 and 60 minutes and finally decreases slowly again for destinations over 60 minutes. What can be intuited from this result is that commuters have different time sensitivities for local, regional and interregional interaction. However, in our study we are only dealing with local commuting, which suggests that the linearity assumption may not be an issue. Figure 10.3 displays the average willingness to commute over time for the OD Zones. The curve pattern does not seem to resemble the nonlinear relation observed by Johansson et al.

The travel time was calculated by a transit engineering firm, which used Equilibre Multimodal, Multimodal Equilibrium (EMME) software. They estimated the travel times both by private vehicles and by public transportation. For private vehicles, the estimations included only the travel time, and for public transportation, it considered walking, waiting, and in-vehicle times. Therefore, two indices were possible:

$$(a)\, A_{i,pv} = \sum_{j=1}^{460} \frac{E_j}{e^{0.01154 \times t_{ij}}}$$

$$(b)\, A_{i,pt} = \sum_{j=1}^{460} \frac{E_j}{e^{0.01154 \times t_{ij}}} \qquad (10.5)$$

where (a) calculates the accessibility A by private vehicle for each region i, and (b) the accessibility A by public transportation also for each region i.

4. RESULTS

4.1 General Results

The accessibility values for the private vehicle mode are higher than the values for public transportation for all the quartile break values (Table 10.1). The average value for private vehicle is 22 percent higher than the average value for public transportation, and the standard deviation is 18 percent higher.

The histograms (Figure 10.4) show that the main difference between the two distributions is that accessibility by private vehicle surpasses 6 million in 25 percent of the regions, but none in the case of public transportation.

Table 10.1 Basic statistics for the accessibility indices

	Private vehicle	Public transportation
Minimum	444,496	107,324
1st quartile	3,619,281	3,243,575
Median	4,789,450	4,113,647
3rd quartile	6,081,871	4,881,718
Maximum	6,984,029	5,835,243
Average	4,721,267	3,871,235
Std Deviation	1,533,880	1,293,130

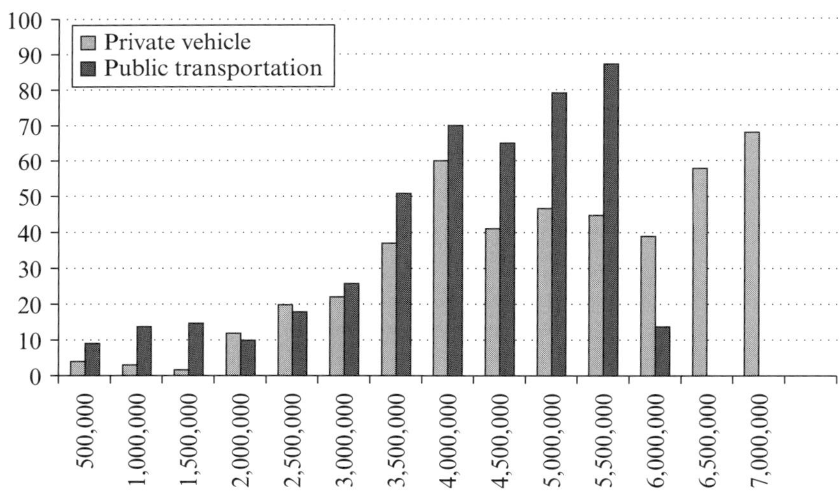

Figure 10.4 Histograms for the accessibility indices

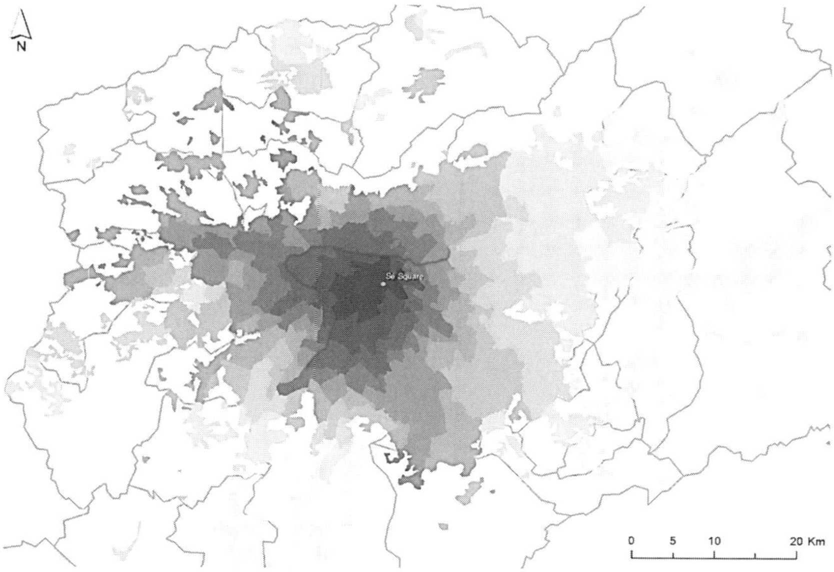

Figure 10.5 *Spatial distribution of accessibility by the private vehicle mode*

4.2 Spatial Distribution of Results

Figures 10.5 and 10.6 show the spatial distribution of the two indices, and both maps are shaded according to a division of the 460 zones into ten groups with 46 zones in each group); the darker the shade the higher the accessibility of the group.

From Figure 10.5, it becomes clear that accessibility by private vehicle has a spatial distribution in the shape of concentric rings, with higher accessibility the closer the zone is to the center.

However, the center of the distribution does not seem to be the *Sé*, but at some point to its west. By plotting this map over a satellite picture of the city, it can be observed that the central point of the distribution seems to be somewhere around Paulista Avenue (shown in Appendix 2).

Regarding accessibility by public transportation, Figure 10.6 displays its spatial distribution. Although it also has a pattern of higher accessibility the closer the zone is to the center, it is not possible to observe the concentric rings of Figure 10.5.

Although the center of the distribution seems to be the *Sé* Square, from plotting it over a satellite picture of the city, it can be observed that there is

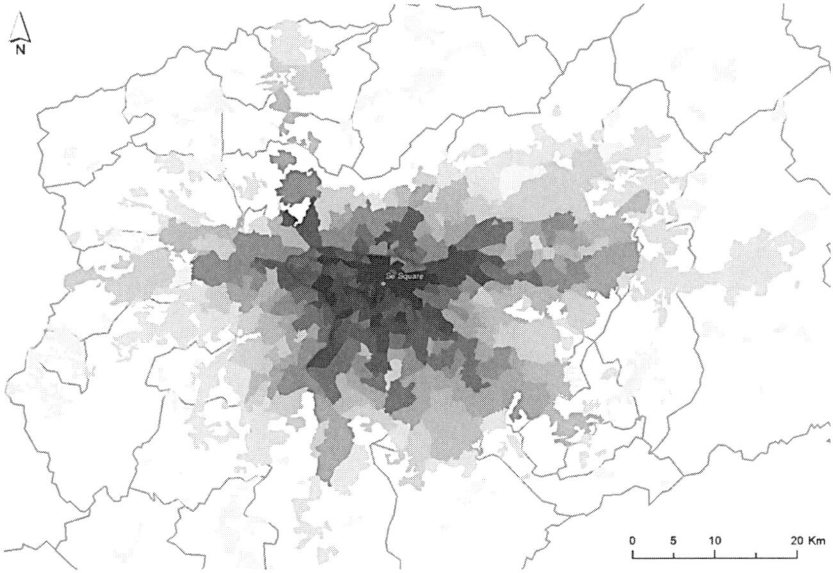

Figure 10.6 Spatial distribution of accessibility by public transportation mode

a relationship between the spatial distribution of the index and the urban railway network of the city (Appendix 2).

We also analyzed the difference between the two indices, which is shown in Figure 10.7. Surprisingly, there are a few regions where accessibility is higher for public transportation, for example in some peripheral zones to the east, south, and southeast of the city, which are regions served by the public railway network. The probable explanation for this result might be that the eastern and southern parts of the city do not have as many high speed roads as the western; however, it is in these areas that a huge proportion of the population is concentrated, and because their jobs are located downtown, this large number of people commuting leads to traffic jams on the streets of the few high speed roads connecting these peripheries to the city center. Such congestion does not affect the users of the rail system, increasing their relative accessibility.

The western part, however, has a higher accessibility by private vehicle, independent of whether the zones are closer to or farther from the city center, and the explanation might be the same as the one given above, that is, this part of the city has fewer inhabitants and greater high speed road infrastructure.

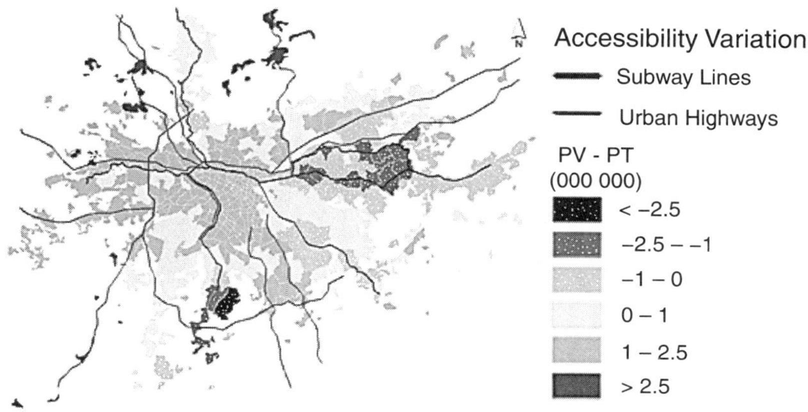

Figure 10.7 Difference between private and public accessibility

4.3 Spatial Correlation Between Income and Accessibility

Villaça (2011) argued that the richer households live in central areas with higher accessibility, whereas the poorer households live in the peripheral regions with lower accessibility; therefore, we calculated a spatial multivariate local indicator of spatial association (LISA) for per capita income and the accessibility indices; the significant clusters are presented in Figure 10.8.

Both maps were calculated with a spatial weighting matrix of the queen type, and they show significant clusters of high income and high

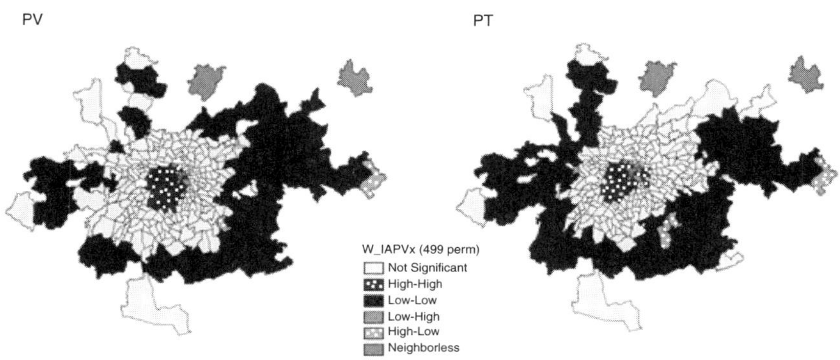

Figure 10.8 Multivariate LISA clusters for accessibility indices and income per capita

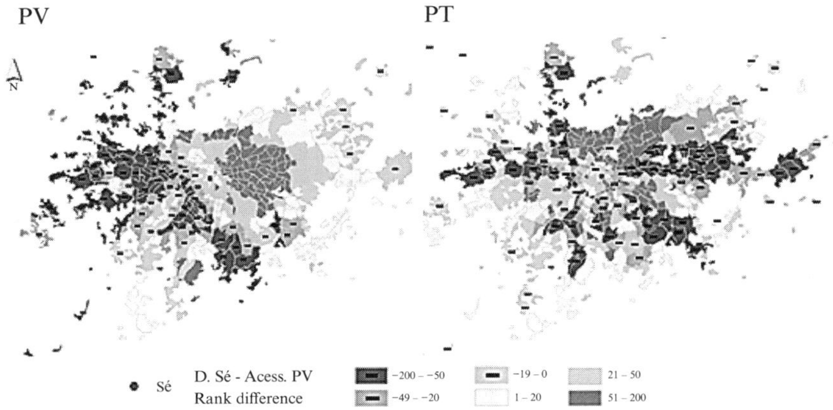

Figure 10.9 Difference between the indices and distance to Sé

accessibility in the central-western part of São Paulo and a low income, low accessibility cluster at the periphery, confirming Villaça's proposition. However, we also observed an interesting outlier; for both maps, in the central part of the city, there are some zones with low income and high accessibility, contrary to the pattern observed for almost all other zones. The city center has the best public transportation infrastructure of the city, with several subway stations and also the highest density of jobs; however, it is a poor neighborhood.

4.4 Comparing this Index to Other Measurements

Figure 10.9 compares the difference between the indices calculated in this study and the measurement used by Hermann and Haddad (2005), that is, Euclidian distance to downtown São Paulo (Sé Square). The darkest regions indicate zones where the Euclidian distance overestimates accessibility, whereas the slightly lighter ones indicate underestimation. For the private vehicle, the distance to Sé does not capture the differences between the eastern and western parts of the city, overestimating accessibility on the eastern part and underestimating on the western. Meanwhile, when we compare it to the public transportation index, the main difference is related to the proximity of a region to train and subway stations, which is not considered when calculating the distance to Sé.

From Figure 10.9 it is clear that the gravity-based accessibility indices capture a broader picture of accessibility distribution, including the transport infrastructure and the heterogeneities of the spatial distribution of employment.

5. CONCLUSION

This study developed an accessibility index to employment for the Metropolitan Region of São Paulo, and was constructed according to Hansen's gravity-based formulation. From the database, it was possible to create two indices, one for the private vehicle mode and a second for public transportation.

The first observation was an average higher accessibility by the private vehicle mode in the majority of the city's zones, which was expected. However, for a few regions located on the edges of eastern, southern, and southwestern parts of the city, the values for the accessibility by public transportation were higher, probably as a consequence of road congestion and the availability of train and subways, making public transportation a faster option to reach the highest density employment areas.

A similarity between both indices was also noted, in the sense that zones have higher accessibility the closer they are to the city center. However, the private vehicle index distribution is shaped as concentric rings, which are centered somewhere near Paulista Avenue. Meanwhile, the map for public transportation is aligned with the railway network.

Finally, a significant spatial correlation between income and accessibility was observed, confirming the observation that the richer households live in regions with better accessibility and closer to the central parts of the city and the poorer households in the distant periphery with lower accessibility. The main exception to this pattern was the area around downtown, which although having high accessibility, is inhabited by poor people.

It must be noted that this study is limited to a static analysis of the spatial distribution of accessibility over a single metropolitan region. Therefore we do not address the dynamic relationship between accessibility and the spatial allocation of workers and firms.

For now, we make the following recommendation for further topics of research: (i) reproduce the index for other metropolitan areas to allow a comparison of the results; (ii) compare this formulation with other accessibility indicators; and (iii) assess the dynamic effects of accessibility over the structure of the urban economy (e.g. land value).

REFERENCES

Carruthers, D. and Lawson, G. The contribution of transport to the quality of life. In: Blessington, H.K., *Urban Transport*. London, Thomas Telford. 1995, pp. 11–20.

Du, H. and Mulley, C. Relationship between transport accessibility and land value. *Transportation Research Record*, v. 1977, 2006, pp. 197–205.
Geurs, K., Krizek, K. and Reggiani, A. *Accessibility Analysis and Transport Planning: Challenges for Europe and North America*. Cheltenham, UK and Northampton, MA: Edward Elgar Publishing. 2012.
Gomes, A., Maciel, V. and Kuwahara, M. *Determinantes dos Preços de Imóveis Residenciais Verticais no Município de São Paulo*. ANPEC XL. Porto de Galinhas. 2012.
Hansen, W. How accessibility shapes land use. *Journal of the American Institute of Planners*, v. 25, n. 2, 1959, pp. 73–76.
Hermann, B and Haddad, E. Mercado Imobiliário e Amenidades Urbanas: A view through the window. *Estudos Econômicos*, v. 35, n. 2, 2005, pp. 237–269.
IBGE. *Sinópse do Censo Demográfico 2010*. Instituto Brasileiro de Geografia e Estatística - IBGE. Rio de Janeiro. 2011.
Johansson, B., Klaesson, J. and Olsson, M. Commuters' non-linear response to time distances. *Journal of Geographical Systems*, v. 5, n. 3, 2003, pp. 315–329.
Nadalin, V. *Três ensaios sobre economia urbana e mercado de habitação em São Paulo*. Tese (Doutorado em Economia) – FEA-USP. São Paulo. 2010.
Raia Jr., A. *Acessibilidade e mobilidade na estimativa de um índice de potencial de viagens utilizando redes neurais artificiais e sistemas de informação geográfica*. Tese (Doutorado em Engenharia Civil) – Escola de Engenharia de São Carlos – USP. São Carlos. 2000.
Rolnik, R. and Klintowitz, D. (I)Mobilidade na cidade de São Paulo. *Estudos avançados*, São Paulo, v. 25, n. 71, Apr. 2011.
Spiekermann, K. and Neubauer, J. *European Accessibility and Peripherality: Concepts, Models and Indicators*. Stockholm, Sweden: Nordregio – Nordic Centre for Spatial Development. 2002.
Vasconcellos, E. *Circular é preciso, viver não é preciso: a história do trânsito na cidade de São Paulo*. São Paulo: Annablume. 1999.
Villaça, F. São Paulo: segregação urbana e desigualdade. *Estudos avançados*, São Paulo, v. 25, n. 71, Apr. 2011.

APPENDIX 1: DEMOGRAPHIC FIGURES FOR THE METROPOLITAN REGION OF SÃO PAULO

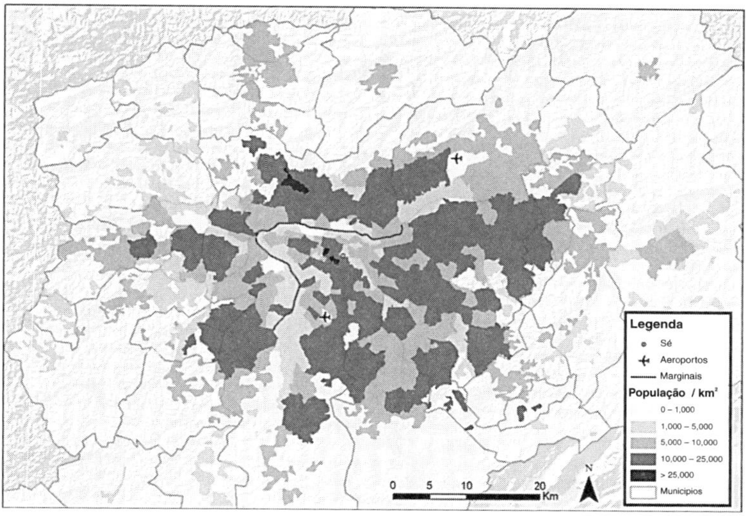

Figure 10.A1.1 Population density

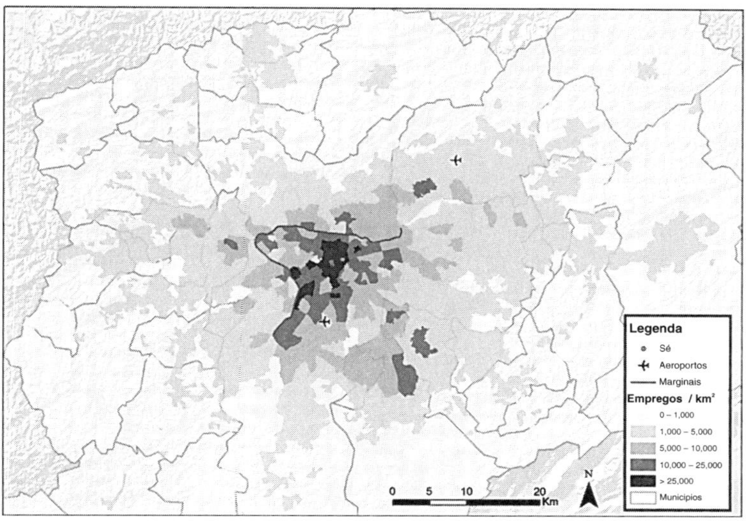

Figure 10.A1.2 Employment density

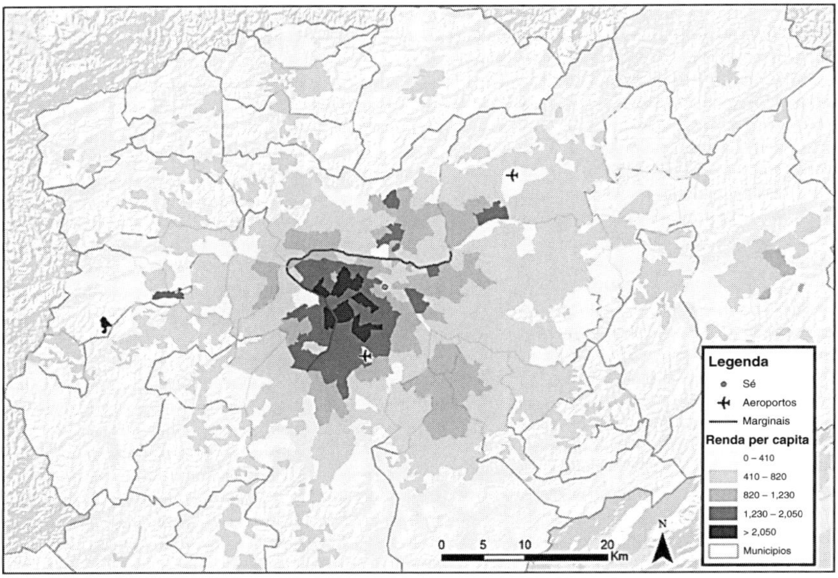

Figure 10.A1.3 Income per capita

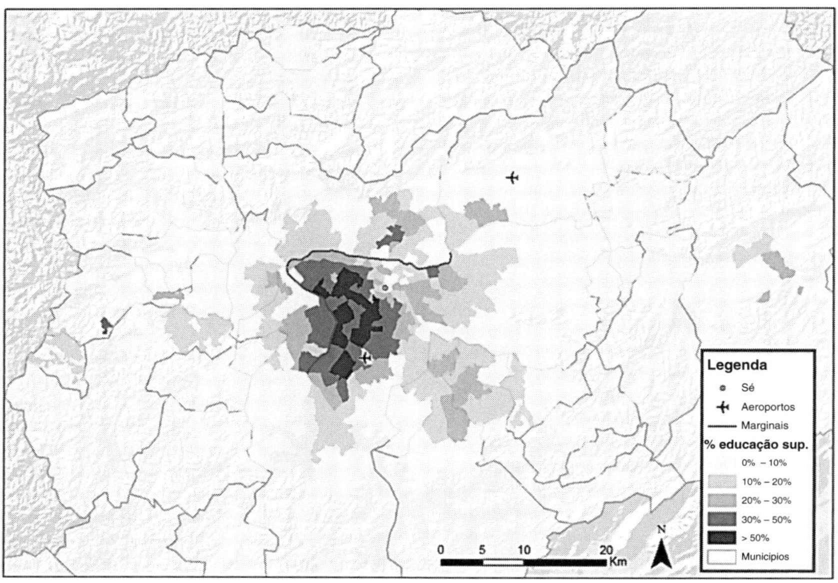

Figure 10.A1.4 Proportion of population with tertiary education

APPENDIX 2: SPATIAL DISTRIBUTION OF ACCESSIBILITY AND THE TRANSPORT INFRASTRUCTURE

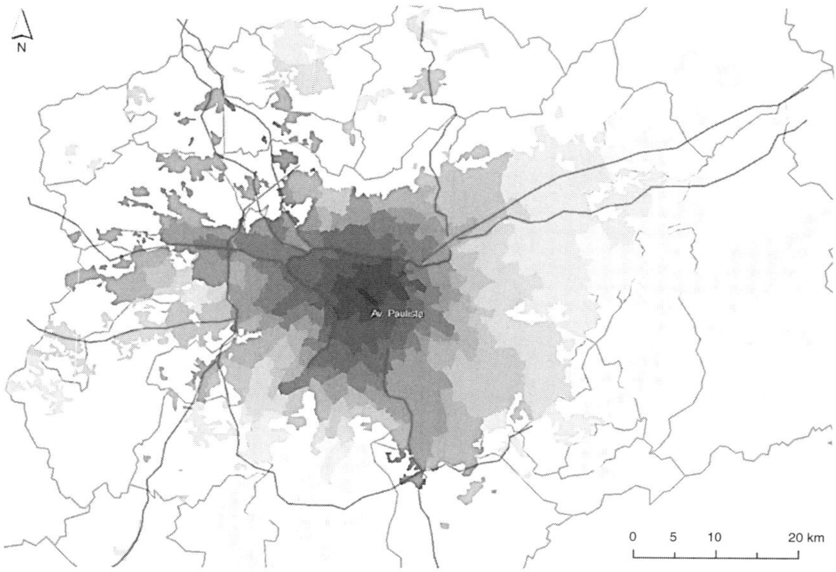

Figure 10.A2.1 Accessibility by private vehicle, Paulista Avenue and main roads

Figure 10.A2.2 Accessibility by public transportation, subway and train network

11. Urbanization and quality of life: an overview of the health impacts of urban and rural residential patterns*

Noriko Ishikawa, Karima Kourtit and Peter Nijkamp

1. INTRODUCTION

The worldwide rise in urbanization leads to a "New Urban World"[1] (see Kourtit and Nijkamp, 2013) which is characterized by higher population densities and higher spatial concentrations of human activity in designated places. This phenomenon may create more options for education, innovation, and choice variety. However, it may also prompt various externalities, such as environmental decay or decline in human health. These studies will address the health outcomes of the urban way of life, in contrast with other settlement patterns (e.g., in rural areas).

Social determinants of health, defined as "the full set of social conditions in which people live and work" (see Solar and Irwin, 2007), have been studied extensively for nearly five decades. A series of studies have shown that health outcomes are affected not only by individual socioeconomic status, but also by the physical environment, and socioeconomic and political circumstances. In March 2005, the Commission on Social Determinants of Health (CSDH) was set up by the World Health Organization (WHO) to collect, collate, and synthesize global evidence on the social determinants of health and their impact on health inequity, and to make recommendations for action to address that inequity (see CSDH, 2008). As the CSDH indicates, to explore social determinants of health is still a major issue to be addressed.

As the CSDH indicates in its final report, it is important to shed light

* This work was supported by Grant-in-Aid for Young Scientists (B) 23730291 from JSPS.

1 "The New Urban World" is that in our age of urbanization – with ever increasing urbanization rates in most countries of the world, in particular in emerging and developing economies – more and more people will move towards urban areas, so that these areas become the "new home of humankind" (Kourtit et al., 2015).

on whether there exist health inequities within and between countries (see CSDH, 2008). The WHO defines health equity as "the absence of unfair and avoidable or remediable differences in health among population groups defined socially, economically, demographically or geographically" (see Solar and Irwin, 2007). In other words, health inequities can (should) be reduced by social and economic policies. This is a good reason to find the social determinants of health inequity to close the health gap within and between countries.

Social determinants of health inequity have been explored in various interdisciplinary approaches including economics, epidemiology, political science, spatial planning, and social psychology. A number of studies have explored factors affecting the health status and causes of health inequity. Many researchers have estimated the impact of both the individual characteristics such as gender, race/ethnicity, socioeconomic status and health-related behaviors, and the socioeconomic circumstances including regional deprivation (see Reijneveld and Schene, 1998; Benach and Yasui, 1999; Haynes and Gale, 2000; Barnett et al., 2001; Stafford and Marmot, 2003; Hanlon et al., 2005; Connolly et al., 2007; Fukuda et al., 2007; Winkleby et al., 2007; Havard et al., 2008; Brown and Leyland, 2010; Pampalon et al., 2010), accessibility to and utilization of health services (see Matteson et al., 1998; Basu and Cooper, 2000; Campbell et al., 2001; Gulliford, 2002; Jordan et al., 2003; Arcury et al., 2005a; Morris et al., 2005; Laditka et al., 2009; Sarrazin et al., 2009), social capital (see Kennedy et al., 1998; Veenstra, 2000; Drukker et al., 2003; Smith and Polanyi, 2003; Greiner et al., 2004; Ziersch, 2005; Bell et al., 2006; Kim and Kawachi, 2006; Sirven, 2006; Folland, 2007; Engstrom et al., 2008; Mansyur et al., 2008; Fujisawa et al., 2009; Nogueira, 2009; D'Hombres et al., 2010; Giordano and Lindstrom, 2010; Mair et al., 2010; Mohnen et al., 2011), regional income inequality (see Kawachi and Kennedy, 1997; Kahn et al., 1998; Judge et al., 1998; Soobader and LeClere, 1999; Diez-Roux et al., 2000; McLaughlin and Stokes, 2002; Shibuya et al., 2002; McLeod et al., 2003; De Vogli et al., 2005; Hou and Miles, 2005; Dahl et al., 2006; Ram, 2006; Babones, 2008; Lorgelly and Lindley, 2008), socio-political factors (see Coburn, 2004; Chung and Muntaner, 2006; Navarro et al., 2006; Bartley, 2012), environmental conditions (see Dockery et al., 1993; Schwartz, 1994; Bobak and Leon, 1999; Hoek et al., 2002; Takano et al., 2002; Finkelstein et al., 2003; Jerrett et al., 2003; Frank et al., 2004; Maas et al., 2006; Mitchell and Popham, 2007, 2008; Richardson and Mitchell, 2010), and urbanization (see Senior et al., 2000; Paykel et al., 2000; Vlahov and Galea, 2002; Parks et al., 2003; Woods, 2003; Eberhardt and Pamuk; 2004; O'Reilly et al., 2007; Pampalon et al., 2010; Peen et al., 2010; Monnat and Beeler Pickett, 2011). In general, these effects of socioeconomic circumstances can be separated into compositional and contextual effects. A concise explanation of these definitions has been given by various researchers (see Congdon et al., 1997; Curtis and Jones, 1998; Cummins et al., 2005; Bernard et al., 2007; Mansyur et al., 2008). According to these definitions, compositional effects are related to characteristics of individuals residing in the area, whereas contextual effects depend on spatial and environmental characteristics of the area itself. Although some earlier studies have indicated a considerably smaller magnitude of contextual effect or have found no contextual effects on health outcomes, it is now commonly accepted that the contextual characteristics are important factors in understanding spatial variations in health outcomes.

Most of the effects of socioeconomic circumstances on health outcome seem to be intuitively plausible. In terms of regional deprivation, for example, nearly all studies have shown a statistically significant negative relationship between health outcome and area-level deprivation measured by various indices. Accessibility and utilization of health services, and social capital may positively affect health, while some studies have shown a significant negative relationship between regional income inequality and health outcomes. As for environmental conditions, the level of air pollution is likely to have a negative effect and the amount of green space tends to have a positive effect on cause-specific mortality.

Although the final report of CSDH focuses on health risks in urban areas (see CSDH, 2008), the effect of urbanization on health remains as yet obscure. Some papers have demonstrated that urban environment may have a positive effect on self-rated health (see Kim and Kawachi, 2006; Ziller et al., 2010; Monnat and Beeler Pickett, 2011) and on mortality rate (see Matteson et al., 1998; Lorant et al., 2001; Kindig et al., 2002; Cosby et al., 2008). Other studies, however, have shown that residents living in rural areas may have an advantage in health compared to their counterparts in urban areas (see Congdon et al., 1997; Reijneveld et al., 1999; Rosenberg and Wilson, 2000; Levin, 2003; Maas et al., 2006; Weich et al., 2006; Riva et al., 2009). Additionally, some studies conclude that there exists no significant effect of urbanization on health (see Auster et al., 1969; Campbell et al., 2001; Hyyppa and Maki, 2001; Greiner et al., 2004; Levin and Leyland, 2006). Why do these estimated effects of urbanization vary across countries and studies? And how do we disentangle the independent effects of urban/rural characteristics on health outcomes? The aim of the present chapter is to offer an inventory of studies that have addressed the relationship between urban conditions (sometimes in contrast with rural conditions) and health outcomes.

This chapter consists of eight sections. We first examine key outcomes addressed in regional health surveys (section 2) and overview previous studies dealing with the relationship between urbanization and health (section 3). In the following section, we show the various notions of urbanity across studies. Then we shed light on critical issues in estimating the independent effect of urbanity (rurality) in section 5, and propose six critical contextual factors that may affect health outcomes in section 6. In section 7, we analyze in-depth the externalities associated with a higher population density. A new perspective for future studies investigating the urban/rural effects on health and some concluding remarks are given in the last section.

2. MEASUREMENT OF HEALTH OUTCOMES

Before going into detail, we pay attention to specific health outcomes that are dealt with in the previous studies. The WHO defines outcomes as "the effect the process has had on the people targeted by it (WHO-HIA, 2015)." In our chapter, we specify health outcome as "the health status indicator which may depend on social, economic, demographic or geographic factors."

Self-rated health (SRH) is one of the most common health outcomes used in general health surveys. Although SRH is a subjective measure which quantifies individuals' health conditions assessed by themselves, SRH is thought to be a good predictor of health outcome, which is similar to some objective measures of health status, such as mortality and morbidity (see Kaplan et al., 1996; Miilunpalo et al., 1997; Benjamins et al., 2004; Singh-Manoux et al., 2007; Wu et al., 2013).

Some papers which have revealed the existence of health inequities in England and Wales employ limiting long-term illness (LLTI) as a proxy of health outcome. LLTI is a dichotomous measure of whether or not an individual has a long-term illness. According to the Census 2001 in England and Wales conducted by Office for National Statistics (ONS), LLTI is defined as "anyone who felt they have any long-term illness, health problem or disability which limits their daily activities or the work they can do (ONS, 2001)." Along with SRH, LLTI is also a good self-reported measure of ill health and is commonly used in order to estimate geographical health inequalities. Although Bentham et al. (1995) and Cohen et al. (1995) have raised some concerns about the reliability of LLTI, this indication has been shown to be strongly associated with other health status indicators. In fact, Manor et al. (2001) have proven that LLTI as well as SRH are reliable and valid as health status measures.

Both mortality and morbidity rates are commonly used as objective indicators of health status. In particular, a cause-specific mortality rate, calculated by the number of deaths from a specified cause during a specified time period, is often adopted as a health outcome. Some papers have shown that cause of death is affected by social determinants. Mitchell and Popham (2008) have estimated the impact of the exposure to the natural environment on some cause-specific mortality rates using data in England. They have shown mortality from circulatory diseases is significantly and strongly affected by the exposure to green space, whereas mortality from lung cancer and intentional self-harm is not. Gartner et al. (2011) have examined differences in mortality between rural and urban areas in England and Wales and have concluded that the living environment in rural areas is likely to be desirable for patients with lung cancer and respiratory disease but no significant urban/rural difference could be found for all-cause mortality as well as mortality due to circulatory diseases and cancer. When it comes to morbidity, acute/chronic disease and physical/psychiatric morbidity are often employed in addition to disease-specific morbidity. The cause of death and disease is either classified according to the International Classification of Diseases (ICD), which is maintained by the WHO and has been used in WHO Member States since 1994. The other measure of morbidity is the General Health Questionnaire (GHQ), which is a screening test introduced by Goldberg (1978) to identify psychological distress among adults. The findings of previous studies have indicated that care should be taken to choose the health outcome: Inappropriate health outcomes may skew the results because the impact of socioeconomic factors may differ depending on the disease or cause of death.

Availability of and accessibility to health care facilities and health service utilization are also regarded as health outcomes (see Evashwick et al., 1984; Basu and Cooper, 2000; Dempsey et al., 2003; Gilthorpe and Wilson, 2003; Caldwell et al., 2004; Jordan et al., 2004; Chaix et al., 2005; Morris et al., 2005). Moreover, we find papers have considered hospitalization (see Haynes, 1991; Johnson and Richter, 2002; Corburn et al., 2006; Lostao et al., 2007), the prevalence of disease risk factors and health-related behaviors (see Duncan et al., 1993; Ettner, 1996; Diez-Roux et al., 2000; Frank et al., 2004; Fogelholm et al., 2006; Van Lenthe et al., 2007; Folland, 2008; Hajat et al., 2010), low birthweight and infant mortality rates (see Reading et al., 1994; Lee et al., 1997; Judge et al., 1998; Chung and Muntaner, 2006, 2007; Grady, 2006; Folland, 2007; Luo and Wilkins, 2008; Auger et al., 2009), life expectancy (see Walberg et al., 1998; Gravelle et al., 2002; De Vogli et al., 2005; Navarro et al., 2006; Pampalon et al., 2006; Backhans et al., 2007; Laditka et al., 2007; Whiting and Unwin, 2008) and preventive health care exams and regular checkup care (see Martin et al., 2001; Arcury et al., 2005a, 2005b; Larson and Correa-de-Araujo, 2006) as health outcomes.

Thus, it seems to be difficult to draw an accurate conclusion of whether socioeconomic factors might precisely and steadily affect health outcomes because of the variety of health outcomes. In other words, there may be the possibility of overlooking the influence of key factors on health outcomes if an appropriate indicator of health outcomes were not selected. Moreover, we still need to unravel the processes underlying the effects of socioeconomic as well as geographical factors on health outcomes, although some papers have demonstrated the mechanisms and potential pathways underlying the relationship between income equality and health (see Kaplan et al., 1996; Kawachi and Kennedy, 1999; Marmot and Wilkinson, 2001; Subramanian and Kawachi, 2004).

3. ESTIMATION OF URBAN/RURAL EFFECTS ON HEALTH OUTCOME

As we noted above, urban/rural effects on health outcomes seem not to be clear. From analyzing 105 papers mentioning health inequality between urban and rural areas using quantitative analysis, 29 papers have shown that urban living may offer health benefits, while 42 papers have proven that residents in rural areas are likely to enjoy a healthy life. The remainder of the papers have yielded different results depending on health outcomes (13 papers), or have not been able to find any significant differences between urban and rural areas (five papers). We also note that it is difficult to judge which region has a health advantage from the findings of some papers. Larson and Correa-de-Araujo (2006), for example, have shown that 18 year olds and older females in rural areas are less likely to obtain blood cholesterol tests, dental exams and mammograms in the United States. Although it is well known that these screening tests may lead to early detection of some serious diseases and help to reduce morbidity and mortality, we cannot make a definite assertion that females residing in rural areas are less healthy compared to their counterparts in urban areas. Jordan et al. (2004) have estimated accessibility to both primary and secondary health care in south-west England and have concluded a higher need for health care services in the areas furthest from them after pointing out that "rural" does not always mean remoteness from health care. That is, this chapter has not offered enough evidence to identify the presence of health inequalities due to differences in urban and rural characteristics.

As we noted in the previous section, a series of studies have found a definite relationship between regional deprivation and population health. Some of them have stressed that regional deprivation which estimates some neighborhood socioeconomic indicators could largely account for regional inequalities in health. As Senior et al. (2000) noted, a tendency for lower mortality in more rural areas is substantially reduced after controlling for differences in socioeconomic characteristics using deprivation measures in Wales. Monnat and Beeler Pickett (2011) have shown that individuals living in nonmetropolitan counties are likely to be less healthy compared to their counterparts in metropolitan counties in the United States. But after controlling for county-level socioeconomic factors, the differences in health status between residents in metropolitan versus nonmetropolitan counties would diminish or even vanish completely if some individual-level variables were introduced. Some studies, however, have stressed that it may be important to take into account contextual effects including urbanity in health surveys. House et al. (2000) have estimated prospective effects of urban/suburban/rural residence on mortality among individuals 25 years or older living in the United States and have shown the existence of a higher mortality risk among urban residents. They have concluded that "psychosocial factors" in urban areas which might affect health status should be explored further. Lorant et al. (2001) have shown the significant impact of spatial autocorrelation measured by Moran's I on the relationship between mortality and socioeconomic deprivation and have stated that "location acts as a confounding variable." That is, health inequity may be accounted for by spatial distribution of individuals and the lack of spatial structure data may give biased results when analyzing the relationship between mortality and regional deprivation. In addition to these facts, some papers have clarified the difference of effectiveness between urban and rural areas. Levin and Leyland (2006) and Pampalon et al. (2010) have estimated the difference in mortality rates between the most affluent and the most deprived areas using data from Scotland and Canada respectively. Both of them have concluded that the impact of deprivation is larger on the health of residents living in urban areas than that of their counterparts in rural areas. Maas et al. (2006) have confirmed the positive relationship between the proximity to green spaces and self-rated health in the Netherlands and have identified that the effectiveness of green spaces is likely to be higher for residents living in very highly urban areas than those living in other areas. Mohnen et al. (2011) have shown individuals in urban areas may receive more health benefits from neighborhood-level social capital in the Netherlands. Auger et al. (2009) have demonstrated an educational gradient in birth outcomes among residents living in all areas using data from Quebec, Canada, and the gradient does diminish as rurality increases. These findings imply that the contextual effects of regions should not be ignored in assessing regional health inequities even though these effects may be modest or inconsistent. Hereinafter, we discuss the notion of urbanity which is a key issue for predicting the urban/rural effects on health outcomes.

4. THE NOTION OF URBANITY

The difference in urban/rural effects on health outcomes seems to be partly due to an ambiguous definition of urbanity. The definition of urbanity varies across countries and during different periods reflecting their geographical and socioeconomic differences. The various definitions of "urban" provided by each government (the national census office) are used even when making international comparisons (see the United Nations, 2013).

So it is not surprising that we find various urban/rural definitions across health studies. In previous studies, levels of urbanity are distinguished not only by the definitions which were derived from the census or were set by the government offices in each country but by population size, population density or whether people are living in a core city or not. We should stress the fact that some studies classify areas into "urban areas" and "rest of urban areas." It may be because the majority of the population is concentrated in urban areas. This classification, however, may conceal considerable heterogeneity in rural areas and may lead to inconsistent results.

In the following subsection, we describe some urban/rural definitions commonly used in health studies and highlight a key difference in the definitions.

4.1 Urban Influence Codes and Rural-Urban Continuum Codes

Two kinds of classification schemes are often used in studies on health inequalities in the United States: One is urban influence codes (UIC) and the other is Rural-Urban Continuum Codes (RUCC), both of which are developed by the United States Department of Agriculture Economic Research Service (USDA ERS). The UIC, which was first released in Ghelfi and Parker (1997) and was last modified in 2013 based on the Office of Management and Budget (OMB) metropolitan classification, divides the 3,143 counties, county equivalents, and independent cities in the United States into 12 groups (see USDA, 2013a). Groups are distinguished between metropolitan and nonmetropolitan counties by population size as well as by their adjacency to metropolitan areas. Some studies have grouped these scales and have estimated the difference between urban and rural areas (see Stearns et al., 2000; Auchincloss and Hadden, 2002; Eberhardt and Pamuk, 2004; Larson and Correa-de-Araujo, 2006; Laditka et al., 2009).

RUCC is also commonly used in order to distinguish between urban and rural (see Ziller et al., 2006, 2010; Basu and Mobley, 2007; Cosby et al., 2008; Cossman et al., 2008). First introduced by Hines et al. (1975) and updated in 1974, 1983, 1993, 2003 and 2013 by the USDA ERS, it distinguishes metropolitan counties by the population size of their metro area, and nonmetropolitan counties by degree of urbanity and adjacency to metro areas (see USDA, 2013b). While the UIC classifies a nonmetropolitan county according to whether it includes micropolitan or noncore as defined by the OMB classification, the RUCC classifies a nonmetropolitan county by the size of the urban population. We also note that adjacency to metropolitan areas is determined by geographical proximity as well as the mobility of people measured by commuting to work, in both classifications. Although some studies have applied other urban/rural classification schemes according to metropolitan statistical areas (MSAs) and non-MSAs (see Ingram and Gillum, 1989; Barnett et al., 2000; Kindig et al., 2002; Kim and Kawachi, 2006; King et al., 2009), population size (see Gerdtham and Johannesson, 1999; Barnett and Halverson, 2000; Campbell et al., 2001) or population density (see Lorant et al., 2001; Greiner et al., 2004; Sundquist et al., 2004; Chaix et al., 2006; Maas et al., 2006; Van Hooijdonk, 2007; Verheij et al., 2008; Kroneman et al., 2010; Mohnen et al., 2011), the adjacency to metropolitan areas is considered a key element to capture heterogeneity within rural areas (see Hewitt, 1989; Higgs, 1999; Luo and Wilkins, 2008).

Some researchers have verified whether these measures would lead to different results. Langlois et al. (2009) have concluded that the UIC and RUCC classifications are likely to be almost identical when examining the regional difference of the prevalence of birth defects in Texas. Basu and Mobley (2007) and Cossman et al. (2008) have also indicated that both the UIC and RUCC may lead to the same results in terms of severity of illness and age-adjusted mortality rates respectively. In contrast, Berke et al. (2009) have compared seven urban/rural classification systems including the UIC and RUCC in estimating Veterans Administration utilization in the United States and have concluded that an appropriate classification system should be used according to policy issues and spatial scale since the results may highly depend on the definition of rurality. Hall et al. (2006) have shown that the urban/rural differences in breast cancer incidence may be associated with various measures of urbanity including the UIC, RUCC, MSAs/non-MSAs, and the census based-classifications, which are commonly used in health surveys in the United States. The above results warn us that we should not employ a classification scheme without explicitly considering the impact on the results.

Additionally, we also note that the French National Statistics and Economic Studies Institute (INSEE) classifies municipalities into six (three urban and three rural) categories based on population size and employment clusters (see Viel et al., 2011; Fournel et al., 2012), whereas the Rural, Remote and Metropolitan Index (RRMA) classification commonly employed as urban/rural classification among the health studies in Australia is stratified into seven (two metropolitan, three rural and two remote) zones (see Roberts and Algert, 2000; Dempsey et al., 2003; Caldwell et al., 2004). The RRMA classification uses population size and the degree of remoteness calculated by some geographic distance factors. Like the UIC and RUCC, these measures also take into account the proximity to urban cores (see AIHW, 2014).

4.2 The ONS Area Classifications and a Classification of Residential Neighborhoods

The ONS Area Classifications is one of the common measures used to assess neighborhood environments in England, Wales and Scotland, although it was not designed to define urban or rural areas (see DCLG, 2006). This classification, based on the United Kingdom Census 1991, groups wards into 43 clusters and classifies them into 14 groups. In contrast to the UIC and RUCC classifications, the clusters are calculated by 37 census variables, not only variables of demographic structure, but also variables related to household composition, housing, socioeconomic character and employment characteristics (see CeLSIUS, 2014). Six of 105 papers have adopted a dichotomized (urban/rural) or trichotomized (urban/rural/rural fringe) scale according to the ONS classifications (see Barnett et al., 2001; Pearce et al., 2003; Weich et al., 2003, 2006; Jordan et al., 2004; McCulloch, 2006). Three of them have demonstrated a rural advantage in health compared to urban areas and the remainder of the papers have not been able to find any significant difference between urban and rural (see Jordan et al., 2004; McCulloch, 2006; Weich et al., 2006).

A Classification of Residential Neighbourhoods (ACORN) is a geodemographic segmentation of residential neighborhoods in the United Kingdom (see CASI, 2013), which is also used when examining regional differences in health outcomes (see Haynes, 1991; Langford and Bentham, 1996; Chandola, 2001; Boys et al., 2003). The latest ACORN classification, which was rebuilt in 2013, classifies postcodes into six categories (affluent achievers, rising prosperity, comfortable communities, financially stretched, urban adversity, and not private households), 18 groups and 62 types (see CASI, 2013). Since the ACORN classification is a measurement of prosperity based on a wide range of variables including demographic, geographic, socioeconomic, and lifestyle factors using a multivariate classification method, it is difficult to determine whether these categories belong to urban or rural areas. As Langford and Bentham (1996) have shown the regional difference in mortality rates can be explained by the difference between the types of areas defined by the ACORN classification scheme, and Boys et al. (2003) have confirmed that young people aged 13–15 years residing in a "thriving" area, which is defined as "populated by wealthy achievers living in suburban areas, affluent 'greys' (middle-aged people) in rural communities and prosperous pensioners in retirement areas (Boys et al., 2003)" are more likely to drink alcohol regularly. These results indicates that the ACORN classification scheme seems to be a valid classification to clarify the regional differences in health although it is difficult to determine whether the urban health advantage exists.

To conclude, demographic-based measurements are often employed when estimating the impact of urban/rural areas in the Unites States, whereas multidimensional measurements are used in the United Kingdom. These measurements have pros and cons. Since a demographic-based measurement focuses on population distribution within an area and spatial proximity to other areas, it may be useful to estimate regional differences in health outcomes due to the demographic distribution but it is not adequate to fully capture the contextual effects that urban and rural might themselves have. On the other hand, a multidimensional measurement may be available for confirming the existence of regional differences. As for the ACORN classification, for example, all four studies as noted above have shown statistically significant regional differences, although ACORN areas may defy classification into urban/rural categories. Although Reading et al. (1994) have stressed the usefulness of multidimensional classifications in health service research, the classifications may make it difficult to identify which contextual factors significantly affect health outcomes. In terms of policy implication, it may be preferable to estimate the "decomposed" effects of contextual factors that may affect health outcomes.

We also note that substantial differences in effects of urbanity are also found between studies conducted in the same country. Out of 105 studies highlighting the urban/rural differences in health, 42 studies are from the United States and 31 studies from the UK. As for the studies' focus on the United States, 18 studies have demonstrated health benefits to residents in urban areas whereas 10 studies have found the opposite results. Among studies from the UK, however, 19 studies have shown that residents living in rural areas tend to have better health while only one study supported the existence of urban advantage.

Various classification schemes are used to categorize areas according to the level of urbanity across countries as well as studies. Although these schemes accurately reflect the geographical and demographical characteristics and environmental changes due to urbanization in each country, the results obtained have been inconsistent between countries, and even within a country. A more precise identification of the differences in results between the studies may provide additional clues to unravel the mechanism underlying the contextual effects on health outcomes. In the following section, we discuss some defects in the urban/rural classification schemes.

5. URBAN AND RURAL DIFFERENTIALS IN HEALTH OUTCOMES

5.1 Defects in the Dichotomous Classification

A series of studies have argued against the use of the urban/rural dichotomy (see Higgs, 1999; McDade and Adair, 2001; Vlahov and Galea, 2002; Hall et al., 2006; Laditka et al., 2007; Berke et al., 2009; Peen et al., 2010). Higgs (1999) has pointed out that an urban/rural dichotomy is inappropriate because of its simplistic approach; it ignores multidimensional complexity. Some studies have underlined the necessity of finding a solid criterion for distinguishing urban from rural (see Christie and Fone, 2003; Laditka et al., 2007; Peen et al., 2010). A lack of appropriate classification criterion would cause an underestimate of the effect of urbanity (see Wang, 2004; Peen et al., 2010) or would lead to a different result (see Gillanders et al., 1997; Laditka et al., 2007; Berke et al., 2009; Langlois et al., 2009) which may lead to wrong conclusions. Eberhardt and Pamuk (2004) have indicated that the definition of rurality varying according to time period may impair the ability to assess trends in regional inequalities. To conclude, we maintain that a dichotomous classification scheme would lead to inconsistent results across countries, time, as well as studies even if a more definitive classification could be made.

Berke et al. (2009) have stressed the need of "more granular" classifications instead of the urban/rural dichotomy. Cossman et al. (2008), however, have confirmed that a further classification may bring unstable and ambiguous results by using a ten-category RUCC classification. On the other hand, they also verified that the area-based differences would be masked if regional categories were aggregated to represent an urban/rural dichotomy or grouped into larger clusters, and have concluded "it is not a matter of finding the 'right' number of categories." Moreover, Paykel et al. (2000) interpret the definition of urbanity as "impressionistic," Peen et al. (2010) describe urban and rural as "relative concepts," and Hart et al.

(2005) conclude that the definition should be applied depending on the study. That is, a robust method of urban–rural comparison remains to be established and seems to be nearly impossible to be widely accepted across borders.

Two main threads can be now identified in a series of works concerning urban/rural differences in health and wellbeing. Some of the studies have explored intra-regional differences in health outcomes, and the others have suggested a well-designed classification scheme to capture differences between urban and rural areas. In the following subsections, we overview these studies and detail some issues to be addressed.

5.2 Intra-regional Heterogeneity

The ambiguity of the urban–rural differences may arise from intra-regional heterogeneity. A series of studies have revealed the existence of intra-urban or intra-rural heterogeneity.

For intra-urban differences, some studies have focused on inner-city areas with poor environmental quality and most of them have observed a higher prevalence of poor health among inner-city residents (see McCarthy et al., 1985; Haynes, 1991; Chandola, 2001; Middleton et al., 2006). McCarthy et al. (1985) have shown that householders living in a metropolitan district in the north-east of England in high-rise flats built in the 1960s that are classified as "difficult to let" and which are located in the inner city are likely to report higher psychological distress. Middleton et al. (2006) have investigated regional differences in suicide rates and have identified the existence of "bull's-eye pattern," which has the highest rates in core parts of cities and relatively lower rates in their peripheries within densely populated cities in England and Wales. These facts may reveal the existence of the "urban health penalty," which draws a harmful effect of urban negatives on health that have been exacerbated since the Industrial Revolution (see Harpham and Molyneux, 2001; Leon 2008; Sverdlik, 2011).

Other studies have distinguished suburban areas from other urban areas and have referred to significant differences (see Ingram and Gillum, 1989; Rahkonen et al., 1997; Singh and Siahpush, 2002; Parks et al., 2003; Eberhardt and Pamuk, 2004). Ingram and Gillum (1989) have examined regional and urban differentials in coronary heart disease (CHD) mortality among white adult males aged 35–74 years in the United States and have identified the lowest risk of mortality from CHD in fringe metropolitan areas defined as the counties not containing the central city of MSAs with populations of at least 1,000,000 or more. Interestingly, the core metropolitan area in one region appears to have an advantage in terms of

CHD mortality whereas a disadvantage exists in the other regions: these are seemingly inconsistent results on the effect of urban areas on health. Parks et al. (2003) have shown the relationship between physical activity and level of urbanization, which they categorized by urban, suburban, and rural areas according to the census data from the United States, and have indicated that suburban residents are the most likely to meet physical activity recommendations compared to urban and rural residents. We should be careful about using the terms "suburban" or "urban fringe" areas. Some studies seem to use the term "rural fringe" as a rough synonym for "urban fringe" (see Jordan et al., 2003; Levin, 2003). These terms may just be regarded as an intermediate area between urban and rural areas and it may lead to inconsistent results due to the ambiguity of their definitions. In fact, although some studies have proven the health advantage of living in urban-fringe areas, other studies have specified that "urban sprawl" areas may have some adverse health effects using some urban sprawl indices (see Freudenberg et al., 2005 and the following section for more details). A finer categorization scheme might reduce the heterogeneity within grouped areas. But we cannot correctly and accurately evaluate the contextual effects of these "intermediate areas" without a precise definition of the areas.

Some researchers have maintained the existence of intra-rural heterogeneity which may impede the reliable detection of regional effects (see Haynes and Gale, 2000; Martin et al., 2000; Barnett et al., 2001; Levin, 2003; Gartner et al., 2008; Hall et al., 2006). Barnett et al. (2001) have identified a significant intra-rural variation in premature LLTI among residents living in the south-west regions of England. They have stressed that rurality is likely to be less associated with premature LLTI regardless of the definition used because of its heterogeneity, and the definition of rurality may require further consideration. Haynes and Gale (2000) have shown a lesser association between social deprivation scores and both death and illness rates in rural areas compared to that in urban areas using data from East Anglia, in the United Kingdom. They have pointed out that average deprivation scores may not accurately predict urban–rural differentials in health outcomes due to the heterogeneity within rural areas. They also concluded that using aggregate census indicators may mask the rural poor who suffered additional disadvantage posted by geographical distance: Car ownership is used as a proxy for the level of household wealth although a car is an essential mode for people living in areas with lower residential mobility.

"Rural" is sometimes poorly defined. As we noted in the previous section, in some papers, urban areas are identified according to well-defined criteria established by governments whereas rural areas are classified as "those areas that are not urban areas." It means that intra-rural heterogeneity is likely to be greater than intra-urban heterogeneity although most individuals live in urban areas. This heterogeneity does not merely mean "individual heterogeneity" within areas but "geographical heterogeneity." As we further illustrate in the following section, the geographical as well as the economic proximity to urban core areas may be a good element, accounting for heterogeneity within rural areas. Judd et al. (2002) have reviewed studies that discussed the urban/rural differences in the prevalence of mental/psychiatric disorders in order to assess the contribution of contextual effects, and accordingly have stressed that the existence of intra-regional heterogeneity should not be ignored by using a "one size does fit all," which focuses on location rather than place. It may be inadequate to examine contextual effects on health outcomes within the urban and rural settings. We should explore contextual factors in explaining the differences between urban and rural areas and estimate more accurately how they affect health outcomes.

5.3 Reclassifications of Urban/Rural Categories

Although a number of studies have employed the classification schemes developed by the government, some researchers have developed a more reliable classification framework to reduce heterogeneity within urban and rural areas.

Several studies have proposed a new classification scheme in order to eliminate intra-urban heterogeneity (see McDade and Adair, 2001; Weich et al., 2001; Dahly and Adair, 2007). McDade and Adair (2001) have explored multiple definitions of urbanity using longitudinal data from Metro Cebu, the Philippines, by factor analysis of household and community variables and have found the factor scores, representing the dimensions of basic infrastructure, health services, education, and affluence. They have concluded the inadequacy of a simple dichotomous classification and have stressed the importance of taking into account the spatiotemporal dynamics of urbanization. Dahly and Adair (2007) have also constructed a continuous measure of urbanity that allows a more precise analysis of the relationship between urban environment and health outcome based on seven components including population size, population density, the availability of communication services, transportation system, educational facilities, health services, and markets in Metro Cebu, the Philippines. Weich et al. (2001) have suggested a subjective measure of the built environment which may affect the prevalence of depression in the inner city in north London. They have shown evidence of statistically significant relationships between the prevalence of depression and living areas with specific housing characteristics. This measurement may be one way to find out the causes of the health differences between wards in the inner city.

Other studies have developed a classification scheme to capture intra-rural heterogeneity. Some studies have focused on the degree of rural isolation, estimated by the degree of geographical remoteness (see Middleton et al., 2003), the accessibility of services and social opportunities (see Murray et al., 2004), and the size of work-commuting flow (see Luo and Wilkins, 2008). Ocaña-Riola and Sánchez-Cantalejo (2005) have explored rurality index, which can be regularly updated to meet the change in socioeconomic conditions in Spanish municipalities using a principal components factor analysis, and have stressed the importance of exploring a country-specific "optimal rurality index." Kristiansen et al. (2012) have assessed the regional differences in injury and death from pediatric trauma by using three measures of rurality among children aged 16 years and under in Norway and have shown "municipal centrality," which is a proxy for both the population size of the area and the accessibility of other cities, is likely to be a better predictor of high risk of death compared to settlement density and population density. Teljeur and Kelly (2008) have suggested a new urban–rural classification for the smallest administrative units (Electoral Divisions; EDs) in Ireland, where most EDs are likely to be categorized as rural. They subdivided rural areas into smaller groups based on settlement size, population density, proximity to urban centers, and land use. Congdon et al. (1997) have examined the impact of socioeconomic factors on morbidity and mortality in England and Wales using the "rurality index" calculated from population density, proportions of residents working in agriculture, the levels of detached housing, and children in households.

The results obtained from the current studies have shown that the existence of heterogeneity within areas may mask urban/rural disparities in health outcomes considerably. Taking these results into account, it may be important to find a classification scheme that minimizes the heterogeneity within groups rather than evaluating the usefulness of dichotomous and continuum classifications. It does not simply mean that we should develop an adequate multidimensional classification that demonstrates a clear difference between urban and rural areas. We assert that the primary purpose of a health survey is to reveal which and what extent regional components affect health outcomes, not to conclude which region has an absolute advantage.

5.4 Health Benefits in Urban/Rural Living

The concept of urban penalty is well known, and quite a few researchers have been concerned with the issues. As the WHO and UN-HABITAT point out in their global report "Hidden cities: Unmasking and overcoming health inequities in urban settings," there exist large health disparities among urban residents and it is important to shed light on the poor living conditions in urban informal settlements or slums (see WHO-CHD, 2010). Although more than 90% of slums are in the developing world, some studies have demonstrated the existence of health disparities among urban residents in developed countries. Some researchers, however, have argued against the "urban penalty approach" (see Freudenberg et al., 2005; Vlahov et al., 2004). Vlahov et al. (2004) have stressed that this approach may overlook the health advantages enjoyed by urban residents. Freudenberg et al. (2005) have suggested a more comprehensive framework for determining urban living conditions that affect health outcomes instead of the urban penalty and urban sprawl approaches, both of which focus on the adverse health effects of urban living.

In comparison with urban and rural areas, is it possible to determine which area has definite advantages in achieving better health outcomes? We find some researchers have predicted a non-linear relationship between urbanity and health outcomes (see Curtis and Jones, 1998; Barnett et al., 2001; Rosenblatt et al., 2001; Hillemeier et al., 2007; Auger et al., 2009). Barnett et al. (2001) have demonstrated a "U-shape relation" with rurality in terms of the prevalence of LLTI in the south-west regions of England. Hillemeier et al. (2007) have investigated the prevalence of preterm birth and low birthweight among singleton first births in Pennsylvania. They have classified areas into four categories (urban-focused area, large rural city-focused/town-focused area, small rural town-focused area, and isolated small rural town-focused area) based on the Rural-Urban Commuting Areas (RUCA) taxonomy, developed by the WWAMI Rural Health Research Center (RHRC) at the University of Washington, the Health Resources and Service Administration's Office of Rural Health Policy and the USDA ERS (see RUCA, 2014), and shown that the prevalence of both preterm birth and low birthweight in large rural city-focused areas is likely to be lower than that in urban-focused areas after controlling for individual risk factors. Moreover, Curtis and Jones (1998) have indicated "health does not improve straightforwardly as rurality increases" from a review of previous studies. Hartley (2004) has stressed "suburban versus rural disparity" is of concern rather than "urban versus rural disparity."

It should be noted that the urban/rural differences in health can be compared, but it cannot simply be concluded that one region is superior to the other regions in health and wellbeing. There, however, still exist significant differences between urban and rural areas in terms of living environment that affect health outcomes. We identify the components of the living environment that have a critical influence on health outcomes so as to better understand the determinants of health inequities.

6. CONTEXTUAL IMPACTS ON HEALTH OUTCOMES

The CSDH final report stresses the improvement of urban living conditions "applying healthy urban design principles" as an urgent priority (see CSDH, 2008). What are healthy urban design principles? And how can we achieve the objectives of closing the health gap between regions? It may not be enough to identify living conditions that achieve and maintain "optimal" health through a series of studies for the reasons listed above. As the WHO and UN-HABITAT indicate, it is important to figure out health inequalities within cities using disaggregated health and health determinants data (see WHO-CHD, 2010). That is, it is better to decompose the neighborhood contextual effects on health outcomes in order to unravel the determinants underlying health inequities between urban and rural areas. We propose six critical contextual factors (housing conditions, environmental hazards, land use mix and regional segregation, residential proximity to the CBD, accessibility to and affordability of medical services, and population density), each of which may be a considerable predictor of health outcomes.

6.1 Housing Conditions

Houses are the major components of a city and one of the most important elements for one's life. A lack of access to safe water and adequate sanitation facilities in dwellings may be a critical factor that triggers a range of health problems (see WHO-CHD, 2010). Carneiro et al. (2002) have shown that availability of water in their houses may reduce the risk of *Ascaris lumbricoides* infection among children living in overcrowded housing in rural areas of Brazil. D'Hombres et al. (2010) have proven that access to good quality water may be positively and significantly associated with self-reported health among individuals living in eight former Soviet countries. Inadequate sanitation is also likely to be a significant risk factor for diarrheal and parasitic disease, including schistosomiasis (see Moore et al., 2003). Krieger and Higgins (2002) have indicated the relationship between poor housing conditions and a wide range of health problems from a review of studies.

As Jackson (2003) indicates, poor sanitation is no longer the leading health threat in the United States, and Shaw (2004) emphasizes that housing is now used as an indicator for the material socioeconomic status of the household rather than as an element that has "direct" impact on health outcomes, the impact of housing itself seems to be less of an issue in most developed countries.

In fact, quite a few studies have shown relationships between housing tenure and risk of mortality (see Malmstrom et al., 2001), self-rated morbidity (see Haynes, 1991), LLTI (see Levin, 2003), and self-rated health (see Ziersch, 2005; Poortinga, 2006; Sundquist and Yang, 2007; Ichida et al., 2009; Snelgrove et al., 2009). In addition, the homeownership rate at the neighborhood level is used to measure another "indirect" impact: It is considered a proxy for residential stability, which is known as a measure of social capital (see Browning et al., 2003; Franzini and Spears, 2003). Moreover, the non-homeownership rate is one of the elements that comprise some area deprivation indices (see Shouls et al., 1996; Ross and Mirowsky, 2001; Middleton et al., 2006; Connolly et al., 2007). The Townsend index, which was developed as a measure of material deprivation (see Jarman et al., 1991) and is commonly used to describe spatial distribution of deprivation in England and Wales, also employs the percentage of households living in non-owner-occupied housing as a key indicator.

Although many studies have shifted focus to "indirect" effect of housing, we assert that we should take into account the effect of the structural type of dwelling when examining regional inequities in health, that is, we should not ignore the "direct" effect of housing and living environment. According to Evans (2003), the built environment including housing type, floor level and quality may affect mental health both directly and indirectly. Some papers have shown high-rise living is likely to have a statistically and significantly negative impact on health outcomes (see Wells, 2000; Evans et al., 2000; Jackson, 2003; Gifford, 2007). Moreover, the structural characteristics of housing units can be also be considered to be elements which determine the quality of the physical environment in the area. Interestingly, mental disorder may result from residential dissatisfaction with their dwellings (see Krieger and Higgins, 2002; Guite et al., 2006; Gifford, 2007). A lack of indicators of housing characteristics might give biased results since spatial heterogeneity is not fully captured by the distribution of the population.

6.2 Environmental Hazards

It is generally considered that exposure to environmental hazards has a negative impact on health outcomes. Air pollution is well known as one of the environmental health hazards and has proven to significantly affect stroke mortality (see Maheswaran and Elliott, 2003), mortality from ischemic heart disease (see Nafstad et al., 2004), cardiopulmonary mortality (see Dockery et al., 1993; Hoek et al., 2002; Heinrich et al., 2013), lung cancer mortality and cancer risk (see Dockery et al., 1993; Nafstad et al., 2004; Apelberg et al., 2005; Chakraborty, 2009; Heinrich et al., 2013), circulatory disease mortality (see Finkelstein et al., 2005), coronary artery calcification (see Dragano, 2009), asthma hospitalization rates (see Corburn et al., 2006; Maantay, 2007), and the risk of hospital admission for cardiovascular and respiratory diseases (see Dominici et al., 2006; Chakraborty, 2009). Although Finkelstein et al. (2005) have maintained that there exists no evidence to support the presence of socioeconomic disparities in exposure to air pollution in European countries, socioeconomic inequalities in exposure to environmental pollutants, most of which are airborne pollutants including nitrogen dioxide (NO_2) and particulate matter ($PM_{2.5}$ and PM_{10}), might be found in the United States and Canada (see Finkelstein et al., 2003; Corburn et al., 2006; Gray et al., 2013) as well as in European countries (see Chaix et al., 2006; Havard et al., 2009; Viel et al., 2011). These results have proven the existence of "environmental injustice" (see Pellow, 2000) within urban areas.

These studies have also demonstrated that some cause-specific morbidity and mortality may depend on where one lives. Residents living near a major road or highway (see Hoek et al., 2002; Apelberg et al., 2005; Finkelstein et al., 2005; Brugge el al., 2007; Chakraborty, 2009; Dragano, 2009; Heinrich et al., 2013) or near noxious facilities (see Corburn et al., 2006; Maantay, 2007; Viel et al., 2011) would be highly exposed to air pollution. These results indicate that environmental hazards would widen health inequities within areas. The differences between urban and rural with respect to exposure to environmental hazards remain to be delineated, although Viel et al. (2011) have shown that the relatively high risk of exposure to noxious facilities can be estimated in urban areas. Further studies are needed to confirm the advantage of living in rural areas in terms of the natural environment. We also note that these contextual impacts on health outcomes should be more precisely estimated, taking into account the spatial location of the air/water/noise pollutant emission sources through geographic information systems (GIS) techniques.

6.3 Land Use Mix and Regional Segregation

Land use mix, an indicator of proximity of different land uses (see Handy et al., 2002), is found to be associated with health status and health behaviors related to obesity (see Saelens et al., 2003; Frank et al., 2004; Mobley et al., 2006; Rundle et al., 2007; Li et al., 2008; Brown et al., 2009). Closer residential proximity to food retailers, restaurants, or commercial establishments (see Liu et al., 2007; Nagel et al., 2008; Zick et al. 2009), to workplace (see Smith et al., 2008; Brown et al., 2009, Zick et al., 2009), and to green space (see Grahn and Stigsdotter, 2003; Maas et al., 2006; Liu et al., 2007; Nielsen and Hansen, 2007; Mitchell and Popham, 2008) would reduce the risk of obesity, stress or mortality, and increase self-perceived health. Land use mix is used as a component of "urban sprawl index" and it has been shown that a higher degree of land use mix may lead to an increase in better health outcomes through the index.

A series of studies have highlighted the disadvantageous effects of urban sprawl on health status and health behaviors using some urban sprawl indices (see Ewing, 2003; Lopez, 2004; Sturm and Cohen, 2004). Although there seems not to be one unique definition of urban sprawl, Johnson (2001) gives six clear dimensions of sprawl (less mixed land use, lesser neighborhood diversity, lower population density, higher automobile dependency, closer proximity to metropolitan area, and governments' inability to address regional issues rather than metropolitan areas), each of which except the last one is thought to have a contextual effect on health outcomes and to be used as a component of the urban sprawl index. Sturm and Cohen (2004) have examined the relationship between suburban sprawl and self-rated chronic health conditions and mental health disorders in the United States and have found a disproportionate impact of suburban areas on the chronic health of the elderly and possibly the poor. This result has highlighted the geographical disadvantage of urban sprawl areas in terms of mobility and accessibility. A walkability index which integrates residential density, street connectivity, extent of mixed land use and retail floor area ratio is also an indicator of accessibility to services and facilities and is likely to be positively related to physical activity and less obesity (see Frank et al., 2006; Owen et al., 2007; Sallis et al., 2009).

We also note that racial segregation, representing an aspect of social heterogeneity, may be one of the key factors affecting health outcomes. Racial segregation is measured by some indices such as the isolation index, the spatial proximity index, and the dissimilarity index all of which represent the degree of spatial separation between different race groups. And a higher level of racial segregation would increase the risk of low birthweight (see Bell et al., 2006; Grady, 2006; Walton, 2009) and mortality risk (see Fang et al. 1998; Jackson et al. 2000) and would lower self-rated health (see Subramanian et al., 2005; Lee and Ferraro, 2007). Although we could not find studies examining the relationship between racial segregation and health outcomes in countries other than the United States and some studies have shown that the effect of racial segregation appears to be obscure (see Kramer and Hogue, 2009; White and Borrell, 2011), racial segregation is a critical factor to be considered when assessing health inequities.

As for land use mix, living in the urban core and in metropolitan areas may have advantages for health compared to living in urban sprawl areas with more segregated land use or living in rural areas with less public transport accessibility. As far as we know, there are no studies which have addressed the urban/rural differences in racial segregation, although a considerable difference in racial segregation is expected between urban and rural areas. It is worth estimating the impact of geographical as well as social separation on health outcomes.

6.4 Residential Proximity to the CBD

The monocentric city model, which is also known as the Alonso-Muth-Mills model, simply and theoretically describes the urban residential structure assuming all workers living outside the CBD commute to the CBD (see Alonso, 1964; Mills, 1967, 1972; Muth, 1969). In this model, the trade-off between commuting costs and housing costs is a key factor when workers choose their residences. The reality, however, seems to be more complicated than this simple model. Cities have been growing independently but influence each other. Residents can access "employment subcenters" in suburban areas which are defined as smaller sites which benefit from a lower level of agglomeration economies compared to the CBD (see White, 1999). Although the monocentric city model seems to be too simple to capture spatial heterogeneity, some empirical studies have also shown that commuting distance (time) is one of the most important determinants of residential location choice (see Cho et al., 2008).

According to urban economic theory, households choose their residence to maximize their utility subject to budget constraints including commuting costs. And it assumes that households should incur higher commuting costs if they choose longer commutes. Commuting costs, which often refer to the monetary cost of travel and the opportunity cost of travel time, also include non-monetary costs caused by environmental factors affecting commuters' physical and mental health such as overcrowding on trains, traffic jams, and confined spaces. That is, commuting distance may be associated with negative health outcomes.

In fact, previous studies have shown the negative impact of commuting on health. Commuting is likely to not only cause additional psychological stress and affect the mood of commuters (see Costa et al., 1988; Novaco et al., 1990; Koslowsky et al., 1996; O'Regan and Buckley, 2003; Wener et al., 2005; Evans and Wener, 2006; Gottholmseder et al., 2009; Wener and Evans, 2011; Sposato et al., 2012) and cardiac autonomic activity (see Kageyama et al., 1998), but also yield other risk factors such as increased body mass index (BMI) and blood pressure (see Hoehner et al., 2012).

In these studies, commuting distance, time, and impedance (calculated by both distance and time) are commonly used as determinants of objective or subjective health status. There are other indicators such as control, predictability (see Schulz, 1976), and variability (see Kluger, 1998), each of which is also a good predictor of commuting stress. Although these indicators are not directly related to distance or time, a spatial proximity between the CBD and the residential area can be considered as a proxy for the exposure to the risk arising from commuting. Taking into account the fact that the extent of commuting stress is likely to depend on transportation mode (see O'Regan and Buckley, 2003; Gatersleben and Uzzell, 2007; Wener and Evans, 2011), we should consider a variety of public and private transport modes to the CBD when examining the spatial inequalities in health. Some economists might emphasize that the burden of commuting is not much of a problem if its cost is compensated with a wage. However, Stutzer and Frey (2008) have proven that commuting time may have a significantly negative impact on self-rated satisfaction with life using panel data from Germany and have demonstrated the existence of the "commuting paradox:" workers seem to accept the burden associated with commuting without appropriate compensation.

Some studies have identified the existence of a strong spatial autocorrelation in mortality (see Rosenberg, 1999; Burnett et al., 2001; Lorant et al., 2001; Sridharan et al., 2007). And other studies have pointed out that adjacency to metropolitan areas may also be one of the significant determinants of health outcomes (see Barnett et al., 2000; Auchincloss and Hadden, 2002; Middleton et al., 2003; Luo and Wilkins, 2008; Laditka et al., 2009; Monnat and Beeler Pickett, 2011). In Quebec, Canada, Luo and Wilkins (2008) have found a significant negative association between the risk of neonatal and postneonatal deaths and the degree of rural isolation based on the size of the workforce commuting flows into any metropolitan areas, which remains even after controlling for maternal characteristics. Middleton et al. (2003) have highlighted the usefulness of the population potential index which captures the degree of geographical remoteness from large concentrations of population as a criterion for classifying an area as urban or rural when examining suicide trends among young adults in England and Wales. These results indicate that the degree of socioeconomic isolation in addition to geographical isolation may be a key determinant when examining health inequity. That is, we should estimate the impact on regional health status based on the characteristics of the area itself, as well as the social and economic influence from its surroundings.

6.5 Accessibility to and Availability of Medical Services

Access to medical services is also considered as a key element that describes both health outcome and a determinant of health outcomes. According to Penchansky and Thomas (1981), access can be classified into five broad categories: availability, accessibility, accommodation, affordability, and acceptability. The first two dimensions are regarded as factors explaining contextual effects. From a health inequity point of view, availability is a factor that determines whether a sufficient number of general practitioners, medical specialists, or health care facilities are provided to meet residents' demand, while accessibility indicates whether there are time and distance barriers preventing residents from using medical services. A number of studies have demonstrated the relationship between health outcomes and availability of (see Matteson et al., 1998; Gulliford, 2002; Kindig et al., 2002; Jerrett et al., 2003; Macinko et al., 2007) and accessibility to (see Haynes et al., 1999; Campbell et al., 2001; Jordan et al., 2004; Basu and Mobley, 2007) health care facilities or services. As for availability, some studies have shown that residential health status would be improved if the supply of doctors in an area increased. Bloor et al. (2006), however, have strongly emphasized that expansion of the medical workforce does not directly redress the inequitable geographic distribution of physicians. Moreover, Starfield et al. (2005) have concluded that benefits from the availability of physicians on health outcomes may depend on their type: An increase in primary care physician supply may reduce mortality, but in the United States the same effect cannot be observed for specialists.

A shortage of physicians is an important issue that still needs to be addressed in some developed countries such as the United States and Japan (see Colwill, 2008; Goodman and Fisher, 2008; Shinjo and Aramaki, 2012), while there is little consensus on the "ideal" physician-to-population ratios (see Bloor et al., 2006). Taking into account the continuous rise in health care costs due to the ageing population, we should pay much more attention to the improvement in accessibility to health care services, that is, every effort should be made to eliminate regional imbalances in the distribution of services rather than to expand the availability of physicians. To make the policy implementation more effective, more detailed research is needed to clarify the respective roles of not only generalists/specialists, but the roles of acute/chronic services and medical/nursing care services.

6.6 Population Density

Some studies classify an area as rural if the population density is below a certain threshold. However, the results derived from the studies on the basis of this classification seem to be inconsistent. Lorant et al. (2001) and Mohnen et al. (2011) have shown a positive impact of urbanity on mortality in Belgium and on self-rated health in the Netherlands respectively, while Sundquist et al. (2004) and Chaix et al. (2006) have demonstrated a rural advantage in some cause-specific mortality using data from Sweden, and Greiner et al. (2004) have concluded urban/rural effects on self-rated health are both insignificant in the United States. How should these results be interpreted? Moreover, some deficiencies in the urban/rural classification scheme based on population density have been pointed out (see Watt et al., 1994; Weich et al., 2006; Teljeur and Kelly, 2008). As Teljeur and Kelly (2008) have emphasized, a single variable such as population density may be insufficient for the proper classification of areas into urban or rural. Although some researchers have developed alternative measures of urbanity, and population density seems to be no longer a fundamental element accounting for the level of urbanity, we assert that population density is still a key factor affecting health outcomes. Population density is a simple and adequate proxy of living conditions. Concentration of population has a significant impact on individuals. In general, high population density would not only cause a deterioration in living conditions through small houses, a lack of open/green spaces, traffic congestion, and high exposure to pollution but also provide benefits including lower transportation costs, higher accessibility to services and amenities, better neighborhood walkability, higher employment opportunities, and higher human capital accumulation. If population density only is used to measure the level of urbanization, different results would be obtained across studies because these two opposite effects of population density may cancel each other out. It depends on the socioeconomic and environmental conditions of urban areas whether the health benefits of urban living exceed the urban costs. To find the underlying determinants of urban health, we should carefully consider each dimension of urban living in addition to population density. Moreover, population density may affect the extent of social capital (see Veenstra, 2002; Greiner et al. 2004; Kim et al. 2011). As Fisher et al. (2004) have indicated in their paper, population density has been overlooked as a potential influence on physical activity behaviors, and a detailed analysis would be needed to find the effects of population density. In the following section, we focus on human capital accumulation, one of the externalities arising from higher population density.

7. EXTERNALITIES IN DENSELY POPULATED AREAS

7.1 Aggregate Human Capital Externalities

Density populated areas can be characterized by an accumulation of human capital. Human capital is the potential capacity for the production of embodied knowledge and skills (see Becker et al., 1994). The existence of the benefits of human capital on the individual, which is commonly measured by one's educational attainment, has been proven in a number of studies (see Moretti, 2004). On the other hand, the individual stock of human capital may not only positively affect an individual's own productivity, but also enhance other workers' productivity. This spillover effect of human capital is thought of as an important factor of economic development, and human capital accumulation is one of the key determinants in the theory of urban growth (see Black and Henderson, 1999). That is, the more highly populated areas, such as metropolitan areas, are more productive compared to sparsely populated areas (see Glaeser and Gottlieb, 2009).

Grossman (1972, 1999) has proposed a health demand model incorporating human capital. He assumes gross investments in health capital may be produced by the household production function determined by the individual's human capital such as educational attainment. That is, the better educated would demand a higher level of health if education increases their efficiency. Evidence has been accumulated which shows that individual educational attainment has a positive impact on an individual's health outcomes (see Furnée et al., 2008). We can then conclude that the well-educated are more likely to enjoy favorable health outcomes.

If individual human capital imposes externalities on others, and individuals with more human capital have incentives for investing in their own health, residents living in an area with higher concentrations of human capital may receive health benefits from the area. That is, human capital accumulation can be deemed to enhance regional health status, just as it boosts regional productivity.

Some papers have confirmed the relationship between human capital accumulation and health outcomes. Wen et al. (2003) have demonstrated a significant, independent, and positive impact of individual as well as aggregated educational attainment on self-rated health even after controlling for other contextual effects, including neighborhood affluence, physical environment, and social capital among residents in the city of Chicago. Zhang et al. (2011) have also shown the benefits of education at individual and neighborhood levels on self-perceived health in Hawaii. In this paper, both economic wellbeing estimated by income level, household size, and employment status, and social wellbeing defined as self-perceived social circumstance and functioning, are assumed to be mediators of education effects. In terms of self-rated physical health, educational attainments at both individual and neighborhood levels have significant independent effects even though the two mediators reduce the direct effects of education. Zhang et al. (2011) have also emphasized the necessity that the effect of human capital accumulation in an area should be measured separately, distinguishing between effects at individual and neighborhood levels.

Since neither Wen et al. (2003) nor Zhang et al. (2011) have investigated urban/rural difference in health outcomes, these findings may provide insufficient evidence to support the positive "population agglomeration effect" on health. So we have identified six studies (Ross and Mirowsky, 2001, 2008; Kim and Kawachi, 2006; Winkleby et al., 2007; Monnat and Beeler Pickett, 2011; Debrand et al., 2012) in which both individual and neighborhood effects of education and urbanity have been examined. In the following subsections, we further investigate these studies and clarify the effect of agglomeration.

7.2 The Effect of Human Capital Accumulation on Health Outcomes

We find that four out of the six studies above have shown the positive effects of human capital accumulation on health outcomes even when the urban/rural difference is taken into account (see Table 11.1).

Both Ross and Mirowsky (2001) and Kim and Kawachi (2006) have found no effect of neighborhood education level on self-reported health. Ross and Mirowsky (2001) have examined the effect of neighborhood disadvantage on self-reported physical health among adults living in Illinois, the United States. They have applied two indices composed of contextual factors affecting health outcome. One is the index of objective neighborhood disadvantage, comprising four items that reflect poverty, mother-only households, housing tenure, and educational attainment and the other is the perceived neighborhood disorder index of physically and socially deprived neighborhoods as identified by residents. The effect of human capital accumulation captured by the former index seems to disappear when the latter index is added to the model. This result indicates that the neighborhood disorder may act as a mediator of neighborhood

Table 11.1 Effects of human capital on health

Author (year)	Health outcomes	Targets	Independent variables	The effects of human capital on positive health outcomes	The effects of urbanity on positive health outcomes
Ross and Mirowsky (2001)	self-reported physical health	2,482 households (18–92 years) in Illinois interviewed by telephone	• individual sociodemographic disadvantage (index adds the prevalence of poverty, of mother-only households, and subtracts the prevalence of home ownership and of educated residents) • objective neighbourhood disadvantage (including the percentage of college educated adults) • perceived neighbourhood disorder (physical and social signs of disorder) • frequency in walking • frequency of feeling fear • urbanicity (dichotomous measure: living in the city of Chicago or not)	• the educational effect on oneself: significant positive • the educational effect on neighbourhood (estimated by an "objective neighbourhood disadvantage"): insignificant if "disorder" variable is added	insignificant (although urbanicity has significant positive impact on "disorder", "fear" and "walking")
Kim and Kawachi (2006)	self-reported general health	24,835 individuals (18–99 years) nested within 40 U.S. communities from the Social Capital Benchmark Survey	• individual-level characteristics: sociodemographic, socioeconomic (including educational attainment), and social capital characteristics • community-level characteristics: socioeconomic status (including educational attainment) and social capital characteristics • urbanicity (within core urban areas (i.e., in the center city of an MSA); non-core urban areas (outside the center city of an MSA but inside the county of the center city); suburban areas (inside a suburban county of an MSA); and rural areas (not in an MSA)	• the educational effect on oneself: unknown (estimated as a confounder) • the educational effect on neighbourhood: insignificant	significant (the non-core urban areas has the highest health advantage)

Winkleby et al. (2007)	CHD (coronary heart disease) incidence and one year case fatality from CHD	all Swedish individual data (35–74 years) provided by the Swedish Statistics Bureau	• individual-level variables (including educational attainment) • neighbourhood deprivation index (including low educational status, low income, unemployment, and social welfare recipient) • urbanicity (large cities (Stockholm, Gothenburg, and Malmo); middle sized towns, and small towns/rural areas)	• the educational effect on oneself: significant negative (individuals with compulsory school or less education have higher risk of CHD compared to those with theoretical high school and/or college education) • the educational effect on neighbourhood (estimated by neighbourhood deprivation): significant positive	• CHD incidence insignificant for women and significant negative (higher risk in small towns/rural areas compared to large cities) for men • fatality from CHD significant positive (higher risk in large cities compared to small towns/rural areas)
Ross and Mirowsky (2008)	self-rated physical functioning	2,482 English-speaking adults (18–92 years) in Illinois interviewed by telephone	• individual socioeconomic status (including educational attainment) • neighbourhood socioeconomic status (including education, homeownership and poverty(reverse scored)) • urbanicity (dichotomous measure: living in the city of Chicago or not)	• the educational effect on oneself: significant positive • the educational effect on neighbourhood (estimated by an "neighbourhood SES"): significant positive	insignificant
Monnat and Pickett (2011)	self-rated health	a sample of 1,661,961 adults aged 18 and older in the U.S.	• individual-level variables (including educational attainment) • individual health behaviours • country-level social disorganization and economic disadvantage variables (including low education) • urbanicity (five levels of rurality based on the USDA-ERS classification: metropolitan, large nonmetropolitan adjacent to metropolitan area, large nonmetropolitan remote, rural adjacent to metropolitan area, and rural remote)	• the educational effect on oneself: significant positive • the educational effect on neighbourhood: significant positive	insignificant if individual SES and county disadvantage variables are added

Table 11.1 (continued)

Author (year)	Health outcomes	Targets	Independent variables	The effects of human capital on positive health outcomes	The effects of urbanity on positive health outcomes
Debrand et al. (2012)	self-reported health	16,505 individuals aged over 18 years of CUA (critical urban areas) residents and 14,492 of non-CUA residents in France	• individual characteristics (including education level) • three synthetic context factors: factor1: social and economic condition (mostly composed of unemployed, foreigners, unqualified and people living in social housing); factor2: residential stability (positively linked with the percentage of people living in the same household, region and town of residence since 1990, and negatively linked with the percentage of people having moved during or after 1990, people with lower education level, people between 20 and 39 years old, and private renters); factor3: generational factor (positively linked with the percentage of people under 20 years old, homes built after 1982 and negatively linked with the percentage of people over 60 years of age and houses built before 1948) • inhabitants of or outside CUA • urbanity (categorized size of town: less than 50,000 people; between 50,000 and 200,000 people; more than 200,000 people; and Paris)	• the educational effect on oneself: significant positive • the educational effect on neighbourhood (estimated by a factor2): significant positive	significant (areas with 50,000 to 200,000 people has the highest health advantage)

disadvantage. Interestingly, they have concluded that social disorder in the area is likely to have a larger negative effect on health than physical disorder. These findings can be interpreted that lower human capital accumulation causes a deterioration of physical and social living conditions and, as a result, impairs health status.

In the paper of Kim and Kawachi (2006), both individual and community-level social capital have been proven as key determinants for perceived health status, and community-level socioeconomic factors such as levels of income and educational attainment have appeared to have no significant effect if added to individual-level social capital among the US adult population. In their paper, social capital is classified into eight indicators: social trust, formal/religious group involvement, giving and volunteering, electoral/non-electoral political participation, diversity of friendship networks and informal social interactions, and all social capital except the last two indicators are likely to have significant effects on self-reported health. These findings are enough to indicate that some individual-level social capital indicators may be regarded as mediators of neighborhood socioeconomic status. That is, those living in communities with higher income or educational levels may enhance health through greater individual social capital.

To conclude, the human capital accumulation estimated as neighborhood-level educational attainment may significantly and positively affect health outcomes directly and in some cases indirectly through living conditions or individual social capital.

7.3 The Contextual Effect of Urbanity (Rurality) on Health Outcomes

If we assume that human capital accumulation is a key factor accounting for the level of urbanity, the effect of urbanity would diminish or possibly even disappear after taking human capital accumulation into account. Three out of six studies have demonstrated a significant urban/rural effect on health outcomes whereas the other three have not. In the papers of Kim and Kawachi (2006), Winkleby et al. (2007) and Debrand et al. (2012) level of urbanity is likely to have a significant impact on self-rated health although these impacts vary between these studies. Kim and Kawachi (2006) have shown that residents living in noncore urban areas defined as areas outside the center city of an MSA but inside the county of the center city seem to have more favorable health status than those living within urban core areas. Debrand et al. (2012) have demonstrated the existence of a neighborhood effect on perceived health status in France. They have employed three types of contextual variables: a variable representing the size of towns classified into four categories by population size;

a dichotomous variable indicating whether the area is located within or outside the critical urban areas (CUA); and three synthetic factors including social and economic condition (factor 1), residential stability (factor 2) and generational factor (factor 3) obtained from a principal component analysis. Since the CUA is defined as an area of "high-rise buildings and a marked imbalance between housing and employment," we can regard CUA as a proxy of urban areas along with the city size variable. As shown in the paper, although living in the CUA is likely to increase health risks, the CUA no longer has a significant negative impact on self-rated health if the three synthetic factors are added to the model, whereas residents living in a middle-sized town (with 50,000–200,000 people) are still likely to be healthier compared to their counterparts in Paris. Winkleby et al. (2007) have shown regional inequities in the incidence and one-year case fatality of CHD among all Swedish women and men aged from 35 to 74 years. Their results have revealed that the level of urbanity differently affects each of the health outcomes. In particular, men living in a small town or rural areas are likely to have higher risk of CHD incidence, but there exists no significant urban effect on incidence among women. In contrast, both men and women living in large cities may have disadvantage in one-year case fatality from CHD.

Considering the findings from Kim and Kawachi (2006), the effect of urbanity may include the effect of geographical conditions since they have employed no physical environment variables which may contribute to regional health inequities. As for the findings from Debrand et al. (2012), the effect of the CUA may be large and diminish the difference in population size but may disappear after controlling for the three synthetic factors. One of the reasons for the results may be that the synthetic factors are comprised of variables related to housing conditions. More precise classification may be needed for estimating the contextual effect caused by the built environment because the effect of population size is unstable due to other factors including the CUA and the synthetic factors. Moreover, although we could find no clear description of the classification of urbanity in Winkleby et al. (2007), a lack of consideration of contextual factors in the model may lead to ambiguous results.

In contrast to the above three studies, Ross and Mirowsky (2001, 2008) and Monnat and Beeler Pickett (2011) have proven that the level of urbanity is likely to have little effect on self-rated health using a multilevel model analysis. In the studies of Ross and Mirowsky (2001, 2008), they defined urban as a dichotomous variable (whether or not the respondents live in the city of Chicago) and have estimated no urban effect on self-rated health, although they have employed no contextual factors representing geographical or physical conditions. The result, however, is not enough evidence to confirm that neither geographical/physical conditions nor urbanity have any effect on health outcomes. It seems that the real effect of urbanity may be obscured and furthermore may be overlooked due to the relatively large individual-level error variance.

Monnat and Beeler Pickett (2011) have examined the urban/rural differences in self-rated health by applying a multilevel logistic model with random effects among US adults. They have employed some county-level "structural disadvantages," some of which are compositional variables such as elderly, race/ethnicity, poverty, unemployment, income and low education, and two other variables that are contextual and represent areas that have experienced population loss over the last decade and areas supported by the federal government in order to overcome a shortage of health professionals. Both of the contextual variables appeared to have significant and relatively large effects on self-reported health in addition to the other compositional variables. They have also examined the effect of urbanization, classified into five categories (metropolitan, large metropolitan adjacent to metropolitan area, large non metropolitan remote, rural adjacent to metropolitan area, and rural remote) based on the USDA ERS classification scheme.

As the first step of analysis, they have proven that residents living in remote rural counties are more likely to report poor health compared to their counterparts living in other counties after controlling for individual demographic and social characteristics except education, income, employment status, and with/without health insurance (hereinafter, these individual characteristics are referred to as individual socioeconomic factors). They have, however, shown that the negative effect of rurality seems to disappear after further controlling for county-level variables. This indicates that the rural effect may arise from the compositional and contextual factors at the county level, and as the authors stated in their paper, it is the combination of all these variables, rather than some specific variables, that seems to better describe the effect of rurality. Moreover, the model with county-level variables indicates that individuals living in relatively urban counties are more likely to experience unfavorable health conditions in contrast to the model without these variables. These findings allow us to conclude that the urban environment may have other factors that exert a negative influence on health outcomes. However, if individual socioeconomic factors are added to the model, the difference between urban and rural diminishes and becomes statistically insignificant. Although the negative effect of urbanity may be partially explained by the compositional and contextual effects, and may be fully absorbed by the effect of individual characteristics, it is worth exploring other contextual factors that bring about regional differences in health outcomes, as the authors concluded.

Through these six studies examining the impact of human capital accumulation and level of urbanity, we find that urban/rural effect may vary greatly depending on independent variables in the model. The urban/rural effect seems to be inconsistent across different independent variables in the three studies, Ross and Mirowsky, 2001, Monnat and Beeler Pickett, 2011 and Debrand et al., 2012. That is, the relationship between level of urbanity and health outcomes may become statistically significant or even may be reversed after controlling for additional variables. This instability makes it difficult to state a definite conclusion.

If the effect of urbanity is estimated as insignificant in a model, it is thought to be partly because other neighborhood-level characteristics such as compositional factors including accumulation of human capital (i.e., better-educated people) and contextual factors related to physical characteristics can fully account for the effect of urbanity. However, urban/rural effect would also be masked due to a high error variance if the appropriate independent variables were not used. These results suggest that further attention is needed to examine the potential impact of urban/rural environments.

8. CONCLUDING REMARKS

This chapter reviews a series of studies assessing compositional and contextual effects on health outcomes. As we indicated above, it cannot simply be concluded that one region is advantageous in health compared to other regions on the basis of the urban/rural dichotomy or even on continuum classification. The effect of urbanity seems to be inconsistent across countries and studies as well as over time. This inconsistency may due to the following three reasons. First is the ambiguity of the definition. Since urban/rural characteristics largely depend on demographic, socioeconomic, and geographical factors, each country should develop their own urban/rural definition to satisfy their conditions and the definition should be revised to reflect the changing situation. Furthermore, the distinction between urban and rural areas becomes blurred partly because suburban areas have been extensively developed to meet the demand of the population growth. These facts make it difficult to give a unique definition of urbanity/rurality and to make a clear distinction between areas. Second is the existence of intra-urban/intra-rural heterogeneity. Positive and negative effects on health outcomes have been identified in both urban and rural areas. The coexistence of positive and negative factors in an area masks disparities between regions and causes the underestimation of the true effect that the area has on health outcomes. The third reason is the inappropriate selection of independent variables. If health outcome can be fully explained by individual and regional factors, and compositional and contextual factors of urban/rural areas can be fully identified, the difference between urban and rural areas would disappear. However, the urban/rural effect would also be diminished if crucial variables were omitted from the model.

Is it meaningful to identify the existence of health inequities across regions as well as countries in the context of urban/rural differences? We are convinced that the implication from these findings is important. A number of studies have found significant contextual effects due to urban/rural areas and some of them have maintained the importance of spatial correlation between areas. We should not invest too much effort in finding a significant difference between urban and rural areas, but should identify key elements affecting health outcomes that characterize the urban/rural environment.

Some studies have explored a new urban/rural classification scheme to capture intra-regional heterogeneity. Other studies have developed an index that more accurately describes regional characteristics such as rurality index, or urban sprawl index using a principal components analysis. Constructing an index is also useful to reduce the number of independent variables. In contrast, a regional index masks the effects of each component. Taking into account the fact that, generally, controlled variables interact with each other, a regional index should be carefully used in accordance with the research objectives. Furthermore, we should also pay attention to "inter-regional" relationships in terms of not only geographical but also socioeconomic aspects. We also find a series of studies examining the impact of inter-regional migration on health outcomes. Although most of those studies have concluded that the impact of migration is not significantly large (see Brimblecombe et al., 1999; O'Reilly et al., 2001; Boyle et al., 2002; Connolly et al., 2007, 2011; Martikainen et al., 2008; Jongeneel-Grimen et al., 2011), we should address the problems from the perspective of urban dynamics.

Broadly speaking, urbanity seems to have two dimensions that affect health outcomes: One is the productivity spillovers that arise from human capital accumulation. Previous studies have produced evidence that higher productivity, usually represented as level of educational attainment, leads to better health status. The productivity spillovers improve regional productivity and, as a result, may positively affect regional health status. Unsurprisingly, concentration of population is considered to exert a substantial influence on the extent of social capital, although several studies have raised questions about the relationship between human capital and social capital. Some papers have shown that the accumulation of social capital is likely to be lower among residents in urban areas (see Veenstra,

2002; Greiner et al., 2004; Mohnen et al. 2011). Veenstra (2002) has proven in Saskatchewan, Canada, that social capital may be higher in areas with smaller populations or with a lower population density. Greiner et al. (2004) have demonstrated that residents living in an urban area are likely to rate their community higher and their community involvement lower, and that self-rated health and behaviors are not associated with community involvement but with community ratings among adults living in Kansas, the United States. Mohnen et al. (2011) have concluded that neighborhood social capital may have a positive effect on self-rated health for respondents living in urban areas but not for those in rural areas in the Netherlands, although social capital accumulation decreases as the degree of urbanity increases. Moreover, the prevalence of crime, sometimes regarded as an indicator of lack of social cohesion, may negatively affect population health (see Kennedy et al., 1998; Walberg et al., 1998; Wilcox et al., 2000; Franzini and Spears, 2003). The perceived safety may closely relate to walking activity (see Fisher et al., 2004; Suminski et al., 2005) and self-rated health (see Chandola, 2001; Ross and Mirowsky, 2001; Ziersch et al. 2005, Bowling and Stafford, 2007). Although some papers have stressed that it is unclear whether higher population density results in an increase in crime or not (see Patterson, 1991; Browning et al., 2010; Hipp et al., 2013), examining how the effect of social capital on health outcomes varies over levels of urbanity is still one of the outstanding issues.

The other is the physical environment. Agglomeration economies would provide benefits for consumers. Higher productivity in urban areas would be expected to generate higher wage rates and to enhance accessibility to a wider variety of goods and services. Moreover, greater land use mix would reduce commuting cost as well as car dependency and increase walkability. In contrast, overcrowding due to a concentration of population would cause deterioration in quality of living. Higher population density negatively affects health outcomes via high-rise buildings, overcrowded households, and less green space. Residents living in areas with a high density of buildings may also face a higher level of exposure to pollution.

In general, living in urban areas confers advantages for people in terms of the spatial accessibility and availability of goods or services. Many studies, however, have shown the health advantages of rural living. These results are obtained in three cases where net benefits in urban areas are estimated to be smaller than those in rural areas because (1) urban losses are relatively high, (2) urban benefits are relatively low, and (3) losses in deprived areas within urban areas (e.g., inner areas) cancel out benefits in urban areas. We should separately examine the effect of individual factors that compose urbanity/rurality before concluding the superiority of one region over the other.

From the economic point of view, it matters little if individual consumers could choose their health status based on their own preferences. However, it may be a critical issue if their health suffers from negative externalities caused by environmental degradation. Further research will be needed to identify the components of the living environment that have a critical influence on health outcomes so as to reveal the mechanism underlying inequalities in health and to find "optimal" cities where residents can enjoy the benefits of health. A few researchers have analyzed the impact of some factors which may affect health outcomes using a meta-analysis method (Schwartz, 1994; Peen et al., 2010; Jenkinson et al., 2013). Schwartz (1994) has examined the impact of the exposure to air pollution on mortality. Jenkinson et al. (2013) have demonstrated the benefit of volunteering on mental health and survival. Peen et al. (2010) have revealed a clear difference in prevalence rates of psychiatric disorders between urban and rural areas in comparing 20 selected studies on developed countries. They have found that rates of mental disorders including mood and anxiety disorders may be relatively higher in urban areas. A meta-analysis is one of the effective approaches for estimating the effect size assumed to be constant across studies. Although it seems to be difficult to simply compare the impacts of contextual factors on health outcomes, we are sure that more reliable results would be expected from further studies applying a meta-analysis.

The previous integrated, substantive conclusions from an inventory of (case) studies that have addressed the relationship between (urban) socioeconomic conditions and human health in the previous sections can be further supported by the use of a visual content analysis of the key concepts in sections 5–7. To that end, we use a "content cloud" analysis. A "content cloud" offers a hierarchically decomposed and visual presentation – often in a multi-color format – of the most relevant terms used in a scientific text, based on the frequency of their use. It is not a research tool in itself, but merely a visualization method of qualitative contents. The "content cloud" related to sections 5–7 of this chapter is presented in Figure 11.1.

The results in Figure 11.1 show that various core concepts in our case studies, for example population, housing, density, living, sprawl, mortality, accessibility, residential, spatial, services, pollution, segregation and status, appear rather prominently. These are clearly the key terms used in the analysis of urban conditions in relation to sustainable human health and regional growth. These results confirm the essence of our applied research on the key socioeconomic conditions of cities (and their actors) on health outcomes, from the perspective of the "New Urban World."

In conclusion, the urban pattern of living and working to improve health and wellbeing in today's urbanized world needs a broad explanatory

Figure 11.1 *A 'content cloud' of the key concepts in sections 5–7*

assessment framework through which we are able to understand the motives and behavior of citizens, visitors, firms, and other stakeholders (see also Nijkamp, 2008, p. 5; Nijkamp and Kourtit, 2011; Kourtit et al., 2015).

From the above overview, it is clear that further studies will be needed to clarify the urban/rural differences using an empirical modeling approach in order to identify the effect of urbanity more precisely. We call this approach "urban medico-metrics." It will be a key challenge to reveal the components of the urban/rural environment that affect health outcomes. Urban medico-metrics could offer a clue to the mechanism that helps to clarify the causes of health inequities within and between countries.

REFERENCES

AIHW (Australian Institute of Health and Welfare). (2014). Rural, Remote and Metropolitan Areas. (RRMA) classification. Available from: https://www.aihw.gov.au/rural-health-rrma-classification/ (21 February, 2014).

Alonso, William. (1964). *Location and Land Use: Toward a General Theory of Land Rent*. Cambridge, MA, Harvard University Press.

Apelberg, Benjamin J., Timothy J. Buckley, and Ronald H. White. (2005). Socioeconomic and racial disparities in cancer risk from air toxics in Maryland. *Environmental Health Perspectives*, 113(6), 693–699.
Arcury, Thomas A., Wilbert M. Gesler, John S. Preisser, Jill Sherman, John Spencer, and Jamie Perin. (2005a). The effects of geography and spatial behavior on health care utilization among the residents of a rural region. *Health Services Research*, 40(1), 135–155.
Arcury, Thomas A., John S. Preisser, Wilbert M. Gesler, and James M. Powers. (2005b). Access to transportation and health care utilization in a rural region. *The Journal of Rural Health*, 21(1), 31–38.
Auchincloss, Amy H., and Wilbur Hadden. (2002). The health effects of rural–urban residence and concentrated poverty. *Journal of Rural Health*, 18(2), 319–336.
Auger, Nathalie, Marie-Andree Authier, Jerome Martinez, and Mark Daniel. (2009). The association between rural–urban continuum, maternal education and adverse birth outcomes in Quebec, Canada. *The Journal of Rural Health*, 25(4), 342–351.
Auster, Richard, Irving Leveson, and Deborah Sarachek. (1969). The production of health, an exploratory study. *The Journal of Human Resources*, 411–436.
Babones, Salvatore J. (2008). Income inequality and population health: Correlation and causality. *Social Science and Medicine*, 66(7), 1614–1626.
Backhans, Mona C., Michael Lundberg, and Anna Mansdotter. (2007). Does increased gender equality lead to a convergence of health outcomes for men and women? A study of Swedish municipalities. *Social Science and Medicine*, 64(9), 1892–1903.
Barnett, Elizabeth, and Joel Halverson. (2000). Disparities in premature coronary heart disease mortality by region and urbanicity among Black and White adults ages 35–64, 1985–1995. *Public Health Reports*, 115(1), 52–64.
Barnett, Elizabeth, Joel A. Halverson, Gregory A. Elmes, and Valerie E. Braham. (2000). Metropolitan and non-metropolitan trends in coronary heart disease mortality within Appalachia, 1980–1997. *Annals of Epidemiology*, 10(6), 370–379.
Barnett, S., P. Roderick, D. Martin, and I. Diamond. (2001). A multilevel analysis of the effects of rurality and social deprivation on premature limiting long term illness. *Journal of Epidemiology and Community Health*, 55(1), 44–51.
Bartley, Mel. (2012). Explaining health inequality: Evidence from the UK. *Social Science and Medicine*, 74(5), 658–660.
Basu, Jayasree, and James Cooper. (2000). Out-of-area travel from rural and urban counties: A study of ambulatory care sensitive hospitalizations for New York state residents. *The Journal of Rural Health*, 16(2), 129–138.
Basu, Jayasree, and Lee R. Mobley. (2007). Illness severity and propensity to travel along the urban–rural continuum. *Health and Place*, 13(2), 381–399.
Becker, Gary S., Kevin M. Murphy, and Robert Tamura. (1994). Human capital, fertility, and economic growth. In *Human Capital A Theoretical and Empirical Analysis with Special Reference to Education* (3rd Edition). Chicago, IL, The University of Chicago Press, 323–350.
Bell, Janice F., Frederick J. Zimmerman, Gunnar R. Almgren, Jonathan D. Mayer, and Colleen E. Huebner. (2006). Birth outcomes among urban African-American women: A multilevel analysis of the role of racial residential segregation. *Social Science and Medicine*, 63(12), 3030–3045.
Benach, Joan, and Yutaka Yasui. (1999). Geographical patterns of excess mortality

in Spain explained by two indices of deprivation. *Journal of Epidemiology and Community Health*, 53(7), 423–431.
Benjamins, Maureen Reindl, Robert A. Hummer, Isaac W. Eberstein, and Charles B. Nam. (2004). Self-reported health and adult mortality risk: An analysis of cause-specific mortality. *Social Science and Medicine*, 59(6), 1297–1306.
Bentham, Graham, Jane Eimermann, Robin Haynes, Andrew Lovett, and Julii Brainard. (1995). Limiting long-term illness and its associations with mortality and indicators of social deprivation. *Journal of Epidemiology and Community Health*, 49(suppl 2), S57–S64.
Berke, Ethan M., Alan N. West, Amy E. Wallace, and William B. Weeks. (2009). Practical and policy implications of using different rural–urban classification systems: A case study of inpatient service utilization among Veterans Administration users. *The Journal of Rural Health*, 25(3), 259–266.
Bernard, Paul, Rana Charafeddine, Katherine L. Frohlich, Mark Daniel, Yan Kestens, and Louise Potvin. (2007). Health inequalities and place: A theoretical conception of neighbourhood. *Social Science and Medicine*, 65(9), 1839–1852.
Black, Duncan, and Vernon Henderson. (1999). A theory of urban growth. *Journal of Political Economy*, 107(2), 252–284.
Bloor, Karen, Vivien Hendry, and Alan Maynard. (2006). Do we need more doctors? *Journal of the Royal Society of Medicine*, 99(6), 281–287.
Bobak, Martin, and David A. Leon. (1999). Pregnancy outcomes and outdoor air pollution: An ecological study in districts of the Czech Republic 1986–8. *Occupational and Environmental Medicine*, 56(8), 539–543.
Bowling, Ann, and Mai Stafford. (2007). How do objective and subjective assessments of neighbourhood influence social and physical functioning in older age? Findings from a British survey of ageing. *Social Science and Medicine*, 64(12), 2533–2549.
Boyle, Paul, Paul Norman, and Philip Rees. (2002). Does migration exaggerate the relationship between deprivation and limiting long-term illness? A Scottish analysis. *Social Science and Medicine*, 55(1), 21–31.
Boys, A., M. Farrell, C. Taylor, J. Marsden, R. Goodman, T. Brugha, P. Bebbington, R. Jenkins, and H. Meltzer. (2003). Psychiatric morbidity and substance use in young people aged 13–15 years: Results from the Child and Adolescent Survey of Mental Health. *British Journal of Psychiatry*, 182(6), 509–517.
Brimblecombe, Nic, Danny Dorling, and Mary Shaw. (1999). Mortality and migration in Britain, first results from the British Household Panel Survey. *Social Science and Medicine*, 49(7), 981–988.
Brown, Barbara B., Ikuho Yamada, Ken R. Smith, Cathleen D. Zick, Lori Kowaleski-Jones, and Jessie X. Fan (2009). Mixed land use and walkability: Variations in land use measures and relationships with BMI, overweight, and obesity. *Health and Place*, 15(4), 1130–1141.
Brown, Denise, and Alastair H. Leyland. (2010). Scottish mortality rates 2000–2002 by deprivation and small area population mobility. *Social Science and Medicine*, 71(11), 1951–1957.
Browning, Christopher R., Kathleen A. Cagney, and Ming Wen. (2003). Explaining variation in health status across space and time: Implications for racial and ethnic disparities in self-rated health. *Social Science and Medicine*, 57(7), 1221–1235.
Browning, Christopher R., Reginald A. Byron, Catherine A. Calder, Lauren J. Krivo, Mei-Po Kwan, Jae-Yong Lee, and Ruth D. Peterson. (2010). Commercial density, residential concentration, and crime: Land use patterns and violence in

neighborhood context. *Journal of Research in Crime and Delinquency*, 47(3), 329–357.
Brugge, Doug, John L. Durant, and Christine Rioux. (2007). Near-highway pollutants in motor vehicle exhaust: A review of epidemiologic evidence of cardiac and pulmonary health risks. *Environmental Health*, 6(1), 23.
Burnett, Richard, Renjun Ma, Michael Jerrett, Mark S. Goldberg, Sabit Cakmak, C.A. Pope 3rd, and Daniel Krewski. (2001). The spatial association between community air pollution and mortality: A new method of analyzing correlated geographic cohort data. *Environmental Health Perspectives*, 109(suppl 3), 375–380.
Caldwell, T.M., A.F. Jorm, S. Knox, D. Braddock, K.B.G. Dear, and H. Britt. (2004). General practice encounters for psychological problems in rural, remote and metropolitan areas in Australia. *Australian and New Zealand Journal of Psychiatry*, 38(10), 774–780.
Campbell, N.C., A.M. Elliott, L. Sharp, L.D. Ritchie, J. Cassidy, and J. Little. (2001). Rural and urban differences in stage at diagnosis of colorectal and lung cancers. *British Journal of Cancer*, 84(7), 910–914.
Carneiro, Fernando Ferreira, Enrique Cifuentes, Martha Maria Tellez-Rojo, and Isabelle Romieu. (2002). The risk of *Ascaris lumbricoides* infection in children as an environmental health indicator to guide preventive activities in Caparao and Alto Caparao, Brazil. *Bulletin of the World Health Organization*, 80(1), 40–46.
CASI. (2013). ACORN user guide. Available from: http://acorn.caci.co.uk/downloads/Acorn-User-guide.pdf.
CeLSIUS. (2014). Classification: CLUST91. Available from: http://www.celsius.lshtm.ac.uk/newDataDict/getClassification.php?shortname=CLUST91 (13 January, 2014).
Chaix, B., P.-Y. Boelle, P. Guilbert, and P. Chauvin. (2005). Area-level determinants of specialty care utilization in France: A multilevel analysis. *Public Health*, 119(2), 97–104.
Chaix, Basile, Maria Rosvall, John Lynch, and Juan Merlo. (2006). Disentangling contextual effects on cause-specific mortality in a longitudinal 23-year follow-up study: Impact of population density or socioeconomic environment? *International Journal of Epidemiology*, 35(3), 633–643.
Chakraborty, Jayajit. (2009). Automobiles, air toxics, and adverse health risks: Environmental inequities in Tampa Bay, Florida. *Annals of the Association of American Geographers*, 99(4), 674–697.
Chandola, Tarani. (2001). The fear of crime and area differences in health. *Health and Place*, 7(2), 105–116.
Cho, Eun Joo, Daniel Rodriguez, and Yan Song. (2008). The role of employment subcenters in residential location decisions. *Journal of Transport and Land Use*, 1(2), 121–151.
Christie, S.M.L., and D.L. Fone. (2003). Does car ownership reflect socio-economic disadvantage in rural areas? A cross-sectional geographical study in Wales, UK. *Public Health*, 117(2), 112–116.
Chung, Haejoo, and Carles Muntaner. (2006). Political and welfare state determinants of infant and child health indicators: An analysis of wealthy countries. *Social Science and Medicine*, 63(3), 829–842.
Chung, Haejoo, and Carles Muntaner. (2007). Welfare state matters: A typological multilevel analysis of wealthy countries. *Health Policy*, 80(2), 328–339.
Coburn, David. (2004). Beyond the income inequality hypothesis: Class,

neo-liberalism, and health inequalities. *Social Science and Medicine*, 58(1), 41–56.
Cohen, Geoff, John Forbes, and Michael Garraway. (1995). Interpreting self reported limiting long term illness. *British Medical Journal*, 311(7007), 722.
Colwill, Jack M., James M. Cultice, and Robin L. Kruse. (2008). Will generalist physician supply meet demands of an increasing and aging population? *Health Affairs*, 27(3), w232–w241.
Congdon, P., S. Shouls, and S. Curtis. (1997). A multi-level perspective on small-area health and mortality: A case study of England and Wales. *International Journal of Population Geography*, 3(3), 243–263.
Connolly, Sheelah, Dermot O'Reilly, and Michael Rosato. (2007). Increasing inequalities in health: Is it an artefact caused by the selective movement of people? *Social Science and Medicine*, 64(10), 2008–2015.
Connolly, Sheelah, Michael Rosato, and Dermot O'Reilly. (2011). The effect of population movement on the spatial distribution of socio-economic and health status: Analysis using the Northern Ireland mortality study. *Health and Place*, 17(4), 1007–1010.
Corburn, Jason, Jeffrey Osleeb, and Michael Porter. (2006). Urban asthma and the neighbourhood environment in New York City. *Health and Place*, 12(2), 167–179.
Cosby, Arthur G., Tonya T. Neaves, Ronald E. Cossman, Jeralynn S. Cossman, Wesley L. James, S. Neal Feierabend, David M. Mirvis, Carol A. Jones, and Tracey Farrigan. (2008). Preliminary evidence for an emerging nonmetropolitan mortality penalty in the United States. *American Journal of Public Health*, 98(8), 1470–1473.
Cossman, Ronald E., Jeralynn S. Cossman, Arthur G. Cosby, and Rebel M. Reavis. (2008). Reconsidering the rural–urban continuum in rural health research: A test of stable relationships using mortality as a health measure. *Population Research and Policy Review*, 27(4), 459–476.
Costa, Giovanni, Laurie Pickup, and Vittorio Di Martino. (1988). Commuting a further stress factor for working people: Evidence from the European Community. II. An empirical study. *International Archives of Occupational and Environmental Health*, 60(5), 377–385.
CSDH. (2008). Closing the gap in a generation: Health equity through action on the social determinants of health. Final Report of the Commission on Social Determinants of Health. Geneva, World Health Organization.
Cummins, Steven, Sally Macintyre, Sharon Davidson, and Anne Ellaway. (2005). Measuring neighbourhood social and material context: Generation and interpretation of ecological data from routine and non-routine sources. *Health and Place*, 11(3), 249–260.
Curtis, Sarah, and Ian Rees Jones. (1998). Is there a place for geography in the analysis of health inequality? *Sociology of Health and Illness*, 20(5), 645–672.
D'Hombres, B., L. Rocco, M. Suhrcke, and M. McKee. (2010). Does social capital determine health? Evidence from eight transition countries. *Health Economics*, 19(1), 56–74.
Dahl, Espen, Jon Ivar Elstad, Dag Hofoss, and Melissa Martin-Mollard. (2006). For whom is income inequality most harmful? A multi-level analysis of income inequality and mortality in Norway. *Social Science and Medicine*, 63(10), 2562–2574.
Dahly, Darren L., and Linda S. Adair. (2007). Quantifying the urban environment:

A scale measure of urbanicity outperforms the urban–rural dichotomy. *Social Science and Medicine*, 64(7), 1407–1419.

DCLG. (2006). Urban and rural area definitions: A user guide. Department for Communities and Local Government. Available from: http://webarchive.nationalarchives.gov.uk/20120919132719/http://www.communities.gov.uk/index.asp?id=1147752.

De Vogli, Roberto, Ritesh Mistry, Roberto Gnesotto, and Giovanni Andrea Cornia. (2005). Has the relation between income inequality and life expectancy disappeared? Evidence from Italy and top industrialised countries. *Journal of Epidemiology and Community Health*, 59(2), 158–162.

Debrand, Thierry, Aurélie Pierre, Caroline Allonier, and Véronique Lucas-Gabrielli. (2012). Critical urban areas, deprived areas and neighbourhood effects on health in France. *Health Policy*, 105(1), 92–101.

Dempsey, Paula, David Wilson, Anne Taylor, and David Wilkinson. (2003). Self-reported patterns of health services utilisation: An urban–rural comparison in South Australia. *Australian Journal of Rural Health*, 11(2), 81–88.

Diez-Roux, Ana V., Bruce G. Link, and Mary E. Northridge. (2000). A multilevel analysis of income inequality and cardiovascular disease risk factors. *Social Science and Medicine*, 50(5), 673–687.

Dockery, Douglas W., C. Arden Pope, Xiping Xu, John D. Spengler, James H. Ware, Martha E. Fay, Benjamin G. Ferris, Jr., and Frank E. Speizer. (1993). An association between air pollution and mortality in six U.S. cities. *The New England Journal of Medicine*, 329(24), 1753–1759.

Dominici, Francesca, Roger D. Peng, Michelle L. Bell, Luu Pham, Aidan McDermott, Scott L. Zeger, and Jonathan M. Samet. (2006). Fine particulate air pollution and hospital admission for cardiovascular and respiratory diseases. *The Journal of the American Medical Association*, 295(10), 1127–1134.

Dragano, Nico, Barbara Hoffmann, Susanne Moebus, Stefan Möhlenkamp, Andreas Stang, Pablo Emilio Verde, Karl-Heinz Jöckel, Raimund Erbel, and Johannes Siegrist. (2009). Traffic exposure and subclinical cardiovascular disease: Is the association modified by socioeconomic characteristics of individuals and neighbourhoods? Results from a multilevel study in an urban region. *Occupational and Environmental Medicine*, 66(9), 628–635.

Drukker, Marjan, Charles Kaplan, Frans Feron, and Jim van Os. (2003). Children's health-related quality of life, neighbourhood socio-economic deprivation and social capital. A contextual analysis. *Social Science and Medicine*, 57(5), 825–841.

Duncan, Craig, Kelvyn Jones, and Graham Moon. (1993). Do places matter? A multilevel analysis of regional variations in health-related behaviour in Britain. *Social Science and Medicine*, 37(6), 725–733.

Eberhardt, Mark S., and Elsie R. Pamuk. (2004). The importance of place of residence: Examining health in rural and nonrural areas. *American Journal of Public Health*, 94(10), 1682–1686.

Engstrom, Karin, Fredrik Mattsson, Anders Jarleborg, and Johan Hallqvist. (2008). Contextual social capital as a risk factor for poor self-rated health: A multilevel analysis. *Social Science and Medicine*, 66(10), 2268–2280.

Ettner, Susan L. (1996). New evidence on the relationship between income and health. *Journal of Health Economics*, 15(1), 67–85.

Evans, Gary W. (2003). The built environment and mental health. *Journal of Urban Health*, 80(4), 536–555.

Evans, Gary W., and Richard E. Wener. (2006). Rail commuting duration and passenger stress. *Health Psychology*, 25(3), 408–412.
Evans, Gary W., Nancy M. Wells, Hoi-Yan Erica Chan, and Heidi Salzman. (2000). Housing quality and mental health. *Journal of Consulting and Clinical Psychology*, 68(3), 526–530.
Evashwick, Connie, Genevieve Rowe, Paula Diehr, and Laurence Branch. (1984). Factors explaining the use of health care services by the elderly. *Health Services Research*, 19(3), 357–382.
Ewing, Reid, Tom Schmid, Richard Killingsworth, Amy Zlot, and Stephen Raudenbush. (2003). Relationship between urban sprawl and physical activity, obesity, and morbidity. *American Journal of Health Promotion*, 18(1), 47–57.
Fang, Jing, Shantha Madhavan, William Bosworth, and Michael H. Alderman. (1998). Residential segregation and mortality in New York City. *Social Science and Medicine*, 47(4), 469–476.
Finkelstein, Murray M., Michael Jerrett, and Malcolm R. Sears. (2005). Environmental inequality and circulatory disease mortality gradients. *Journal of Epidemiology and Community Health*, 59(6), 481–487.
Finkelstein, Murray M., Michael Jerrett, Patrick DeLuca, Norm Finkelstein, Dave K. Verma, Kenneth Chapman, and Malcolm R. Sears. (2003). Relation between income, air pollution and mortality: A cohort study. *Canadian Medical Association Journal*, 169(5), 397–402.
Fisher, K. John, Fuzhong Li, Yvonne Michael, and Minot Cleveland. (2004). Neighborhood-level influences on physical activity among older adults a multilevel analysis. *Journal of Aging and Physical Activity*, 12(1), 45–63.
Fogelholm, Mikael, Raisa Valve, Pilvikki Absetz, Heikki Heinonen, Antti Uutela, Kristiina Patja, Antti Karisto, Riikka Konttinen, Tiina Mäkelä, Aulikki Nissinen, Piia Jallinoja, Olli Nummela, and Martti Talja. (2006). Rural–urban differences in health and health behaviour: A baseline description of a community health-promotion programme for the elderly. *Scandinavian Journal of Public Health*, 34(6), 632–640.
Folland, Sherman. (2007). Does "community social capital" contribute to population health? *Social Science and Medicine*, 64(11), 2342–2354.
Folland, Sherman. (2008). An economic model of social capital and health. *Health Economics, Policy and Law*, 3(4), 333–348.
Fournel, Isabelle, Vanessa Cottet, Christine Binquet, Valérie Jooste, Jean Faivre, Anne Marie Bouvier, and Claire Bonithon-Kopp. (2012). Rural–urban inequalities in detection rates of colorectal tumours in the population. *Digestive and Liver Disease*, 44(2), 172–177.
Frank, Lawrence D., Martin A. Andresen, and Thomas L. Schmid. (2004). Obesity relationships with community design, physical activity, and time spent in cars. *American Journal of Preventive Medicine*, 27(2), 87–96.
Frank, Lawrence D., James F. Sallis, Terry L. Conway, James E. Chapman, Brian E. Saelens, and William Bachman. (2006). Many pathways from land use to health: Associations between neighborhood walkability and active transportation, body mass index, and air quality. *Journal of the American Planning Association*, 72(1), 75–87.
Franzini, Luisa, and William Spears. (2003). Contributions of social context to inequalities in years of life lost to heart disease in Texas, USA. *Social Science and Medicine*, 57(10), 1847–1861.

Freudenberg, Nicholas, Sandro Galea, and David Vlahov. (2005). Beyond urban penalty and urban sprawl: Back to living conditions as the focus of urban health. *Journal of Community Health*, 30(1), 1–11.
Fujisawa, Yoshikazu, Tsuyoshi Hamano, and Shogo Takegawa. (2009). Social capital and perceived health in Japan: An ecological and multilevel analysis. *Social Science and Medicine*, 69(4), 500–505.
Fukuda, Yoshiharu, Keiko Nakamura, and Takehito Takano. (2007). Higher mortality in areas of lower socioeconomic position measured by a single index of deprivation in Japan. *Public Health*, 121(3), 163–173.
Furnée, Carina A., Wim Groot, and Henriëtte Maassen van Den Brink. (2008). The health effects of education a meta-analysis. *The European Journal of Public Health*, 18(4), 417–421.
Gartner, Andrea, Daniel Farewell, Frank Dunstan, and Emma Gordon. (2008). Differences in mortality between rural and urban areas in England and Wales, 2002–04. *Health Statistics Quarterly*, 39(39), 6–13.
Gartner, Andrea, Daniel Farewell, Paul Roach, and Frank Dunstan. (2011). Rural/urban mortality differences in England and Wales and the effect of deprivation adjustment. *Social Science and Medicine*, 72(10), 1685–1694.
Gatersleben, Birgitta, and David Uzzell. (2007). Affective appraisals of the daily commute comparing perceptions of drivers, cyclists, walkers, and users of public transport. *Environment and Behavior*, 39(3), 416–431.
Gerdtham, U.-G., and Magnus Johannesson. (1999). New estimates of the demand for health: Results based on a categorical health measure and Swedish micro data. *Social Science and Medicine*, 49(10), 1325–1332.
Ghelfi, Linda M., and Timothy S. Parker. (1997). A county-level measure of urban influence. *Rural Development Perspectives*, 12, 32–41.
Gifford, Robert. (2007). The consequences of living in high-rise buildings. *Architectural Science Review*, 50(1), 2–17.
Gillanders, W.R., Terry F. Buss, and C. Richard Hofstetter. (1997). Urban/rural elderly health status differences. *Journal of Aging and Social Policy*, 8(4), 7–24.
Gilthorpe, Mark S., and Richard C. Wilson. (2003). Rural/urban differences in the association between deprivation and healthcare utilisation. *Social Science and Medicine*, 57(11), 2055–2063.
Giordano, Giuseppe N., and Martin Lindstrom. (2010). The impact of changes in different aspects of social capital and material conditions on self-rated health over time: A longitudinal cohort study. *Social Science and Medicine*, 70(5), 700–710.
Glaeser, Edward L., and Joshua D. Gottlieb. (2009). The wealth of cities: Agglomeration economies and spatial equilibrium in the United States. *Journal of Economic Literature*, 47(4), 983–1028.
Goldberg, David P. (1978). *Manual of the General Health Questionnaire*. London, NFER.
Goodman, David C., and Elliott S. Fisher. (2008). Physician workforce crisis? Wrong diagnosis, wrong prescription. *New England Journal of Medicine*, 358(16), 1658–1661.
Gottholmseder, Georg, Klaus Nowotny, Gerald J. Pruckner, and Engelbert Theurl. (2009). Stress perception and commuting. *Health Economics*, 18(5), 559–576.
Grady, Sue C. (2006). Racial disparities in low birthweight and the contribution of residential segregation: A multilevel analysis. *Social Science and Medicine*, 63(12), 3013–3029.

Grahn, Patrik, and Ulrika A. Stigsdotter. (2003). Landscape planning and stress. *Urban Forestry and Urban Greening*, 2(1), 1–18.

Gravelle, Hugh, John Wildman, and Matthew Sutton. (2002). Income, income inequality and health: What can we learn from aggregate data? *Social Science and Medicine*, 54(5), 577–589.

Gray, Simone C., Sharon E. Edwards, and Marie Lynn Miranda. (2013). Race, socioeconomic status, and air pollution exposure in North Carolina. *Environmental Research*, 126, 152–158.

Greiner, K. Allen, Chaoyang Li, Ichiro Kawachi, D. Charles Hunt, and Jasjit S. Ahluwalia. (2004). The relationships of social participation and community ratings to health and health behaviors in areas with high and low population density. *Social Science and Medicine*, 59(11), 2303–2312.

Grossman, Michael. (1972). On the concept of health capital and the demand for health. *Journal of Political Economy*, 80(2), 223–255.

Grossman, Michael. (1999). The human capital model of the demand for health. Working Paper 7078, Amsterdam, North-Holland, National Bureau of Economic Research.

Guite, H.F., C. Clark, and G. Ackrill. (2006). The impact of the physical and urban environment on mental well-being. *Public Health*, 120(12), 1117–1126.

Gulliford, Martin C. (2002). Availability of primary care doctors and population health in England: Is there an association? *Journal of Public Health Medicine*, 24(4), 252–254.

Hajat, A., J.S. Kaufman, K.M. Rose, A. Siddiqi, and J.C. Thomas. (2010). Do the wealthy have a health advantage? Cardiovascular disease risk factors and wealth. *Social Science and Medicine*, 71(11), 1935–1942.

Hall, Susan A., Jay S. Kaufman, and Thomas C. Ricketts. (2006). Defining urban and rural areas in U.S. epidemiologic studies. *Journal of Urban Health*, 83(2), 162–175.

Handy, Susan L., Marlon G. Boarnet, Reid Ewing, and Richard E. Killingsworth. (2002). How the built environment affects physical activity views from urban planning. *American Journal of Preventive Medicine*, 23(2), 64–73.

Hanlon, P., R.S. Lawder, D. Buchanan, A. Redpath, D. Walsh, R. Wood, M. Bain, D.H. Brewster, and J. Chalmers. (2005). Why is mortality higher in Scotland than in England and Wales? Decreasing influence of socioeconomic deprivation between 1981 and 2001 supports the existence of a "Scottish Effect". *Journal of Public Health*, 27(2), 199–204.

Harpham, Trudy, and Catherine Molyneux. (2001). Urban health in developing countries: A review. *Progress in Development Studies*, 1(2), 113–137.

Hart, L. Gary, Eric H. Larson, and Denise M. Lishner. (2005). Rural definitions for health policy and research. *American Journal of Public Health*, 95(7), 1149–1155.

Hartley, David. (2004). Rural health disparities, population health, and rural culture. *American Journal of Public Health*, 94(10), 1675–1678.

Havard, Sabrina, Séverine Deguen, Julie Bodin, Karine Louis, Olivier Laurent, and Denis Bard. (2008). A small-area index of socioeconomic deprivation to capture health inequalities in France. *Social Science and Medicine*, 67(12), 2007–2016.

Havard, Sabrina, Séverine Deguen, Denis Zmirou-Navier, Charles Schillinger, and Denis Bard. (2009). Traffic-related air pollution and socioeconomic status: A spatial autocorrelation study to assess environmental equity on a small-area scale. *Epidemiology*, 20(2), 223–230.

Haynes, Robin. (1991). Inequalities in health and health service use: Evidence from the General Household Survey. *Social Science and Medicine*, 33(4), 361–368.
Haynes, Robin, and Susan Gale. (2000). Deprivation and poor health in rural areas: Inequalities hidden by averages. *Health and Place*, 6(4), 275–285.
Haynes, Robin, Graham Bentham, Andrew Lovett, and Susan Gale. (1999). Effects of distances to hospital and GP surgery on hospital inpatient episodes, controlling for needs and provision. *Social Science and Medicine*, 49(3), 425–433.
Heinrich, Joachim, Elisabeth Thiering, Peter Rzehak, Ursula Krämer, Matthias Hochadel, Knut M. Rauchfuss, Ulrike Gehring, and Heinz-Erich Wichmann. (2013). Long-term exposure to NO2 and PM10 and all-cause and cause-specific mortality in a prospective cohort of women. *Occupational and Environmental Medicine*, 70(3), 179–186.
Hewitt, Maria. (1989). *Defining 'Rural' Areas: Impact on Health Care Policy and Research*. Darby, PA, DIANE Publishing.
Higgs, Gary. (1999). Investigating trends in rural health outcomes: A research agenda. *Geoforum*, 30(3), 203–221.
Hillemeier, Marianne M., Carol S. Weisman, Gary A. Chase, and Anne-Marie Dyer. (2007). Individual and community predictors of preterm birth and low birthweight along the rural–urban continuum in central Pennsylvania. *The Journal of Rural Health*, 23(1), 42–48.
Hines, Fred K., David L. Brown, and John M, Zimmer. (1975). *Social and Economic Characteristics of the Population in Metro and Nonmetro Counties, 1970*. Washington, DC, Economic Research Service, US Department of Agriculture.
Hipp, John R., Carter T. Butts, Ryan Acton, Nicholas N. Nagle, and Adam Boessen. (2013). Extrapolative simulation of neighborhood networks based on population spatial distribution. Do they predict crime? *Social Networks*, 35(4), 614–625.
Hoehner, Christine M., Carolyn E. Barlow, Peg Allen, and Mario Schootman. (2012). Commuting distance, cardiorespiratory fitness, and metabolic risk. *American Journal of Preventive Medicine*, 42(6), 571–578.
Hoek, Gerard, Bert Brunekreef, Sandra Goldbohm, Paul Fischer, and Piet A. van den Brandt. (2002). Association between mortality and indicators of traffic-related air pollution in the Netherlands: A cohort study. *The Lancet*, 360(9341), 1203–1209.
Hou, Feng, and John Myles. (2005). Neighbourhood inequality, neighbourhood affluence and population health. *Social Science and Medicine*, 60(7), 1557–1569.
House, James S., James M. Lepkowski, David R. Williams, Richard P. Mero, Paula M. Lantz, Stephanie A. Robert, and Jieming Chen. (2000). Excess mortality among urban residents: How much, for whom, and why? *American Journal of Public Health*, 90(2), 1898–1904.
Hyyppa, Markku T., and Juhani Maki. (2001). Individual-level relationships between social capital and self-rated health in a bilingual community. *Preventive Medicine*, 32(2), 148–155.
Ichida, Yukinobu, Katsunori Kondo, Hiroshi Hirai, Tomoya Hanibuchi, Goshu Yoshikawa, and Chiyoe Murata. (2009). Social capital, income inequality and self-rated health in Chita peninsula, Japan: A multilevel analysis of older people in 25 communities. *Social Science and Medicine*, 69(4), 489–499.
Ingram, Deborah D., and Richard F. Gillum. (1989). Regional and urbanization differentials in coronary heart disease mortality in the United States, 1968–1985. *Journal of Clinical Epidemiology*, 42(9), 857–868.

Jackson, Laura E. (2003). The relationship of urban design to human health and condition. *Landscape and Urban Planning*, 64(4), 191–200.
Jackson, Sharon A., Roger T. Anderson, Norman J. Johnson, and Paul D. Sorlie. (2000). The relation of residential segregation to all-cause mortality: A study in black and white. *American Journal of Public Health*, 90(4), 615–617.
Jarman, Brian, Peter Townsend, and Vera Carstairs. (1991). Deprivation indices. *British Medical Journal*, 303(6801), 523.
Jenkinson, Caroline E., Andy P. Dickens, Kerry Jones, Jo Thompson-Coon, Rod S. Taylor, Morwenna Rogers, Clare L. Bambra, Iain Lang, and Suzanne H. Richards. (2013). Is volunteering a public health intervention? A systematic review and meta-analysis of the health and survival of volunteers. *BMC Public Health*, 13(1), 773.
Jerrett, Michael, Richard Burnett, Alette Willis, Daniel Krewski, Mark Goldberg, Patrick DeLuca, and Norm Finkelstein. (2003). Spatial analysis of the air pollution-mortality relationship in the context of ecologic confounders. *Journal of Toxicology and Environmental Health, Part A: Current Issues*, 66(16–19), 1735–1777.
Johnson, Michael P. (2001). Environmental impacts of urban sprawl: A survey of the literature and proposed research agenda. *Environment and Planning A*, 33(4), 717–735.
Johnson, Patrick B., and Linda Richter. (2002). The relationship between smoking, drinking, and adolescents' self-perceived health and frequency of hospitalization: Analyses from the 1997 National Household Survey on Drug Abuse. *Journal of Adolescent Health*, 30(3), 175–183.
Jongeneel-Grimen, Birthe, Mariel Droomers, Karien Stronks, and Anton E. Kunst. (2011). Migration does not enlarge inequalities in health between rich and poor neighbourhoods in the Netherlands. *Health and Place*, 17(4), 988–995.
Jordan, H., P. Roderick, and D. Martin. (2003). The index of multiple deprivation 2000 and accessibility effects on health. *Journal of Epidemiology and Community Health*, 58(3), 250–257.
Jordan, Hannah, Paul Roderick, David Martin, and Sarah Barnett. (2004). Distance, rurality and the need for care: Access to health services in South West England. *International Journal of Health Geographics*, 3(1), 21.
Judd, Fiona K., Henry J. Jackson, Angela Komiti, Greg Murray, Gene Hodgins, and Caitlin Fraser. (2002). High prevalence disorders in urban and rural communities. *Australian and New Zealand Journal of Psychiatry*, 36(1), 104–113.
Judge, Ken, Jo-Ann Mulligan, and Michaela Benzeval. (1998). Income inequality and population health. *Social Science and Medicine*, 46(4), 567–579.
Kageyama, Takayuki, Noriko Nishikido, Toshio Kobayashi, Yoshika Kurokawa, Tetsuya Kaneko, and Michinori Kabuto. (1998). Long commuting time, extensive overtime, and sympathodominant state assessed in terms of short-term heart rate variability among male white-collar workers in the Tokyo megalopolis. *Industrial Health*, 36(3), 209–217.
Kahn, Henry S., Lilith M. Tatham, Elsie R. Pamuk, and Clark W. Health Jr. (1998). Are geographic regions with high income inequality associated with risk of abdominal weight gain? *Social Science and Medicine*, 47(1), 1–6.
Kaplan, George A., Elsie R. Pamuk, John W. Lynch, Richard D. Cohen, and Jennifer L. Balfour. (1996). Inequality in income and mortality in the United

States: Analysis of mortality and potential pathways. *British Medical Journal*, 312(7037), 999.
Kawachi, Ichiro, and Bruce P. Kennedy. (1997). The relationship of income inequality to mortality: Does the choice of indicator matter? *Social Science and Medicine*, 45(7), 1121–1127.
Kawachi, Ichiro, and Bruce P. Kennedy. (1999). Income inequality and health: Pathways and mechanisms. *Health Services Research*, 34(1 Pt2), 215–227.
Kennedy, Bruce P., Ichiro Kawachi, and Elizabeth Brainerd. (1998). The role of social capital in the Russian mortality crisis. *World Development*, 26(11), 2029–2043.
Kim, Daniel, Christopher F. Baum, Michael L. Ganz, S.V. Subramanian, and Ichiro Kawachi. (2011). The contextual effects of social capital on health: A cross-national instrumental variable analysis. *Social Science and Medicine*, 73(12), 1689–1697.
Kim, Daniel, and Ichiro Kawachi. (2006). A multilevel analysis of key forms of community- and individual-level social capital as predictors of self-rated health in the United States. *Journal of Urban Health*, 83(5), 813–826.
Kindig, David A., Christopher L. Seplaki, and Donald L. Libby. (2002). Death rate variation in US subpopulations. *Bulletin of the World Health Organization*, 80(1), 9–15.
King, Malcolm, Alexandra Smith, and Michael Gracey. (2009). Indigenous health part 2: The underlying causes of the health gap. *Lancet*, 374(9683), 76–85.
Kluger, Avraham N. (1998). Commute variability and strain. *Journal of Organizational Behavior*, 19(2), 147–165.
Koslowsky, Meni, Asher Aizer, and Moshe Krausz. (1996). Stressor and personal variables in the commuting experience. *International Journal of Manpower*, 17(3), 4–14.
Kourtit, Karima, and Peter Nijkamp. (2013). In praise of megacities in a global world. *Regional Science Policy and Practice*, 5(2), 167–182.
Kourtit, Karima, Peter Nijkamp, and H. Scholten. (2015). The Future of the New Urban World. *International Planning Studies*, 20(1–2), 4–20.
Kramer, Michael R., and Carol R. Hogue. (2009). Is segregation bad for your health? *Epidemiologic Reviews*, 31(1), 178–194.
Krieger, James, and Donna L. Higgins. (2002). Housing and health: Time again for public health action. *American Journal of Public Health*, 92(5), 758–768.
Kristiansen, Thomas, Marius Rehn, Hans Magne Gravseth, Hans Morten Lossius, and Petter Kristensen. (2012). Paediatric trauma mortality in Norway: A population-based study of injury characteristics and urban–rural differences. *Injury*, 43(11), 1865–1872.
Kroneman, Madelon, Robert Verheij, Margot Tacken, and Jouke van der Zee. (2010). Urban–rural health differences: Primary care data and self reported data render different results. *Health and Place*, 16(5), 893–902.
Laditka, James N., Sarah B. Laditka, Bankole Olatosi, and Keith T. Elder. (2007). The health trade-off of rural residence for impaired older adults: Longer life, more impairment. *The Journal of Rural Health*, 23(2), 124–132.
Laditka, James N., Sarah B. Laditka, and Janice C. Probst. (2009). Health care access in rural areas: Evidence that hospitalization for ambulatory care-sensitive conditions in the United States may increase with the level of rurality. *Health and Place*, 15(3), 761–770.

Langford, Ian H., and Graham Bentham. (1996). Regional variations in mortality rates in England and Wales: An analysis using multi-level modelling. *Social Science and Medicine*, 42(6), 897–908.
Langlois, Peter H., Angela Scheuerle, Scott A. Horel, and Susan E. Carozza. (2009). Urban versus rural residence and occurrence of septal heart defects in Texas. *Birth Defects Research Part A: Clinical and Molecular Teratology*, 85(9), 764–772.
Larson, Sharon, and Rosaly Correa-de-Araujo. (2006). Preventive health examinations: A comparison along the rural–urban continuum. *Women's Health Issues*, 16(2), 80–88.
Lee, Kwang-sun, Sang-Chul Park, Babak Khoshnood, Hal-Lung Hsieh, and Robert Mittendorf. (1997). Human development index as a predictor of infant and maternal mortality rates. *The Journal of Paediatrics*, 131(3), 430–433.
Lee, Min-Ah, and Kenneth F. Ferraro. (2007). Neighborhood residential segregation and physical health among Hispanic Americans: Good, bad, or benign? *Journal of Health and Social Behavior*, 48(2), 131–148.
Leon, David A. (2008). Cities, urbanization and health. *International Journal of Epidemiology*, 37(1), 4–8.
Levin, Kate A. (2003). Urban–rural differences in self-reported limiting long-term illness in Scotland. *Journal of Public Health Medicine*, 25(4), 295–302.
Levin, Kate A., and Alastair H. Leyland. (2006). A comparison of health inequalities in urban and rural Scotland. *Social Science and Medicine*, 62(6), 1457–1464.
Li, Fuzhong, Peter A. Harmer, Bradley J. Cardinal, Mark Bosworth, Alan Acock, Deborah Johnson-Shelton, and Jane M. Moore. (2008). Built environment, adiposity, and physical activity in adults aged 50–75. *American Journal of Preventive Medicine*, 35(1), 38–46.
Liu, Gilbert C., Jeffrey S. Wilson, Rong Qi, and Jun Ying. (2007). Green neighborhoods, food retail and childhood overweight: Differences by population density. *American Journal of Health Promotion*, 21(4s), 317–325.
Lopez, Russ. (2004). Urban sprawl and risk for being overweight or obese. *American Journal of Public Health*, 94(9), 1574–1579.
Lorant, Vincent, Isabelle Thomas, Denise Deliege, and Rene Tonglet. (2001). Deprivation and mortality: The implications of spatial autocorrelation for health resources allocation. *Social Science and Medicine*, 53(12), 1711–1719.
Lorgelly, Paula K., and Joanne Lindley. (2008). What is the relationship between income inequality and health? Evidence from the BHPS. *Health Economics*, 17(2), 249–265.
Lostao, Lourdes, Enrique Regidor, Siegfried Geyer, and Pierre Aiach. (2007). Patient cost sharing and social inequalities in access to health care in three western European countries. *Social Science and Medicine*, 65(2), 367–376.
Luo, Zhong-Cheng, and Russell Wilkins. (2008). Degree of rural isolation and birth outcomes. *Paediatric and Perinatal Epidemiology*, 22(4), 341–349.
Maantay, Juliana. (2007). Asthma and air pollution in the Bronx: Methodological and data considerations in using GIS for environmental justice and health research. *Health and Place*, 13(1), 32–56.
Maas, Jolanda, Robert A. Verheij, Peter P. Groenewegen, Sjerp de Vries, and Peter Spreeuwenberg. (2006). Green space, urbanity, and health: How strong is the relation? *Journal of Epidemiology and Community Health*, 60(7), 587–592.
Macinko, James, Barbara Starfield, and Leiyu Shi. (2007). Quantifying the health

benefits of primary care physician supply in the United States. *International Journal of Health Services*, 37(1), 111–126.
Maheswaran, Ravi, and Paul Elliott. (2003). Stroke mortality associated with living near main roads in England and Wales: A geographical study. *Stroke*, 34(12), 2776–2780.
Mair, Christina, Ana V. Diez Roux, and Jeffrey D. Morenoff. (2010). Neighborhood stressors and social support as predictors of depressive symptoms in the Chicago Community Adult Health Study. *Health and Place*, 16(5), 811–819.
Malmstrom, Marianne, Sven-Erik Johansson, and Jan Sundquist. (2001). A hierarchical analysis of long-term illness and mortality in socially deprived areas. *Social Science and Medicine*, 53(3), 265–275.
Manor, Orly, Sharon Matthews, and Chris Power. (2001). Self-rated health and limiting longstanding illness: Inter-relationships with morbidity in early adulthood. *International Journal of Epidemiology*, 30(3), 600–607.
Mansyur, Carol, Benjamin C. Amick, Ronald B. Harrist, and Luisa Franzini. (2008). Social capital, income inequality, and self-rated health in 45 countries. *Social Science and Medicine*, 66(1), 43–56.
Marmot, Michael, and Richard G. Wilkinson. (2001). Psychosocial and material pathways in the relation between income and health: A response to Lynch et al. *British Medical Journal*, 322(7296), 1233–1236.
Martikainen, Pekka, Petteri Sipila, Jenni Blomgren, and Frank J. van Lenthe. (2008). The effects of migration on the relationship between area socioeconomic structure and mortality. *Health and Place*, 14(2), 361–366.
Martin, David, Philip Brigham, Paul Roderick, Sarah Barnett, and Ian Diamond. (2000). The (mis) representation of rural deprivation. *Environment and Planning A*, 32(4), 735–751.
Martin, Richard M., Jonathan A.C. Sterne, Punam Mangtani, and Azeem Majeed. (2001). Social and economic variation in general practice consultation rates amongst men aged 16–39. *Health Statistics Quarterly*, (9), 29–36.
Matteson, Donald W., Jefferey A. Burr, and James R. Marshall. (1998). Infant mortality: A multi-level analysis of individual and community risk factors. *Social Science and Medicine*, 47(11), 1841–1854.
McCarthy, P., D. Byrne, S. Harrison, and J. Keithley. (1985). Housing type, housing location and mental health. *Social Psychiatry*, 20(3), 125–130.
McCulloch, Andrew. (2006). Variation in children's cognitive and behavioural adjustment between different types of place in the British National Child Development Study. *Social Science and Medicine*, 62(8), 1865–1879.
McDade, Thomas W., and Linda S. Adair. (2001). Defining the 'urban' in urbanization and health: a factor analysis. *Social Science and Medicine*, 53(1), 55–70.
McLaughlin, Diane K., and C. Shannon Stokes. (2002). Income inequality and mortality in US counties: Does minority racial concentration matter? *American Journal of Public Health*, 92(1), 99–104.
McLeod, Christopher B., John N. Lavis, Cameron A. Mustard, and Greg L. Stoddart. (2003). Income inequality, household income, and health status in Canada: A prospective cohort study. *American Journal of Public Health*, 93(8), 1287–1293.
Middleton, Nicos, David Gunnell, Stephen Frankel, Elise Whitley, and Daniel Dorling. (2003). Urban–rural differences in suicide trends in young adults: England and Wales, 1981–1998. *Social Science and Medicine*, 57(7), 1183–1194.
Middleton, Nicos, Jonathan A.C. Sterne, and David Gunnell. (2006). The

geography of despair among 15–44-year-old men in England and Wales: Putting suicide on the map. *Journal of Epidemiology and Community Health*, 60(12), 1040–1047.
Miilunpalo, Seppo, Ilkka Vuori, Pekka Oja, Matti Pasanen, and Helka Urponen. (1997). Self-rated health status as a health measure: The predictive value of self-reported health status on the use of physician services and on mortality in the working-age population. *Journal of Clinical Epidemiology*, 50(5), 517–528.
Mills, Edwin S. (1967). An aggregative model of resource allocation in a metropolitan area. *The American Economic Review*, 57(2), 197–210.
Mills, Edwin S. (1972). *Studies in the Structure of the Urban Economy*. Baltimore, MD, The Johns Hopkins University Press.
Mitchell, Richard, and Frank Popham. (2007). Greenspace, urbanity and health: Relationships in England. *Journal of Epidemiology and Community Health*, 61(8), 681–683.
Mitchell, Richard, and Frank Popham. (2008). Effect of exposure to natural environment on health inequalities: An observational population study. *Lancet*, 372(9650), 1655–1660.
Mobley, Lee R., Elisabeth Root, Luc Anselin, Nancy Lozano-Gracia, and Julia Koschinsky. (2006). Spatial analysis of elderly access to primary care services. *International Journal of Health Geographics*, 5(1), 19.
Mohnen, Sigrid M., Peter P. Groenewegen, Beate Völker, and Henk Flap. (2011). Neighborhood social capital and individual health. *Social Science and Medicine*, 72(5), 660–667.
Monnat, Shannon M., and Camille Beeler Pickett. (2011). Rural/urban differences in self-rated health: Examining the roles of county size and metropolitan adjacency. *Health and Place*, 17(1), 311–319.
Moore, Melinda, Philip Gould, and Barbara S. Keary. (2003). Global urbanization and impact on health. *International Journal of Hygiene and Environmental Health*, 206(4), 269–278.
Moretti, Enrico. (2004). Human capital externalities in cities. *Handbook of Regional and Urban Economics*, 4, 2243–2291.
Morris, Stephen, Matthew Sutton, and Hugh Gravelle. (2005). Inequity and inequality in the use of health care in England: An empirical investigation. *Social Science and Medicine*, 60(6), 1251–1266.
Murray, Greg, Fiona Judd, Henry Jackson, Caitlin Fraser, Angela Komiti, Gene Hodgins, Pip Pattison, John Humphreys, and Garry Robins. (2004). Rurality and mental health: The role of accessibility. *Australian and New Zealand Journal of Psychiatry*, 38(8), 629–634.
Muth, Richard. (1969). *Cities and Housing: The Spatial Patterns of Urban Residential Land Use*. Chicago, IL, University of Chicago Press.
Nafstad, Per, Lise Lund Håleim, Torbjørm Wisløff, Frederick Gram, Bente Oftedal, Ingar Holme, Ingvar Hjermann, and Paul Leren. (2004). Urban air pollution and mortality in a cohort of Norwegian men. *Environmental Health Perspectives*, 112(5), 610–615.
Nagel, Corey L., Nichole E. Carlson, Mark Bosworth, and Yvonne L. Michael. (2008). The relation between neighborhood built environment and walking activity among older adults. *American Journal of Epidemiology*, 168(4), 461–468.
Navarro, Vicente, Carles Muntaner, Carme Borrell, Joan Benach, Águeda Quiroga, Maica Rodríguez-Sanz, Núria Vergés, and M. Isabel Pasarín (2006). Politics and health outcomes. *Lancet*, 368(9540), 1033–1037.

Nielsen, Thomas, Alexander Sick, and Karsten Bruun Hansen. (2007). Do green areas affect health? Results from a Danish survey on the use of green areas and health indicators. *Health and Place*, 13(4), 839–850.

Nijkamp, Peter. (2008). XXQ factors for sustainable urban development: A systems economics view. *Romanian Journal of Regional Science*, 2(1), 1–34.

Nijkamp, Peter, and Karima Kourtit. (2011). Urban Europe scoping document, Joint Programming Initiative, Urban Europe, VU University, Amsterdam.

Nogueira, Helena. (2009). Healthy communities: The challenge of social capital in the Lisbon Metropolitan Area. *Health and Place*, 15(1), 133–139.

Novaco, Raymond W., Daniel Stokols, and Louis Milanesi. (1990). Objective and subjective dimensions of travel impedance as determinants of commuting stress. *American Journal of Community Psychology*, 18(2), 231–257.

O'Regan, Brendan, and Finian Buckley. (2003). The psychological effects of commuting in Dublin. Working paper, Dublin, Centre for Research in Management Learning and Development Working Paper Series.

O'Reilly, D., S. Browne, Z. Johnson, and A. Kelly. (2001). Are cities becoming more unhealthy? An analysis of mortality rates in Belfast and Dublin between 1981 and 1991 to illustrate a methodological difficulty with ecological studies. *Journal of Epidemiology and Community Health*, 55(5), 354–355.

O'Reilly, Gareth, Dermot O'Reilly, Michael Rosato, and Sheelah Connolly. (2007). Urban and rural variations in morbidity and mortality in Northern Ireland. *BMC Public Health*, 7(1), 123.

Ocaña-Riola, Ricardo, and Carmen Sánchez-Cantalejo. (2005). Rurality index for small areas in Spain. *Social Indicators Research*, 73(2), 247–266.

ONS (Office for National Statistics). (2001). Limiting long-term illness (Census 2001): Facts and Figures. Available from: https://www.google.co.jp/url?sa=t&rct=j&q=&esrc=s&source=web&cd=1&cad=rja&uact=8&ved=0CB0QFjAA&url=http%3A%2F%2Ffactsandfigures.herefordshire.gov.uk%2Fdocs%2FSoH%2FLimiting_long-termillness%2528Census2001%2529.xls&ei=lcIUVdLjCuX6mQWm9oDoBA&usg=AFQjCNHf8ycpVSAG_uh1giBmzZwwECIdvA.

Owen, Neville, Ester Cerin, Eva Leslie, Lorinne duToit, Neil Coffee, Lawrence D. Frank, Adrian E. Bauman, Graeme Hugo, Brian E. Saelens, and James F. Sallis. (2007). Neighborhood walkability and the walking behavior of Australian adults. *American Journal of Preventive Medicine*, 33(5), 387–395.

Pampalon, Robert, Jerome Martinez, and Denis Hamel. (2006). Does living in rural areas make a difference for health in Quebec? *Health and Place*, 12(4), 421–435.

Pampalon, Robert, Denis Hamel, and Philippe Gamache. (2010). Health inequalities in urban and rural Canada: Comparing inequalities in survival according to an individual and area-based deprivation index. *Health and Place*, 16(2), 416–420.

Parks, S.E., R.A. Housemann, and R.C. Brownson. (2003). Differential correlates of physical activity in urban and rural adults of various socioeconomic backgrounds in the United States. *Journal of Epidemiology and Community Health*, 57(1), 29–35.

Patterson, E. Britt. (1991). Poverty, income inequality, and community crime rates. *Criminology*, 29(4), 755–776.

Paykel, E.S., R. Abbott, R. Jenkins, T.S. Brucha, and H. Meltzer. (2000). Urban–rural mental health differences in Great Britain: Findings from the National Morbidity Survey. *Psychological Medicine*, 30(2), 269–280.

Pearce, Jamie, Paul Boyle, and Robin Flowerdew. (2003). Predicting smoking behaviour in census output areas across Scotland. *Health and Place*, 9(2), 139–149.
Peen, J., R.A. Schoevers, A.T. Beekman, and J. Dekker. (2010). The current status of urban–rural differences in psychiatric disorders. *Acta Psychiatrica Scandinavica*, 121(2), 84–93.
Pellow, David N. (2000). Environmental inequality formation toward a theory of environmental injustice. *American Behavioral Scientist*, 43(4), 581–601.
Penchansky, Roy, and J. William Thomas. (1981). The concept of access definition and relationship to consumer satisfaction. *Medical Care*, 19(2), 127–140.
Poortinga, Wouter. (2006). Social relations or social capital? Individual and community health effects of bonding social capital. *Social Science and Medicine*, 63(1), 255–270.
Rahkonen, Ossi, Eero Lahelma, and Minna Huuhka. (1997). Past or present? Childhood living conditions and current socioeconomic status as determinants of adult health. *Social Science and Medicine*, 44(3), 327–336.
Ram, Rati. (2006). Further examination of the cross-country association between income inequality and population health. *Social Science and Medicine*, 62(3), 779–791.
Reading, Richard, Stan Openshaw, and Stephen Jarvis. (1994). Are multidimensional social classifications of areas useful in UK health service research? *Journal of Epidemiology and Community Health*, 48(2), 192–200.
Reijneveld, Sijmen A., and Aart H. Schene. (1998). Higher prevalence of mental disorders in socioeconomically deprived urban areas in the Netherlands: Community or personal disadvantage? *Journal of Epidemiology and Community Health*, 52(1), 2–7.
Reijneveld, Sijmen A., Robert A. Verheij, and Dinny H. de Bakker. (1999). Relative importance of urbanicity, ethnicity and socioeconomic factors regarding area mortality differences. *Journal of Epidemiology and Community Health*, 53(7), 444–445.
Richardson, Elizabeth A., and Richard Mitchell. (2010). Gender differences in relationships between urban green space and health in the United Kingdom. *Social Science and Medicine*, 71(3), 568–575.
Riva, Mylene, Sarah Curtis, Lise Gauvin, and James Fagg. (2009). Unravelling the extent of inequalities in health across urban and rural areas: Evidence from a national sample in England. *Social Science and Medicine*, 68(4), 654–663.
Roberts, Christine L., and Charles S. Algert. (2000). The urban and rural divide for women giving birth in NSW, 1990–1997. *The Australian and New Zealand Journal of Public Health*, 24(3), 291–297.
Rosenberg, Mark W. and Kathleen Wilson. (2000). Gender, poverty and location: How much difference do they make in the geography of health inequalities? *Social Science and Medicine*, 51(2), 275–287.
Rosenberg, Michael S., Robert R. Sokal, Neal L. Oden, and Donna DiGiovanni. (1999). Spatial autocorrelation of cancer in Western Europe. *European Journal of Epidemiology*, 15(1), 15–22.
Rosenblatt, R.A., L.M. Baldwin, L. Chan, M.A. Fordyce, I.B. Hirsch, J.P. Palmer, G.E. Wright, and L.G. Hart. (2001). Improving the quality of outpatient care for older patients with diabetes: Lessons from a comparison of rural and urban communities. *The Journal of Family Practice*, 50(8), 676–680.
Ross, Catherine E., and John Mirowsky. (2001). Neighborhood disadvantage, disorder, and health. *Journal of Health and Social Behavior*, 42(3), 258–276.

Ross, Catherine E., and John Mirowsky. (2008). Neighborhood socioeconomic status and health: Context or composition? *City and Community*, 7(2), 163–179.
RUCA. (2014). Rural-Urban Commuting Area Codes. (RUCAs). WWAMI RUCA Rural Health Research Center. Available from: http://depts.washington.edu/uwruca/index.php (6 March, 2014).
Rundle, Andrew, Ana V. Diez Roux, Lance M. Freeman, Douglas Miller, Kathryn M. Neckerman, and Christopher C. Weiss. (2007). The urban built environment and obesity in New York City: A multilevel analysis. *American Journal of Health Promotion*, 21(4s), 326–334.
Saelens, Brian E., James F. Sallies, and Lawrence D. Frank. (2003). Environmental correlates of walking and cycling: Findings from the transportation, urban design, and planning literatures. *Annals of Behavioral Medicine*, 25(2), 80–91.
Sallis, James F., Brian E. Saelens, Lawrence D. Frank, Terry L. Conway, Donald J. Slymen, Kelli L. Cain, James E. Chapman, and Jacqueline Kerr. (2009). Neighborhood built environment and income: Examining multiple health outcomes. *Social Science and Medicine*, 68(7), 1285–1293.
Sarrazin, Mary Vaughan, Mary Campbell, and Gary E. Rosenthal. (2009). Racial differences in hospital use after acute myocardial infarction: Does residential segregation play a role? *Health Affairs*, 28(2), w368–w378.
Schulz, Richard. (1976). Effects of control and predictability on the physical and psychological well-being of the institutionalized aged. *Journal of Personality and Social Psychology*, 33(5), 563–573.
Schwartz, Joel. (1994). Air pollution and daily mortality: A review and meta analysis. *Environmental Research*, 64(1), 36–52.
Senior, Martyn, Huw Williams, and Gary Higgs. (2000). Urban–rural mortality differentials: Controlling for material deprivation. *Social Science and Medicine*, 51(2), 289–305.
Shaw, Mary. (2004). Housing and public health. *Annual Review of Public Health*, 25, 397–418.
Shibuya, Kenji, Hideki Hashimoto, and Eiji Yano. (2002). Individual income, income distribution, and self rated health in Japan: Cross sectional analysis of nationally representative sample. *British Medical Journal*, 324(7328), 16.
Shinjo, Daisuke, and Toshiharu Aramaki. (2012). Geographic distribution of healthcare resources, healthcare service provision, and patient flow in Japan: A cross sectional study. *Social Science and Medicine*, 75(11), 1954–1963.
Shouls, Susanna, Peter Congdon, and Sarah Curtis. (1996). Modelling inequality in reported long term illness in the UK: Combining individual and area characteristics. *Journal of Epidemiology and Community Health*, 50(3), 366–376.
Singh, Gopal K., and Mohammad Siahpush. (2002). Increasing rural–urban gradients in US suicide mortality, 1970–1997. *American Journal of Public Health*, 92(7), 1161–1167.
Singh-Manoux, Archana, Alice Guéguen, Pekka Martikainen, Jane Ferrie, Michael Marmot, and Martin Shipley. (2007). Self-rated health and mortality: Short-and long-term associations in the Whitehall II study. *Psychosomatic Medicine*, 69(2), 138–143.
Sirven, Nicolas. (2006). Endogenous social capital and self-rated health: Cross-sectional data from rural areas of Madagascar. *Social Science and Medicine*, 63(6), 1489–1502.
Smith, Ken R., Barbara B. Brown, Ikuho Yamada, Lori Kowaleski-Jones, Cathleen

D. Zick, and Jessie X. Fan. (2008). Walkability and body mass index: Density, design, and new diversity measures. *American Journal of Preventive Medicine*, 35(3), 237–244.
Smith, Peter, and Michael Polanyi. (2003). Social norms, social behaviours and health: An empirical examination of a model of social capital. *The Australian and New Zealand Journal of Public Health*, 27(4), 456–463.
Snelgrove, John W., Hynek Pikhart, and Mai Stafford. (2009). A multilevel analysis of social capital and self-rated health: Evidence from the British Household Panel Survey. *Social Science and Medicine*, 68(11), 1993–2001.
Solar, Orielle, and Arec Irwin. (2007). A conceptual framework for action on the social determinants of health. Social Determinants of Health Discussion Paper 2, Policy and Practice. Geneva, World Health Organization.
Soobader, Mah-Jabeen, and Felicia B. LeClere. (1999). Aggregation and the measurement of income inequality: Effects on morbidity. *Social Science and Medicine*, 48(6), 733–744.
Sposato, Robert G., Kathrin Röderer, and Renate Cervinka. (2012). The influence of control and related variables on commuting stress. *Transportation Research Part F: Traffic Psychology and Behaviour*, 15(5), 581–587.
Sridharan, Sanjeev, Helena Tunstall, Richard Lawder, and Richard Mitchell. (2007). An exploratory spatial data analysis approach to understanding the relationship between deprivation and mortality in Scotland. *Social Science and Medicine*, 65(9), 1942–1952.
Starfield, Barbara, Leiyu Shi, Atul Grover, and James Macinko. (2005). The effects of specialist supply on populations' health: Assessing the evidence. *Health Affairs*, w5.97–107.
Stafford, Mai, and Michael Marmot. (2003). Neighbourhood deprivation and health: Does it affect us all equally? *International Journal of Epidemiology*, 32(3), 357–366.
Stearns, Sally C., Rebecca T. Slifkin, and Heather M. Edin. (2000). Access to care for rural Medicare beneficiaries. *The Journal of Rural Health*, 16(1), 31–42.
Sturm, R., and D.A. Cohen. (2004). Suburban sprawl and physical and mental health. *Public Health*, 118(7), 488–496.
Stutzer, Alois, and Bruno S. Frey. (2008). Stress that doesn't pay: The commuting paradox. *The Scandinavian Journal of Economics*, 110(2), 339–366.
Subramanian, S.V., and Ichiro Kawachi. (2004). Income inequality and health: What have we learned so far? *Epidemiologic Reviews*, 26(1), 78–91.
Subramanian, S.V., Dolores Acevedo-Garcia, and Theresa L. Osypuk. (2005). Racial residential segregation and geographic heterogeneity in black/white disparity in poor self-rated health in the US: A multilevel statistical analysis. *Social Science and Medicine*, 60(8), 1667–1679.
Suminski, Richard R., Walker S. Carlos Poston, Rick L. Petosa, Emily Stevens, and Laura M. Katzenmoyer. (2005). Features of the neighborhood environment and walking by US adults. *American Journal of Preventive Medicine*, 28(2), 149–155.
Sundquist, Kristina, and Min Yang. (2007). Linking social capital and self-rated health: A multilevel analysis of 11,175 men and women in Sweden. *Health and Place*, 13(2), 324–334.
Sundquist, Kristina, Golin Frank, and Jan Sundquist. (2004). Urbanisation and incidence of psychosis and depression: Follow-up study of 4.4 million women and men in Sweden. *The British Journal of Psychiatry*, 184(4), 293–298.

Sverdlik, Alice. (2011). Ill-health and poverty: A literature review on health in informal settlements. *Environment and Urbanization*, 23(1), 123–155.
Takano, T., K. Nakamura, and M. Watanabe. (2002). Urban residential environments and senior citizens' longevity in megacity areas: The importance of walkable green spaces. *Journal of Epidemiology and Community Health*, 56(12), 913–918.
Teljeur, Conor, and Alan Kelly. (2008). An urban–rural classification for health services research in Ireland. *Irish Geography*, 41(3), 295–311.
United Nations. (2013). *Demographic Yearbook 2012*. New York, United Nations.
USDA. (2013a). Urban Influence Codes documentation. United States Department of Agriculture, Economic Research Services. Available from: http://www.ers.usda.gov/data-products/urban-influence-codes/documentation.aspx (11 January, 2014).
USDA. (2013b). Rural-Urban Continuum Codes documentation. United States Department of Agriculture, Economic Research Services. Available from: http://www.ers.usda.gov/data-products/rural-urban-continuum-codes/documentation.aspx#.UwMeAEJdXrU (11 January, 2014).
Van Hooijdonk, C., Mariël Droomers, I.M. Deerenberg, J.P. Mackenbach, and A.E. Kunst. (2007). Higher mortality in urban neighbourhoods in The Netherlands: Who is at risk? *Journal of Epidemiology and Community Health*, 62(6), 499–505.
Van Lenthe, Frank J., Pekka Martikainen, and Johan P. Mackenbach. (2007). Neighbourhood inequalities in health and health-related behaviour: Results of selective migration? *Health and Place*, 13(1), 123–137.
Veenstra, Gerry. (2000). Social capital, SES and health: an individual-level analysis. *Social Science and Medicine*, 50(5), 619–629.
Veenstra, Gerry. (2002). Social capital and health (plus wealth, income inequality and regional health governance). *Social Science and Medicine*, 54(6), 849–868.
Verheij, R.A., J. Maas, and P.P. Groenewegen. (2008). Urban–rural health differences and the availability of green space. *European Urban and Regional Studies*, 15(4), 307–316.
Viel, Jean-Francois, Mathieu Hagi, Erika Upegui, and Lucie Laurian. (2011). Environmental justice in a French industrial region: Are polluting industrial facilities equally distributed? *Health and Place*, 17(1), 257–262.
Vlahov, David, and Sandro Galea. (2002). Urbanization, urbanicity, and health. *Journal of Urban Health*, 79(1), S1–S12.
Vlahov, D., S. Galea, and N. Freudenberg. (2004). The urban health "advantage". *Journal of Urban Health*, 82(1), 1–4.
Walberg, Peder, Martin McKee, Vladimir Shkolnikov, Laurent Chenet, and David A. Leon. (1998). Economic change, crime, and mortality crisis in Russia: Regional analysis. *British Medical Journal*, 317(7154), 312–318.
Walton, Emily. (2009). Residential segregation and birth weight among racial and ethnic minorities in the United States. *Journal of Health and Social Behavior*, 50(4), 427–442.
Wang, Jian Li. (2004). Rural–urban differences in the prevalence of major depression and associated impairment. *Social Psychiatry and Psychiatric Epidemiology*, 39(1), 19–25.
Watt, Ian S., Antony J. Franks, and Trevor A. Sheldon. (1994). Health and health care of rural populations in the UK: Is it better or worse? *Journal of Epidemiology and Community Health*, 48(1), 16–21.

Weich, S., L. Twigg, G. Holt, G. Lewis, and K. Jones. (2003). Contextual risk factors for the common mental disorders in Britain: A multilevel investigation of the effects of place. *Journal of Epidemiology and Community Health*, 57(8), 616–621.

Weich, Scott, Elizabeth Burton, Martin Blanchard, Martin Prince, Kerry Sproston, and Bob Erens. (2001). Measuring the built environment: Validity of a site survey instrument for use in urban settings. *Health and Place*, 7(4), 283–292.

Weich, Scott, Liz Twigg and Glyn Lewis. (2006). Rural/non-rural differences in rates of common mental disorders in Britain. *British Journal of Psychiatry*, 188(1), 51–57.

Wells, Nancy M. (2000). At home with nature: Effects of "greenness" on children's cognitive functioning. *Environment and Behavior*, 32(6), 775–795.

Wen, Ming, Christopher R. Browning, and Kathleen A. Cagney. (2003). Poverty, affluence, and income inequality: Neighborhood economic structure and its implications for health. *Social Science and Medicine*, 57(5), 843–860.

Wener, Richard E., and Gary W. Evans. (2011). Comparing stress of car and train commuters. *Transportation Research Part F*, 14(2), 111–116.

Wener, Richard, Gary W. Evans, and Pier Boately. (2005). Commuting stress: Psychophysiological effects of a trip and spillover into the workplace. *Transportation Research Record: Journal of the Transportation Research Board*, 1924(1), 112–117.

White, Kellee, and Luisa N. Borrell. (2011). Racial/ethnic residential segregation: Framing the context of health risk and health disparities. *Health and Place*, 17(2), 438–448.

White, Michelle J. (1999). Urban areas with decentralized employment: Theory and empirical work. *Handbook of Regional and Urban Economics*, 3, 1375–1412.

Whiting, David, and Nigel Unwin. (2008). Cities, urbanization and health. *International Journal of Epidemiology*, 38(6), 1737–1738.

WHO-CHD (World Health Organization-Centre for Health Development). (2010). *Hidden Cities: Unmasking and Overcoming Health Inequities in Urban Settings*. Geneva, World Health Organization.

WHO-HIA (World Health Organization-Health Impact Assessment). (2015). Outcomes from Glossary of terms used. Available from: http://www.who.int/hia/about/glos/en/index1.html.

Wilcox, Sara, Cynthia Castro, Abby C. King, Robyn Housemann, and Ross C. Brownson. (2000). Determinants of leisure time physical activity in rural compared with urban older and ethnically diverse women in the United States. *Journal of Epidemiology and Community Health*, 54(9), 667–672.

Winkleby, Marilyn, Kristina Sundquist, and Catherine Cubbin. (2007). Inequities in CHD incidence and case fatality by neighborhood deprivation. *American Journal of Preventive Medicine*, 32(2), 97–106.

Woods, Robert. (2003). Urban–rural mortality differentials: An unresolved debate. *Population and Development Review*, 29(1), 29–46.

Wu, Shunquan, Rui Wang, Yanfang Zhao, Xiuqiang Ma, Meijing Wu, Xiaoyan Yan, and Jia He. (2013). The relationship between self-rated health and objective health status: A population-based study. *BMC Public Health*, 13(1), 320.

Zhang, Wei, Qi Chen, Hamilton McCubbin, Laurie McCubbin, and Shirley Foley. (2011). Predictors of mental and physical health: Individual and neighborhood levels of education, social well-being, and ethnicity. *Health and Place*, 17(1), 238–247.

Zick, Cathleen D., Ken R. Smith, Jessie X. Fan, Barbara B. Brown, Ikuho Yamada, and Lori Kowaleski-Jones. (2009). Running to the store? The relationship between neighborhood environments and the risk of obesity. *Social Science and Medicine*, 69(10), 1493–1500.
Ziersch, Anna M. (2005). Health implications of access to social capital: Findings from an Australian study. *Social Science and Medicine*, 61(10), 2119–2131.
Ziersch, Anna M., Fran E. Baum, Colin MacDougall, and Christine Putland. (2005). Neighbourhood life and social capital: The implications for health. *Social Science and Medicine*, 69(1), 71–86.
Ziller, Erika C., Andrew F. Coburn, and Anush E. Yousefian. (2006). Out-of-pocket health spending and the rural underinsured. *Health Affairs*, 25(6), 1688–1699.
Ziller, Erika C., Nathaniel J. Anderson, and Andrew F. Coburn. (2010). Access to rural mental health services: Service use and out-of-pocket costs. *The Journal of Rural Health*, 26(3), 214–224.

12. Dynamic analysis of the energy rebound effects in megacities: evidence from Beijing and Shanghai, China (1990–2011)*

Yuyuan Wen

1. INTRODUCTION

As early as in the 1860s, Jevons (1865) proposed that the idea to reduce total energy consumption by improving energy efficiency is not consistent with the actual situation. He found that every improvement of the engine would only accelerate the consumption of coal, and it occurs repeatedly in later history. To save energy, people continuously improve technology and develop many related preferential energy-saving policies to enhance energy efficiency, which in turn increases total energy consumption. Taking China as an example, since the economic reform in the late 1970s, and the rapid economic development, energy consumption of 987.03 million tons of standard coal equivalent (SCE) in 1990 rose to 3620.00 million tons of SCE in 2012, increasing nearly 2.7 times in the last two decades. In the same period, energy intensity in China declined from 5.273 tons of SCE in 1990 to 1.867 tons of SCE in 2012, which is only 35.4% of that in 1990 (Figure 12.1). That is to say, with the decrease of energy intensity and the increase of energy efficiency, the total energy consumption did not decrease but grew at a faster rate, which is the so-called energy rebound effect, now a hot issue in the field of energy economics. Energy rebound effects can be understood as the following: technology progress may reduce energy consumption by improving energy efficiency but may also accelerate economic growth and stimulate more energy consumption because of extra energy consumption induced by the rapid economic

* The author is indebted to two anonymous referees for their very helpful comments. The author gratefully acknowledges financial support from the Fundamental Research Funds for the Central Universities and the Decision Consultation and Pre-research Project Funds of Renmin University of China (Grant No. 15XNQ007).

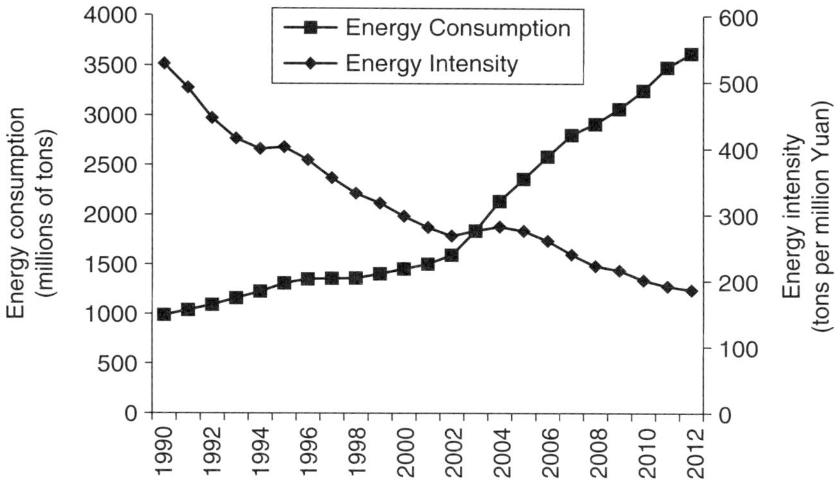

Source: National Bureau of Statistics (1991–2012c).

Figure 12.1 Trend of total energy consumption and energy intensity in China

growth offsetting and even surpassing the energy conservation gained by energy efficiency improvement. Therefore, the idea to simply reduce energy consumption through technological advances is biased and inappropriate. Some scholars even wonder whether a successful energy policy depends on considering rebound effects or not (UK Energy Research Centre, 2007).

With sustained and rapid economic growth, China's energy consumption is increasing rapidly, and China, surpassing the US, has become the largest energy consumer in the world since 2011. With the severe constraints of domestic resources and environmental capacity, as well as the tremendous pressure from global energy security and climate change, China has been committed to reducing the dependence of economic growth on intensive energy consumption. However, in China, energy use intensity is continuously declining while total energy consumption continues to increase, demonstrating the existence of the rebound effect of energy. In fact, the main share of China's energy consumption lies in the cities. For example, in 2011, the prefecture-level and above cities, 287 in total, were responsible for about 60% of the national energy consumption, and therefore the cities play a critical role in energy saving and emission reduction in the country. In this chapter, the author uses two megacities, Beijing and Shanghai, China, as cases to analyze their energy consumption and energy rebound effects. For both cities, the energy consumption intensities decrease while total energy consumption tends to increase year by year, which indicates that the energy rebound effect possibly exists. To test this possibility, energy rebound effect models are constructed and estimated with the extended Cobb-Douglas (C-D) production function and constant elasticity of substitution (CES) production function respectively.

The chapter is organized as follows. Section 2 provides a brief overview of the literature on energy rebound effects. Section 3 gives the analytical framework. Section 4 presents the empirical estimation and analyzes the results. Section 5 concludes.

2. LITERATURE REVIEW

The issue of energy rebound effects has become a hot one in energy economics. The research focuses on five aspects: the definition of rebound effect, direct rebound effects, indirect rebound effects, macro-level rebound effects and rebound effects methodologies.

2.1 Definition of Rebound Effect

Although how the energy rebound effect works is accepted by most researchers, the definitions of how to measure it are disputed and different. These are usually categorized into two perspectives.

One perspective is to define the rebound effect using macro-economics. For instance, Saunders (1992, 2000a, 2000b, 2008), Howarth (1997), Barker (2005) and Wei (2007) think that the rebound effect is the elasticity of energy consumption relative to energy efficiency. This type of definition is usually used in studies on economy-wide rebound effects. Based on this definition, Saunders (2008) found the estimated results were directly affected under different production functions with various policy implications.

Another perspective is to define the rebound effect using micro-economics. According to the definition of micro-level rebound effect summarized by Sorrell (2007), it has five types: (1) Energy rebound effect is the elasticity of total energy consumption relative to energy efficiency. (2) Rebound effect is the price elasticity of energy consumption. (3) Rebound effect can be thought of as a correlation coefficient of energy efficiency and the cost of other input factors (capital, for instance). (4) Taking energy efficiency or technology progress as an endogenous variable when defining rebound effect. (5) Considering time cost when defining rebound effect, that is, for consumers either energy production or energy-based services will consume time. These five definitions vary widely although all of them are called rebound effects. As a consequence, very different estimated results may occur when using different definitions, especially in the case when the rebound effect is defined as the price elasticity of energy consumption.

2.2 Three Types of Rebound Effect

Based on an empirical study of the American economy, Greening et al. (2000) think energy rebound effects exist and may have important impacts on energy efficiency. They divide rebound effects into three types, that is, direct effects, indirect effects and economy-wide effects, which bring us a step closer to the economic mechanism of rebound effects. Direct rebound effects means improved energy efficiency will decrease the marginal cost of supplying that service and should therefore lead to an increase in consumption of the service, which will tend to offset the expected energy conserved from the energy efficiency improvement. Today, most empirics focus on the direct rebound effect because it is easy to measure relative to the indirect rebound effect and the economy-wide effect. When measuring the direct rebound effect for consumers (or producers), it is usually decomposed into a substitution effect and an income (or output) effect. Actually, the direct rebound effect is difficult to completely decompose. Khazzoom (1980), considering energy consumption increases when there are energy efficiency improvements, decomposed the direct rebound effect in his model. But he only considered energy products and ignored that the rebound effect may affect other non-energy products. Berkhout et al. (2000) explained the direct rebound effect theoretically and illustrated the magnitude of it. Lovins et al. (1988) believe that the direct rebound effect is related to the price elasticity of energy demand. Greening et al. (2000) studied energy consumption in the US and proved the rebound effect, but it varied in different situations. Haas and Biermayr (2000) found a nearly 30% rebound effect in heater service in Australia. Bentzen (2004) found, based on time series data from manufacturing industries during 1949–1999 in the US and employing translog cost function, that the direct rebound effect was only about 24% when the energy price decreased. Despite debates in the literature, the direct rebound effect is confirmed and the research has arrived at almost consistent conclusions. Direct rebound effects in developed countries usually are 10–30%. Fewer studies of developing countries have been carried out, but it is generally believed that their direct rebound effects are higher than those of developed countries.

Indirect rebound effects focus on what further impacts energy efficiency improvement has on other products and services. For consumers, energy efficiency improvement will decrease the energy price and then change the demand for other goods and services in the market, which is called the indirect energy rebound effect. In fact, the indirect rebound effect will occur for either producers or consumers. For producers, energy efficiency improvements will change the input of other production factors and, in addition, the reduction of the production costs of upstream products will, to some extent, decrease the production costs of downstream products, which could then lead to a series of adjustments in the prices and quantities of goods and services supplied and demanded throughout an economy. Binswanger (2001) thinks that energy efficiency improvements may themselves change the demand for other goods and services. Actually, the net impact of such secondary effects is very difficult to estimate. However, many scholars, such as Lovins et al. (1988), Greening and Greene (1998) and Schipper and Grubb (2000), claim that the secondary effects from energy efficiency improvements in consumer technologies are relatively small. This is because energy occupies a small share of total consumer expenditure and the energy content of most other goods and services is also small. Greening and Greene (1998) calculated and thought that the secondary effect should be around one tenth of the direct effect. Bränlund et al. (2007) examined the energy rebound effects of transport and heating in Sweden with an input–output and lifecycle analysis model and found energy efficiency improvements led to total rebound effects (direct plus indirect) of 120% and 170% respectively. Mizobuchi (2008) examined the rebound effects of Japanese households with a similar approach to Bränlund et al. (2007) and got almost the same results. Up to now, the available evidence from empirical literature on indirect rebound effects is relatively scarce and general conclusions on indirect rebound are difficult to determine although the existence of indirect rebound effects is confirmed.

The economy-wide rebound effect represents the sum of the direct and indirect effects on the national-level economy involved, which makes it more difficult to measure or estimate because the rebound effects of different mechanisms are individually complex, mutually interdependent and likely to vary from one type of energy efficiency improvement to another. In the present theories on economy-wide rebound effect, neoclassical economic growth models and computable general equilibrium (CGE) models are popular. Brookes (1990) found that improvements in energy productivity are generally associated with greater improvements in total factor productivity (TFP), which then boost the productivity of other inputs and thereby save costs on more than energy alone. Saunders (1992, 2000b) pointed out that Khazzoom's research was constrained to individual energy services, and other possible situations, for example substitution between multiple energy services, are ignored. Based on neoclassic economic growth theory and employing C-D and CES production functions, Saunders (2008) tested and proved that the Khazzoom-Brookes postulate is still correct under the condition of multiple energy services. Howarth (1997), Sorrell and Dimitropoulos (2007) and Aghion and Howitt (1998) called into question the reliability of the economy-wide rebound effect calculation with neoclassic economic growth. Another model, the CGE model, is also widely used to estimate the economy-wide rebound effect. However, various variables and many equations are involved in CGE models, the calculation is very complicated and different models appear to produce widely varying results for similar policy questions. So a number of limitations in CGE models have led many scholars to question their realism and policy relevance (Barker, 2005). In summary, it is very difficult to test economy-wide rebound effects either theoretically or empirically. However, overall, the issue of the economy-wide rebound effect is much more important than the individual rebound effect.

2.3 Models of Rebound Effect

In all the rebound effect models, most empirical research focuses on the direct rebound effect and generally from the consumers' perspective rather than the producers' perspective. In addition, most of empirical studies estimate the direct rebound effects by employing transportation and heating data and seldom calculate the indirect rebound effects because it's difficult to separate them. However, the economy-wide effect is more difficult to measure because of the many parameters involved and the complicated relationships between parameters which are not easy to represent with mathematical expressions. Generally, rebound effect research is implemented from the view of the substitution effect or income effect within energy economics. However, how best to study the economy-wide rebound effect has so far not been conclusive. The specific methodologies for the rebound effect, according to related literature, include direct estimation, price elasticity estimation, lifecycle analysis or input–output analysis, decomposition analysis, substitution elasticity estimation, CGE modeling and neoclassic economic growth modeling (Sorrell and Dimitropoulos, 2005a, 2005b; Saunders, 2008).

2.4 Summary Review

On the whole, the energy rebound effect has become a hot issue academically. Empirically, many studies are focused on the direct rebound effect and prove its existence. However, empirical results vary widely even for the same sample dataset with different models, and usually are not consistent with each other. Most of the estimations for rebound effects are limited to household heating and transportation while studies on economy-wide rebound effects are relatively rare. No general conclusions are drawn although the existence of the economy-wide rebound effect has been proved.

Energy rebound effects have caused widespread concern in developed countries but this concern has not arisen in developing countries. Studies on energy rebound effects are just beginning in many emerging economies, including China.

Rebound effect studies usually take countries as spatial units, while sub-regions in a country, especially megacities where there is a concentration of energy demand growth and energy consumption, are seldom involved. Actually, in a practical operational way, to save energy and control the rebound effect effectively, rebound effect studies should be focused on sub-regions or city-level areas within a country and the research conclusions will then be more practical for determining the explicit energy policy implications. Based on this thought, this chapter selects the two largest megacities, Beijing and Shanghai, in China, and comparatively investigates their energy rebound effects.

3. REBOUND EFFECT MODEL

Saunders (2008) pointed out that estimation results would vary widely with different models and different models need various datasets. Practically, various factors should be considered when setting a proper model. A practicable method is to analyze a specific rebound effect with more than two models.

3.1 Rebound Effect Model Selection

There are many rebound effect models and empirical research available in the literature. Generally three methodologies are popular as follows. The first is to directly measure the direct rebound effect. Small and Dender (2007) estimated the direct rebound effects of transportation in US. This method is not practical in China because it needs various detailed sector data which are not available. The second is the CGE model, considered as the most difficult of all rebound effect models. The CGE model not only needs a large amount of data from various sectors but its computation is also very complicated. The CGE model has been widely spread in recent years, for example Turner (2009) investigated the rebound effects in Britain with the CGE model. The third is the neoclassic economic growth model which has various specifications, and different production functions have different impacts on estimation results. So how to select a proper model is very important and critical for solving real problems.

Direct measurement and the CGE model needs detailed data, especially energy prices to reflect the supply and demand in the market, which are difficult to obtain in China. So this chapter, based on the neoclassic economic growth theory, selects the C-D and CES production functions as the basic models to estimate the rebound effects.

Neoclassic economic growth models take technology progress as a determinant of economic growth but at the same time technology progress is excluded by assuming it is an exogenous variable, which is considered a flaw for neoclassic economic growth theories. When analyzing different economies, the neoclassic growth model and endogenous growth model must be treated differently because the two models are applicable to different economic issues.

In fact, technology progress in an economy cannot be simply considered either completely exogenous or completely endogenous. A more applicable model should be employed for an economy according to its specific characteristics. As for China, its technology progress is determined with both exogenous and endogenous factors. According to Liu et al. (2006), China's technology progress included 23.1% endogenous components and 76.9% exogenous components during 1978–2003, which indicates that the exogenous factor (for example, natural diffusion of technology, technology introduction) is dominant. This conclusion seems to support the neoclassic growth model with exogenous technology progress selected in this chapter.

3.2 Production Function Selection for the Rebound Effect

Saunders (1992) introduced the Khazzoom-Brookes postulate in his paper and further research was done with the neoclassic economic growth theory, in which a conclusion was drawn that the rebound effect was induced by energy efficiency improvements. Later, Howarth (1997) questioned Saunders' theory and thought Saunders did not distinguish energy production and energy services and overestimated the rebound effects. Again Saunders (2000a) confirmed that the neoclassic growth model was able to predict the rebound effect. Saunders (2005) illustrated, with a mathematical simulation method, that there would be greater rebound effects under conditions of improvements in both energy efficiency and the productivity of other input factors at the same time.

Production functions defined by Saunders (2008) include output Y and three input factors (capital K, labor L and energy E):

$$Y = f\,(K, L, E) \tag{12.1}$$

In order to reflect the relationship between energy consumption and energy efficiency, Saunders (2008) defines energy efficiency parameter τ, which multiplies energy use to improve its effective use:

$$Y = f\,(K, L, \tau F) \tag{12.2}$$

where $\tau F = E$ defines the relationship between energy and energy services. Saunders (2008) finds, by comparative analysis, that the rebound effect depends on the selected production function or cost function, and the a priori elasticity parameter of factor substitution selected will determine the magnitude of the rebound effect directly. As Saunders (2008) points out, Fourier cost function is the best method to estimate the rebound effect but it is not applicable in China as the necessary data are unavailable. The C-D production function will produce estimates of more than 100% for either the short-term or long-term rebound effect, which indicates that only backfire effects exist and is therefore not consistent with reality. The C-D model is easy to calculate, has explicit implications and has been employed in many empirical studies even though it is not the best model. So the C-D model is used in this chapter as a comparison model.

The CES production function is the only one with constant elasticity of substitution in the eight models introduced by Saunders (2008). Within energy economics, the CES model is usually extended with the three-factor CES model. Hogan and Manne (1977) introduced a version wherein they embedded a C-D production function for capital and labor within a CES function. Saunders (2008) proved that the nested form $(K, L)E$ is the only one consistent with the Khazzoom-Brookes postulate. The CES function including the energy factor is:

$$Y = [a(K^{\alpha}L^{1-\alpha})^{\rho} + b(\tau E)^{\rho}]^{1/\rho} \tag{12.3}$$

where Y is output, K is capital input, L is labor input, E is energy input, τ is energy efficiency, a and b are parameters of factor shares, $0 < a, b < 1$, $a + b = 1$, α is the capital–labor substitution parameter, $\rho = (\sigma - 1)/\sigma$ is the substitution parameter, and σ is the elasticity of substitution between energy ($=\tau F$) and the capital/labor combination. For fixed $L > 0$, transform (12.3) into:

$$y = [ak^{\alpha\rho} + b(\tau e)^{\rho}]^{1/\rho} + \varepsilon \tag{12.4}$$

where $y = Y/L$, $k = K/L$ and $e = E/L$.

In the CES function, elasticity is not constant and is related to capital equipment ratio (technological coefficient) *K*/*L*. According to Saunders (2008), the nested CES function embedded with the C-D function is enough to exhibit all the possible rebound conditions except super-conservation and is appropriate for rebound effect analysis. But the CES estimation results should be interpreted with caution because of their highly specific form and nesting scheme selected a priori.

The Leontief production function has a simple form which enables understanding of the illustration of the roles played by energy share and substitution elasticity in the determination of rebound and its components. However, the Leontief production function cannot be rigorously used in empirical analyses (Saunders, 2008). It will not be dwelled on here.

This chapter selects the nested CES function as the basic model and at the same time the C-D function is used as the comparative model.

3.3 Solutions to Rebound Effect under the CES Function

Here solutions to rebound effects under the CES function are given mathematically. The rebound effect can be decomposed into two effects, that is, energy intensity effect (can be explained as a substitution effect) and output or income effect.

For the form $Y = [a(K^{\alpha}L^{1-\alpha})^{\rho} + b(\tau E)^{\rho}]^{1/\rho}$, define ξ as energy actually used $\xi = \tau E$, τ is energy efficiency and η_{τ}^{E} is the elasticity of energy consumption to energy efficiency. The elasticity of output to energy consumption is $S_E = \frac{\partial Y}{\partial E} \cdot \frac{E}{Y}$, the elasticity of output to labor is $S_L = \frac{\partial Y}{\partial L} \cdot \frac{L}{Y}$, the elasticity of output to capital is $S_K = \frac{\partial Y}{\partial K} \cdot \frac{K}{Y}$, the rebound effect is *R*, *R* is the ratio of the change rate of energy actually used to the change rate of energy efficiency, then

$$R = \frac{\partial \xi / \xi}{\partial \tau / \tau} = 1 + \frac{\tau}{E} \cdot \frac{\partial E}{\partial \tau} = 1 + \eta_{\tau}^{E} \qquad (12.5)$$

According to the definition of rebound effect, energy consumption will increase *R*% every 1% increment in energy efficiency. If $R > 1$ or $\eta_{\tau}^{E} > 0$, indicating a rebound effect greater than 100%, the backfire effect occurs. If $R = 1$ or $\eta_{\tau}^{E} = 0$, full rebound occurs. If $0 < R < 1$ or $-1 < \eta_{\tau}^{E} < 0$, partial rebound occurs. If $R = 0$ or $\eta_{\tau}^{E} = -1$, zero rebound occurs. If $R < 0$ or < -1, super-conservation occurs.

In the short term, *K*, *L* and the energy price are fixed; only energy consumption *E* is free. We get

$$\frac{\partial Y}{\partial E} = b\tau^{\rho}\left(\frac{Y}{E}\right)^{1-\rho} = \frac{p_E}{C} \qquad (12.6)$$

Here $\frac{p_E}{C}$ denotes the real energy price.

Solve the equations (12.4) and (12.6) with the Jacobi matrix and the short-term rebound effect under $\sigma = 1/(1-\rho)$ should be.

$$R_{short} = \frac{\sigma}{1 - S_E} = \frac{1}{(1-\rho)[1 - b\tau^{\rho}(Y/E)^{-\rho}]} \tag{12.7}$$

From (12.7) we know, conditional on exogenous technology progress, that the short-term rebound effect is only related to the elasticity of substitution between energy and the capital/labor combination σ and the elasticity of output to energy consumption S_E.

As for the long term, energy price and capital price are fixed, capital, labor and energy consumption are free. Then

$$\frac{\partial Y}{\partial K} = a\alpha Y^{1-\rho} L^{(1-\alpha)\rho} K^{\alpha\rho - 1} = \frac{p_K}{C},$$

$$\text{i.e. } Y = \left(\frac{P_K}{Ca\alpha L^{(1-\alpha)\rho}}\right)^{\frac{1}{1-\rho}} K^{\frac{\rho-\alpha\rho}{1-\rho}} K \tag{12.8}$$

As $S_K = \frac{P_K K}{CY}, \frac{Y}{K} = \frac{P_K}{S_K} = \left(\frac{P_K}{C\alpha a L^{(1-\alpha)\rho}}\right)^{\frac{1}{1-\rho}} K^{\rho \frac{\rho-\alpha}{1-\rho}}$, then

$$Y = \frac{P_K}{CS_K} K \tag{12.9}$$

Solve the equations (12.4), (12.6) and (12.9) with the Jacobi matrix to get the long-term rebound effect.

$$R_{long} = \frac{S_E + S_L + (\sigma - 1)(1-\alpha)}{S_L} = \frac{1 - a\alpha Y^{-\rho} L^{(1-\alpha)\rho} K^{\alpha\rho} + \dfrac{\rho(1-\alpha)}{1-\rho}}{a(1-\alpha) Y^{-\rho} L^{(1-\alpha)\rho} K^{\alpha\rho}} \tag{12.10}$$

From (12.10) we know that the two determinants of the long-term rebound effect are the elasticity of substitution between energy and the capital/labor combination σ and the substitution parameter α of capital and labor. If $\sigma > 1$ and $\alpha < 1$, or if $0 > \sigma > 1$ and $\alpha > 1$, then the elasticity of output to energy consumption S_E will be positively related to the long-term rebound effect R_{long}, that is, the greater S_E, the greater R_{long}, which indicates output is sensitive to energy consumption and the long-term rebound effect is greater when energy efficiency is higher. Here it is impossible to reduce energy consumption by improving energy efficiency unless other approaches are adopted. The elasticity of output to labor S_L is negatively related to the long-term rebound effect R_{long}, that is, the greater S_L, the less R_{long}. If $0 > \sigma > 1$ and < 1, or if $\sigma > 1$ and $\alpha > 1$, the elasticity of energy consumption S_E and the elasticity of output to labor S_L have no explicit relationship with the long-term rebound effect R_{long}.

3.4 Solutions to Rebound Effect under the C-D Function

The specification of the C-D production function is

$$Y = AK^{\alpha}L^{\beta}(\tau E)^{1-\alpha-\beta} \tag{12.11}$$

then

$$\frac{\partial Y}{\partial E} = \frac{p_E}{C} = (1 - \alpha - \beta)\frac{Y}{E}, \ E = \frac{(1 - \alpha - \beta)C}{P_E}Y \tag{12.12}$$

Substitute (12.12) with the production function (12.11) and the solution to short-term rebound effect is

$$R_{short} = 1 + \eta_{\tau}^{E} = 1 + \frac{S_E}{1 - S_E} = \frac{1}{\alpha + \beta} \tag{12.13}$$

In the long term, the return rate of capital is fixed, then

$$K = \alpha\frac{Y}{R} \tag{12.14}$$

Substitute (12.14) with the production function (12.11) and the solution to long-term rebound effect is

$$R_{long} = 1 + \eta_{\tau}^{E} = 1 + \frac{S_E}{S_L} = 1 + \frac{1 - \alpha - \beta}{\beta} = \frac{1 - \alpha}{\beta} \tag{12.15}$$

4. EMPIRICAL ANALYSIS

4.1 Data Description

4.1.1 Data sources

The dataset is compiled from various data sources including the *Beijing Statistical Yearbooks*, the *Shanghai Statistical Yearbooks*, the *China Statistical Yearbooks* and the *China Energy Statistical Yearbooks* from the years 1991–2012.

1. Gross domestic product Y: GDP with the constant prices of 1990. The unit is 100 million Chinese Yuan Renminbi (CNY).

2. GDP per capita/worker y: GDP divided by population/total number of employed persons. The unit is CNY/person.
3. Labor input L: Yearly total number of employed persons. The unit is 10,000 persons.
4. Capital input K: China does not publish data on capital stock. The perpetual inventory method (PIM) is employed to estimate the capital stock of Beijing, Shanghai and China. The formula is

$$K_t = K_{t-1}(1 - \delta_t) + I_t \tag{12.16}$$

K_t is the capital stock in year t, K_{t-1} is the capital stock in year $t - 1$. δ_t is depreciation rate of capital. I_t is the investment in fixed assets in year t. 1990 constant price is used here. The unit is 100 million CNY.
5. Capital input per capita/worker k: Capital input K divided by population/total number of employed persons. The unit is CNY/person.
6. Energy consumption E: The total energy consumption in primary, secondary and tertiary industries, and not including household energy consumption. The unit is 10,000 tons of SCE.
7. Energy consumption per capita/person: Energy consumption divided by population/total number of employed persons. The unit is ton of SCE per capita.

4.1.2 Energy intensity and energy consumption changes over the study period

To better understand the energy use situation in Beijing and Shanghai, their energy intensity is illustrated before the rebound effect analyses. Energy intensity is energy consumption per output. The energy intensity and energy consumption development trends in Beijing and Shanghai between 1990 and 2011 as well as China are shown in Figures 12.2 and 12.3 respectively.

As can be seen in Figure 12.2, the energy intensity in Beijing, Shanghai and the country as a whole shows a decreasing trend over the past 20 years on the whole. The sharpest decline of energy intensity occurs in Beijing, where the energy intensity decreased from 5.41 tons of SCE per 10,000 CNY GDP in 1990 to 1.39 tons of SCE per 10,000 CNY GDP. A reduction of 4.02 tons of SCE per 10,000 CNY GDP occurred in the 20-year period, which is more than the whole country (3.34 tons of SCE per 10,000 CNY GDP) and Shanghai (2.16 tons of SCE per 10,000 CNY GDP). The decline of energy intensity resulted either from the contributions from energy efficiency improvements or from economic and energy restructuring.

However, as shown in Figure 12.3, the energy consumption in Beijing and Shanghai increases yearly, as does the country as a whole, although

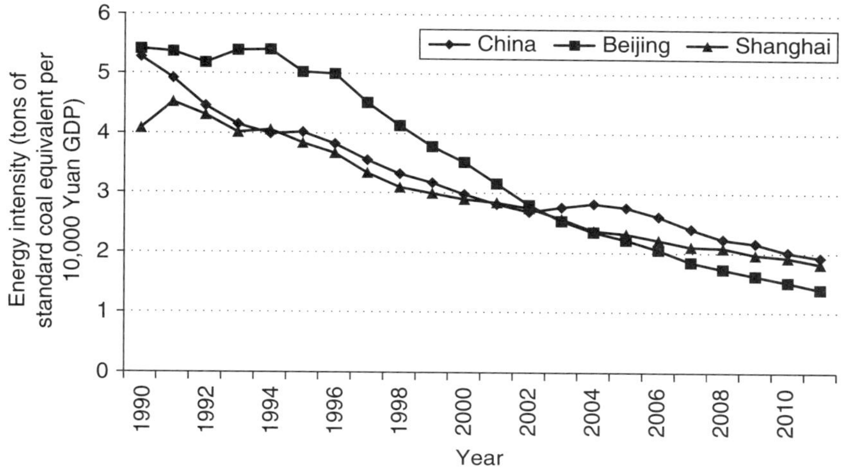

Figure 12.2 *Energy intensity comparison of Beijing, Shanghai and China, 1990–2011 (unit: ton of SCE per 10,000 CNY GDP)*

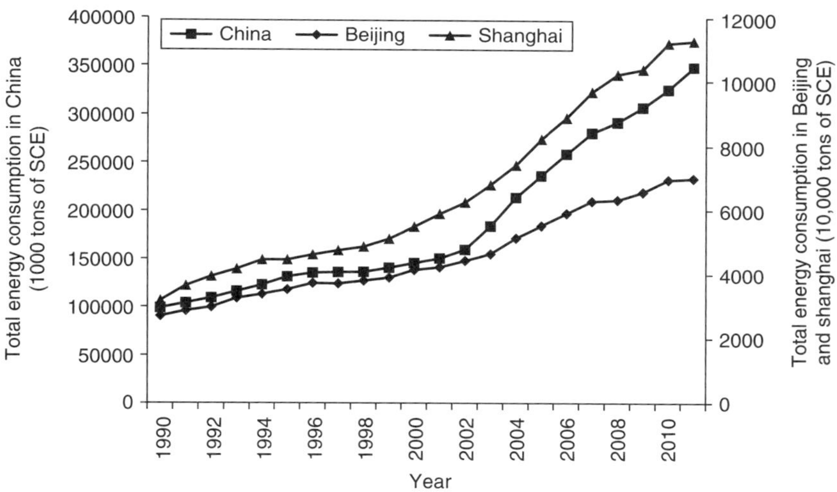

Figure 12.3 *Comparison of total energy consumption in Beijing, Shanghai and China (unit: 10,000 tons of SCE)*

Table 12.1 Estimation results of the rebound effects under the CES function for Beijing, Shanghai and China

Parameters	Beijing	Shanghai	China
a	0.9553 (3.1637)***	0.7924 (3.1442)***	0.8874 (1.6533)*
$b = 1 - a$	0.0447 (3.1637)***	0.2076 (3.1442)***	0.1126 (1.6533)*
α	0.5459 (2.1231)***	0.8568 (2.7163)***	0.7891 (4.1336)***
τ	0.6648 (2.7673)***	0.6233 (1.7147)*	0.6114 (2.8112)***
ρ	−0.3182 (1.6675)*	−0.4277 (1.8762)**	−0.9766 (1.6722)*
$\sigma = 1/(1 - \rho)$	0.7586 (1.6675)*	0.7004 (1.8762)**	0.5059 (1.6722)*
# of obs.	22	22	22

Sources: National Bureau of Statistics (1991–2012a, b, c, d).

Notes:
The numbers in ( ) are t-values.
*, ** and *** denote significance at the 1, 5 and 10% levels, respectively.

their energy intensity declines gradually over the period and, in addition, since 2002, energy consumption has tended to increase more rapidly than it did in the period 1990–2001. The average growth rates of energy consumption in the country as a whole, Beijing and Shanghai between 1990 and 2002 are 4.08%, 4.19% and 5.76% respectively, while the average growth rates between 2002 and 2011 are 9.06%, 5.19% and 6.77% respectively. The growth rates in Beijing and Shanghai are significantly lower than the country as a whole. This phenomenon indicates the possible existence of the energy rebound effect for both the megacities as well as the country.

4.2 Model Estimation and Results Analyses

The estimation results of the CES function model (12.4) with weighted Nonlinear Least Squares (NLS) regression are listed in Table 12.1. The estimation results of the C-D function (12.11) with Ordinary Least Squares (OLS) regression are listed in Table 12.2.

We know from the results shown in Table 12.1 that the values of energy use efficiency τ in Beijing, Shanghai and the country as a whole are not all high and show large variations, which indicates energy use efficiency in the megacities in China is not adequate and needs a great deal of improvement. The difference in energy efficiency between the two megacities and the country as a whole is possibly related to the differences in their industrial and energy structures.

Table 12.2 Estimation results of the rebound effects and the short-/long-term rebound effects under the C-D function for Beijing, Shanghai and China

Parameters	Beijing	Shanghai	China
α	0.3092 (3.1598)***	0.5037 (2.4741)***	0.3224 (2.1008)***
β	0.4505 (5.8114)***	0.4021 (3.8210)***	0.5946 (4.2133)***
$R_{short} = 1/(\alpha+\beta)$	131.63%	110.40%	109.05%
$R_{long} = (1-\alpha)/\beta$	153.34%	123.43%	113.96%
# of obs.	22	22	22

Sources: National Bureau of Statistics (1991–2012a, b, c, d).

Notes:
The numbers in ( ) are t-values.
*** denotes significance at the 10% level.

Table 12.3 The short-term rebound effect under the CES model for Beijing, Shanghai and China (unit: %)

Year	Beijing	Shanghai	China	Year	Beijing	Shanghai	China
1990	78.19	81.37	62.85	2001	78.64	83.65	64.70
1991	78.19	80.81	63.01	2002	78.75	83.88	64.87
1992	78.22	81.08	63.26	2003	78.85	84.38	64.76
1993	78.19	81.46	63.45	2004	78.92	84.99	64.68
1994	78.19	81.40	63.56	2005	78.98	85.15	64.77
1995	78.24	81.72	63.54	2006	79.06	85.52	64.98
1996	78.25	81.99	63.68	2007	79.18	85.93	65.32
1997	78.33	82.57	63.90	2008	79.25	86.00	65.64
1998	78.40	83.07	64.11	2009	79.33	86.48	65.78
1999	78.48	83.29	64.27	2010	79.41	86.68	66.11
2000	78.54	83.52	64.49	2011	79.50	87.18	66.34

Sources: National Bureau of Statistics (1991–2012a, b, c, d).

4.2.1 The short-term rebound effect

Substituting the parameters in Table 12.1 into the short-term rebound effect formula (12.7) will give the results listed in Table 12.3 for the years 1991–2011.

We know from Table 12.3 that the short-term rebound effects in Beijing, Shanghai and the country as a whole are under 100%, which indicates no backfire effects. So, for the short term, theoretically it is possible to

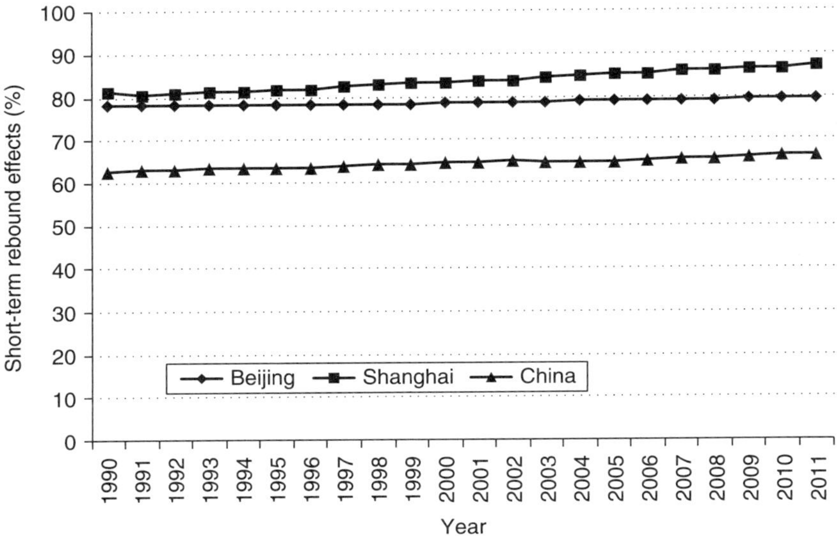

Source: Data from Table 12.3.

Figure 12.4 The trend of short-term rebound effect

reduce energy consumption by improving energy efficiency. The short-term rebound effects in Beijing and Shanghai between 1990 and 2011 are located in the 78.19–79.50% and 81.37–87.18% ranges respectively, which are higher than the 62.85–66.34% range for the country as a whole. In the last two decades, the changes in the short-term rebound effects had shown a gently rising trend. With rapid urbanization and industrialization, high economic growth makes energy intensive industries, such as the petrochemical and metal smelting industries, account for a large proportion of the industries in the two megacities. As a result, energy use efficiency becomes lower as does the output elasticity of energy and thus increases the rebound effects. Therefore, the industry structure in a region will have direct impact on its rebound effect and then on its energy savings. Figure 12.4 shows that the short-term rebound effects in Shanghai are always higher than in Beijing and the gap between the two cities has been increasing, which suggests that the changes in industry structure in the two megacities are not synchronous. Actually, the proportions of primary, secondary and tertiary industries were adjusted from 8.76 : 52.39 : 38.85 in 1990 to 0.9 : 23.4 : 75.7 in 2011 for Beijing, and from 4.38 : 64.68 : 30.94 in 1990 to 0.65 : 41.47 : 57.88 in 2011 for Shanghai. The proportion of secondary industry

Table 12.4 Long-term rebound effect under the CES model for Beijing, Shanghai and China (unit: %)

Year	Beijing	Shanghai	China	Year	Beijing	Shanghai	China
1990	185.62	277.09	378.72	2001	168.21	263.61	348.77
1991	184.27	280.94	354.51	2002	162.50	261.43	341.24
1992	182.37	269.93	326.81	2003	157.17	246.07	334.64
1993	181.97	265.30	313.59	2004	155.56	229.78	324.42
1994	189.82	276.37	316.23	2005	152.21	221.95	318.44
1995	190.64	291.04	332.91	2006	147.96	215.13	305.07
1996	192.76	298.58	340.36	2007	140.60	206.48	286.04
1997	190.12	292.95	345.19	2008	139.64	215.05	282.73
1998	184.29	287.86	354.42	2009	136.06	216.45	293.65
1999	179.46	282.67	357.76	2010	130.94	207.96	271.49
2000	173.13	268.31	351.89	2011	128.74	206.66	257.16

Sources: National Bureau of Statistics (1991–2012a, b, c, d).

declined from 52.39% in 1990 to 23.4% in 2011 for Beijing, a 29 percentage point decrement in the last two decades, while for Shanghai the same proportion declined from 64.68% in 1990 to 41.47% in 2011, a decrement of only 23 percentage points in the same period. Obviously, the secondary industry share of GDP is much greater in Shanghai than in Beijing. As we know, secondary industries are usually energy intensive, especially in the heavy-industry stage, as in Shanghai, thus it is not difficult to understand why the short-term rebound effects are higher in Shanghai than in Beijing.

4.2.2 The long-term rebound effect

Similarly, substituting the parameters in Table 12.1 into the long-term rebound effect formula (12.10) will give the results are listed in Table 12.4 and drawn in Figure 12.5.

As shown in Table 12.4 and Figure 12.5, unlike the short-term rebound effect, on the whole, long-term rebound effects in Beijing, Shanghai and the country as a whole show declining trends, although with fluctuations in some years, which indicates that the energy-saving policy introduced in the mid-1990s in China has had positive impacts on the reduction of energy consumption. However, the long-term rebound effects in Beijing and Shanghai are significantly higher than 100% (as shown in Tables 12.2 and 12.4 and Figure 12.5), which indicates that backfire effects exist in the long term and the energy saving task is a difficult issue for Beijing, Shanghai and the country as a whole in the future.

Now let's discuss some details about various phases of the long-term

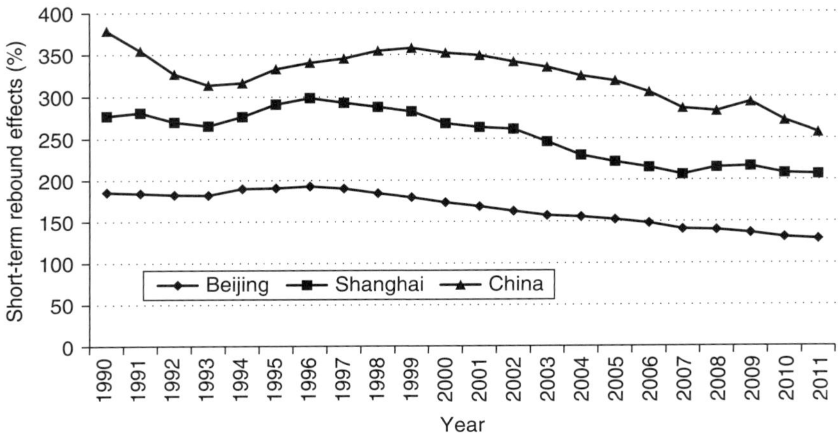

Sources: Data from Table 12.4.

Figure 12.5 The trend of the long-term rebound effect

rebound effects. At the beginning of the 1990s, the long-term rebound effects in both Beijing and Shanghai declined and then went up until they peaked in 1996 (1999 for the country as a whole), followed by a continuous decrease in the subsequent years although the declining rates were low, which is consistence with the national energy-saving-industry development policy advocated in the Ninth Five-Year Plan "to reduce material consumption especially energy consumption". However, the energy saving policy had different effects on various regions. In the full sample period, the long-term rebound effects in Shanghai were always greater than those in Beijing for the same reason as the short-term rebound effects above. However, the long-term rebound effects in both megacities were lower than those in the country as a whole as both Beijing and Shanghai are experiencing the later stage of industrialization while the country as a whole is predominantly in the mid-industrialization stage. Considering that the long-term rebound effects in both Beijing and Shanghai are above 100%, there is still a lot of opportunity to enhance energy efficiency in both megacities and the country as a whole in the future. In addition, with the slope of the curve of the long-term rebound effects for Beijing, Shanghai and China getting flatter since the later 1990s, this means that the marginal effects of energy savings induced by energy efficiency improvements are becoming less, which indicates that the limitations of energy saving with energy efficiency enhancement should be taken into consideration in energy policy-making in China in the future.

5. CONCLUSIONS AND DISCUSSION

How an energy policy can be scientifically developed is a critical issue for the megacities as well as the country as a whole. The chapter provides an energy rebound effect analytical framework and estimates both short-term and long-term energy rebound effects in Beijing and Shanghai. Comparisons between the two megacities and the country as a whole are analyzed. The main conclusions and policy implications are as follows.

1. Based on the neoclassic economic growth framework and the definition of rebound effect by Saunders (2008), employing the nested CES production function, the C-D production function and assuming exogenous technology progress, estimation methods of short/long term are derived and energy rebound effect models are constructed. The results show that the short-term rebound effect is only related to the elasticity of substitution between energy and the capital/labor combination and the elasticity of output to energy consumption. The two determinants of the long-term rebound effect are the elasticity of substitution between energy and the capital/labor combination and the substitution parameters of capital and labor.
2. The estimation results for 1990–2011 show, in the short term, that short-term rebound effects in Beijing, Shanghai and the country as a whole are under 100% thus, theoretically, it is possible to reduce energy consumption by improving energy efficiency.
3. In the long term, on the one hand, the long-term rebound effects in Beijing, Shanghai and the country as a whole have predominantly been declining over the last two decades, which indicates that the energy saving policy has had positive impacts on the reduction of energy consumption. On the other hand, the long-term rebound effects in Beijing, Shanghai and the country as a whole are much greater than 100%, suggesting that energy efficiency improvement plays a limited role in total energy consumption control for the current period as well as for the next few years. Therefore, this situation should be taken into consideration in future energy saving policy-making. How the backfire effects in the long term can be overcome is a difficult issue for China to address in the future.
4. All factors including energy efficiency improvements, economic and energy restructuring and effective institution design should be considered together to develop the appropriate energy policy. Firstly, because energy efficiency improvements will not be able to reduce the total energy consumption in the short term, speeding up industrial and energy consumption restructuring is an essential way to solve

energy saving problems for the current period. Secondly, it is necessary to constantly promote science and technology progress in the field of energy saving. On the one hand, energy efficiency improvement is partly helpful for energy saving; on the other hand, technology progress will still play an important role in energy conservation after industrial structuring. Finally, to implement the policies of industrial and energy consumption restructuring and promote energy-saving technology progress, the incentive mechanism needs to be improved, and an access system for energy efficiency and an exit mechanism of backward production capacity established. Only in this way can the two megacities and the country as a whole achieve significant energy consumption reductions.

The analysis can be extended in several directions in the future. (1) The models in this chapter do not consider the energy price and other policy factors, which may influence the results and conclusions. These factors should be included in future research. (2) The mechanism of the energy rebound effects should be investigated further. (3) Because of limited available data, only macro-level rebound effects are analyzed in this chapter. Future research should be extended to the micro-level, for example sector, even firm-level, rebound effects, which is more useful for energy policy-making. (4) More production functions should be tested and their appropriateness investigated.

REFERENCES

Aghion, P., Howitt, P.W. (1998) *Endogenous Growth Theory*. MIT Press, Cambridge, MA and London.

Barker, T. (2005) The transition to sustainability: a comparison of general equilibrium and space-time economics approaches. Working Paper Number 62, Tyndall Centre for Climate Change Research, University of East Anglia, Norwich, UK.

Bentzen, J. (2004) Estimating the rebound effect in US manufacturing energy consumption. *Energy Economics* 26(1): 123–134.

Berkhout, P.H.G., Muskens, J.C., Velthuijsen, J.W. (2000) Defining the rebound effect. *Energy Policy* 28(6–7): 425–432.

Binswanger, M. (2001) Technological progress, sustainable development: what about the rebound effect. *Ecological Economics* 36(1): 119–132.

Bränlund, R., Ghalwash, T., Nordstrom, J. (2007) Increased energy efficiency and the rebound effect: effects on consumption and emissions. *Energy Economics* 29(1): 1–17.

Brookes, L.G. (1990) The greenhouse effect: the fallacies in the energy efficiency solution. *Energy Policy* 18(2): 199–201.

Greening, L.A., Greene, D.L. (1998) *Energy Use, Technical efficiency, and the Rebound Effect: A Review of the Literature*. Center for Transportation Analysis, Oak Ridge National Laboratory, Oak Ridge, TN.

Greening, L.A., Greene, D.L., Difiglio, C. (2000) Energy efficiency and consumption—the rebound effect—a survey. *Energy Policy* 28(6–7): 389–401.
Haas, R., Biermayr, P. (2000) The rebound effect for space heating: empirical evidence from Austria. *Energy Policy* 28(6–7): 403–410.
Hogan, W., Manne, A. (1977) Energy-economy interaction: the fable of the elephant and the rabbit? Energy and the Economy, EMF Report 1 of the Energy Modeling Forum. Institute for Energy Studies, Stanford University, Stanford, CA.
Howarth, R.B. (1997) Energy efficiency and economic growth. *Contemporary Economic Policy* 15(4): 1–9.
Jevons, W.S. (1865) The coal question: can Britain survive? In A.W. Flux (ed.), *The Coal Question: An Inquiry Concerning the Progress of the Nation and the Probable Exhaustion of Our Coal-mines*. Augustus M. Kelley, New York.
Khazzoom, J.D. (1980) Economic implications of mandated efficiency standards for household appliances. *The Energy Journal* 11(2): 21–40.
Liu, Y.Q., Huang, T. Sh., Zhang, D.Y. (2006) The situation of endogenous and exogenous technology progress in China and policy proposals. *Chinese Science & Technology Translators Journal* 5(3): 60–64 (in Chinese).
Lovins, A.B., Henly, J., Ruderman, H., Levine, M.D. (1988) Energy saving resulting from the adoption of more efficient appliances: another view; a follow up. *The Energy Journal* 9(2): 155–160.
Mizobuchi, K. (2008) An empirical study on the rebound effect considering capital costs. *Energy Economic* 30(5): 2486–2516.
National Bureau of Statistics (1991–2012a) *Beijing Statistical Yearbooks (1991–2012)*. China Statistics Press, Beijing, China.
National Bureau of Statistics (1991–2012b) *China Energy Statistical Yearbooks (1991–2012)*. China Statistics Press, Beijing, China.
National Bureau of Statistics (1991–2012c) *China Statistical Yearbooks (1991–2012)*. China Statistics Press, Beijing, China.
National Bureau of Statistics (1991–2012d) *Shanghai Statistical Yearbooks (1991–2012)*. China Statistics Press, Beijing, China.
Saunders, H.D. (1992) The Khazzoom-Brookes postulate and neoclassical growth. *The Energy Journal* 13(4): 131–137.
Saunders, H.D. (2000a) Does predicted rebound depend on distinguishing between energy and energy services? *Energy Policy* 28(6–7): 497–500.
Saunders, H.D. (2000b) A view from the macro side: rebound, backfire, Khazzoom-Brookes. *Energy Policy* 28(6–7): 439–449.
Saunders, H.D. (2005) A calculator for energy consumption changes arising from new technologies. *Topics in Economic Analysis and Policy* 5(1): 1–31.
Saunders, H.D. (2008) Fuel conserving (and using) production functions. *Energy Economics* 30: 2184–2235.
Schipper, L., Grubb, M. (2000) On the rebound? Feedback between energy intensities and energy uses in IEA countries. *Energy Policy* 28: 367–388.
Small, K.A., Dender, K.V. (2007) Fuel efficiency and motor vehicle travel: the declining rebound effect. *The Energy Journal* 28(1): 25–51.
Sorrell, S. (2007) The rebound effect: an assessment of the evidence for economy-wide energy savings from improved energy efficiency. UK Energy Research Centre. http://www.ukerc.ac.uk/Downloads/PDF/07/ 0710ReboundEffect/0710 ReboundEffectReport.pdf.
Sorrell, S., Dimitropoulos, J. (2005a) An assessment of evidence for a rebound

effect from improvements in energy efficiency: assessment protocol. A report for the UK energy Research Centre, Sussex Energy Group, Science, Technology Policy Research (SPRU), University of Sussex, Brighton.

Sorrell, S., Dimitropoulos, J. (2005b) An assessment of evidence for rebound effect from improvements in energy efficiency: scoping note. Report for the Technology Policy Assessment function of the UK Energy Research Centre, Science, Technology Policy Research (SPRU), University of Sussex, Brighton.

Sorrell, S., Dimitropoulos, J. (2007) Computable general equilibrium modeling studies. UKERC Review of Evidence for the Rebound Effect, Technical Report 4. UK Energy Research Centre, London.

Turner, K. (2009) Negative rebound and disinvestment effects in response to an improvement in energy efficiency in the UK economy. *Energy Economics* 31(5): 648–666.

UK Energy Research Centre (2007) The rebound effect: an assessment of the evidence for economy-wide energy savings from improved energy efficiency. UK Energy Research Centre, London.

Wei, T. (2007) Impact of energy efficiency gains on output and energy use with Cobb-Douglas production function. *Energy Policy* 35(4): 2023–2030.

13. How should cities manage economic development? Highlights from theory and practice*

Marlon G. Boarnet and Richard K. Green

INTRODUCTION

In the world's first urban century, cities are increasingly economic engines and agglomeration benefits appear to be more important than ever. Against that backdrop, it is likely that cities will compete ever more fiercely for mobile capital. Virtually every city of even modest size has formal and informal efforts to boost economic development. Many localities offer place-based tax breaks, targeted infrastructure, job training, or programs that streamline or waive regulatory reviews to promote job or income growth.

At the local level, officials often promote real estate development as a path toward economic development. Economic development is often combined or even conflated with real estate development. While we believe the two activities are not the same, place-based economic development policy deals with the most place-based of all resources – land – and real estate development and local economic development will often be linked in practice. Economic and real estate development policies are often animated by a need to "do something," and the political pressures can be immense. All of this means that the world of policy and practice combines economics and planning (or land development) in a political environment. The implication of combining those two activities has rarely been appreciated.

In this chapter, we hope to speak both to practitioners and to the scholars who train, advise, and critique those practitioners. First, we define economic development and real estate development principles, highlighting

* We are grateful to participants of a one-day economic development symposium held at the USC Sol Price School of Public Policy in June, 2012. We particularly thank Ravaut Benitez and Suzanne Ekerling for their skill in organizing that workshop. The authors alone are responsible for all facts, interpretations, and policy recommendations in this chapter.

insights from economic theory. After defining those theoretical principles, we summarize the experience of four U.S. cities – Austin, Texas, New York, New York, San Diego, California, and Washington, D.C. Each of those cities has experienced robust economic growth over the past two decades, each has a reputation for innovative policy, and the cities represent a broad range of metropolitan types in terms of size, industrial structure, geographic location, and the broader policy setting defined by the relationship to state and national governments. The last section includes policy suggestions that flow from the lessons from theory and practice.

We note that our focus is explicitly local – at the scale of large cities in major metropolitan areas. Practice and policy in those cities is not macroeconomic per se, which is usually a matter for national governments. Hence we do not discuss factors that lead to stronger national growth – which of course would often be correlated with more rapid city economic growth. Instead we focus on local economic development policy as it is usually practiced, taking aggregate national (or even supra-national) growth rates as exogenous, and asking how cities might best manage their locally oriented policies.

To set the stage for later analysis, we discuss economic development and real estate development principles in turn, below. To be consistent with the fact that practice usually combines (and at times conflates) real estate development and economic development, we focus on the nexus between economic and real estate development, while being alert to the fact that those are different but overlapping activities.

1. ECONOMIC DEVELOPMENT PRINCIPLES

The leading authorities on economic development policy have been Ladd, Bartik and Zimbalist.[1] Our reading of these scholars leads us to suggest that economic development policy be guided by four principles. Economic development policy should: (1) address one or more market failures; (2) spend no more public money, either explicitly or implicitly, than is necessary; (3) generate new economic activity rather than simply shifting economic activity across the landscape; and (4) make any guarantees explicit and transparent. In this chapter, we consider the first three of these.

[1] All three are prolific authors. For examples of their economic development research, see Bartik (1991), Ladd (1994) and Siegfried and Zimbalist (2002).

Market Failures

We divide market failures into four types: positive externalities, negative externalities, public goods, and "herding." Economic development policy has a role with respect to all.

Externalities

A positive externality is a phenomenon where conduct that is beneficial to the market is not priced by the market; as a consequence, we see under-provision of the phenomenon. Real estate development decisions produce many externalities, both positive and negative. To give but one example of a positive externality, consider an anchor department store. The store not only draws shoppers to itself, but also to surrounding stores – yet in the absence of some coordinating mechanism among stores, the anchor receives no compensation for the benefit it provides to other stores. This leads to the under-provision of anchors.

Regional shopping centers largely solve the problem by "internalizing the externalities." Anchors in malls often pay very low rents – and in-line stores pay high rents. As such, the in-line stores are essentially paying for the benefit of being close to anchor stores – the positive externality is priced, and there is appropriate provision of both types of stores.

This puts old downtowns at a disadvantage relative to regional shopping malls, because parcels are generally owned by large numbers of owners, which in turn prevents the possibility of strategic interaction among shops. It is no accident that some of the most successful downtowns in the United States either have "vertical malls," or have Business Improvement Districts that have members that agree to something akin to a mall operating agreement. North Michigan Avenue in Chicago, one of the most productive shopping areas in America, uses both.

Networks also produce positive externalities via increasing returns to scale. As nodes get added to a network, nodes previously in the network become more valuable. There is a tendency for markets to under-provide networks, and so there is a role for governments to subsidize or provide networks in particular, or activities with increasing returns to scale in general.

Just as positive externalities are activities that produce uncompensated benefits, negative externalities are activities that impose unbilled costs on society. Blight is a potential source of negative externalities, in that it can attract crime and, more generally, cause neighboring properties to lose value. Some planners maintain that urban sprawl generates negative externalities, because it leads to congestion and pollution, although other planners maintain that sprawl is a socially efficient land use.

The most direct method for dealing with a negative externality is to tax it or to regulate it. Taxes intended to reduce negative externalities are called "Pigou taxes" and are named for the economist who showed that a properly calibrated *ad valorem* tax on an activity that generates negative externalities can lead to a socially optimal provision of that activity. Economists like such taxes because they produce a "double-dividend;" they lead to socially optimal outcomes and they raise revenue.

Pigou taxes, however, have very little political support. The most widely used Pigou tax – the tax on gasoline at the pump – is among the least politically popular of taxes. As a consequence, governments are left scrambling to find other tools to cure externalities. One is direct regulation – this, too, is arguably less popular than it once was. Another is economic development policy.

As we shall discuss elsewhere in this chapter, one of the justifications for many years for economic development policy was blight removal. In particular, local governments have used tax increment financing as a tool for eliminating blight. Eminent domain is another tool for blight removal. But many analysts have found that local governments have used these tools in places where the existence of blight was questionable, to say the least.

With respect to sprawl, it is arguable that eminent domain may be used as a tool to put infill development on a level playing field with greenfield development. Parcel assembly in downtowns (plottage) is very difficult, while subdividing green fields on the edge of cities (plattage) is relatively easy. To the extent that suburban sprawl is (1) a beneficiary of the relative ease of plattage and (2) actually does produce negative externalities, one could justify an economic development policy that incorporates eminent domain as a method for central city parcel assembly.

Public goods

Some goods contribute to economic well-being, but cannot be priced optimally by private markets. These goods are known as public goods. Using the terminology of economics, these goods are "non-rival" and "non-excludable."

Non-rival means that one person's use of the good does not diminish the enjoyment of another person using the good. We can think, for example, about an uncongested highway – each car or truck that enters the highway has little impact on other cars' or trucks' use of that highway.

Non-excludable means that it is difficult to prevent anyone from using the good. For example, if the police prevent crime from happening, the benefit of that crime prevention accrues to everyone, whether they pay for it or not. To some extent, gated communities attempt to make public safety excludable, but work by leading urban economists suggests that they generally simply push crime elsewhere (see Helsley and Strange, 1999).

Economic development policy often creates a nexus between how capital expenses for public goods can be financed and the beneficiaries of those public goods through increases in property values. Economically feasible public goods (those that pass a benefit–cost test) that are specific to a place get reflected in higher property values in the location that benefits. For instance, a road can convert an agricultural field, which may have relatively less value, into a newly urbanized area, which can have considerably more value. Increased property value can create a steam of revenue via *ad valorem* taxes. That revenue can in turn retire bonds that might have been used to fund the infrastructure.

Herd mentality

Lenders are well known for being able to forecast backward. If property values rose in the past year, lenders will assume they will continue to rise; if property values fell, lenders will assume they will continue to fall. Some scholars have suggested that herd mentality was one of the underlying causes of the recent financial crisis (see Davis and Madura, 2012).

One frustration that communities (and developers) face when they attempt to do a new type of development is that it is difficult to get financing, because new types of development lack a track record. The natural funders of new types of development might be venture capitalists, except that venture capitalists are generally seeking returns that are considerably higher than those one observes from any kind of development deal.

There is, to our knowledge, no evidence on whether individual developments (on the scale of a few acres) that create mixed use, higher density, walking- and transit-oriented neighborhoods improve agglomeration economies, but there is evidence that larger locations with higher densities have agglomeration benefits (see, e.g., Ciccone and Hall, 1996, for a well known reference in this literature.) We note that the more dense, mixed use, and urban characteristics that are associated with higher productivity at the metropolitan level are built from individual developments that are, in turn, mixed use, dense, and often transit- or walking-oriented. Currently, it is difficult for developers to get financing for projects as simple as those with ground floor retail space beneath apartments – despite the fact that this use has been very successful in New York, Paris, and many Asian cities. One should be cautious about how well government can see opportunity where the private sector does not, but in the case of mixed use development, it seems that the private sector is missing out. Of course, in cases where a beneficial form of development cannot obtain private funding due to "herd behavior" on the part of lenders, the role of public financing may be to provide demonstration or proof-of-concept until private capital becomes more widely available. More generally, if there were broad external benefits, some public financing may be justified even in the long run.

Minimizing Expenditures

There is a long literature on how governments spend more than is necessary to induce the development of sport arenas, factories, housing, and high-end shopping areas (Ladd, 1994; Siegfried and Zimbalist, 2002). Government should do its best to figure out the minimum amount of money it needs to spend to make a project feasible. While the ideal of a lean, waste-free public sector is as unrealistic as the idea that large private companies would never waste a penny, the fact that public funds are a public trust creates particular responsibilities to pursue goals with a minimum of expenditures. We know of many instances where government spends many multiples of what is necessary to accomplish a development goal. For example, analyses of the Section 42 Low Income Housing Tax Credit program show that investors receive far more in benefits from the program than they give up in foregone rents (Burge, 2011).

At the same time, government can use its ownership of land and zoning power to extract benefits from developers. Hong Kong has for years given developers ground leases in exchange for both rent and financing of infrastructure – this is how one of the densest cities in the world functions quite well. Recently, Washington, D.C. induced property owners to help pay for a new Metro station at New York Avenue in exchange for density bonuses.[2]

Producing More Than Shifting Activity

Economic development policy is touted as triumphant when it helps to reinvigorate a neighborhood, or when it brings jobs to a community. This, however, is not sufficient evidence of policy success.

A city that has had tremendous apparent success in economic development is Washington, D.C. The city has been redeveloping from west to east – over the past 30 years, a corridor of seven blocks has transformed from an area characterized by poor housing, drug dealing, and prostitution into among the nicest urban environments in the United States.

The problem is that the people who lived in the area got pushed out, and have left for adjacent Prince George's County, Maryland, which now has

[2] See http://www.ncppp.org/resources/case-studies/transportation-infrastructure/new-york-avenue-metro-station/, accessed September 28, 2014.

its own troubles with poor quality housing, drugs, and prostitution. This issue is not specific to the Washington area – to some extent, economic development policy can seem like a game of whack-a-mole – push down troubles in one place, and they just pop up somewhere else. But for economic development policy to be meaningful, it needs to judge itself based on its net impact on a region, not just on a particular city or neighborhood.

2. REAL ESTATE DEVELOPMENT REGULATION PRINCIPLES

Land value is deeply entwined with regulation, for two reasons. First, regulation is necessary to "make the market." Laws, regulations, government activity, and social norms define the conditions for private property rights in land. The "commons" of early colonial America reflected the idea that land was held as a community resource – a principal applied to many rivers, lakes, and oceans today. Yet the U.S., like virtually all developed countries, moved to a system where property rights in land are held privately. That system relies on formal legal structures for establishing, enforcing, and conveying title and also on laws that establish how one can use land (see, e.g., Kim, 2004, for an example and discussion). Second, the potential to use land (and hence land value) is affected by a host of activities that governments pursue. The most obvious link is from transportation infrastructure to land value.[3] Yet other government functions – waste removal, water, and public amenities such as parks, street cleaning, public schools, and public safety – all affect the value of property.

The net effect is that land value is strongly influenced by the legal and regulatory environment that both defines the property right and that provides infrastructure and defines allowed uses for the land. While any private property is a result of social and legal norms that create the market, the ways that government influences land value is more complex than for simpler commodities. The value of a sofa, a pair of pants, or a wristwatch are unlikely to be affected positively or negatively by government provision of public goods such as infrastructure, education, or public safety, except of course for the transportation infrastructure that allows moving the goods to market. Land is different. Land value is tied more closely to government activity that confers place-based amenities (infrastructure, school systems, public safety) and to regulations determining, when, how,

[3] See, for example, Alonso (1964) for theory and Mohring (1961) for early evidence or Boarnet and Chalermpong (2001) for more recent evidence.

and under what conditions land can be developed. With that background, consider some principles of "best practices" in land use regulation.

Have a Clear Economic Rationale for Land Use Regulation

Land use planning, and associated regulations, flow from three classes of "problems of the commons," each of which requires some form of intervention or coordination.

a. Separation of incompatible land uses: Traditional zoning is based on the idea that some land uses are not compatible in close proximity. Separating noxious industrial uses from residences and schools is an obvious example. What planners call Euclidean Zoning typically segregates land uses, creating zones where land can be developed in particular categories.[4] The separation of incompatible land uses can be justified by negative externalities that one land use imposes on another – for example externalities imposed by industrial uses on nearby residents (e.g. Fischel, 1985).
b. City building: Planning extends beyond externality management to the form and meaning of the city. Historically cities have encompassed an element of inspiration and aspiration, with great works of architecture and urban plans that were intended to project images of power, promote fealty to a ruler, celebrate or commemorate religious sanctity, or elevate the humanity of daily life through aesthetically pleasing environments. The Haussmann Plan that resulted in the modernization of Paris and the construction of the city's great boulevards in the late 1800s is an example of planning, and hence government intervention, not to manage externalities but to engage in the task of building and transforming the city. Similar examples include L'Enfant's plan for the capital of a young republic in Washington, D.C., and plans for similar world or capital cities.
c. Regional planning to manage common resource pool externalities: Problems of traffic congestion and air quality, as an example, may be addressed in part by arranging the form of the city in ways that reduce travel along particular corridors. The arrangement of land uses, in this perspective, is not to separate incompatible uses but instead to coordinate land use in ways that reduce common resource pool externalities (e.g. those associated with driving) or in ways that produce public goods associated with street life or amenities (more like the Haussmann Plan).

[4] The name is a reference to the 1926 case *Village of Euclid, Ohio* v. *Ambler Realty Co.*, in which the U.S. Supreme Court upheld the practice of local zoning.

Each of these motives – separating incompatible land uses, building cities with civic amenities, and using regional land use patterns to address issues of public goods or externalities – all relate to common resource pool issues associated with regulation. Land use regulation should be justified as a response to a problem of the commons that (a) cannot be easily addressed by private markets, due to coordination problems across dispersed landowners, and that (b) targets a clearly specified market failure, whether that market failure is externality reduction or amenity production.

Beware of Rent Seeking

Because land value is influenced by government action, there are obvious incentives to use regulation to increase private land values. Fischel (2005) has argued a "home voter" hypothesis – that homeowners have incentives to use regulation to reduce the supply of new lots in their neighborhoods, thereby driving up the price of existing lots and hence increasing the price of their own homes. A recent literature has conjectured that land use regulation reduces land supply and hence raises home prices, benefiting existing residents at the expense of potential newcomers to the community (e.g. Glaeser et al., 2005). Bogart (1993), among others, discussed exclusionary zoning – the use of zoning not to manage externalities but to exclude minorities or lower income residents. Identifying the motives associated with exclusionary zoning can be difficult. If, as some research suggests, lower income residents purchase low-value homes that yield property tax revenues that are less than the cost of serving those residents, fiscal motives for exclusion may be correlated with efforts to exclude the poor or minority groups that are predominantly poor (e.g. Bogart, 1993). Hence motives for rent seeking range from clearly self-interested efforts to raise private home values, to objectionable (and, in many countries, illegal) efforts to exclude based on race, to exclusionary motives based on the intersection of local public finances and land use or a desire to mitigate perceived or real impacts of growth. Regulations should be justified in relation to the common good – a point that holds for all regulation but a caution that is particularly pertinent for land use regulations given the various ways that government action can confer private property value gains or losses.[5]

Be Alert to the Public and Private Motives for Land Use Regulation

Protecting the local tax base may be a public good or a common resource pool. Yet the result, when exclusionary zoning is in play, is rent seeking.

[5] For a discussion, see, for example, Hagman and Misczynski, 1977.

Ideally, the design of tax mechanisms will provide localities with an ability to safeguard their fiscal position without presenting motives to exclude persons of lower income. In California, for example, redevelopment was often a tool to address some of the difficulties caused by the way that the state's fiscal and land use policies interact. Redevelopment agencies in California served two purposes – land assembly (including exercising the power of eminent domain) and tax increment financing to fund infrastructure or other amenities. Proposition 13 limited property tax revenues, making tax increment financing an attractive alternative to an overburdened local fisc. This often confounded redevelopment motives with fiscal objectives, including motives to finance infrastructure or public goods that would have been more appropriately funded through local property tax revenues, had Proposition 13 allowed property tax increases.

Predictable, By Right, Land Use Regulation

"By right" development means that the zoning code has clear provisions for what can be developed. Uses, densities, and other requirements (e.g. parking requirements, aesthetic treatments, or the like), are clearly specified under "by right" zoning and uses that are consistent with those conditions are presumed allowable and if reviewed are reviewed quickly and without much provision for challenge. This requires clarity in the zoning code and a zoning code that reflects existing market conditions. In some cases, preferred market uses evolve beyond the zoning code and the code is not uniformly updated, requiring conditional use permits. As an example, in a growing city some parcels may have economically viable uses that exceed densities allowed by the code, or in new transit-oriented developments parking requirements may be outdated and may not reflect lower vehicle use associated with transit. Extensive use of conditional use permits, often following from a zoning code that does not reflect market realities, creates uncertainty, as the ability to approve a use lies with the discretionary authority of a planning commission and city council. Developers consistently say that departures from "by right" development create delays and uncertainties that increase the cost of real estate development.

Another departure from "by right" development is the practical effect of the California Environmental Quality Act (CEQA). CEQA requires environmental impact reports (EIRs) for any project undertaken by a public agency or requiring a permit from a public agency – hence most any new development.[6] Compared to its counterpart, the U.S. National

[6] For information on CEQA, see, for example, http://www.aqmd.gov/ceqa/faq.html, accessed December 1, 2012.

Environmental Policy Act (NEPA), CEQA decisions are more open to being contested through litigation. The EIR does not require that development have no impact – a statement of overriding concerns can be filed – but the analysis is open to legal challenge.[7] This creates risks for developers. Many EIRs in California urban areas bring traffic impacts or possibly air quality or other impacts that are above the threshold of significance, and legal challenges are common. This causes delay and cost as the developer defends the CEQA analysis, and CEQA challenges create political pressure in cases where planning commission action is also needed, for example to obtain a conditional use permit. The question of CEQA reform is an active subject of political debate (e.g. Stephens, 2012.)

3. FROM THEORY TO PRACTICE

The economic development and real estate development principles outlined in the previous two sections can be summarized as follows. Efficient policies focus government activity on market failures, particularly common resource pool externalities or public goods that would be inefficiently addressed by dispersed private actors. Those policies should be crafted to produce aggregate increases in economic activity rather than simply shifting jobs or production from one part of the city to another, and the policies should guard against private rent seeking and form a predictable, often "by right," land development regulatory framework. In our case studies, we found that economic development practitioners rarely talk in the abstract language of microeconomic theory. Economic development agencies are operational bodies, defined by their organizational structure, financing arrangements, and the scope of their duties, and these characteristics are often the most salient aspects to both agency insiders and practitioners. Hence it is necessary for us to link our theoretical observations to questions of agency structure, organization, financing, and functions. In our interviews with economic development practitioners and in our background research the agencies were described in ways that link to five characteristics, listed below.

1. Independence from direct political pressure: This is the extent to which economic development efforts are shielded, formally or informally, from the pressure of elected officials.
2. Financing/fiscal arrangements: How are economic development efforts financed? What tax instruments are used and how much local control does the city have over its revenue streams?

[7] See, for example, the discussion in Bilir (2012).

3. Functions: Economic development agencies vary in their functions. Possible roles include real estate redevelopment, business attraction/retention, workforce training, long-term land use planning (often to support redevelopment), research and analysis, and in some cases long-term strategizing.
4. Timeframe: Does the economic development agency focus mostly on near-term initiatives, for example defined by the span of a few years or constrained to terms of elected office? Or does the agency strategize over a longer span that may include decades?
5. Scope of action: Does the economic development agency have authority for land use planning or permitting? Does the agency influence (or simplify) environmental approval? Is housing policy (particularly affordable housing policy) handled within the economic development agency?

There is a link between these organizational characteristics and the theoretical, outcome-oriented characteristics discussed in Sections 1 and 2. Efforts to shield agencies from political pressure can limit rent seeking and focus attention on broader metropolitan area or citywide criteria, possibly limiting "beggar thy neighbor" efforts that simply move economic activity from one location to another. Independence from direct political influence, independent financing (a concomitant of political influence), and a long timeframe all can assist in reducing rent seeking or the capture of agencies by privately interested actors that can lead to rent seeking. The functions and scope of actions can be tailored to create a focus on common resource pool externalities or public goods, such as infrastructure, public safety, or general labor force training. While it would be ideal to classify our case study entities by measures that correspond directly to the ideas in Sections 1 and 2, our information and, more to the point, our study agencies' self-conceptions, relate more to the organizational and functional elements summarized by the five characteristics listed above.

We also note that it is possible to engage in economic development for equity rather than efficiency concerns. Efforts to redistribute economic development or to boost the prospects of lagging regions (e.g. Appalachia in the U.S. or many of the formerly eastern bloc countries in Europe) are often motivated by equity rather than efficiency concerns. We do not intend to diminish the role for regional economic equity, but our analysis focuses on efficiency criteria and the organizational characteristics that are likely to be associated with those efficiency criteria. Particularly in the large city cases that we examined, the agencies perceived their role more in efficiency than in equity terms, and analyzing regional equity would require both a different theoretical lens and different case study information.

4. LESSONS FROM FOUR CITIES

How well the principles for economic and real estate development are met depends on the outcome of a political process. The outcome cannot be mandated or ensured, no more than "wise policy" can be mandated. (Of course, what constitutes "wisdom" is also part of the political debate.) Instead, we focus on what political and institutional arrangements are more or less likely to yield results consistent with the principles outlined above. How might governments approach economic and real estate development in ways that will best meet policy needs? We examined the experience of four U.S. cities – Austin, New York, San Diego, and Washington D.C., and then we summarize each city's experience based on the five characteristics listed in Section 3.

The summary information below is taken, in part, from a one-day economic development summit held at the University of Southern California's Sol Price School of Public Policy on June 8, 2012. The summaries below list the representative who attended and presented at the June 8 economic development summit. Certainly the representatives listed do not necessarily condone any facts or policy interpretations in this chapter. We thank each of the local economic development officials listed, but the authors of this chapter are solely responsible for the facts, interpretations, and policy suggestions presented here.

Austin, Texas

Rodney Gonzalez, Deputy Director, Economic Development Department

Austin's Economic Development Department (hereafter also economic development office) is a city agency, answering to the assistant city manager, with authority for economic development. Austin has a council/manager form of government, with six council members and the mayor elected at large.[8] The economic development office has a large focus on redevelopment and associated real estate development projects. Eleven of the 52-member staff have responsibility for long-range planning efforts that support catalytic redevelopment, much of which has been focused in downtown. Recent projects have a large role for mixed use, urban infill developments that will return underutilized land to the tax rolls and create both construction and ongoing, post-construction jobs. Yet the planning that occurs within the economic development department is not formal planning or permitting, but instead is more about facilitating partnerships

[8] Effective in 2015 the Austin City Council will be ten members and a mayor.

with the private sector. The economic development department also operates programs to support small businesses, but the Austin Chamber of Commerce, with more than 20 staff members, has primary responsibility for business recruitment and retention. The economic development department contracts out workforce development and career training to several local non-profit organizations. Housing is handled by a separate city agency, and the economic development department does not focus on housing policy per se or affordable housing, but the department's redevelopment projects produce affordable housing units and millions of dollars to an established city housing trust fund.[9]

1. Independence from direct political pressure: As a city agency, the economic development department is subject to political direction, although the council/manager form of city government is intended to buffer agencies from direct political influence and build a spirit of professional management.
2. Financing/fiscal arrangements: Austin, like other cities in Texas, has authority to set the property tax rate. Properties are reassessed periodically to reflect market value. Even with market value assessment, property tax revenue tends to be less sensitive to economic expansions or downturns than either the sales or income taxes. Hence Austin has more local control over its revenue instruments and a more stable revenue stream than cities in states with property tax limitations, particularly in California where cities cannot set property or sales tax rates and which rely in part on transfers from a state government heavily dependent on volatile income, business, and capital gains taxes.
3. Functions: The economic development department sees itself as an economic development agency, but as a practical matter, with housing handled elsewhere and workforce development contracted out, the economic development department operates more as the city's redevelopment agency, focused on stimulating real estate development on under utilized land. Since being established in 2003, the economic development department has created 6.3 million square feet of new development in commercial, office, industrial, and residential space. Another 6.1 million square feet of new development is under contract through master development agreements. All projects are catalysts intended to spur new development in Austin, specifically with an eye toward new urbanism. The 700-acre former municipal airport

[9] This information is from comments from Rodney Gonzalez at a USC Price School of Public Policy – Lusk Center for Real Estate Economic Development Summit, June 8, 2012, Los Angeles, California and from the Austin Economic Growth Office web page, http://austintexas.gov/department/economic-growth, accessed December 1, 2012.

(Mueller) is one of several marquee projects led by the economic development department. At completion, Mueller will house 11,000 residents and have 10,000 jobs on-site. The economic development department is leading two waterfront development projects totaling in excess of $650 million and 2.1 million square feet.[10]

4. Timeframe: The timeframe seems typical for real estate redevelopment efforts, and is generally dictated by the cycle of real estate activity. This may span a few years, from conceptualization to redevelopment. As an example, the Mueller redevelopment project originated in 1996 and is not scheduled to be completed for another 10 years.[11] Longer-term visioning about industry structure, workforce issues, or large scale infrastructure investment seems to be a second-order question for the economic development department although the department is working on several long-term projects, including the development of a logistics and distribution center in proximity to the city airport.
5. Scope of action: The function in some other cities to "cut through the red tape" seems not as important in relation to land use in Austin, although the city manager can expedite projects. Note that Texas has a more limited and simpler land use regulatory environment than, for example, California or New York, and the existence of more "by right" development throughout Texas may reduce the need for an agency to cut through land use regulatory barriers. The economic development department has a business enhancement and retention low-interest loan program along a t-shaped corridor down Congress Street, from Town Lake to the border of the University of Texas campus and down 8th Street to Interstate 35.

New York City, New York

Kyle Kimball, Chief Financial Officer, New York Economic Development Authority

The New York Economic Development Corporation (NYEDC), while "culturally" part of the mayor's office, is a non-profit corporation. The president of its board is appointed by the mayor.

1. Independence from direct political pressure: The "privateness" of the NYEDC allows it to go through streamlined procurement processes. It

[10] Comments from Rodney Gonzales, deputy director, Austin Economic Development Department, via email, October, 2014.

[11] Comments from Rodney Gonzales, deputy director, Austin Economic Development Department, via email, October, 2014.

also has its own revenue stream, about which we will say more below. The key to the corporation's independence is likely that it returns a profit to New York City's taxpayers. In the end, however, the mayor of New York has considerable influence over the activities of the NYEDC – the fact that he can "protect" it reflects in part the strength of the mayor's position in New York City's government charter.

2. Financing/fiscal arrangements: The NYEDC is a landlord. It owns considerable real estate that generates rents that it can use to encourage economic development. It also acts as a bond guarantor, and makes money through a fee schedule. Finally, NYEDC provides consulting services, for a fee, to investors interested in doing economic development projects.
3. Functions: NYEDC does fairly large scale projects for the city. Three examples are particularly noteworthy. The NYEDC financed the high line, a project that converted abandoned, elevated railroad tracks in the southern part of Manhattan into a park. There is no controversy that the project is beautiful, and it has arguably raised surrounding property values, which is evidence that it was an economically feasible project.

   The NYEDC has also been instrumental in the early stages of planning a research university campus on Roosevelt Island. Cornell and Technion (a technical university in Israel) have committed to spending $2 billion on the development of that campus; New York is providing the universities a substantial amount of land on Roosevelt Island.

   The NYEDC/New York Industrial Development Authority have also been a partner with the Hudson Yards development authority, collaborating on a major transformation of previously manufacturing land uses into what will become a large expansion of Midtown New York's business district.[12] According to the Hudson Yards Development Corporation website, key components of the development program include:[13]

   - rezoning Hudson Yards and the Western Rail Yard, in 2005 and 2009, from manufacturing to commercial and residential, creating capacity for 20,000 housing units (5,000 affordable units), 2 million square feet of retail, and 3 million square feet of hotel space;
   - extension of the No. 7 subway to a new terminal in the Hudson Yards area;

[12] See Hudson Yards website, http://www.hydc.org/html/home/home.shtml, accessed September 26, 2013.

[13] Quoted and paraphrased from Hudson Yards website, http://www.hydc.org/html/home/home.shtml, accessed September 26, 2013.

- mixed use developments containing several million square feet of office space, 12 acres of open space, and a public school.

4. Timeframe: Because the authority works on such a wide variety of projects, from consulting to large scale economic development, the timing of what it does varies considerably. It argues that its ability to avoid a standard government procurement process means that it does get things done more rapidly than would be the case if it were a government agency.
5. Scope of action: The mission statement and scope for the New York City Industrial Development Agency (NYCIDA, which is the implementation arm of the NYEDC) is:

> . . . to encourage economic development throughout the five boroughs, and to assist in the retention of existing jobs, and the creation and attraction of new ones. NYCIDA programs are discretionary and provide companies with access to triple tax-exempt bond financing and/or tax benefits to acquire or create capital assets, such as purchasing real estate, constructing or renovating facilities, and acquiring new equipment.[14]

San Diego, California

Jeff Graham, Vice President, Redevelopment, Centre City Development Corporation

The Centre City Development Corporation (CCDC) was created as a non-profit entity in 1975. With the elimination of redevelopment agencies in California in 2012, the CCDC's functions now rest with a new entity, Civic San Diego, but the discussion here focuses on the CCDC's role. The city and the city's redevelopment agency entered into an operating agreement with CCDC that allowed CCDC to implement redevelopment powers in an area encompassing the whole of downtown, 1,450 acres. From the earliest days, the mission of CCDC was to redevelop downtown, which as of the 1970s had entered a decline. Early projects included Horton Plaza and the Gaslamp Quarter, both influential downtown developments in their time. The opening of San Diego's light rail system in the 1980s, with substantial service in downtown, provided an opportunity to pursue transit-oriented development, and CCDC was a leader in those efforts (Boarnet and Compin, 1999). In 1992, all planning and entitlement functions in the CCDC redevelopment area were delegated to the CCDC, creating a "one

[14] Quoted from the NYEDC website, http://www.nycedc.com/nycida, accessed September 26, 2013.

stop shop" for land use permitting.[15] The CCDC stated that environmental approval takes 90 to 100 days in the redevelopment zone, compared with one to five years in other parts of the city.[16] The CCDC also funded a program environmental impact report (PEIR) for the entire 1,450-acre zone, allowing individual projects to use the results of the PEIR to get approved.[17] By showing compliance with the PEIR, the CEQA compliance process is expedited for projects in the zone. CCDC policy is to provide a minimum 20% affordable housing set aside.[18] More generally, CCDC and the city have innovated by pursuing long-term agreements with private developers. As an example, the city sold parkland to a developer for below-ground parking, on the condition that the developer use the proceeds that the CCDC would have otherwise received from the sale to design, construct, secure, and maintain the park in perpetuity.[19] As a redevelopment agency, the CCDC had the power of eminent domain to assist in land assembly, and the CCDC could issue bonds against the tax increment created by the increased property values resulting from CCDC projects. Following the state's decision to dissolve redevelopment, the City of San Diego chose to become the successor agency to the CCDC's redevelopment authority, and the non-profit corporation merged with Southeastern Economic Development Corporation to form Civic San Diego, a new City-owned non-profit corporation.[20] Civic San Diego is now responsible for redevelopment and economic development activities in all of the City's former 14 redevelopment project areas.

1. Independence from direct political pressure: The fact that CCDC was a non-profit with redevelopment authority and an independent revenue stream provided exceptional independence from direct political pressure. This provided an ability to engage in a coherent, decades-long process of transforming downtown San Diego. The CCDC Board of Directors, nominated by the mayor and confirmed by City Council, approved a majority of all entitlements and permits. Only projects requiring investment or a sale of redevelopment agency property were

15 See, for example, memo to San Diego City Council, http://docs.sandiego.gov/councilcomm_agendas_attach/2012/LUH_120411_6.pdf, accessed December 1, 2012.

16 Comments by Jeff Graham at USC Price School of Public Policy – Lusk Center for Real Estate Economic Development Summit, June 8, 2012, Los Angeles, California.

17 Ibid.

18 Ibid.

19 Comments from Jeff Graham and Gail Goldberg (former San Diego Planning Director) at USC Price School of Public Policy – Lusk Center for Real Estate Economic Development Summit, June 8, 2012, Los Angeles, California.

20 Roger Showley, SD Redevelopment Agency Holds Last Meeting. *San Diego Union-Tribune*. Available at http://www.utsandiego.com/news/2012/jun/28/ccdc-holds-final-meeting-becoming-civic-san-diego/, accessed December 1, 2012.

required to be considered and approved by City Council. The CCDC Board and its committees typically thoroughly vetted a proposed public-private partnership agreement prior to its consideration by the City Council.

2. Financing/fiscal arrangements: As a redevelopment agency, the CCDC had a dedicated revenue stream from the incremental increase in property tax revenues above what would have occurred absent CCDC projects.
3. Functions: Because the CCDC funding was tax increment financing, increasing property tax revenues was essential. The CCDC's functions were largely physical redevelopment, including large commercial centers and transit-oriented developments. The 20% affordable housing set aside implied that housing affordability was an important part of CCDC's residential development portfolio, but that nested within a primary focus on redevelopment.
4. Timeframe: The CCDC's planning efforts spanned decades, and the CCDC viewed itself as leading the transformation of downtown. The vision of the effort spanned beyond particular mayoral terms or city councils.
5. Scope of action: The CCDC's scope was centered on land development, and the associated land assembly and tax increment financing functions authorized by California redevelopment law. The long-term nature of CCDC's existence and the fact that the CCDC could engage in physical infrastructure projects allowed for efforts that included building a sense of place and aesthetics. Efforts such as workforce training, business attraction and retention, and education programs or public safety were outside of the CCDC's scope, as those functions were not allowed uses of funds under California law governing redevelopment.

Washington, D.C.

Michael Stevens, Capitol Riverfront Business Improvement District

The Capitol Riverfront Business Improvement District (CRBID) is a BID whose purpose is to attract developers, retailers, residents, and visitors to a new 500-acre neighborhood along the Anacostia River waterfront in Washington, D.C. The mixed use nature of the area included in the BID is a new phenomenon – for many years, the area was (unusually for D.C.) made up of industrial uses.

The BID was created by the District of Columbia City Council and approved by Mayor Fenty in August 2007. To some extent, the BID operates in a manner similar to a mall developer – it collects a management fee from "tenants" (area businesses) and uses the proceeds to make common area improvements. The BID was created at the time that the Washington Nationals were building a ballpark in the area; the U.S. Department of Transportation also moved its headquarters there.

1. Independence from direct political pressure: Because the Capitol Riverfront Business Improvement District is just that, a BID, it operates more like a private sector entity than a political entity, answering to the businesses and residents within the BID area. The CRBID is organized as a non-profit entity, responsible to stakeholders represented by its board of directors.
2. Financing/fiscal arrangements: The BID is funded through a self-imposed tax on property owners in the area, at rates that vary based on use (hotel, residential, and commercial properties are assessed at different rates) and occupancy. Funds are used to provide improved services in the BID area.[21]
3. Functions: The BID attempts to develop common areas in a way that improves business conditions within a fairly narrowly defined area. According to the CRBID annual report, their functions include:[22]
   - trash removal and beautification in the public realm;
   - public safety and hospitality greeters on the streets;
   - marketing efforts to promote the district and produce special events; and
   - efforts to attract commercial tenants to the area and advocate for infrastructure improvements.
4. Timeframe: Many of the CRBID's functions are more short term in nature. While the area along the Anacostia waterfront has developed rapidly in recent years, the CRBID is not a redevelopment agency and does not pursue long-term development projects. The CRBID works with city agencies and private entities to encourage long-term public and private investment that will improve the quality of life along the Anacostia waterfront area, but it is not a redevelopment agency.
5. Scope of action: The BID is focused on providing services and marketing the attractiveness of the BID area, through a broad range of activities, including neighborhood cleaning and maintenance, safety and hospitality efforts, marketing and branding initiatives that promote

[21] For more information, see http://www.capitolriverfront.org/about/bid-tax-information, accessed September 26, 2013.

[22] From the Capitol Riverfront BID web page, http://www.capitolriverfront.org/about/what-we-do, accessed September 26, 2013.

the waterfront area, and coordination with city agencies and the local community.

Summary of Lessons from the Four Cities

Table 13.1 summarizes the key elements from each city. All but the City of Austin economic growth office are independent entities, shielded from direct political influence and with their own revenue streams. The agencies have a heavy real estate development focus, with only the NYEDC engaging in long-term strategic planning that goes beyond land development. The Capitol Riverfront BID is unique in providing services within a distinct, and narrowly defined, area.

Some of these agencies illustrate best practices. The NYEDC combines long-term strategic planning with a real estate development function. It is shielded from direct political influence, in part by the city's strong mayor form of government and also by the agency's own revenue streams. The NYEDC is also comprehensive in scope, engaging in activities that range from partnering on major real estate redevelopment projects to long-term strategic study and planning. The San Diego CCDC was also shielded from direct political influence, at arm's length from city council oversight and with its own revenue stream. It engaged in a decades-long planning, policy, and investment program that helped transform downtown San Diego. Compared to these two cases, both the city agency in Austin and Washington D.C.'s CRBID are more limited in functions and timeframe. Austin's economic development agency is, essentially, a real estate development entity, and the CRBID provides important services (public safety, aesthetics, branding) in the Anacostia waterfront area. While neither Austin nor Washington have large, independent, long-serving economic development entities that compare to the NYEDC or the CCDC, the more focused missions in Austin and Washington and the neighborhood orientation of CRBID also play useful roles. Hence we suggest that an ideal combination would partner a quasi-independent economic growth office with more localized, neighborhood oriented entities. This suggestion is described in more detail in Section 5.

5. ECONOMIC DEVELOPMENT AND REAL ESTATE DEVELOPMENT POLICY LESSONS

Most economic development has been conflated with real estate development. Yes, the task of taking underused land and facilitating economically productive uses for that land is important. Yet a too-heavy focus on real

Table 13.1 Summary of organization of economic development agencies

	New York EDC	Washington D.C. Capitol Riverfront BID	Austin economic growth office	San Diego CCDC
Independence from direct political pressure	Independent	Independent	City agency	Independent
Financing/ revenue sources	Own revenue: Income on land and building holdings	Own revenue: Tax on property values in BID	General revenue: City revenues primarily local property tax and tax increment financing	Own revenue: Tax increment financing
Functions	Real estate development, long-term strategic economic development planning	Aesthetics, infrastructure maintenance, safety, business retention and attraction in BID area	Real estate development, also business recruitment and expansion (mostly contracted)	Real estate development and 20% affordable housing goal
Timeframe	Years (real estate activities) to decades (long-term strategic planning)	Short-term	Years	Years
Scope	Real estate primarily	Focused on services in BID area	Real estate development	Real estate development and affordable housing; substantial transit-oriented development efforts

estate development overlooks the broader context for economic growth. Cities increasingly are sources for innovative, knowledge-based industries, and cities that have a well-educated labor force, with clear and predictable business regulations and infrastructure that provides the quality-of-life amenities sought by mobile, educated workers, will be more competitive. Those functions go beyond land development, to include education, infrastructure, and environmental stewardship.

As a general model of economic development in large cities in the modern, knowledge-based economy we suggest two different agencies, with authority over the broad-based economic climate and local, real estate development respectively. Each task is distinct, and each is important enough to warrant its own entity.

A Quasi-independent Economic Growth Office

We suggest an economic growth office, whose duties would focus on long-term strategic planning that would include policy issues related to education and labor force training, infrastructure, and the health of the business environment. We do not suggest a short-term focus on business attraction or retention, as that leads to efforts that are driven by the needs of particular businesses or firms, but instead a focus on the overall business environment. The agency's staff should include a strong analytic capability. The analytics should focus on strategy and policy development and on *ex post* evaluations of policies and plans.

The agency should be shielded from direct political pressure, possibly by a board of directors appointed by the mayor and council, with terms of service staggered over multiple council terms. The primary role for this entity would be strategy and long-term policy advice. We note that the membership of the board should be inclusive and should allow for appointees from the business and labor communities, including representatives appointed by the mayor and council but with outreach and membership beyond the traditional political or business communities. The structure of the board should be carefully calibrated to allow for fact-based analyses of long-term issues, including issues that would be politically controversial and possibly too difficult for electoral realms. An agency dominated by political appointees may become too cautious about taking on key long-term issues such as tax structure, and, likewise, any one interest group (i.e. large businesses or labor), while they should be represented on the agency board, ought not to dominate the board's policy-making. The entity should be structured to be a long-term voice, with funds that are secure from day-to-day politics.

The most successful economic development efforts in our study cities had secure funding streams that were not subject to political review. Allocations from general revenue budgets of the city or county would bring political pressure. Hence funding would require creative thought. Funding may come from dedicated portions of, for example, visitor tax or business license revenues. The funding source should be long term, not subject to year-to-year political review. The analytic portion of this agency would be lean and would require stable, long-term, shielded, but not lavish funding.

We suggest three key foci for this agency: (1) education and workforce training, (2) infrastructure and public safety, and (3) a business climate including studying reforms that will lead to more manageable "by right" development. Each of these functions is a public good, and each flows from the general economic and land development principles articulated in the early sections of this chapter.

We note that questions of education are fundamental in an increasingly knowledge-based economy. An economic growth office could and should focus on education and entry-level workforce training. There may be other innovations. One role of the economic growth office should be to analyze and advocate for policy options that would further overall economic growth and to evaluate those programs.

A more ambitious version of this model would provide larger dedicated tax revenues to the economic growth office, allowing it to become a grant-making agency. This would require a dedicated funding stream. Under this model, the office might follow a grant-making business model, inviting a competition for resources and evaluating outcomes consistently as part of a grant-making program. While in some ways attractive, we caution against this. The grant-making apparatus would come to dominate the analytic and policy planning portion of the agency. The distribution of substantial financial resources would create political pressure on grant-making decisions and evaluations, which would overshadow the policy evaluation and planning function. In most cities, there are private foundations which make grants, but few cities have an entity charged with overall public sector strategic policy planning.

Place-based, Neighborhood Specific Real Estate Development Entities

In addition to an economic development "strategic planning" agency, we suggest a separate but complementary entity (or entities) focused on land development in specific locations. These entities (there may be several for various locations in the city) would combine the functions of land development (sometimes called "redevelopment") agencies and business improvement districts. Redevelopment agencies, for example in some U.S. states, have assisted with land assembly and tax-increment financing. Those agencies typically assembled land from private owners (at times through eminent domain, which has become controversial), and the agencies often built infrastructure with bonds issued against anticipated future increases in tax revenues that would be created by increases in land value caused by the public infrastructure. The redevelopment agencies were in part financing instruments, allowing governments to pursue projects that would increase land value by, in effect, borrowing against that future increase in land value. Many cities will still have needs for both the land assembly and financing function of such agencies, and hence spatially focused real estate development agencies could in part serve that function.

We believe that, in some instances, the business improvement district functions of a spatially delimited real estate development entity of the sort we propose may be more important than the land assembly or infrastructure financing characteristics. City leadership could choose targeted areas for local services that would include public safety and infrastructure enhancement that could be financed through fees assessed on property owners. The fact that the rebirth of downtowns in many U.S. cities occurred coincident with the substantial drop in urban crime rates over the past two decades suggests that services, including but not limited to public safety, serve an important role for businesses.

We note that these more locally (even neighborhood) focused entities, particularly those focused on real estate development, can bring both social costs and social benefits. For example, redevelopment could increase traffic congestion, imposing external costs, or it might gentrify neighborhoods in ways that reduce the stock of affordable housing. We further note, though, that those impacts could be consistent either with policies that improve social welfare (despite increases in traffic externalities or gentrification) or that on net decrease social welfare. Particular cases will vary, and we caution that focusing on localized impacts may miss the larger role for neighborhood revitalization in a coherent citywide economic development strategy. We suggest that the vision for these more localized entities should be informed in part by a citywide view, and one role for a quasi-independent economic growth office would be to study opportunities for and the performance of these more localized entities. Yet to maintain a position above the political fray, it might be necessary for an economic growth office, or other strategic planning entity, to merely have authority to study and strategize, rather than any direct ability to authorize or renew the operation of these local real estate development entities.

Summary

It is often easy for cities to run their economic and real estate development efforts on an "autopilot" of sorts, continuing what they have done in the past or responding to the crisis of the moment while lacking an overall strategy. A better approach would be to recognize that the most effective economic development policies respond to either externalities or public goods, playing roles that the private sector cannot. Such a solution should, ideally, be cognizant of the dual role of economic development, fostering competitiveness through strategic policies while also providing a way to foster the public goods aspects of land assembly, tax increment financing, and local service provision that are associated with and at times necessary for successful land development. We suggest that those two functions may be housed in separate agencies, with coordination between the entities. Regardless of the specific form, cities should focus on an economic development structure that can provide long-term analytic thinking that reflects input from a broad range of voices in the city, while separate entities focus on land development issues specific to smaller neighborhoods.

REFERENCES

Alonso, William. 1964. *Location and Land Use: Toward a General Theory of Land Rent*. Cambridge, MA: Harvard University Press.

Bartik, Timothy J. 1991. *Who Benefits From State and Local Economic Development Policies?* Kalamazoo, MI: W.E. Upjohn Institute for Employment Research.

Bilir, C. Aylin. 2012. Stopping the Runaway Train of CEQA Litigation: Proposals for Non-Judicial Substantive Review. *Environs: Environmental Law and Policy Journal*. Davis, CA: UC Davis School of Law. Available at http://environs.law.ucdavis.edu/issues/35/2/bilir.pdf, accessed December 1, 2012.

Boarnet, Marlon G. and Saksith Chalermpong. 2001. New Highways, House Prices, and Urban Development: A Case Study of Toll Roads in Orange County, California. *Housing Policy Debate* 12(3): 575–605.

Boarnet, Marlon G. and Nick Compin. 1999. Transit-Oriented Development in San Diego County: The Incremental Implementation of a Planning Idea. *Journal of the American Planning Association* 65(1): 80–95.

Bogart, William T. 1993. "What Big Teeth You Have:" Identifying the Motives for Exclusionary Zoning. *Urban Studies* 30(0): 1669–1681.

Burge, Gregory S. 2011. Do Tenants Capture the Benefits from the Low-income Housing Tax Credit Program? *Real Estate Economics* 39(1): 71–96.

Ciccone, Antonio and Robert E. Hall. 1996. Productivity and the Density of Economic Activity. *American Economic Review* 86(1): 54–70.

Davis, Sean M. and Jeff Madura. 2012. How the Shift to Quality Distinguished Winners from Losers During the Financial Crisis. *Journal of Behavioral Finance* 13(2): 81–92.

Fischel, William A. 1985. *The Economics of Zoning Laws: A Property Rights Approach to American Land Use Controls*. Baltimore, MD: Johns Hopkins University Press.
Fischel, William A. 2005. *The Homevoter Hypothesis: How Home Values Influence Local Government Taxation, School Finance, and Land-Use Policies*. Cambridge, MA: Harvard University Press.
Glaeser, Edward L., Joseph Gyourko and Raven E. Saks. 2005. Why Have Housing Prices Gone Up? Harvard Institute of Economic Research discussion paper number 2061. Available at http://post.economics.harvard.edu/hier/2005papers/2005list.html, accessed December 1, 2012.
Hagman, Donald G. and Dean J. Misczynski. 1977. *Windfalls for Wipeouts: Land Value Capture and Compensation*. Chicago, IL: American Planning Association.
Helsley, Robert W. and William C. Strange. 1999. Gated Communities and the Economic Geography of Crime. *Journal of Urban Economics* 46(1): 80–105.
Kim, Annette M. 2004. A Market without the "Right" Property Rights. *Economics of Transition* 12(2): 275–305.
Ladd, Helen F. 1994. Spatially Targeted Economic Development Strategies: Do They Work? *Cityscape* 1(1): 193–218.
Mohring, Herbert. 1961. Land Values and the Measurement of Highway Benefits. *Journal of Political Economy* 79: 236–249.
Siegfried, John and Andrew Zimbalist. 2002. A Note on the Local Economic Impact of Sports Expenditures. *Journal of Sports Economics* 3(4): 361–366.
Stephens, Josh. 2012. Lawmakers Reject Major CEQA Reform (Update). California Planning and Development Report. Available at www.cp-dr.com/node/3254, accessed December 1, 2012.

Index